· THE ·
BEST OF MY
· LIFE ·

· THE ·
BEST OF MY
· LIFE ·

AUTOBIOGRAPHIES IN LARGE PRINT

Edited by Judith Leet

G. K. HALL & CO.
Boston, Massachusetts
1987

Copyright 1987 by G.K. Hall & Co.

Set in 16 pt. Plantin.

Library of Congress Cataloging-in-Publication Data

The Best of my life.

In large print.
Includes index.
1. United States—Biography. 2. Autobiographies.
3. Celebrities—United States—Biography. 4. Large
type books. I. Leet, Judith.
CT216.B47 1987   920'.073 [B]   87–8468
ISBN 0–8161–4036–7

TABLE OF CONTENTS

v

Introduction

What would it be like, we all ask ourselves at some point, to live someone else's life and to see the world with someone else's eyes. How, for instance, does it feel to be a young surgeon pressing the scalpel into someone's skin to make an incision for the first time? Dr. William Nolen wittily describes his own bungled first attempt, a near-disaster that was not particularly amusing to him at the time. What would it be like to commit oneself to a spiritual life of intense solitude, as described by Thomas Merton, who gradually realized his calling as a young, questing adult; or how does it feel to grow up as an heiress in a very wealthy (and quarrelsome) family, as was the fate of Gloria Vanderbilt? Or to discover oneself a musical prodigy at a very early age, the experience of Arthur Rubinstein? The autobiography allows us some insights into how others have experienced their lives; it allows us to enter the minds of often highly accomplished individuals, and it allows us to explore very different ways of living — had our destiny been otherwise.

My personal impetus for reading autobiographies is to search for the means others have used to survive their lives — the major and minor setbacks that beset everyone. What methods, what strategies, did they adopt to help them through the hard times, the losses, the failures that everyone faces at one point or another? How did Anne Morrow Lindbergh cope with the kidnapping of her first-born toddler son? What strengths did she develop to help her through this extreme ordeal?

Perhaps some of these writers have discovered and described useful tricks of the trade of living — how to live well or at least better — that we might apply to our own lives. Perhaps we can adapt to our own situation certain useful attitudes that have helped others, or some of their self-motivation, or their goals for achieving what they wanted to achieve. Or we might come upon some valuable insights about the mysteries of human relationships — how to get along productively with one's fellow humans, whether friend, family, or even those we look upon as foes.

Another impetus for reading autobiographies is the opportunity to study human character. We are invited to hear someone explain his or her acts and the reasons that such actions were taken — and the consequences. But how much does this individual know about himself or herself? From an outsider's perspective, we can often grasp more clearly what is going on than can the person who is in the middle of the personal storm. And what can we figure out about this person from what is left unmentioned or by what is overemphasized? Is this person likable or smug, generous or self-serving? Do we admire this person's strength and spirit or not?

Individual readers have many personal reasons that spur them to read autobiography: they admire, for example, the skill or success of a particular individual in their own field, or they share a similar cultural or ideological perspective (they are in the same kind of spiritual exile from their homeland that Scott Momaday or Maxine Hong Kingston describes). Sometimes we readers simply want to be amused, and search for writers, such as James Thurber, Richard Feynman, and Russell Baker, who have found joy, humor, and often hilarity in their own daily lives and experiences.

But what motivates people to *write* their autobiographies? Some individuals, looking back over their lives, want to search for the patterns, for the unifying threads, for some purposefulness; they are trying to decipher their own lives and put some shape to what appears not altogether clear to them. By remembering and reconstructing the events of a lifetime, they feel they may find such patterns and purposes — the point of it all. So self-understanding is one large reason someone may put fingers to pen or typewriter or computer — even someone who never had felt compelled to write previously.

The natural counterpart to the reader looking for some insights is the writer who wants to teach and explain all that he or she has found out by living a lifetime. Ben Franklin, one of the first to write an autobiography as we know it, immediately explains his (conscious) motivations for writing: he writes for posterity, having himself been interested in the lives of his ancestors, and in case any of his descendants will be interested in how he rose from a modest family background to a position of some wealth and great prestige.

In contrast, the young Anne Frank, living in

cramped, strained conditions in World War II, wrote her diary in lieu of having a friend, in lieu of someone to share her thoughts and dreams of a future — a future she was not to have.

The popular contemporary writer May Sarton keeps an ongoing journal in an attempt to understand her daily existence as it unfolds and to record what she has experienced of great beauty and, conversely, what has sent her into exhausting rages. Her exacting honesty and self-examination probably explain her strong appeal to readers.

For whatever reasons people read autobiographies and for whatever reasons people write them, they are a source of closeness to others with whom we share the earth. In his usual reserved manner Henry Adams, who wrote one of the classics of autobiography, *The Education of Henry Adams*, observed: "Every one must bear his own universe, and most persons are moderately interested in learning how their neighbors have managed to carry theirs."

CHILDHOOD

New to the World

JAMES THURBER

from

MY LIFE AND HARD TIMES

James Thurber (1894–1961) earned his reputation at the *New Yorker* where his twin gifts as a writer of humorous pieces and as an artist and cartoonist flourished. Born in Columbus, Ohio, he attended Ohio State University from 1913 to 1918, but never earned his degree; one of the contributing factors was his very poor eyesight. He had lost an eye in an accident as a young child, and the vision in his other eye grew progressively weaker until he was declared legally blind. He worked around his handicap, however, and continued with his writing, always noted for its characteristic lighthearted wit.

Thurber's fifty-year career was devoted to the *New Yorker*, a magazine tailored for the sophisticated, urbane reader, where he worked with writer E. B. White and with founder Harold Ross. In the following piece he gives us a lively picture of the early days of automobile driving.

———————

7

The Car We Had to Push

MANY autobiographers, among them Lincoln Steffens and Gertrude Atherton, described earthquakes their families have been in. I am unable to do this because my family was never in an earthquake, but we went through a number of things in Columbus that were a great deal like earthquakes. I remember in particular some of the repercussions of an old Reo we had that wouldn't go unless you pushed it for quite a way and suddenly let your clutch out. Once, we had been able to start the engine easily by cranking it, but we had had the car for so many years that finally it wouldn't go unless you pushed it and let your clutch out. Of course, it took more than one person to do this; it took sometimes as many as five or six, depending on the grade of the roadway and conditions underfoot. The car was unusual in that the clutch and brake were on the same pedal, making it quite easy to stall the engine after it got started, so that the car would have to be pushed again.

My father used to get sick at his stomach pushing the car, and very often was unable to go to work. He had never liked the machine, even when it was good, sharing my ignorance and suspicion of all automobiles of twenty years ago and longer. The boys I went to school with used to be able to identify every car as it passed by: Thomas Flyer, Firestone-Columbus, Stevens Duryea, Rambler, Winton, White Steamer, etc.

I never could. The only car I was really interested in was one that the Get-Ready Man, as we called him, rode around town in: a big Red Devil with a door in the back. The Get-Ready Man was a lank unkempt elderly gentleman with wild eyes and a deep voice who used to go about shouting at people through a megaphone to prepare for the end of the world. "GET READY! GET READY!" he would bellow. "THE WORLLLD IS COMING TO AN END!" His startling exhortations would come up, like summer thunder, at the most unexpected times and in the most surprising places. I remember once during Mantell's production of "King Lear" at the Colonial Theatre, that the Get-Ready Man added his bawlings to the squealing of Edgar and the ranting of the King and the mouthing of the Fool, rising from somewhere in the balcony to join in. The theatre was in absolute darkness and there were rumblings of thunder and flashes of lightning offstage. Neither father nor I, who were there, ever completely got over the scene, which went something like this:

Edgar: Tom's a-cold.— O, do de, do de, do de!— Bless thee from whirlwinds, star-blasting, and taking . . . the foul fiend vexes!

(*Thunder off.*

Lear: What! Have his daughters brought him to this pass? —

Get-Ready Man: Get ready! Get ready!

Edgar: Pillicock sat on Pillicock-hill: —

Halloo, halloo, loo, loo!

(*Lightning flashes.*

Get-Ready Man: The Worllld is com-ing to an End!

Fool: This cold night will turn us all to fools and madmen!

Edgar: Take heed o' the foul fiend: obey thy paren —

Get-Ready Man: Get *Rea*-dy!

Edgar: Tom's a-*cold!*

Get-Ready Man: The *Worr*-uld is coming to an end! . . .

They found him finally, and ejected him, still shouting. The Theatre, in our time, has known few such moments.

But to get back to the automobile. One of my happiest memories of it was when, in its eighth year, my brother Roy got together a great many articles from the kitchen, placed them in a square of canvas, and swung this under the car with a string attached to it so that, at a twitch, the canvas would give way and the steel and tin things would clatter to the street. This was a little scheme of Roy's to frighten father, who had always expected the car might explode. It worked perfectly. That was twenty-five years ago, but it is one of the few things in my life I would like to live over again if I could. I don't suppose that I can, now. Roy twitched the string in the middle of a lovely afternoon, on Bryden Road near Eighteenth Street. Father had closed his eyes and, with his hat off, was enjoying a cool breeze. The clatter on the asphalt was tremendously effective: knives, forks, can-openers, pie pans, pot lids, biscuit-cutters, ladles, eggbeaters fell, beautifuly together, in a lingering, clamant crash. "Stop the *car!*" shouted father. "I can't," Roy said. "The engine fell out." "God Almighty!" said father, who knew what *that* meant, or knew what it sounded as if it might mean.

It ended unhappily, of course, because we finally had to drive back and pick up the stuff and even father knew the difference between the works of an automobile and the equipment of a pantry. My mother wouldn't have known, however, nor *her* mother. My mother, for instance, thought — or, rather, knew — that it was dangerous to drive an automobile without gasoline: it fried the valves, or something. "Now don't you dare drive all over town without gasoline!" she would say to us when we started off. Gasoline, oil, and water were much the same to her, a fact that made her life both confusing and perilous. Her greatest dread, however, was the Victrola — we had a very early one, back in the "Come Josephine in My Flying Machine" days. She had an idea that the Victrola might blow up. It alarmed her, rather than reassured her, to explain that the phonograph was run neither by gasoline nor by electricity. She could only suppose that it was propelled by some newfangled and untested apparatus which was likely to let go at any minute, making us all the victims and martyrs of the wild-eyed Edison's dangerous experiments. The telephone she was comparatively at peace with, except, of course, during storms, when for some reason or other she always took the receiver off the hook and let it hang. She came naturally by her confused and groundless fears, for her own mother lived the latter years of her life in the horrible suspicion that electricity was dripping invisibly all over the house. It leaked, she contended, out of empty sockets if the wall switch had been left on. She would go around screwing in bulbs, and if they lighted up she would hastily and fearfully turn off the wall switch and go back to her *Pearson's* or *Everybody's*, happy in the satisfaction that she had stopped not only a costly but a dangerous leakage. Nothing could ever clear this up for her.

Our poor old Reo came to a horrible end, finally. We had parked it too far from the curb on a street with a car line. It was late at night and the street was dark. The first streetcar that came along couldn't get by. It picked up the tired old automobile as a terrier might seize a rabbit and drubbed it unmercifully, losing its hold now and then but catching a new grip a second later. Tires booped and whooshed, the fenders queeled and graked, the steering-wheel rose up like a spectre and disappeared in the direction of Franklin Avenue with a melancholy whistling sound, bolts and gadgets flew like sparks from a Catherine wheel. It was a splendid spectacle but, of course, saddening to everybody (except the motorman of the streetcar, who was sore). I think some of us broke down and wept. It must have been the weeping that caused grandfather to take on so terribly. Time was all mixed up in his mind; automobiles and the like he never remembered having seen. He apparently gathered, from the talk and excitement and weeping, that somebody had died. Nor did he let go of this delusion. He insisted, in fact, after almost a week in which we strove mightily to divert him, that it was a sin and a shame and a disgrace on the family to put the funeral off any longer. "Nobody is dead! The automobile is smashed!" shouted my father, trying for the thirtieth time to explain the situation to the old man. "Was he drunk?" demanded grandfather, sternly. "Was who drunk?" asked father. "Zenas," said grandfather. He had a name for the corpse now: it was his brother Zenas, who, as it happened, *was* dead, but not from driving an automobile while intoxicated. Zenas had died in 1866. A sensitive, rather poetical boy of twenty-one when the Civil War broke out, Zenas had gone to South America — "just," as he wrote back, "until it blows over." Returning after the war had blown over, he caught the same disease that was killing off the chestnut trees in those years, and passed away. It was the only case in history where a tree doctor had to be called in to spray a person, and our family had felt it very keenly; nobody else in the United States caught the blight. Some of us have looked upon Zenas' fate as a kind of poetic justice.

Now that grandfather knew, so to speak, who was dead, it became increasingly awkward to go on living in the same house with him as if nothing had happened. He would go into towering rages in which he threatened to write to the Board of Health unless the funeral were held at once. We realized that something had to be done. Eventually, we persuaded a friend of father's, named George Martin, to dress up in the manner

13

and costume of the eighteen-sixties and pretend to be Uncle Zenas, in order to set grandfather's mind at rest. The impostor looked fine and impressive in sideburns and a high beaver hat, and not unlike the daguerreotypes of Zenas in our album. I shall never forget the night, just after dinner, when this Zenas walked into the living-room. Grandfather was stomping up and down, tall, hawk-nosed, round-oathed. The newcomer held out both his hands. "Clem!" he cried to grandfather. Grandfather turned slowly, looked at the intruder, and snorted. "Who air *you?*" he demanded in his deep, resonant voice. "I'm Zenas!" cried Martin. "Your brother Zenas, fit as a fiddle and sound as a dollar!" "Zenas, my foot!" said grandfather. "Zenas died of the chestnut blight in '66!"

Grandfather was given to these sudden, unexpected, and extremely lucid moments; they were generally more embarrassing than his other moments. He comprehended before he went to bed that night that the old automobile had been destroyed and that its destruction had caused all the turmoil in the house. "It flew all to pieces, Pa," my mother told him, in graphically describing the accident. "I knew 'twould," growled grandfather. "I allus told ye to git a Pope-Toledo."

AGATHA CHRISTIE

from

AN AUTOBIOGRAPHY

In these remembrances of her English childhood, **Dame Agatha Christie** (1890–1976) writes in the same readable and engrossing manner that made her detective mysteries so very popular worldwide. In the first incident, she captures the child's helplessness in communicating her emotions: when a French guide, as a kindness, pins a live butterfly to her hat, she does not know how to express the revulsion she feels in words — and only the insight of her mother finally releases her from her misery.

She also wittily contends that the position of women has definitely deteriorated from what it once was when Victorian women "cleverly" had established themselves as the weaker sex, needing support and protection. "We have clamored to be allowed to work as men work. Men, not being fools, have taken kindly to the idea."

Finally, she recalls the great Victorian Christmas feasts of her childhood. If you find these few excerpts to your taste, you probably will enjoy her entire autobiography from beginning to end.

Girls and Boys Come Out to Play

Father and Madge made a good many excursions on horseback, and in answer to my entreaties one day I was told that on the morrow I should be allowed to accompany them. I was thrilled. My mother had a few misgivings, but my father soon overruled them.

"We have a guide with us," he said, "and he's quite used to children and will see to it that they don't fall off."

The next morning the three horses arrived, and off we went. We zigzagged along up the precipitous paths, and I enjoyed myself enormously perched on top of what seemed to me an immense horse. The guide led it up, and occasionally picking little bunches of flowers, handed them to me to stick in my hatband. So far all was well, but when we arrived at the top and prepared to have lunch at the plateau there, the guide excelled himself. He came running back to us bringing with him a magnificent butterfly he had trapped. *"Pour la petite mademoiselle,"* he cried. Taking a pin from his lapel he transfixed the butterfly and stuck it in my hat! Oh the horror of that moment! The feeling of the poor butterfly fluttering, struggling against the pin, the agony I felt as the butterfly fluttered there. And of course I couldn't *say* anything. There were too many conflicting loyalties in my mind. This was a kindness on the part of the guide. He had brought it to me. It was a special

16

kind of present. How could I hurt his feelings by saying I didn't like it? How I wanted him to take it off. And all the time, there was the butterfly, fluttering, dying. That horrible flapping against my hat. There is only one thing a child can do in these circumstances. I cried.

The more anyone asked me questions the more I was unable to reply.

"What's the matter?" demanded my father. "Have you got a pain?"

My sister said, "Perhaps she's frightened at riding on the horse."

I said no and no. I wasn't frightened and I hadn't got a pain.

"Tired," said my father.

"No," I said.

"Well, then, what *is* the matter?"

But I couldn't say. Of course I couldn't say. The guide was standing there, watching me with an attentive and puzzled face. My father said rather crossly,

"She's too young a child. We shouldn't have brought her on this expedition."

I redoubled my weeping. I must have ruined the day for both him and my sister, and I knew I was doing so, but I couldn't stop. All I hoped and prayed was that presently he, or even my sister, would *guess* what was the matter. Surely they would look at that butterfly, they would see it, they would say, "Perhaps she doesn't like the butterfly on her hat." If *they* said it, it would be all right. But I couldn't *tell* them. It was a terrible day. I refused to eat any lunch. I sat there and cried, and the butterfly flapped. It stopped flapping in the end. That ought to have made me feel better. But by that time I had got into such a state of misery that nothing *could* have made me feel better.

We rode down again, my father definitely out of temper, my sister annoyed, and the guide still sweet, kindly and puzzled. Fortunately, he did not think of getting me a second butterfly to cheer me up. We arrived back, a most woeful party, and went into our sitting room where mother was.

"Oh dear," she said, "what's the matter? Has Agatha hurt herself?"

"I don't know," said my father crossly. "I don't know what's the matter with the child. I suppose she's got a pain or something. She's been crying ever since lunchtime, and she wouldn't eat a thing."

"What is the matter, Agatha?" asked my mother.

I couldn't tell her. I only looked at her dumbly while tears still rolled down my cheeks. She looked at me thoughtfully for some minutes, then said, "Who put that butterfly in her hat?"

My sister explained that it had been the guide.

"I see," said my mother. Then she said to me, "You didn't like it, did you? It was alive and you thought it was being hurt?"

Oh, the glorious relief, the wonderful relief it is when somebody knows what's in your mind and tells it to you so that you are at last released from that long bondage of silence, that seems so inescapable. I flung myself at her in a kind of frenzy, thrust my arms round her neck and said,

"Yes, yes, yes. It's been flapping. It's been *flapping*. But he was so kind and he meant to be kind. I couldn't *say*."

She understood it all and patted me gently. Suddenly the whole thing seemed to recede in the distance.

"I quite see what you felt," she said. "I know. But it's over now, and so we won't talk about it any more."

I personally had no ambition. I knew that I was not very good at anything. Tennis and croquet I used to enjoy playing, but I never played them well. How much more interesting it would be if I could say that I always longed to be a writer, and was determined that some day I would succeed, but, honestly, such an idea never came into my head.

As it happened, I *did* appear in print at the age of eleven. It came about in this way. The trams came to Ealing — and local opinion immediately erupted into fury. A terrible thing to happen to Ealing; such a fine residential neighbourhood, such wide streets, such beautiful houses — to have *trams* clanging up and down! The word Progress was uttered but howled down. Everyone wrote to the press, to their M.P., to anyone they could think of to write to. Trams were common — they were noisy — everyone's health would suffer. There was an excellent service of brilliant red buses, with Ealing on them in large letters, which ran from Ealing Broadway to Shepherds Bush, and another extremely useful bus, though more humble in appearance, which ran from Hanwell to Acton. And there was the good old-fashioned Great Western Railway, to say nothing of the District Railway.

Trams were simply not needed. But they came. Inexorably they came, and there was weeping and gnashing of teeth — and Agatha had her first literary effort published, which was a poem I wrote on the first day of the running of the trams. There were four verses of it, and one of Grannie's old gentlemen, that gallant bodyguard of Generals, Lt.-Colonels, and Admirals, was persuaded by Grannie to visit the local newspaper office and suggest that it should be inserted. It was — and I can still remember the first verse:

> When first the electric trams did run
> In all their scarlet glory,
> 'Twas well, but ere the day was done,
> It was another story.

After which I went on to deride a "shoe that pinched." (There had been some electrical fault in a "shoe," or whatever it was, which conveyed the electricity to the trams, so that after running for a few hours they broke down.) I was elated at seeing myself in print, but I cannot say that it led me to contemplate a literary career.

In fact I only contemplated one thing — a happy marriage. About that I had complete self-assurance — as all my friends did. We were conscious of all the happiness that awaited us; we looked forward to love, to being looked after, to being cherished, and admired, and we intended

20

to get our own way in the things which mattered to us while at the same time putting our husbands' life, career and success before all, as was our proud duty. We didn't need pep pills or sedatives, we had belief and joy in life. We had our own personal disappointments — moments of unhappiness — but on the whole life was *fun*. Perhaps it is fun for girls nowadays — but they certainly don't *look* as if it is. However — a timely thought — they may enjoy melancholy; some people do. They may enjoy the emotional crises that seem always to be overwhelming them. They may even enjoy anxiety. That is certainly what we have nowadays — anxiety. My contemporaries were frequently badly off and couldn't have a quarter of the things they wanted. Why then did we have so much enjoyment? Was it some kind of sap rising in us that has ceased to rise now? Have we cut it off with education and, worse, anxiety over education; anxiety as to what life holds for you?

We were like obstreperous flowers — often weeds maybe, but nevertheless all of us growing exuberantly — pressing violently up through cracks in pavements and flagstones, and in the most inauspicious places, determined to have our fill of life and enjoy ourselves, bursting out into the sunlight, until someone came and trod on us. Even bruised for a time, we would soon lift a head again. Nowadays, alas, life seems to apply weed killer (selective!) — we have no chance to raise a head again. There are said to be those who are "unfit for living." No one would ever have told *us* we were unfit for living. If they had, we shouldn't have believed it. Only a murderer was unfit for living. Nowadays a murderer is the one person you *mustn't* say is unfit for living.

The real excitement of being a girl — of being, that is, a woman in embryo — was that life was such a wonderful gamble. *You didn't know what was going to happen to you.* That was what made being a woman so exciting. No worry about what you should be or do — Biology would decide. You were waiting for The Man, and when the man came, he would change your entire life! You can say what you like, that is an exciting point of view to hold at the threshold of life. What will happen? "Perhaps I shall marry someone in the Diplomatic Service . . . I think I should like that; to go abroad and see all sorts of places. . . ." Or: "I don't think I would like to marry a sailor; you would have to spend such a lot of time living in seaside lodgings." Or: "Perhaps I'll marry someone who builds bridges, or an explorer." The whole world was open to you — not open to your *choice*, but open to what Fate *brought* you. You might marry *anyone;* you might, of course, marry a drunkard or be very unhappy, but that only heightened the general feeling of excitement. And one wasn't marrying the profession, either; it was the *man.* In the words of old nurses, nannies, cooks and housemaids:

"One day Mr. Right will come along."

I remember when I was very small seeing one of mother's prettier friends being helped to dress for a dance by old Hannah, Grannie's cook. She was being laced into a tight corset. "Now then, Miss Phyllis," said Hannah, "brace your foot against the bed and lean back — I'm going to pull. Hold your breath."

"Oh, Hannah, I can't bear it, I can't really. I can't *breathe*."

"Now don't you fret, my pet, you can breathe all right. You won't be able to eat much supper, and that's a good thing, because young ladies shouldn't be seen eating a lot; it's not delicate. You've got to behave like a proper young lady. You're all right. I'll just get the tape measure. There you are — nineteen and a half. I *could* have got you to nineteen."

"Nineteen and a half will do quite well," gasped the sufferer.

"You'll be glad when you get there. Suppose this is the night that Mr. Right's coming along? You wouldn't like to be there with a thick waist, would you, and let him see you like that?"

Mr. Right. He was more elegantly referred to sometimes as "Your Fate."

"I don't know that I really want to go to this dance."

"Oh yes, you do, dear. Think! You might meet your Fate."

And of course that *is* what actually happens in life. Girls go to something they wanted to go to, or they didn't want to go to, it doesn't matter which — and there is their Fate.

Of course, there were always girls who declared they were not going to marry, usually for some noble reason. Possibly they wished to become nuns or to nurse lepers, to do something grand and important, above all self-sacrificial. I think it was almost a necessary phase. An ardent wish to become a nun seems to be far more constant in Protestant than in Catholic girls. In Catholic girls it is, no doubt, more vocational — it is recognized as one of the ways of life — whereas for a Protestant it has some aroma of religious mystery that makes it very desirable. A hospital nurse was also considered a heroic way of life, with all the prestige of Miss Nightingale behind it.

But marriage was the main theme; whom you were going to marry the big question in life.

By the time I was thirteen or fourteen I felt myself enormously advanced in age and experience. I no longer thought of myself as protected by another person, I had my own protective feelings. I felt responsible for my mother. I also began to try to know myself, the sort of person I was, what I could attempt successfully, and the things I was no good at and that I must not waste time over. I knew that I was not quick-witted, I must give myself time to look at a problem carefully before deciding how I would deal with it.

I began to appreciate time. There is nothing more wonderful to have in one's life than time. I don't believe people get enough of it nowadays. I was excessively fortunate in my childhood and youth, just *because* I had so much time. You wake up in the morning, and even before you are properly awake you are saying to yourself, "Now, what shall I do with today?" You have the choice, it is there, in front of you, and you can plan as you please. I don't mean that there were not a lot of things (duties, we called them)

I had to do — of course there were. There were jobs to be done in the house: days when you cleaned silver photograph frames, days when you darned your stockings, days when you learned a chapter of *Great Events in History*, a day when you had to go down the town and pay all the tradesmen's bills. Letters and notes to write, scales and exercises, embroidery — but they were all things that lay in my choice, to arrange as I pleased. I could plan my day, I could say, "I think I'll leave my stockings until this afternoon; I will go down town in the morning and I will come back by the other road and see whether that tree has come into blossom yet."

Always when I woke up, I had the feeling which I am sure must be natural to all of us, a joy in being alive. I don't say you feel it consciously — you don't — but there you *are*, you are *alive*, and you open your eyes, and here is another day; another step, as it were, on your journey to an unknown place. That very exciting journey which is your life. Not that it is necessarily going to be exciting *as* a life, but it will be exciting to you because it is *your* life. That is one of the great secrets of existence, enjoying the gift of life that has been given to you.

Not every day is necessarily enjoyable. After that first delightful feeling of "Another day! How wonderful!" you remember you have to go to the dentist at 10:30, and that is not nearly so good. But the *first* waking feeling has been there, and that acts as a useful booster. Naturally, a lot depends on temperament. You are a happy person, or you are of a melancholic disposition.

I don't know that you can do anything about *that*. I think it is the way one is made — you are either happy until something arises to make you unhappy, or else you are melancholy until something distracts you from it. Naturally happy people can be unhappy and melancholic people enjoy themselves. But if I were taking a gift to a child at a christening that is what I would choose: a naturally happy frame of mind.

There seems to me to be an odd assumption that there is something meritorious about working. Why? In early times man went out to hunt animals in order to feed himself and keep alive. Later, he toiled over crops, and sowed and ploughed for the same reason. Nowadays, he rises early, catches the 8:15, and sits in an office all day — still for the same reason. He does it to feed himself and have a roof over his head — and, if skilled and lucky, to go a bit further and have comfort and entertainment as well.

It's economic and necessary. But why is it *meritorious?* The old nursery adage used to be "Satan finds some mischief still for idle hands to do." Presumably little Georgie Stephenson was enjoying idleness when he observed his mother's tea-kettle lid rising and falling. Having nothing at the moment to do, he began to have ideas about it. . . .

I don't think necessity is the mother of invention — invention, in my opinion, arises directly from idleness, possibly also from laziness. *To save onself trouble.* That is the big secret that has brought us down the ages hundreds of thousands of years, from chipping flints to switching on the washing-up machine.

The position of women, over the years, has definitely changed for the worse. We women have behaved like mugs. We have clamoured to be allowed to work as men work. Men, not being fools, have taken kindly to the idea. Why support a wife? What's wrong with a wife supporting *herself*? She *wants* to do it. By golly, she can go on doing it!

It seems sad that having established ourselves so cleverly as the "weaker sex," we should now be broadly on a par with the women of primitive tribes who toil in the fields all day, walk miles to gather camel-thorn for fuel, and on trek carry all the pots, pans and household equipment on their heads, while the gorgeous, ornamental male sweeps on ahead, unburdened save for one lethal weapon with which to defend his women.

You've got to hand it to Victorian women, they got their menfolk where they wanted them. They established their frailty, delicacy, sensibility — their constant need of being protected and cherished. Did they lead miserable, servile lives, downtrodden and oppressed? Such is not *my* recollection of them. All my grandmother's friends seem to me in retrospect singularly resilient and almost invariably successful in getting their own way. They were tough, self-willed, and remarkably well read and well informed.

Mind you, they admired their men enormously. They genuinely thought men were splendid fellows — dashing, inclined to be wicked, easily led astray. In daily life a woman got her own

27

way while paying due lip service to male superiority, so that her husband should not lose face.

"Your father knows best, dear," was the public formula. The real approach came privately. "I'm sure you are *quite* right in what you said, John, but I wonder if you have considered. . . ."

In one respect man was paramount. He was the Head of the House. A woman, when she married, accepted as her destiny *his* place in the world and *his* way of life. That seems to me sound sense and the foundation of happiness. If you can't face your man's way of life, don't take that job — in other words, don't marry that man. Here, say, is a wholesale draper; he is a Roman Catholic; he prefers to live in a suburb; he plays golf and he likes to go for holidays to the seaside. *That* is what you are marrying. Make up your mind to it and like it. It won't be so difficult.

It is astonishing how much you can enjoy almost everything. There are few things more desirable than to be an accepter and an enjoyer. You can like and enjoy almost any kind of food or way of life. You can enjoy country life, dogs, muddy walks, towns, noise, people, clatter. In the one there is repose, ease for nerves, time for reading, knitting, embroidery, and the pleasure of growing things; in the other theatres, art galleries, good concerts, and seeing friends you would otherwise seldom see. I am happy to say that I can enjoy almost everything.

Once when I was travelling by train to Syria, I was much entertained by a fellow traveller's dissertation on the stomach.

"My dear," she said, "never give in to your stomach. If a certain thing doesn't agree with you, say to yourself 'Who's going to be master, me or my stomach?' "

"But what do you actually do about it?" I asked with curiosity.

"Any stomach can be trained. Very small doses at first. It doesn't matter what it is. Eggs, now, used to make me sick, and toasted cheese gave me the most terrible pains. But just a spoonful or two of boiled egg two or three times a week, and then a little more scrambled egg and so on. And now I can eat any amount of eggs. It's been just the same with toasted cheese. Remember this, *your stomach's a good servant, but a bad master.*"

I was much impressed and promised to follow her advice, and I have done so — though it has not presented much difficulty, my stomach being definitely a servile one.

Christmas we used to spend in Cheshire, going up to the Wattses. Jimmy usually got his yearly holiday about then, and he and Madge used to go to St. Moritz for three weeks. He was a very good skater, and so it was the kind of holiday he liked most. Mother and I used to go up to Cheadle, and since their newly built house, called Manor Lodge, was not ready yet, we spent Christmas at Abney Hall, with the old Wattses and their four children and Jack. It was a wonderful house to have Christmas in if you were a child. Not only was it enormous Victorian

29

Gothic, with quantities of rooms, passages, unexpected steps, back staircases, front staircases, alcoves, niches — everything in the world that a child could want — but it also had three different pianos that you could play, as well as an organ. All it lacked was the light of day; it was remarkably dark, except for the big drawing room with its green satin walls and its big windows.

Nan Watts and I were fast friends by now. We were not only friends but drinking companions — we both liked the same drink, *cream*, ordinary plain, neat cream. Although I had consumed an enormous amount of Devonshire cream since I lived in Devonshire, raw cream was really more of a treat. When Nan stayed with me at Torquay, we used to visit one of the dairies in the town, where we would have a glass of half-milk and half-cream. When I stayed with her at Abney we used to go down to the home farm and drink cream by the half-pint. We continued these drinking bouts all through our lives, and I still remember buying our cartons of cream in Sunningdale and coming up to the golf course and sitting outside the club house waiting for our respective husbands to finish their rounds of golf, each drinking our pinta cream.

Abney was a glutton's paradise. Mrs. Watts had what was called her storeroom off the hall. It was not like Grannie's storeroom, a kind of securely locked treasure house from which things were taken out. There was free access to it, and all round the walls were shelves covered with every kind of dainty. One side was entirely chocolates, boxes of them, all different, chocolate creams in labelled boxes. . . . There were biscuits, gingerbread, preserved fruits, jams and so on.

Christmas was the supreme Festival, something never to be forgotten. Christmas stockings in bed. Breakfast when everyone had a separate chair heaped with presents. Then a rush to church and back to continue present opening. At two o'clock Christmas dinner, the blinds drawn down and glittering ornaments and lights. First, oyster soup (not relished by me), turbot, then boiled turkey, roast turkey and a large roast sirloin of beef. This was followed by plum pudding, mince pies and a trifle full of sixpences, pigs, rings, bachelors' buttons and all the rest of it. After that, again, innumerable kinds of dessert. In a story I once wrote, *The Affair of the Christmas Pudding*, I have described just such a feast. It is one of those things that I am sure will never be seen again in this generation; indeed I doubt nowadays if anyone's digestion would stand it. However, *our* digestions stood it quite well then.

I usually had to vie in eating prowess with Humphrey Watts, the Watts son next to James in age. I suppose he must have been twenty-one or twenty-two to my twelve or thirteen. He was a very handsome young man, as well as being a good actor and a wonderful entertainer and teller of stories. Good as I always was at falling in love with people, I don't think I fell in love with him, though it is amazing to me that I should *not* have done so. I suppose I was still at the stage where my love affairs had to be romantically impossible

31

— concerned with public characters, such as the Bishop of London and King Alfonso of Spain, and of course with various actors. I know I fell deeply in love with Henry Ainley when I saw him in *The Bondman,* and I must have been just getting ripe for the K.O.W.'s (Keen on Waller), who were all to a girl in love with Lewis Waller in *Monsieur Beaucaire.*

Humphrey and I ate solidly through the Christmas dinner. He scored over me in oyster soup, but otherwise we were neck and neck. We both first had roast turkey, then boiled turkey, and finally four or five slashing slices of sirloin of beef. It is possible that our elders confined themselves to only one kind of turkey for this course, but as far as I remember old Mr. Watts certainly had beef as well as turkey. We then ate plum pudding and mince pies and trifle. I ate rather sparingly of trifle, because I didn't like the taste of wine. After that there were the crackers, the grapes, the oranges, the Elvas plums, the Carlsbad plums and the preserved fruits. Finally, during the afternoon, various handfuls of chocolates were fetched from the storeroom to suit our taste. Do I remember being sick the next day? Having bilious attacks? No, never. The only bilious attacks I ever remember were those that seized me after eating unripe apples in September. I ate unripe apples practically every day, but occasionally I must have overdone it.

What I do remember was when I was about six or seven years old and had eaten mushrooms. I woke up with a pain about eleven o'clock in the evening, and came rushing down to the drawing room, where Mother and Father were entertaining a party of people, and announced dramatically: "I am going to die! I am poisoned by mushrooms!" Mother rapidly soothed me and administered a dose of ipecacuanha wine — always kept in the medicine cupboard in those days — and assured me that I was not due to die this time.

At any rate I never remember being ill at Christmas. Nan Watts was just the same as I was; she had a splendid stomach. In fact, really, when I remember those days, everyone seemed to have a pretty good stomach. I suppose people had gastric and duodenal ulcers and had to be careful, but I cannot remember anybody living on a diet of fish and milk. A coarse and gluttonous age? Yes, but one of great zest and enjoyment. Considering the amount that I ate in my youth (for I was always hungry) I cannot imagine how I managed to remain so thin — a scrawny chicken indeed.

After the pleasurable inertia of Christmas afternoon — pleasurable, that is, for the elders: the younger ones read books, looked at their presents, ate more chocolates, and so on — there was a terrific tea, with a great iced Christmas cake as well as everything else, and finally a supper of cold turkey and hot mince pies. About nine o'clock there was the Christmas tree, with more presents hanging on it. A splendid day, and one to be remembered till next year, when Christmas came again.

Jack and I nearly drowned ourselves one summer. It was a rough day; we had not gone as far as Meadfoot, but instead to the Ladies' Bathing Cove, where Jack was not yet old enough to cause a tremor in female breasts. He could not swim at that time, or only a few strokes, so I was in the habit of taking him out to the raft on my back. On this particular morning we started off as usual, but it was a curious kind of sea — a sort of mixed swell and chop — and, with the additional weight on my shoulders, I found it almost impossible to keep my mouth and nose above water. I was swimming, but I couldn't get any breath into myself. The tide was not far out, so that the raft was quite close, but I was making little progress, and was only able to get a breath about every third stroke.

Suddenly I realized that I could not make it. At any moment now I was going to choke. "Jack," I gasped, "get off and swim to the raft. You're nearer that than the shore." "Why?" said Jack, "I don't want to." "Please — do —" I bubbled. My head went under. Fortunately, though Jack clung to me at first, he got shaken off and was able therefore to proceed under his own steam. We were quite near the raft by then, and he reached it with no difficulty. By that time I was past noticing what anyone was doing. The only feeling in my mind was a great sense of indignation. I had always been told that when you were drowning the whole of your past life came before you, and I had also been told that you heard beautiful music when you were dying. There was no beautiful music, and I couldn't think about anything in my past life; in fact I could think of nothing at all but how I was going to get some breath into my lungs. Everything went black and — and — and the next thing I knew was violent bruises and pains as I was flung roughly into a boat. The old Sea-Horse, crotchety and useless as we had always thought him, had had enough sense to notice that somebody was drowning and had come out in the boat allowed him for the purpose. Having thrown me into the boat he took a few more strokes to the raft and grabbed Jack, who resisted loudly saying, "I don't want to go in yet. I've only just got here, I want to play on the raft. I won't come in!" The assorted boatload reached the shore, and my sister came down the beach laughing heartily and saying, "What were you doing? What's all this fuss?"

"Your sister nearly drowned herself," said the old man crossly. "Go on, take this child of yours. We'll lay her out flat, and we'll see if she needs a bit of punching."

I suppose they gave me a bit of punching, though I don't think I had quite lost consciousness.

"I can't see how you knew she was drowning. Why didn't she shout for help?"

"I keeps an eye. Once you goes down you can't shout — water's comin' in."

We both thought highly of the old Sea-Horse after that.

RUSSELL BAKER

from

GROWING UP

Born in Virginia in 1925, **Russell Baker** recounts his father's premature death in 1932 and his widowed mother's subsequent economic struggle in the midst of the depression. Baker here recalls how he was sent out to sell magazines to help the family and sold nothing, but his younger sister had the right "gumption." Prize-winning *New York Times* writer and humorist, Baker is well known through his widely syndicated column, the "Observer," and through his autobiography *Growing Up*, a classic tale of American success despite every kind of obstacle.

———————

I began working in journalism when I was eight years old. It was my mother's idea. She wanted me to "make something" of myself and, after a levelheaded appraisal of my strengths, decided I had better start young if I was to have any chance of keeping up with the competition.

The flaw in my character which she had already spotted was lack of "gumption." My idea of a

36

perfect afternoon was lying in front of the radio rereading my favorite Big Little Book, *Dick Tracy Meets Stooge Viller*. My mother despised inactivity. Seeing me having a good time in repose, she was powerless to hide her disgust. "You've got no more gumption than a bump on a log," she said. "Get out in the kitchen and help Doris do those dirty dishes."

My sister Doris, though two years younger than I, had enough gumption for a dozen people. She positively enjoyed washing dishes, making beds, and cleaning the house. When she was only seven she could carry a piece of short-weighted cheese back to the A&P, threaten the manager with legal action, and come back triumphantly with the full quarter-pound we'd paid for and a few ounces extra thrown in for forgiveness. Doris could have made something of herself if she hadn't been a girl. Because of this defect, however, the best she could hope for was a career as a nurse or schoolteacher, the only work that capable females were considered up to in those days.

This must have saddened my mother, this twist of fate that had allocated all the gumption to the daughter and left her with a son who was content with Dick Tracy and Stooge Viller. If disappointed, though, she wasted no energy on self-pity. She would make me make something of myself whether I wanted to or not. "The Lord helps those who help themselves," she said. That was the way her mind worked.

She was realistic about the difficulty. Having sized up the material the Lord had given her to mold, she didn't overestimate what she could do with it. She didn't insist that I grow up to be President of the United States.

Fifty years ago parents still asked boys if they wanted to grow up to be President, and asked it not jokingly but seriously. Many parents who were hardly more than paupers still believed their sons could do it. Abraham Lincoln had done it. We were only sixty-five years from Lincoln. Many a grandfather who walked among us could remember Lincoln's time. Men of grandfatherly age were the worst for asking if you wanted to grow up to be President. A surprising number of little boys said yes and meant it.

I was asked many times myself. No, I would say, I didn't want to grow up to be President. My mother was present during one of these interrogations. An elderly uncle, having posed the usual question and exposed my lack of interest in the Presidency, asked, "Well, what *do* you want to be when you grow up?"

I loved to pick through trash piles and collect empty bottles, tin cans with pretty labels, and discarded magazines. The most desirable job on earth sprang instantly to mind. "I want to be a garbage man," I said.

My uncle smiled, but my mother had seen the first distressing evidence of a bump budding on a log. "Have a little gumption, Russell," she said. Her calling me Russell was a signal of unhappiness. When she approved of me I was always "Buddy."

When I turned eight years old she decided that the job of starting me on the road toward making something of myself could no longer be safely delayed. "Buddy," she said one day, "I want you to come home right after school this afternoon. Somebody's coming and I want you to meet him."

When I burst in that afternoon she was in conference in the parlor with an executive of the Curtis Publishing Company. She introduced me. He bent low from the waist and shook my hand. Was it true as my mother had told him, he asked, that I longed for the opportunity to conquer the world of business?

My mother replied that I was blessed with a rare determination to make something of myself.

"That's right," I whispered.

"But have you got the grit, the character, the never-say-quit spirit it takes to succeed in business?"

My mother said I certainly did.

"That's right," I said.

He eyed me silently for a long pause, as though weighing whether I could be trusted to keep his confidence, then spoke man-to-man. Before taking a crucial step, he said, he wanted to advise me that working for the Curtis Publishing Company placed enormous responsibility on a young man. It was one of the great companies of America. Perhaps the greatest publishing house in the world. I had heard, no doubt, of the *Saturday Evening Post?*

Heard of it? My mother said that everyone in our house had heard of the *Saturday Evening Post* and that I, in fact, read it with religious devotion.

Then doubtless, he said, we were also familiar with those two monthly pillars of the magazine world, the *Ladies Home Journal* and the *Country Gentleman*.

Indeed we were familiar with them, said my mother.

Representing the *Saturday Evening Post* was one of the weightiest honors that could be bestowed in the world of business, he said. He was personally proud of being a part of that great corporation.

My mother said he had every right to be.

Again he studied me as though debating whether I was worthy of a knighthood. Finally: "Are you trustworthy?"

My mother said I was the soul of honesty.

"That's right," I said.

The caller smiled for the first time. He told me I was a lucky young man. He admired my spunk. Too many young men thought life was all play. Those young men would not go far in this world. Only a young man willing to work and save and keep his face washed and his hair neatly combed could hope to come out on top in a world such as ours. Did I truly and sincerely believe that I was such a young man?

"He certainly does," said my mother.

"That's right," I said.

He said he had been so impressed by what he had seen of me that he was going to make me a representative of the Curtis Publishing Company. On the following Tuesday, he said, thirty freshly printed copies of the *Saturday Evening Post* would be delivered at our door. I would place these magazines, still damp with the ink of the presses, in a handsome canvas bag, sling it over my shoulder, and set forth through the streets to bring the best in journalism, fiction, and cartoons to the American public.

He had brought the canvas bag with him. He presented it with reverence fit for a chasuble. He showed me how to drape the sling over my left shoulder and across the chest so that the pouch lay easily accessible to my right hand, allowing the best in journalism, fiction, and cartoons to be swiftly extracted and sold to a citizenry whose happiness and security depended upon us soldiers of the free press.

The following Tuesday I raced home from school, put the canvas bag over my shoulder, dumped the magazines in, and, tilting to the left to balance their weight on my right hip, embarked on the highway of journalism.

We lived in Belleville, New Jersey, a commuter town at the northern fringe of Newark. It was 1932, the bleakest year of the Depression. My father had died two years before, leaving us with a few pieces of Sears, Roebuck furniture and not much else, and my mother had taken Doris and me to live with one of her younger brothers. This was my Uncle Allen. Uncle Allen had made something of himself by 1932. As salesman for a soft-drink bottler in Newark, he had an income of $30 a week; wore pearl-gray spats, detachable collars, and a three-piece suit; was happily married; and took in threadbare relatives.

With my load of magazines I headed toward Belleville Avenue. That's where the people were. There were two filling stations at the intersection with Union Avenue, as well as an A&P, a fruit

41

stand, a bakery, a barber shop, Zuccarelli's drugstore, and a diner shaped like a railroad car. For several hours I made myself highly visible, shifting position now and then from corner to corner, from shop window to shop window, to make sure everyone could see the heavy black lettering on the canvas bag that said THE SATURDAY EVENING POST. When the angle of the light indicated it was suppertime, I walked back to the house.

"How many did you sell, Buddy?" my mother asked.

"None."

"Where did you go?"

"The corner of Belleville and Union Avenues."

"What did you do?"

"Stood on the corner waiting for somebody to buy a *Saturday Evening Post.*"

"You just stood there?"

"Didn't sell a single one."

"For God's sake, Russell!"

Uncle Allen intervened. "I've been thinking about it for some time," he said, "and I've about decided to take the *Post* regularly. Put me down as a regular customer." I handed him a magazine and he paid me a nickel. It was the first nickel I earned.

Afterwards my mother instructed me in salesmanship. I would have to ring doorbells, address adults with charming self-confidence, and break down resistance with a sales talk pointing out that no one, no matter how poor, could afford to be without the *Saturday Evening Post* in the home.

I told my mother I'd changed my mind about wanting to succeed in the magazine business.

"If you think I'm going to raise a good-for-nothing," she replied, "you've got another think coming." She told me to hit the streets with the canvas bag and start ringing doorbells the instant school was out next day. When I objected that I didn't feel any aptitude for salesmanship, she asked how I'd like to lend her my leather belt so she could whack some sense into me. I bowed to superior will and entered journalism with a heavy heart.

My mother and I had fought this battle almost as long as I could remember. It probably started even before memory began, when I was a country child in northern Virginia and my mother, dissatisfied with my father's plain workman's life, determined that I would not grow up like him and his people, with calluses on their hands, overalls on their backs, and fourth-grade educations in their heads. She had fancier ideas of life's possibilities. Introducing me to the *Saturday Evening Post,* she was trying to wean me as early as possible from my father's world where men left with their lunch pails at sunup, worked with their hands until the grime ate into the pores, and died with a few sticks of mail-order furniture as their legacy. In my mother's vision of the better life there were desks and white collars, well-pressed suits, evenings of reading and lively talk, and perhaps — if a man were very, very lucky and hit the jackpot, really made something important of himself — perhaps there might be a fantastic salary of $5,000 a year to support a big house and a Buick with a rumble seat and a vacation in Atlantic City.

And so I set forth with my sack of magazines. I was afraid of the dogs that snarled behind the doors of potential buyers. I was timid about ringing the doorbells of strangers, relieved when no one came to the door, and scared when someone did. Despite my mother's instructions, I could not deliver an engaging sales pitch. When a door opened I simply asked, "Want to buy a *Saturday Evening Post?*" In Belleville few persons did. It was a town of 30,000 people, and most weeks I rang a fair majority of its doorbells. But I rarely sold my thirty copies. Some weeks I canvassed the entire town for six days and still had four or five unsold magazines on Monday evening; then I dreaded the coming of Tuesday morning, when a batch of thirty fresh *Saturday Evening Post*s was due at the front door.

"Better get out there and sell the rest of those magazines tonight," my mother would say.

I usually posted myself then at a busy intersection where a traffic light controlled commuter flow from Newark. When the light turned red I stood on the curb and shouted my sales pitch at the motorists.

"Want to buy a *Saturday Evening Post?*"

One rainy night when car windows were sealed against me I came back soaked and with not a single sale to report. My mother beckoned to Doris.

"Go back down there with Buddy and show him how to sell these magazines," she said.

Brimming with zest, Doris, who was then

44

seven years old, returned with me to the corner. She took a magazine from the bag, and when the light turned red she strode to the nearest car and banged her small fist against the closed window. The driver, probably startled at what he took to be a midget assaulting his car, lowered the window to stare, and Doris thrust a *Saturday Evening Post* at him.

"You need this magazine," she piped, "and it only costs a nickel."

Her salesmanship was irresistible. Before the light changed half a dozen times she disposed of the entire batch. I didn't feel humiliated. To the contrary. I was so happy I decided to give her a treat. Leading her to the vegetable store on Belleville Avenue, I bought three apples, which cost a nickel, and gave her one.

"You shouldn't waste money," she said.

"Eat your apple." I bit into mine.

"You shouldn't eat before supper," she said. "It'll spoil your appetite."

Back at the house that evening, she dutifully reported me for wasting a nickel. Instead of a scolding, I was rewarded with a pat on the back for having the good sense to buy fruit instead of candy. My mother reached into her bottomless supply of maxims and told Doris, "An apple a day keeps the doctor away."

By the time I was ten I had learned all my mother's maxims by heart. Asking to stay up past normal bedtime, I knew that a refusal would be explained with, "Early to bed and early to rise, makes a man healthy, wealthy, and wise." If I whimpered about having to get up early in the morning, I could depend on her to say, "The early bird gets the worm."

The one I most despised was, "If at first you don't succeed, try, try again." This was the battle cry with which she constantly sent me back into the hopeless struggle whenever I moaned that I had rung every doorbell in town and knew there wasn't a single potential buyer left in Belleville that week. After listening to my explanation, she handed me the canvas bag and said, "If at first you don't succeed . . ."

Three years in that job, which I would gladly have quit after the first day except for her insistence, produced at least one valuable result. My mother finally concluded that I would never make something of myself by pursuing a life in business and started considering careers that demanded less competitive zeal.

One evening when I was eleven I brought home a short "composition" on my summer vacation which the teacher had graded with an A. Reading it with her own schoolteacher's eye, my mother agreed that it was top-drawer seventh grade prose and complimented me. Nothing more was said about it immediately, but a new idea had taken life in her mind. Halfway through supper she suddenly interrupted the conversation.

"Buddy," she said, "maybe you could be a writer."

I clasped the idea to my heart. I had never met a writer, had shown no previous urge to write, and hadn't a notion how to become a writer, but I loved stories and thought that making up stories must surely be almost as much

46

fun as reading them. Best of all, though, and what really gladdened my heart, was the ease of the writer's life. Writers did not have to trudge through the town peddling from canvas bags, defending themselves against angry dogs, being rejected by surly strangers. Writers did not have to ring doorbells. So far as I could make out, what writers did couldn't even be classified as work.

I was enchanted. Writers didn't have to have any gumption at all. I did not dare tell anybody for fear of being laughed at in the schoolyard, but secretly I decided that what I'd like to be when I grew up was a writer.

DAVID NIVEN

from

THE MOON'S A BALLOON

Noted for the many film roles in which he played the debonaire, suave, worldly gentleman, **David Niven** here describes his early experiences as a young schoolboy in England, interrupted by a chance encounter with a young professional street walker who continues his education and teaches him, as he reports, much more than he had in mind.

Niven, a born raconteur, tells his tale with a true comedian's sense of timing. And if he had been less successful as a film star, chances are good he could have succeeded as a writer. Despite the tragic accidental death of his young wife, which was a stunning blow to him and left him with two young children to raise, he reviews his life — and life in general — with a remarkably light and witty touch.

———

Nessie, when I first saw her, was nineteen, honey-blond, pretty rather than beautiful, a figure like a two-armed Venus de Milo who had been on a sensible diet, had a pair of legs that went on forever, and a glorious sense of the ridiculous. She was a Piccadilly whore. I was a fourteen-year-old heterosexual schoolboy and I met her thanks to my stepfather. (If you would like to skip on and meet Nessie more fully, she reappears on page 72.)

I had a stepfather because my French mother had married a second time. This she did because my father, along with 90 percent of his comrades in the Berkshire Yeomanry, had landed with immense panache at Suvla Bay in 1915. Unfortunately, the Turks were given ample time to prepare to receive them. For days, sweltering in their troopships, the Berkshire Yeomanry had ridden at anchor off Suvla Bay while the high command in London argued as to the best way to get them ashore. Finally, they arrived at their decision. The troops embarked in the ship's whalers and on arrival held their rifles above heads and gallantly leaped into the dark waist-high water. A combination of barbed wire beneath the surface and maching guns to cover the barbed wire provided a devastating welcome.

Wood pigeons were calling on a warm summer evening, and my sister, Grizel (that's a hell of a name for a girl, incidentally), and I were swapping cigarette cards on an old tree trunk in the paddock when a red-eyed maid came and told us our mother wanted to see us and that we were not to stay too long.

The house was near Cirencester, and after a rather incoherent interview with my mother, who displayed a telegram and tried to explain what "missing" meant, we returned to the swapping of cigarette cards and resumed our perusal of endless trains lumbering along a distant embankment loaded with guns and cheering young men . . . 1915.

I am afraid my father's death meant little or nothing to me at the time; later it meant a great deal. I was just five years old and had not seen him much except when I was brought down to be shown off before arriving dinner guests or departing fox-hunting companions. I could always tell which were which because although they all pinched and chucked and clucked in the same hearty manner, the former smelled of soap and perfume and the latter of sweat and spirits.

I lived with Grizel in a nursery presided over by a warm enveloping creature, Whitty.

Rainy days were spent being taught Highland reels by a wounded piper of the Argyll and Sutherland Highlanders, and listening to an "His Master's Voice" gramophone equipped with an immense horn. Our favorite record had "The Ride of the Valkyrie" on one side and, on the other, a jolly little number for those days called "The Wreck of the Troopship." We were specially fascinated by the whinnying of the horses as the sharks moved in (the troops were on the way to the South African War), the horses on the "Valkyrie" sounded very much the same as the ones on the "Troopship," and if I had known as much about show business then as I do now, I might have been suspicious of the entire production.

Occasionally, I was taken to the hospital in

Cirencester to "do my bit." This entailed trying not to fidget or jump while young VAD's practiced bandaging any part of me they fancied.

The war days sped by and the house in Gloucestershire was sold. So, too, was one we had in Argyllshire. Everyone, my mother included, thought that my father was very rich. As a part-time lieutenant in his part-time regiment, he had cheerfully gone off to war like a knight of old, taking with him as troopers his valet, his undergardener and two grooms. He also took his hunter, but these were exchanged for rifles in Egypt en route, and my father and his valet and one groom were duly slaughtered — cavalrymen ordered to land as infantry, at night, on a strongly defended beach without any training whatsoever for it.

He was hugely in debt at the time.

We soon moved to London to a large, damp house in Cadogan Place, and the sweaty, hearty, red-faced country squires were replaced by pale, gay young men who recited poetry and sang to my mother. She was very beautiful, very musical, very sad and lived on cloud nine.

A character called Uncle Tommy* soon made his appearance and became a permanent member of her entourage. Gradually the pale, gay young men gave way to pale, sad, older men.

Uncle Tommy was a second-line politician who

*Sir Thomas Comyn-Platt. Liked to be known as the mystery man of the Conservative Party. Contested Portsmouth Central in the election of 1926 . . . soundly beaten by Miss Jenny Lee, wife of Aneurin Bevan.

did not fight in the war. A tall ramrod-straight creature with immensely high white collars, a bluish nose and a very noisy cuff-link combination which he rattled at me when I made an eating error at mealtime.

I don't believe he was very healthy really. Anyway he got knighted for something to do with the Conservative Party and the Nineteen Hundred Club, and Cadogan Place became a rendezvous for people like Lord Willoughby de Broke, Sir Edward Carson, KC, and Sir E. Marshall Hall, KC. I suppose it bubbled with the sort of brilliant conversation into which children these days would be encouraged to join, but as soon as it started, Grizel and I were removed to a nursery upstairs. It had a linoleum floor and a bag of apples hanging outside the window during the winter. Grizel, who was two years older, became very interested during this period in the shape and form of my private parts; but when after a particularly painful inspection, I claimed my right to see hers too, she covered up sharply and dodged the issue by saying, "Well, it's a sort of flat arrangement."

At about this time, the Germans began their air raids on London. High in the night sky, I saw a Zeppelin go down in flames near Shepherds Bush. The airplanes were to come next. On the day my mother took me down Sloane Street to buy a pair of warm gloves I saw my first Fokkers. Everyone rushed into the street to point them out to each other. Then as the possibility of what might be about to drop out of the Fokkers dawned on them they rushed back indoors again.

My mother never left the glove shop. She was busy giving a splendid discourse on the superior quality of French gloves when the manager said, "This place will come down like a pack of cards." By that time the Fokkers must have been fifty miles away, but I was nevertheless lugged across the street and we joined the undignified Gadarene swine movement down the steps of the Knightsbridge Tube Station. One woman had a parrot. Another had hysterics and, between screams, ate handfuls of marmalade out of a stone jar, a spectacle I found highly enjoyable.

After sufficient time had elapsed for the Fokkers to be cozily bedded down at their home base outside Hamburg, we all emerged well equipped to tell long dull stories about our experience in air raids during World War I. I suppose we gave these up about September, 1940.

Uncle Tommy's marriage to my mother coincided with my sixth birthday. The wedding took place at All Saints, Sloane Street. Purple with embarrassment, I was pressganged into being a page and pressure-fed into a primrose-colored suit with mother-of-pearl buttons, a white lace collar, shorts and socks.

I did everything I could to wreck the show and fidgeted and picked my nose till an aquiline creature, later identified as the famous Lady Oxford and Asquith, came and knelt in the aisle to comfort me. I decided she was a witch and again and again informed the congregation of this discovery in a shrill treble.

I was removed, and Uncle Tommy, forever

politically sensitive, treated me from that moment on with frosty distaste.

My eldest brother, Henri (known as Max), was a naval cadet at Dartmouth, longing to get into the war. My eldest sister, Joyce, was at home helping my mother, and Grizel had gone away to boarding school in Norfolk. I was the youngest.

Cadogan Place we soon could not afford to live in, so it was sold and a smaller house on Sloane Street, across on the unchic side of the garden, was purchased.

A pink Gawblimy cap was obtained for me and I was sent to Mr. Gibb's day school down the street. It became clear to me very early that I was not going to be long in the house on Sloane Street.

The little room which my mother had set aside for me was appropriated by Uncle Tommy as his dressing room and I was packed off to boarding school at Elstree.

I can't say I was miserable at being snatched away from the bosom of my family because the bosom had not seemed, so far, to be a particularly warm and cozy place.

Apart from the Chinese, the only people in the world who pack their sons off to the tender care of unknown and often homosexual schoolmasters at the exact moment when they are most in need of parental love and influence are the British so-called upper and middle classes.

I don't suppose I particularly minded going away, but I had not been long at Elstree before I discovered that life could be hell.

There was a great deal of bullying, and for a

six-year-old, the spectacle of a gang of twelve-year-olds, bearing down, cracking wet towels like whips, can be terrifying.

For the most part, the masters were even more frightening. It would be charitable to think that they were all shell-shocked heroes returned from the hell of Mons and Vimy, but it seems more probable that they were sadistic perverts who had been found at the bottom of the educational barrel and dredged up at a time of acute manpower shortage.

One, a Mr. Christie, when he tired of pulling ears halfway out of our heads (I still have one that sticks out almost at right angles thanks to this son of a bitch) and delivering, for the smallest mistake in declension, backhanded slaps that knocked one off one's bench, delighted in saying, "Show me the hand that wrote this," and then bringing down the sharp edge of a heavy ruler across the offending wrist.

He took the last form on Friday evening, and I remember praying every week that he would die before then so that I could somehow reach the haven of Saturday and Sunday and the comparative safety of the weekend.

I don't think I have ever been so frightened of a human being in my life. Once he made me lean out of a fourth-floor window — a stupefying height for a little boy — then he shut the window across the small of my back, ordered two other equally terrified boys to hold my feet, and laid into me mightily with a cane. All this for some mistake in "common are *sacerdos dux vates parens et conjux.* . . ."

Years later, when I was at Sandhurst and playing in the Rugby football fifteen, big enough and by then ugly enough to take care of myself, I had an overpowering urge to see the bastard again, face-to-face.

I went down to Elstree, filled with vindictiveness. I don't know what I intended to do really, and when I got there I found the school empty. The prisonlike exercise yard was full of rubbish and old newspapers. The fourth-floor window, out of which I had dangled, was broken and open to the rain — it didn't even look very high.

My mother, at that time, would not believe my tales of woe or rather Uncle Tommy persuaded her that they were nonsense, telling her that all boys exaggerated and that anyway she could not be expected to know anything about English schools.

After two years of this purgatory, I got a huge boil as a result of the bad food. "Oh!" said the matron. "That's nothing. Don't make such a fuss!" and lopped off the top of it with a pair of scissors.

The ensuing infection was pretty horrible and put me in the sanatorium.

Finally, greatly urged on by my brother, who believed me, my mother saw the light and at the end of term gave me the glorious news that I would never have to go back to Elstree again.

The next term, I was sent to Heatherdown at Ascot.

At this point, I don't believe my mother was actually taking in washing, but, as sure as hell, she was sending very little out, and it must have been a fearful drain on her resources. Heatherdown was far more expensive than Elstree; certainly only a token subscription to the family coffers was being made by Uncle Tommy and she still had her thumb in the dike of my father's debts; but I was blissfully unconscious of all this and found myself wallowing in a veritable flood of good fortune.

Heatherdown was a very different cup of tea, very carriage trade, very protected; compared to Elstree, very soft and compared to anywhere else, very snobbish. Everybody went from there to Eton. Gone were the sadistic masters and the school bullies tying small boys to hot radiators; no more mad matrons; no more ex-naval cooks with fingernails like toenails doling out their nauseous confections; and receding like a bad dream were the flinty playground and the evil-smelling doorless lavatories, open to the elements and the helpful advice of schoolmates.

Instead, I found a world of cleanliness and kindly masters, motherly matrons, green playing fields, a lake, delicious food and a swimming pool. In short, schoolboy heaven.

The only grown-ups who hit me were the headmaster who, under great provocation, would uncork an occasional dose of the cane, and a dear old gentleman who taught divinity, called Mr. Hodgson, who occasionally wielded a clothes brush known as Dixon and Parker because if, as rarely happened, he hit hard enough, the name of the maker was left imprinted on the bum.

After the appalling apprenticeship of Elstree, I could not believe that life could be so perfect.

Released from fear and oppression, the whole thing went to my head, and I bloomed like a rather questionable rose.

Almost nine, I became something of a clown. This was hastened on when, for some strange reason, my balls dropped three years earlier than they should have done.

I was in the choir at the time, no Eddie Lough to be sure, but the possessor of a voice of guileless purity. Sometimes I was entrusted with solo passages, and it was on such an occasion, and in front of a full house, that disaster struck.

Ascot Sunday, parents staying in smart country houses nearby for the Race Meeting had filled the chapel to capacity. Alone, I was piping my way through "There is a green hill far away, without a city wall. . . ." Suddenly, on the word "wall" a fearful braying sound issued from the angelic face of the soloist. I tried for the note again; this time it sounded like a Rolls-Royce klaxon of the period. The paper-thin discipline of the choir quickly disintegrated . . . repressed laughter became contagious and finally, general.

Almost immediately after chapel, I was caned by the headmaster, Sammy Day. He had once played cricket for England and still had one of the best late cuts in the business. It hurt a lot and considering the medical evidence that was from then on permanently with me, was rather unfair.

Boys are terrible snobs, and I was annually unnerved when the school list came out, to see some of my contemporaries sniggering because in between the young marquesses and dukes with their splendid addresses was:

Niven, D., Rose Cottage, Bembridge, I.W.

It had become necessary for the house in Sloane Street to go and our permanent address was as advertised in the school list — a converted fisherman's cottage which had a reputation for unreliability. When the east wind blew, the front door got stuck, and when the west wind blew, the back door could not be opened; only the combined weight of the family seemed to keep it anchored to the ground. I adored it and was happier there than I had ever been, especially because, with a rare flash of genius, my mother decided that during the holidays she would be alone with her children.

Uncle Tommy was barred — I don't know where he went — to the Carlton Club, I suppose.

After the sudden descent of my testicles, I was removed from the choir as a bad risk and was told to blow the organ; that is to say, I was the "bellows man" and the musical success of each service (we suffered through two a day) depended entirely on me.

I had by now perceived that a certain popularity could be mine if I became a figure of fun, and although this was a position of great trust, the newly found clown in me could not resist the opportunities it offered. For a very small price — two chocolate whirls, one Cadbury's Milk Flake or a brace of Turkish delights—I could be bribed to let the air out of the bellows on important occasions. The whole school, on the selected day, would be in the know, and hugging itself with delicious anticipation, would sit through an endless sermon.

It took careful preparation, but I could generally arrange matters so that a rude noise could be subtly injected into the proceedings usually just after an Amen. I could redress the situation rapidly by quick pumping and only the conoisseurs could detect that it was not a mistake . . . the boys were all connoisseurs.

Once I tried it when the Bishop of Ripon was in the middle of a special address. This was my masterpiece and also my downfall, but the bribes were mountainous.

It was a highly technical job and involved surreptitiously and noiselessly keeping the bellow half-filled for several minutes after the end of the preceding hymn. I had intended to let the air out in a series of well-spaced small squeaks and trills, thus keeping the boys happy during what promised to be a long, trying period, but something went wrong and it all came out at once and on a most unfortunate cue . . . a quotation from Proverbs 7: "I have perfumed my bed with myrrh, aloes and cinnamon. . . ."

It was as if the bellows could not contain themselves any longer — a tremendous fart rent the air. All was confusion.

The school was infiltrated with informers, and I was soon dealt with once more by the long-suffering Sammy Day.

I loved Heatherdown and tried to uphold the agricultural standards of the landed gentry with whom I was rubbing shoulders. Every summer on the First Sunday after the Derby (it is not thus described in the Book of Common Prayer, but so many boys of noble birth had racehorse owner fathers that at Heatherdown, it far outranked Rogation Sunday, the Sunday after Advent, and the twenty-first Sunday after Trinity) a prize was given to the boy with the most beautiful garden.

Each boy had a garden about the size of a lavatory mat in a small commercial hotel, and immense ingenuity and forethought were displayed by the owners. Actually, these gardens were status symbols of the worst kind, and boys whose family estates employed an army of gardeners proudly displayed the most exotic flowers and shrubs, delivered for planting hot from the family greenhouses, while the more modest smallholders nurtured colorful annuals and arranged them in intricate patterns.

I could only manage a biannual crop of mustard and cress.

The year that Humorist won the Derby was the year of one of the phenomena of the world — a drought in England — and my crop, carefully timed for the flower show, failed, burned to a crisp.

By now the self-appointed jester to the upper classes, I decided to fill the gap, and creeping out of the dormitory after dark, I made my way downstairs and flitting from tree to tree in the moonlight, arrived at a well-known gap in the wall which separated Heatherdown from Heathfield, the girls' school next door.

From preliminary reconnaissance, I knew that this gap opened onto the kitchen garden. I selected a huge vegetable marrow plant, pulled it up by the roots, and once safely back on the male side of the wall, hid it behind a piece of corrugated iron.

It took some while and several near heart attacks, but I finally made it back to bed. The next morning I retrieved the marrow and, in the hubbub caused by the arrival of other boys' parents in Daimlers and Rolls-Royces, managed to plant my prize on top of my poor piece of desert.

It didn't go down very well. The Countess of Jersey, one of the parents, presented the prizes.

She didn't give one to me, and later I was caned again by a no-longer-affable Sammy Day: not for making a nonsense of the flower show which could have been justified, but for *stealing* which put a totally different connotation on the thing.

After this, I went rapidly downhill from popular school clown to unpopular school nuisance. Striving to maintain my waning popularity, I fell in the lake and nearly drowned, purposely split my trousers on the school walk through Ascot one Sunday, and was caught trying to get into Ascot Racecourse — a hideous crime. Poor Brian Franks, a Bembridge friend, near death's door with pneumonia at Wixenford, a school nearby, received from me on the day of his "crisis," a large chocolate box inside which was a smaller box, then a smaller box and so on until finally a matchbox with a piece of dog's mess in it.

Not a funny joke, especially for the matron who opened it, but then I didn't know Brian was ill.

Brian overcame his illness and my gift and has remained a lifelong friend, but the matron took a dim view, the smoke signals went up between Wixenford and Heatherdown, and Sammy Day decided that his school could get along without me.*

I was ten and a half when I was expelled.

The English public schools have been operating for a long time; some for a very long time indeed. Eton was founded in 1440, and Winchester even earlier in 1378. Rugby, where that horrible little boy picked up a soccer ball and charged off with it, opened in 1567, and Oundle, thirteen years before that. Cheltenham and Marlborough, having opened their doors for the first time in the early eighteen forties, were probably the youngest additions to the well-known list, until in 1923 Stowe came along.

Stowe School was started not as were the others, by kings, archbishops or lord mayors but by a consortuim of educators and hardheaded businessmen who saw the possibilities for a new public school and hoped to make a good thing out of it.

*Later as a lieutenant colonel in the Special Air Services in World War II, Brian, for great gallantry after being dropped behind the German lines, was decorated with the DSO and MC. It is rather depressing to think that his mother complained to mine because I told him the facts of life when we were both ten years old. He, not believing this phenomenal piece of news, had asked her for up-to-date information.

Stowe House, the vast Georgian home of the extinct dukes of Buckingham, had become the debt-ridden property of a kinsman, the master of Kinloss.

He, like my father, was slaughtered during the war to end all wars, and his mother like mine was forced to liquidate.

The consortium obtained the magnificent house and several hundred acres of grounds. Clough Williams-Ellis, the architect of Portmeirion in North Wales, was enlisted to transform it. A prospectus was issued and Stowe was on its way, heralded as "the new great public school."

In these early postwar years, a whole strata of suddenly well-to-do industrialists found the established public schools, to which they longed to send their sons, already bulging at the seams, so the consortium had no problem whatever in finding clients. Finding an aggressive headmaster with new ideas was far more difficult. They made a most fortuitous choice: a young housemaster from Lancing College, J. F. Roxburgh.

In May of 1923, the school opened with fewer than a hundred boys. Somewhere in the depths of the Carlton Club, Tommy heard rumblings; they could have been fulminations because a leading article in the *Times* and the headmaster of Eton, Edward Lyttelton, both opined that year that instead of starting a new public school it would be far more sensible to enlarge the facilities of the old ones; but whatever they were, the rumblings sank in. Pa Browning was instructed to investigate this last resort, and in July, I was sent over to Stowe, thirty miles in the dilapidated village taxi, to be interviewed by J. F. Roxburgh.

Stowe has to be the most beautiful school in England. Golden stone colonnades, porticoes by Vanbrugh, sweeping lawns, huge lakes, long green valleys, glorious avenues, a Corinthian arch, a Palladian bridge and scores of assorted grottoes and *"temples d'amour"* from each of which, through spectacular beech woods, rides open up to show other more fascinating "Follies." Robert Adam, Grinling Gibbons, William Kent, Valdré and Borra combined to produce glowing, beautifully proportioned interiors.

Roxburgh, in his first public speech as headmaster, said, "Every boy who goes out from Stowe will know beauty when he sees it for the rest of his life."

How true, but the apprehensive small boy who waited in the headmaster's flower-filled garden on that warm summer evening saw nothing of the architectural and landscaped beauties around him. All he knew was that he had never in all his life wanted anything so much as to be accepted for that school — it just felt right and he longed passionately to be part of it.

Roxburgh finally appeared. Very elegant, he seemed, with a spotted bow tie, very tall, curly hair parted in the middle.

He came out through the French windows of his study and crooked his finger at me. Then he smiled, put an arm around my shoulders and led me to a stone bench.

"Now, my dear man," he said, "you seem to have had a lot of ups and downs. Tell me all about it."

I don't pretend to have total recall, but I do remember these words — I will never forget them.

He listened sympathetically as I told him my version of my life so far. When I had finished, he remained silent for what seemed like an eternity. Then he stood up and said, "I'll walk with you to the car." On the way through the school, he showed me the assembly hall and the library and pointed out the fabulous view from the top of the south front steps across sloping, green pastures to a lake, then up to the towering Corinthian arch. Several times he spoke to boys who passed us, each time addressing them by their Christian names.

When he reached the ancient taxi, he looked down at me and smiled again, then he said. "There will be two hundred new boys coming next term and you will be in Chandos House. Your housemaster will be Major Haworth."

I mumbled something, then climbed into the taxi. If I didn't weep then, I should have.

In September I arrived at Stowe along with the other new boys. As we outnumbered the old boys by two to one, everybody, masters included, for the first couple of weeks, sported a piece of white cardboard pinned to his coat showing his name in bold print, rather like a dentists' convention in Chicago.

All the boys wore gray flannel suits, as one of Roxburgh's better new ideas was to break with the traditional prison garb of the older establishments; no top hats, stiff collars or straw boaters for us . . . gray flannel suits on weekdays and blue suits on Sunday.

Rules were sensible and good manners were encouraged; for instance, hands had to be removed from pockets when passing a master. There were no bounds and boys were allowed to have bicycles. However, one still had to pedal three miles to get out of the school grounds so that was a little more strenuous than it sounded.

I could not believe my good fortune. The boys seemed nice and friendly, albeit as bemused for the first few days as I was, and Major Haworth, lately a company commander at Sandhurst, was one of the kindest and gentlest of men.

People are sharply divided about their school days and contrary to what one tells one's children about their being the best days of one's life, most people remember them as being pretty ghastly.

Stowe, in those early days, had to be different from any other school. At the start, we were all the same age — around thirteen. Within four years, as the number of boys swelled from 300 to 500, there was an annual intake of younger ones, but somehow it seemed as though we all grew up together and I for one enjoyed the whole thing immensely. Later, my inherent weakness of not being able to stand prosperity got me into trouble, but for the first couple of years, I was a fairly reliable citizen.

Roxburgh dominated the scene and I worshiped the man.

The first to notice some special interest being shown by a boy, Roxburgh nurtured it, fostered it and made the boy feel a little bit special because of it. How he did this, I shall never know, but he made every single boy at that school feel that he and what he did were of real importance to the headmaster. Boys were always addressed by their first names and encouraged to build radio sets; to fence and play golf and tennis besides the usual school games; to paint, play the piano or the bagpipes; and to keep pets, though this last got a little out of control as the boys grew older and instead of rabbits and ferrets being the status symbols, monkeys, bears, hyenas and skunks filled the cages. Finally, the school zoo was shut down for reasons of noise and smell.

I played the trombone and the drum in the school band and started a house magazine, to which "J. F." subscribed, called *The Chandosian*. I also, by the age of fourteen, fell in love once more with milk chocolate and became almost entirely conical in shape. My nickname was Podger or Binge and I went bright pink after Rugger. Another boy, named Smallman, was even fatter than I was; his nickname was unoriginal — Tiny. Tiny Smallman was very large indeed and we both became self-conscious about our physical defects. Tiny found an ad in a boys' paper and we spent our pocket money on strange tubes containing a foul-smelling green paste which, when rubbed onto the stomach or bottom, was guaranteed to reduce it in size. After football, we waited till the others had left the changing room rather than take a shower in public and thereby risk the ribald remarks and the towel flicking that was apt to accompany our appearance.

Because of my shape, I was enlisted in the school plays usually playing a mushroom or something fairly unobtrusive . . . I got the call of the greasepaint, however, and before I left school, I was running the school concerts and giving myself all the best parts.

I studied fairly hard, though permanently stymied by mathematics, and my immediate goal was the school certificate, a public exam for which one sat between fifteen and sixteen and which, provided one obtained enough credits, was comparable with O and A levels today. One of the credits one had to obtain in order to get the school certificate was mathematics, so from a very early date, "J. F." saw to it that I took special tuition to try and defeat the monster.

My long-term goal, thanks to some pretty nifty salesmanship by Major Haworth, became the Royal Military College, Sandhurst, followed by a commission in the Argyll and Sutherland Highlanders.

School, between thirteen and fifteen, therefore, presented no great problems and the holidays, too, went along very nicely during this period of formation . . . Tommy being persona non grata at Rose Cottage, the summers were bliss. For Christmas Grizel and I were packed off to spend the holiday at Nanpanton, in Leicestershire, with the Paget family, where the children, Peter and Joan, were of identical vintage.

Edmund, the father, was, with a splendid figure named Algy Burnaby, joint master of the Quorn Hunt; and Barbara, the mother, was a garrulous, gossipy, enchanting, shop-talking fox huntress who rode sidesaddle under a top hat bigger than Tommy's, swore like a trooper and, along with the rest of her family, never could grasp the fact that Grizel and I were not actually afraid of horses — we were just too impecunious to hunt. We loved the Pagets.

Easter holidays in English schools being short — three weeks — Tommy would arrange to be away while my mother found a variety of places in which to house us. Sometimes, it was Bembridge, but Rose Cottage was barely habitable at that time of year. Once we were sent to a sister of Tommy's who lived in a noisome little flat in Portsmouth — far too near the Bollards and the scenes of my crimes for comfort — but the worst was when Tommy decided to be a real-estate tycoon.

He bought a poky little house in a back street behind Windsor Castle. It was a dark-paneled purgatory, whose sole charm lay in the fact that it had once belonged to Nell Gwyn and much royal thrashing around was said to have gone on in the four-poster upstairs. It poured with rain for the entire holiday and Grizel and I played mah-jongg in semidarkness for three weeks.

I hope I never again have to set eyes on the bamboos, the flowers, the winds, the seasons and all those miserable dragons. I couldn't wait to get back to Stowe.

The memorable Easter holiday of this period came just after my fourteenth birthday.

Tommy's real-estate operations found us, for a while, the inhabitants of 110 Sloane Street, a small house of many floors which shook as the

70

buses went past the door: gasoline-driven red metropolitan buses, Nos. 19 and 22, and far more fascinating to me because they were driven by steam, the white Nationals, No. 30.

My brother, who had left the Navy because of chronic seasickness and sensibly switched to the Army, was abroad with his regiment in India. Joyce and Grizel both had tiny bedrooms, but there was no room for me, so I slept in a minute cubicle in a boardinghouse in St. James's Place, some distance away.

Every night after dinner, I walked to Sloane Square, boarded a 19 or a 22 headed for Piccadilly, got off at the Ritz Hotel and proceeded down St. James's Street to my iron bed, wooden floor, stained jug and basin and pot under the bed.

The next morning, I had to be back for breakfast at eight o'clock and I was given fourpence a day for the round trip. Even my rudimentary mathematics could work out that by walking four miles a day, I could save almost half a crown a week.

I enjoyed my nocturnal travels very much and soon gave up going straight from Sloane Street to St. James's Place and took to going all the way down Piccadilly to Piccadilly Circus to watch the electric signs.

Every night, I became most adventurous and after a week or so, I knew the area bounded by Park Lane, Oxford Street, Regent Street and Pall Mall like the back of my hand. This was a pretty safe area for a fourteen-year-old — indeed, it never crossed my mind that it could be otherwise — and apart from being spoken to a few times by strange men who asked me if I would like to go home with them to meet their dogs or see their paintings, I tramped around unhindered.

It seemed to me perfectly normal for a boy to be walking around the West End of London at night, so I saw nothing out of the ordinary in the number of girls who were doing the same thing; cloche hats, flesh-colored stockings and the forerunner of the miniskirt being the vogue, I saw a vast amount of female legs and ankles twinkling their way up and down the same streets that I frequented.

Bond Street was a great favorite of mine because many of the shop windows were lit up all night, and I made it a point, after watching BOVRIL, IRON JELLOIDS and OWBRIDGE change colors in Piccadilly Circus, to pause on my way to St. James's Place and check on how things looked in the windows of Garrards, Aspreys and Ciros Pearls.

Some of the girls, I noticed, were walking every night on the same streets, and I was soon on nodding terms with them, although I didn't understand at all the remarks made as I passed, nor the giggles that followed me.

One night, on Bond Street, I noticed a really superior pair of legs in front of me and I became so fascinated by them that I followed them for quite a distance. The girl seemed to have many friends and stopped and spoke to them from time to time.

The next night, I skipped going to watch the electric signs and went looking for those legs instead. I searched up and down Bond Street and cased the side streets too — Clifford Street, Savile Row and even Burlington Street, the scene of my naval debacle.

Just as I was about to give up, the girl came out of a house right in front of me and walked rapidly off toward Piccadilly. I followed, and when she stopped on a corner to talk to a couple of lady friends, I crossed the street and pretended to look into a shop window. I managed to get a fairly good view of her face. She was laughing and talking . . . very lively, very gay, and her face looked beautiful in an open, fresh English rose kind of way — blond, blue eyes, high color — you know the sort of thing.

She stayed there talking to her friends, and as I didn't want to be conspicuous, I moved off toward my boardinghouse.

When I woke up in the morning I knew I must be in love. At least, I suspected that I was because I could think of nothing else but this girl. The day dragged on interminably, a shopping morning with my mother and in the afternoon, playing among the stunted, grimy bushes of the gardens opposite our house with some stunted, grimy Spanish children.

That night, after dinner, I didn't walk. I was in a hurry. I took the bus and was lucky. After I had cruised up and down for what seemed an age, my patience was rewarded and my heart gave a lurch as I saw her lovely, long legs approaching from the Piccadilly direction. She was with a distinguished-looking, gray-haired man in a dinner jacket, about the same age as Tommy. He wore an opera hat and was smoking a cigar — obviously her father. Together they went into a house on Cork Street, and deliriously happy that I had found out where my dream lived, I took myself off to bed.

It took three days or rather nights of patient toil and careful sleuthing before I finally met Nessie.

I was following her down Cork Street at what I imagined to be a discreet distance, my eyes glued to her wondrous underpinnings, when she stopped and turned so suddenly and so unexpectedly that I nearly bumped into her.

"Wot the 'ell are yer followin' me for?" she demanded.

I went purple.

"I wasn't following you," I lied. "I was just on my way to bed."

"Well, for Gawd's sake, go on 'ome, mate. For the last four nights you've been stuck to me like my bleedin' shadow. Wot d'yer want anyway?"

I stammered and looked wildly to right and left. Suddenly she softened and smiled.

"All right, it's still early and you're a bit young but come on home and I'll give yer a good time."

Soon she turned into her doorway, and in a daze I followed, unable to believe my good fortune.

"A good time," she had said — it had to be at least a ginger beer and listening to the gramophone . . . Aileen Stanley singing "When It's Moonlight in Kaluha" or Jack Hulbert and Cicely Courtneidge in excerpts from *Clowns in Clover*. In a high state of expectancy, I mounted to the second floor behind my glorious new friend.

The flat, above a tailor's shop, was small and smelled of cabbage. In the living room there was a large divan with a lot of satin cushions and some dolls on it and nearby a small lamp with a red shade. A small kitchen stove was behind a screen. The other room was a bedroom, also rather poorly lit; a tiny bathroom was just discernible in the gloom beyond the huge bed that seemed to sag quite a lot in the middle.

"Three quid," she said, as she took off her coat.

I didn't quite get the message, so she came very close to me and peered into my eyes.

"Three quid," she repeated. "That too much?"

I gulped and floundered. "For what?"

"For the best yer've ever 'ad, mate, but then you 'aven't 'ad a lot, 'av yer? 'Ow old are yer anyway?"

I was still unsure as to exactly what ground I was on and I kept wondering if her father lived downstairs, but I managed to mumble the truth.

"Fourteen!!" she practically shrieked. "Wot the 'ell d'yer think I am — a bleedin' nannie?"

Then she started giggling. "Oh, my Gawd, wot a larf. 'Ow old d'yer think I am anyway?"

"Twenty," I suggested tentatively.

"Three years yet before that 'appens," she said. "Well, come on, let's get on wiv it. *Fourteen* . . . Gawd, yer are a one aren't yer?"

I watched half in fascination, half in apprehension as she walked about the living room, taking off her little hat and blouse and unhooking her skirt.

" 'Ere, take a look at these in case you need any 'elp." With that she sat me down on the divan and left me to look at a large album of photographs.

"I'll be ready in a jiffy, dear." She disappeared into the bedroom.

I had not so far been exposed to any pornography so the contents of that album very nearly finished off my sex life before it got under way. Hideous overweight ladies, clad only in shoes and stockings, being mounted from every angle by skinny little men with enormous "dongs": combinations of every sort in threes and twos, all with expressions of the greatest sincerity — and all apparently in advanced middle age.

The awful truth began to filter through my brain.

When Nessie appeared in the bedroom door dressed in the same uniform as the buxom ladies in the album — naked except for black stockings, held up above the knees by pink garters with blue roses on them and pink high-heeled shoes — she had a small towel in her hand.

"Come along, ducks, let's see 'ow good yer are . . . yer can wash in 'ere . . . I've put in pomegranate," she added. In a daze I followed her into the dark little bedroom . . . another red-shaded lamp was beside the bed. "Over there, dear," she said, indicating a kidney shaped enamel bowl on a collapsible knee-high stand. She threw me the towel, lay down on the bed, and put a record on a portable gramophone. The tune was one I knew well; it has, rather naturally, haunted me ever since. "Yes . . . we have no bananas." As I was to discover later, Nessie had a wonderful native wit but I still believe her selection at that particular moment was a random one.

"Get a move on, ducks. You don't get all night for three quid, yer know. Get your shirt off for a start."

I took off my coat and my shirt and started to wash my hands in the bowl.

"Christ!" she yelled, sitting bolt upright. "Not yer bleedin' 'ands — yer dickie bird! Just a minute," she went on more gently, "come 'ere, come and sit on me bed. I want to talk to you . . . Now look me in the eye, straight. . . . Is this the first? . . . 'Ave yer ever done it before . . . ever done any fuckin'?"

Miserably, I shook my head.

"And you 'aven't got three quid either, I'll bet?"

Again I shook my head and mumbled some inane explanation.

"Aw, you poor little bastard," she said, "you must be scared out of yer fuckin' wits." She looked at me reflectively. "Ever seen a naked woman before?"

"No," I confessed.

"Well, this is wot it looks like — 'ow d'yer like it?"

I smiled weakly and tried not to lower my eyes. Nessie snuggled down and started to giggle again, a deliciously infectious sound.

"Well, you've got this far — why don't you

77

take the rest of your clobber orf and pop into bed?"

"What about the . . . ," I began.

"Oh, you owe me three quid," she interrupted. "Christ, I never thought I'd be seducing children. . . . FOURTEEN . . . come on, jump in then."

"Yes . . . we have no bananas" was replaced by something a little more encouraging; the bedside lamp with the red shade was left and Nessie with her wondrous skin became a most understanding teacher. "There we are, dear, that's it now — take a little weight on your elbows like a gentleman. Slowly, dear, more slowly. Whoa! yer not a fuckin' woodpecker, yer know . . . slowly . . . *that's* it, enjoy yerself . . . there, that's nice, isn't it, dear? . . . Are yer 'appy? . . . 'Appy now?"

By the time the Easter holidays ended Nessie had become the most important thing in my life; my education at her hands and, in a way, at her expense had continued. She worked at night and slept late, but on many afternoons, we met, usually at the entrance to a small movie house — she loved W. S. Hart — or we went to the music halls, the Coliseum, the Alhambra or the Palladium, to see Herbert Mundin, Lily Morris, Rebla the juggler, or a marvelous pair of young acrobats — Nervo and Knox. The seats cost one shilling and threepence and after the shows we had a cup of tea and a bun in a little tea shop or we skipped the tea and the bun and went directly back to her flat. Afterward, I would walk down to Sloane Street for a dreary family dinner during which Tommy would rattle the damn cuff links in his starched shirt to draw attention to the fact that I was dozing at the table.

Quite early in my relationship with Nessie, I made the elementary mistake of asking her why she did it . . . "a sweet girl like you." She rounded on me like a tigress: "Now don't yer start tryin' to reform me. About three times a week some silly bugger asks the same friggin' question.

"Look . . . I'm three years older than you and I'm doing it because I want to do it . . . Why I want to do it is none of your fuckin' bizness so if yer don't like it, piss off back to school."

Back at school for the summer term, I found that my life had fundamentally changed. Nessie or the thoughts of Nessie became the focal point of my existence. What I saw in her was fairly obvious, but there were other things, too, quite apart from the normal and very special physical attachment to "the first"; she gave me something that so far had been in rather short supply — call it love, understanding, warmth, female companionship or just ingredient X — whatever it was, it was all over me like a tent.

I can't believe that I contributed very much to Nessie's well-being or peace of mind during this period — a fat fourteen and a half with no money and less experience — but apart from the "hurly burly of the chaise longue," as Mrs. Patrick Campbell once described a splendid activity, there also grew up between us a brother-sister relationship that was to last for many years.

Thanks to Nessie's insistence, I lost weight, a lot of extra padding turned to muscle, and I became quite a proficient athlete of the second rank . . . house colors for practically everything and a frequent performer before I left Stowe in the 1st. XI cricket, the 1st. XV Rugby football and on the fencing and boxing teams.

Nessie came down to Stowe to see me in summer and brought a picnic basket and a tartan rug. Together we took full advantage of the beauties of the school grounds. She had never been out of London before, and these trips to the country, she told me later, gave her a peace she never knew existed. She took a great interest in my progress at the school and became so intrigued by my hero worship of Roxburgh that she insisted on meeting him. Basely, I tried to avoid this confrontation, but Nessie was not easily put off.

"Look dear, 'e'll never know I'm an 'ore. 'E'll think I'm yer bleedin' aunt or somefin'." . . . "Do I look like an 'ore?"

I told her she looked beautiful and like a duchess — not that looking like a duchess was much of a compliment but she was as easily flattered as she was hard to dissuade.

"That's 'im, innit?" she cried one Saturday afternoon, looking across toward the cricket pavilion. Roxburgh was approaching our tartan rug, resplendent in a pale-gray suit topped by the inevitable spotted bow tie.

Nessie stood up, bathed in sunlight. She was wearing a short white silk summer dress that clung lovingly to her beautiful body; her honey-colored hair was cut in the fashion of the time — the shingle; she had a small upturned nose; she looked wonderfully young and fresh.

Roxburgh came over smiling his famous smile. "May I join you?"

I introduced him.

" 'E's just like you told me" said Nessie to me. " 'E's beautiful," and then to Roxburgh, "Don't look a bit like a schoolmaster, dew yer, dear?"

J. F. settling himself on the rug, missed a tiny beat but thereafter never gave any indication that he was not talking to a beautiful duchess.

He stayed about ten minutes, extolling the glories of Stowe House and its history, and Nessie bathed in the full glow of his charm. Never once did he ask any loaded questions, and when he got up to leave, he said, "David is very lucky to have such a charming visitor." The charming visitor nearly got me expelled almost a year later, but it was certainly not her fault.

In the summer of 1926, by now a robust sixteen-year-old and appreciably ahead of my time in worldly experience, I must have seemed changed to Roxburgh. He sent for me and told me that I was one of four boys he had selected to become monitors in a new house — Grafton — which was to open the following term.

The housemaster was coming from Fettes, Mr. Freeman, and the boy chosen as prefect or head of the house was Bernard Gadney.* It was a huge

*B. C. Gadney was later to captain the English XV in many Rugby Internationals.

81

compliment, an enormous boost for any boy, but for me to feel that J. F. had this faith in me, it was a bonanza. However, before I could bask in the glories of my new responsibilities, I had to overcome a slight hazard — the school certificate. I was to sit for the exam in two weeks' time. It was a sort of long shot really; if I failed this first time, I would still have three more chances but I had to obtain the certificate soon in order to qualify to sit for the entrance exam to the Royal Military College, Sandhurst, eighteen months hence.

Apart from the dreaded mathematics, I was quite confident that I could pull it off this first time. My prospects in the new house were very exciting, my fat had disappeared, I had many friends at school and at Bembridge, I had Nessie in the background, and I was at last beginning to get to know and to love my mother. In fact, everything was roses for me. Then that damn wind started puffing those weeds in my direction once more.

I sat for the exam in the big school gymnasium and made mincemeat of the first two papers, French and history, and after the science, geography and English papers, I remained supremely confident. The last two papers were mathematics and Latin translation. In mathematics, as already explained, a credit (about 80 percent) was obligatory, otherwise the whole exam was failed. When the questions were put on my desk — and all over the country at that particular moment identical papers were being put in front of thousands of nervous boys — I took a deep breath and started to read.

One glance was enough. It was hopeless. I knew that I just couldn't cope and there is no more suffocating feeling than that when sitting for a public examination.

I made a few vague stabs at the geometry questions and a token effort at the algebra, but there was no point in my even trying to tackle the arithmetic.

I was the first boy to hand in his answers and leave the gymnasium. I went out to the cricket nets and faced the fact that the school certificate was certainly not going to be mine this time.

Nessie was coming to see me the next day — a Saturday — and her train was due at Buckingham Station at midday. The Latin exam was scheduled from ten o'clock till eleven thirty, so I decided to get through this now-useless and unprofitable period as quickly as possible, pedal down to the station, and surprise her there instead of meeting her as planned near the Corinthian arch at twelve thirty.

It so happened that my Latin teacher was the supervisor of the candidates on that Saturday morning; this meant that it was he who would hand out the questions at the start, collect the answers at the end, and in between, wander about the rows of desks making sure that there was no talking, or, perish the thought, any use of notes.

He knew that I could easily pass the Latin exam, but only I knew that it was now useless to try.

However, if I handed in a half-finished paper

in half the allotted time, he would most certainly make me go and sit down again and do the job properly. The trick then was to complete the whole paper in half the time and be on my way to Buckingham Station. Archie Montgomery-Campbell was a good and outstanding friend who occupied the desk on my right during the whole week of exams. He was also an excellent Latin scholar, so I enlisted his help.

The Latin paper was in two parts, prose and verse. It was agreed that I would quickly dispose of the prose while Archie coped first with the verse. Then, after making his fair copy, he would crumple up his first draft and drop it on the floor between the two desks. It was clearly understood between us that if anything went wrong, Archie would merely say that he had thrown away his first translation after he had made his fair copy and if somebody picked it up it was none of his business. The dirty work was to be done by me alone, he was to be blameless.

It all went beautifully according to plan.

I copied out Archie's verse translation beneath my own effort at the prose, handed in my paper, and bicycled happily off in plenty of time to surprise Nessie.

We spent a blissful day together, eating shrimp paste sandwiches and sausage rolls, drinking shandy-gaff* and rolling around on the tartan rug. Nessie had begun to tell me a little more about herself and I listened adoringly that afternoon to her descriptions of her childhood in

*A mixture of beer and ginger-beer.

a Hoxton slum: six children in a tiny room, the three youngest in the bed, the others sleeping on the floor and all cowering away from the Friday night battles between the parents.

At fifteen she and her sister of a year older had run away. For a while, they found work as waitresses in dingy tea shops and restaurants in Battersea and Pimlico. A few months later they were engaged as hostesses in a sleazy "club" in Wardour Street. Then the sister started taking drugs and one night told Nessie she was going north with a boyfriend to avoid the police. Nessie didn't miss her much and soon was employed by Mrs. Kate Merrick at the 43 Club. She had to be on hand in evening dress as a dancing partner, making a fuss of Ma Merrick's rather high-class clientele and persuading them to buy champagne at exorbitant prices.

She was not allowed to solicit on the premises — a rule that was strictly enforced because Ma Merrick's establishment was often infiltrated by police officers in evening clothes, posing as the tipsy aftermath of regimental dinners or bachelor parties — but, in fact, contacts were easily enough made and Nessie soon built up the basis of an enthusiastic clientele.

"I'm not an 'ore wiv an 'eart of bleedin' gold, yer know, dear. I'm out for everything I can get out of this game for another couple of years — then I'm going to marry some nice Yank or Canadian and fuck off abroad and have kids.

"The only reason I work the streets is that I'm on me own. I don't 'ave to sit up all bleedin' night talkin' to a lot of drunks. When I git tired,

I can go 'ome an' lock me door. . . . I make much more money, too, an' the best bit, it's not like bein' one of those who sit on the end of a phone all night. I can see wot I'm gettin'. If I don't like the look of a bloke, I don't ask 'im up, see?"

Watching Nessie while she talked, it seemed incredible that she could be leading this sort of existence — her very youth and, yes, her very freshness were in complete contradiction to everything she was describing.

"A lot of blokes want to 'ave me all to themselves . . . you know, set me up in a bleedin' flat in Maida Vale wiv a maid an' a fuckin' puppy, but when the time comes, I'll set meself up. I've got to move out of Cork Street tho', it's gettin' so fuckin' noisy, dear, with that big ginger who's moved in above. An Army officer by all accounts. 'E goes 'round the coffee stalls at Hyde Park Corner an' picks up them corporals in their red tunics an' all, then 'e brings them 'ome an' dresses 'imself up as a fuckin' bride, makeup, white satin, 'igh 'eels, a bleedin' veil, orange blossom — the lot. Then 'e chooses one of these blokes — 'e always 'as about a 'arf a dozen 'em up there at the same time — and 'e fuckin' *marries* 'im. Goes through a sort of service, then arm in arm wiv 'is 'usband, 'e walks under a fuckin' arch way of swords 'eld up by the other blokes. I've talked to a coupla the soldiers — they're not gingers, mark you, far from it, but they pick up a coupla quid apiece for the job an' a fiver for the 'usband.

" 'E doesn't lay an 'and on any of them, just

shoots 'is wad walking under them fuckin' swords. But the noise, dear — Christ! I can't stand it! Everything is very military, 'im being an ex-officer an' all, an' when it's all over 'e gets back into 'is nice blue suit, sits down be'ind a table with a fuckin' Army blanket on it an' they all form up like a bleedin' pay parade. 'Guardsman so-and-so.' 'Sir!' One pace forward march . . . crash! 'Forty shillings . . . SIR!' 'About turn' . . . crash! 'NEXT MAN' . . . CRASH! 'SIR!!' . . . CRASH! CHRIST! . . . those fuckin' Army boots, dear, I'm goin' to 'ave to move. . . ." She shook with delicious laughter.

"Of course, I don't get mixed up wiv no funny business meself . . . it's just me an' a bloke, that's all. . . . No exhibitions, none of that stuff. Of course, I'm not sayin' I don't occasionally pick up a little fancy money — there's this Aussie millionaire, dear, about fifty, who gets about eight of us up to 'is 'otel, then we all strip down to the stockin's and 'igh 'eels an' 'e takes off everything! Then 'e gives us each an 'en pheasant's tail feather to stuff up the arse — 'ell of a job keepin' it in there, it is, because we 'ave to walk 'round in a circle — then, would you believe it, dear, 'e stands there in the middle wiv a cock pheasant's feather up 'is own arse an' sprinkles corn on the fuckin' carpet — of course we 'ave a terrible time not larfin' but if we do larf, we don't get paid an' it's a tenner each too. . . . Well, there 'e stands, kind of crowin' or whatever the 'ell pheasants do, an' we all 'ave to kinda peck at the fuckin' corn . . . it's amazin' really, he shoots off right there all by 'isself in the

middle of the circle. We never 'ave to touch 'im
. . . pathetic really when you think."

When Nessie went back to London after these
outings, I always felt terribly lonely. I loved
walking about the fields and woods with her.
I've never seen anyone get such real pleasure out
of trees and flowers and birds, and it gave me a
feeling of importance to be able to point out
different animals and to tell her about life in the
country.

Sadly, I waved her away at Buckingham Station
and pedaled up the long avenue in time for
evening chapel.

The whole school attended chapel twice a day,
and after the evening service, announcements of
special importance were made by the headmaster.

In chapel about three weeks after Nessie's
visit, J. F. motioned the boys to remain in their
places; an expectant murmur arose.

"All over the country," J. F. began, "overworked examiners have been correcting several
thousand papers sent in for this year's examinations.

"Stowe is a new school and these same
examiners have been looking at the papers sent
in by us with special interest.

"Boys who sit for a public examination are
representing their schools in public and they,
therefore, have a very great responsibility. Schools
are judged by the boys who represent them —

"It is, therefore, with grief and great disappointment that I have to tell you that two boys
representing Stowe in the school certificate have
been caught cheating. I shall question the two

concerned this evening and I shall deal with them as I see fit."

Only when I saw Archie Montgomery-Campbell's ashen face did the horrible truth sink in. As the school rose to leave the chapel, my legs turned to water.

BENJAMIN FRANKLIN

from

THE AUTOBIOGRAPHY

With his *Autobiography*, **Ben Franklin** (1706–90) wrote what many critics feel is the first truly distinguished American literary work, and at the same time he established the model for the autobiography as a genre.

A man of enormous gifts, Franklin describes his rise from the poverty and obscurity in which he was born to his successful and influential position in the American colonies, particularly as a publisher, a scientist, and an activist in political affairs. (His autobiography breaks off in 1758—before he had helped to draft and sign the Declaration of Independence and later the Constitution.) In this excerpt he begins at age sixty-five (in 1771) to set down his "memoirs" as he calls them. One of his several reasons for writing about his life is that he wishes to make known to his children and grandchildren the means he employed to attain success, both by his actions and by his practical homespun beliefs and philosophy of life—including hard work, discipline, and thrift.

To any modern reader willing to adapt to an

earlier—but still readable and clear—prose style, Franklin's wit and good sense make his life story a very good tale indeed.

TWYFORD* at the Bishop of St. Asaph's, 1771.

Dear Son:†

I have ever had a pleasure in obtaining any little anecdotes of my ancestors. You may remember the inquiries I made among the remains of my relations when you were with me in England, and the journey I undertook for that purpose. Now imagining it may be equally agreeable to you to know the circumstances of *my* life, many of which you are yet unacquainted with, and expecting a week's uninterrupted leisure in my present country retirement, I sit down to write them for you. To which I have besides some other inducements. Having emerged from the poverty and obscurity in which I was born and bred to a state of affluence and some degree of reputation in the world, and having gone so far through life with a considerable share of felicity, the conducing means I made use of, which with the blessing of God so well succeeded, my posterity may like to know, as they may find some of them suitable to their own situations, and therefore fit to be imitated. That felicity, when I reflected on it, has induced me sometimes

*A village fifty miles from London.
†Franklin addressed his autobiography to his son William.

91

to say that were it offered to my choice I should have no objection to a repetition of the same life from its beginning, only asking the advantages authors have in a second edition to correct some faults of the first. So would I, if I might, besides correcting the faults, change some sinister accidents and events of it for others more favorable, but though this was denied, I should still accept the offer. However, since such a repetition is not to be expected, the next thing most like having one's life over again seems to be a *recollection* of that life, and to make that recollection as durable as possible the putting it down in writing. . . .

The notes one of my uncles (who had the same kind of curiosity in collecting family anecdotes) once put into my hands furnished me with several particulars relating to our ancestors. From these notes I learned that the family had lived in the same village, Ecton, in Northamptonshire, for three hundred years, and how much longer he knew not (perhaps from the time when the name Franklin, that before was the name of an order of people, was assumed by them for a surname when others took surnames all over the kingdom), on a freehold of about thirty acres, aided by the smith's business, which had continued in the family till his time, the eldest son being always bred to that business — a custom which he and my father both followed as to their eldest sons. When I searched the register at Ecton, I found an account of their births, marriages, and burials from the year 1555 only, there being no register kept in that parish at any time preceding. By that register I perceived that I was the youngest son of the youngest son for five generations back. My grandfather Thomas, who was born in 1598, lived at Ecton till he grew too old to follow business longer, when he went to live with his son John, a dyer at Banbury in Oxfordshire, with whom my father served an apprenticeship. There my grandfather died and lies buried. We saw his gravestone in 1758. His eldest son, Thomas, lived in the house of Ecton, and left it with the land to his only child, a daughter, who with her husband, one Fisher of Wellingborough, sold it to Mr. Isted, now lord of the manor there. My grandfather had four sons that grew up, viz.: Thomas, John, Benjamin, and Josiah. . . .

Josiah, my father, married young, and carried his wife with three children into New England about 1682. The conventicle* having been forbidden by law and frequently disturbed induced some considerable men of his acquaintance to remove to that country, and he was prevailed with to accompany them thither, where they expected to enjoy their mode of religion with freedom. By the same wife he had four children more born there, and by a second wife ten more, in all seventeen; of which I remember thirteen sitting at one time at his table, who all grew up to be men and women, and married; I was the youngest son and the youngest child but two, and was born in Boston, New England. My mother, the second wife, was Abiah Folger, a daughter of Peter Folger, one of the first settlers of New England, of whom honorable mention is

*Assemblies of religious dissenters.

made by Cotton Mather, in his church history of that country, entitled *Magnalia Christi Americana,* as "a godly, learned Englishman," if I remember the words rightly. I have heard that he wrote sundry small occasional pieces, but only one of them was printed, which I saw now many years since. . . .

My elder brothers were all put apprentices to different trades. I was put to the grammar school at eight years of age, my father intending to devote me, as the tithe of his sons, to the service of the church. My early readiness in learning to read (which must have been early, as I do not remember when I could not read) and the opinion of all his friends that I should certainly make a good scholar encouraged him in this purpose of his. My uncle Benjamin, too, approved of it, and proposed to give me all his shorthand volumes of sermons, I suppose as a stock to set up with, if I would learn his character.* I continued, however, at the grammar school not quite one year, though in that time I had risen gradually from the middle of the class of that year to be the head of it, and farther was removed into the next class above it, in order to go with that into the third at the end of the year. But my father, in the meantime, from a view of the expense of a college education, which having so large a family he could not well afford, and the mean living many so educated were afterwards able to obtain — reasons that he gave to his friends in my hearing — altered his first intention, took

*His system of shorthand.

94

me from the grammar school, and sent me to a school for writing and arithmetic, kept by a then famous man, Mr. George Brownell, very successful in his profession generally, and that by mild, encouraging methods. Under him I acquired fair writing pretty soon, but I failed in the arithmetic, and made no progress in it. At ten years old I was taken home to assist my father in his business, which was that of a tallow-chandler and soap-boiler; a business he was not bred to, but had assumed on his arrival in New England, and on finding his dying trade would not maintain his family, being in little request. Accordingly, I was employed in cutting wick for the candles, filling the dipping mold and the molds for cast candles, attending the shop, going of errands, etc. . . . .

From a child I was fond of reading, and all the little money that came into my hands was ever laid out in books. Pleased with the *Pilgrim's Progress*, my first collection was of John Bunyan's works in separate little volumes. I afterwards sold them to enable me to buy R. Burton's *Historical Collections;* they were small chapman's books, and cheap, forty or fifty in all. My father's little library consisted chiefly of books in polemic divinity, most of which I read and have since often regretted that at a time when I had such a thirst for knowledge, more proper books had not fallen in my way, since it was now resolved I should not be a clergyman. *Plutarch's Lives* there was, in which I read abundantly, and I still think that time spent to great advantage. There was also a book of Defoe's, called an *Essay on Projects*, and another of Dr. Mather's,* called *Essays to do Good,* which perhaps gave me a turn of thinking that had an influence on some of the principal future events in my life.

This bookish inclination at length determined my father to make me a printer, though he had already one son (James) of that profession. In 1717 my brother James returned to England with a press and letters to set up his business in Boston. I liked it much better than that of my father, but still had a hankering for the sea. To prevent the apprehended effect of such an inclination, my father was impatient to have me bound to my brother. I stood out some time, but at last was persuaded, and signed the indentures when I was yet but twelve years old. I was to serve as an apprentice till I was twenty-one years of age, only I was to be allowed journeyman's wages during the last year. In a little time I made great proficiency in the business and became a useful hand to my brother. I now had access to better books. An acquaintance with the apprentices of booksellers enabled me sometimes to borrow a small one, which I was careful to return soon and clean. Often I sat up in my room reading the greatest part of the night, when the book was borrowed in the evening and to be returned early in the morning, lest it should be missed or wanted.

And after some time an ingenious tradesman, Mr. Matthew Adams, who had a pretty collection

*Cotton Mather whose essay inspired Franklin on self-improvement.

of books, and who frequented our printing-house, took notice of me, invited me to his library, and very kindly lent me such books as I chose to read. I now took a fancy to poetry, and made some little pieces; my brother, thinking it might turn to account, encouraged me, and put me on composing two occasional ballads. One was called *The Lighthouse Tragedy*, and contained an account of the drowning of Captain Worthilake with his two daughters; the other was a sailor's song, on the taking of Teach (or Blackbeard), the pirate. They were wretched stuff, in the Grub-street-ballad style; and when they were printed he sent me about the town to sell them. The first sold wonderfully, the event being recent, having made a great noise. This flattered my vanity; but my father discouraged me by ridiculing my performances and telling me verse-makers were generally beggars. So I escaped being a poet, most probably a very bad one; but as prose writing has been of great use to me in the course of my life, and was a principal means of my advancement, I shall tell you how, in such a situation, I acquired what little ability I have in that way. . . .

About this time I met with an odd volume of the *Spectator*.* It was the third. I had never before seen any of them. I bought it, read it over and over, and was much delighted with it. I thought the writing excellent, and wished, if possible, to imitate it. With that view I took

*Periodical (issued daily), written by Joseph Addison and Sir Richard Steele.

some of the papers, and making short hints of the sentiment in each sentence, laid them by a few days, and then, without looking at the book, tried to complete the papers again by expressing each hinted sentiment at length, and as fully as it had been expressed before, in any suitable words that should come to hand. Then I compared my *Spectator* with the original, discovered some of my faults, and corrected them. But I found I wanted a stock of words, or a readiness in recollecting and using them, which I thought I should have acquired before that if I had gone on making verses; since the continual occasion for words of the same import, but of different length to suit the measure, or of different sound for the rhyme, would have laid me under a constant necessity of searching for variety and also have tended to fix that variety in my mind and make me master of it. Therefore, I took some of the tales and turned them into verse, and, after a time, when I had pretty well forgotten the prose, turned them back again. I also sometimes jumbled my collections of hints into confusion, and after some weeks endeavored to reduce them into the best order, before I began to form the full sentences and complete the paper. This was to teach me method in the arrangement of thoughts. By comparing my work afterwards with the original, I discovered many faults and amended them, but I sometimes had the pleasure of fancying that in certain particulars of small import I had been lucky enough to improve the method, or the language, and this encouraged me to think I might possibly in time come to be a tolerable English writer, of which I was extremely ambitious. My time for these exercises and for reading was at night, after work, or before it began in the morning, or on Sundays, when I contrived to be in the printing-house alone, evading as much as I could the common attendance on public worship which my father used to exact of me when I was under his care, and which indeed I still thought a duty, though I could not, as it seemed to me, afford time to practice it. . . .

And now it was that, being on some occasion made ashamed of my ignorance in figures, which I had twice failed in learning when at school, I took Cocker's book of arithmetic, and went through the whole by myself with great ease. I also read Seller's and Sturmy's books of navigation, and became acquainted with the little geometry they contain; but never proceeded far in that science. And I read about this time Locke *On Human Understanding,* and the *Art of Thinking,* by Messrs. du Port Royal.

While I was intent on improving my language, I met with an English grammar (I think it was Greenwood's), at the end of which there were two little sketches of the arts of rhetoric and logic, the latter finishing with a specimen of a dispute in the Socratic method; and soon after I procured Xenophon's *Memorable Things of Socrates,* wherein there are many instances of the same method. I was charmed with it, adopted it, dropped my abrupt contradicton and positive argumentation and put on the humble inquirer and doubter. And being then, from reading

Shaftesbury and Collins,★ become a real doubter in many points of our religious doctrine, I found this method safest for myself and very embarrassing to those against whom I used it; therefore I took a delight in it, practiced it continually, and grew very artful and expert in drawing people, even of superior knowledge, into concessions, the consequences of which they did not foresee, entangling them in difficulties out of which they could not extricate themselves, and so obtaining victories that neither myself nor my cause always deserved. I continued this method some few years, but gradually left it, retaining only the habit of expressing myself in terms of modest diffidence, never using, when I advanced anything that may possibly be disputed, the words *certainly, undoubtedly,* or any others that give the air of positiveness to an opinion; but rather say, I conceive or apprehend a thing to be so or so; it appears to me, or I should think it so or so, for such and such reasons; or I imagine it to be so; or it is so, if I am not mistaken. This habit, I believe, has been of great advantage to me when I have had occasion to inculcate my opinions and persuade men into measures that I have been from time to time engaged in promoting, and, as the chief ends of conversation are to *inform* or to be *informed,* to *please* or to *persuade,* I wish well-meaning, sensible men would not lessen their power of doing good by a positive, assuming manner that seldom fails to disgust,

★Writers on religious issues whose ideas influenced Franklin.

tends to create opposition and to defeat every one of those purposes for which speech was given to us, to wit, giving or receiving information or pleasure. . . .

My brother had, in 1720 or 21, begun to print a newspaper. It was the second that appeared in America, and was called the *New England Courant*. The only one before it was the *Boston News-Letter*. I remember his being dissuaded by some of his friends from the undertaking, as not likely to succeed, one newspaper being, in their judgment, enough for America. At this time (1771) there are not less than five-and-twenty. He went on, however, with the undertaking, and after having worked in composing the types and printing off the sheets, I was employed to carry the papers through the streets to the customers.

He had some ingenious men among his friends, who amused themselves by writing little pieces for this paper, which gained it credit and made it more in demand, and these gentlemen often visited us. Hearing their conversations, and their accounts of the approbation their papers were received with, I was excited to try my hand among them; but, being still a boy, and suspecting that my brother would object to printing anything of mine in his paper if he knew it to be mine, I contrived to disguise my hand and, writing an anonymous paper, I put it in at night under the door of the printing-house. It was found in the morning and communicated to his writing friends when they called in as usual. They read it, commented on it in my hearing, and I had the exquisite pleasure of finding it met with their approbation, and that, in their different guesses at the author, none were named but men of some character among us for learning and ingenuity. I suppose now that I was rather lucky in my judges, and that perhaps they were not really so very good ones as I then esteemed them.

Encouraged, however, by this, I wrote and conveyed in the same way to the press several more papers which were equally approved;* and I kept my secret till my small fund of sense for such performances was pretty well exhausted, and then I discovered† it, when I began to be considered a little more by my brother's acquaintance, and in a manner that did not quite please him, as he thought, probably with reason, that it tended to make me too vain. And perhaps this might be one occasion of the differences that we began to have about this time. Though a brother, he considered himself as my master, and me as his apprentice, and accordingly expected the same services from me as he would from another, while I thought he demeaned me too much in some he required of me, who from a brother expected more indulgence. Our disputes were often brought before our father, and I fancy I was either generally in the right, or else a better pleader, because the judgment was generally in my favor. But my brother was passionate, and had often beaten me, which I took extremely amiss; and, thinking my apprenticeship very tedious, I was

*Franklin's *The Dogwood Papers* (1772), his first published writing.
†Disclosed.

continually wishing for some opportunity of shortening it, which at length offered in a manner unexpected.*

One of the pieces in our newspaper on some political point, which I have now forgotten, gave offense to the Assembly. He was taken up, censured, and imprisoned for a month, by the speaker's warrant, I suppose because he would not discover his author. I too was taken up and examined before the council; but, though I did not give them any satisfaction, they contented themselves with admonishing me, and dismissed me, considering me, perhaps, as an apprentice who was bound to keep his master's secrets.

During my brother's confinement, which I resented a good deal, notwithstanding our private differences, I had the management of the paper; and I made bold to give our rulers some rubs in it, which my brother took very kindly, while others began to consider me in an unfavorable light, as a young genius that had a turn for libeling and satire. My brother's discharge was accompanied with an order of the House (a very odd one), that "James Franklin should no longer print the paper called the *New England Courant*."

There was a consultation held in our printing-house among his friends what he should do in this case. Some proposed to evade the order by changing the name of the paper; but my brother

*"I fancy his harsh and tyrannical treatment of me might be a means of impressing me with that aversion to arbitrary power that has stuck to me through my whole life" [Original footnote by Franklin].

seeing inconveniences in that, it was finally concluded on as a better way to let it be printed for the future under the name of *Benjamin Franklin*, and to avoid the censure of the Assembly, that might fall on him as still printing it by his apprentice, the contrivance was that my old indenture should be returned to me, with a full discharge on the back of it, to be shown on occasion; but to secure to him the benefit of my service, I was to sign new indentures for the remainder of the term, which were to be kept private. A very flimsy scheme it was; however, it was immediately executed, and the paper went on accordingly under my name for several months.

At length, a fresh difference arising between my brother and me, I took upon me to assert my freedom, presuming that he would not venture to produce the new indentures. It was not fair in me to take this advantage, and this I therefore reckon one of the first errata of my life; but the unfairness of it weighed little with me when under the impression of resentment for the blows his passion too often urged him to bestow upon me, though he was otherwise not an ill-natured man; perhaps I was too saucy and provoking.

When he found I would leave him, he took care to prevent my getting employment in any other printing-house of the town, by going round and speaking to every master, who accordingly refused to give me work. I then thought of going to New York, as the nearest place where there was a printer; and I was rather inclined to leave Boston when I reflected that I had already made myself a little obnoxious to the governing party, and, from the arbitrary proceedings of the Assembly in my brother's case, it was likely I might, if I stayed, soon bring myself into scrapes; and farther, that my indiscreet disputations about religion began to make me pointed at with horror by good people as an infidel or atheist. I determined on the point, but my father now siding with my brother, I was sensible that, if I attempted to go openly, means would be used to prevent me. My friend Collins, therefore, undertook to manage a little for me. He agreed with the captain of a New York sloop for my passage, under the notion of my being a young acquaintance of his, that had got a naughty girl with child, whose friends would compel me to marry her, and therefore I could not appear or come away publicly. So I sold some of my books to raise a little money, was taken on board privately, and as we had a fair wind, in three days I found myself in New York, near three hundred miles from home, a boy of but seventeen, without the least recommendation to, or knowledge of, any person in the place, and with very little money in my pocket.

My inclinations for the sea were by this time worn out, or I might now have gratified them. But, having a trade, and supposing myself a pretty good workman, I offered my service to the printer in the place, old Mr. William Bradford,* who had been the first printer in Pennsylvania, but removed from thence upon the quarrel of George Keith. He could give me no

*Philadelphia's first printer (1685).

employment, having little to do and help enough already; but, says he, "My son at Philadelphia has lately lost his principal hand, Aquila Rose, by death; if you go thither, I believe he may employ you." Philadelphia was one hundred miles further; I set out, however, in a boat for Amboy, leaving my chest and things to follow me round by sea.

In crossing the bay, we met with a squall that tore our rotten sails to pieces, prevented our getting into the Kill,★ and drove us upon Long Island. In our way, a drunken Dutchman, who was a passenger too, fell overboard; when he was sinking, I reached through the water to his shock pate, and drew him up, so that we got him in again. His ducking sobered him a little, and he went to sleep, taking first out of his pocket a book, which he desired I would dry for him. It proved to be my old favorite author, Bunyan's *Pilgrim's Progress*, in Dutch, finely printed on good paper, with copper cuts, a dress better than I had ever seen it wear in its own language. I have since found that it has been translated into most of the languages of Europe, and suppose it has been more generally read than any other book, except perhaps the Bible. Honest John was the first that I know of who mixed narration and dialogue, a method of writing very engaging to the reader, who in the most interesting parts finds himself, as it were, brought into the company and present at the discourse. Defoe in his *Crusoe*, his *Moll Flanders, Religious Courtship,*

★Dutch, meaning waterway.

Family Instructor, and other pieces, had imitated it with success; and Richardson has done the same in his *Pamela,* etc.

When we drew near the island, we found it was at a place where there could be no landing, there being a great surf on the stony beach. So we dropped anchor, and swung round towards the shore. Some people came down to the water edge and hallowed to us, as we did to them; but the wind was so high, and the surf so loud, that we could not hear so as to understand each other. There were canoes on the shore, and we made signs, and hallowed that they should fetch us; but they either did not understand us, or thought it impracticable, so they went away, and night coming on, we had no remedy but to wait till the wind should abate, and in the mean time the boatman and I concluded to sleep if we could; and so crowded into the scuttle, with the Dutchman, who was still wet, and the spray, beating over the head of our boat, leaked through to us, so that we were soon almost as wet as he. In this manner we lay all night, with very little rest; but, the wind abating the next day, we made a shift to reach Amboy before night, having been thirty hours on the water, without victuals or any drink but a bottle of filthy rum, the water we sailed on being salt . . . In the morning, crossing the ferry, I proceeded on my journey on foot, having fifty miles to Burlington, where I was told I should find boats that would carry me the rest of the way to Philadelphia . . .

I have been the more particular in this description of my journey, and shall be so of my first entry into that city, that you may in your mind compare such unlikely beginning with the figure I have since made there. I was in my working dress, my best clothes being to come round by sea. I was dirty from my journey; my pockets were stuffed out with shirts and stockings; I knew no soul nor where to look for lodging. I was fatigued with traveling, rowing, and want of rest; I was very hungry; and my whole stock of cash consisted of a Dutch dollar and about a shilling in copper. The latter I gave the people of the boat for my passage, who at first refused it, on account of my rowing, but I insisted on their taking it, a man being sometimes more generous when he has but a little money then when he had plenty, perhaps through fear of being thought to have but little.

Then I walked up the street, gazing about, till near the markethouse I met a boy with bread. I had made many a meal on bread, and, inquiring where he got it, I went immediately to the baker's he directed me to, in Second Street, and asked for biscuit, intending such as we had in Boston; but they, it seems, were not made in Philadelphia. Then I asked for a three-penny loaf, and was told they had none such. So, not considering or knowing the difference of money, and the greater cheapness nor the names of his bread, I bade him give me three-penny-worth of any sort. He gave me, accordingly, three great puffy rolls. I was surprised at the quantity, but took it, and, having no room in my pockets, walked off with a roll under each arm, and eating the other. Thus I went up Market Street as far as Fourth Street, passing by the door of Mr. Read, my future wife's father; when she, standing at the door, saw me, and thought I made, as I certainly did, a most awkward, ridiculous appearance. Then I turned and went down Chestnut Street and part of Walnut Street, eating my roll all the way, and, coming round, found myself again at Market Street wharf, near the boat I came in, to which I went for a draught of the river water; and, being filled with one of my rolls, gave the other two to a woman and her child that came down the river in the boat with us, and were waiting to go farther.

Thus refreshed, I walked again up the street, which by this time had many clean-dressed people in it, who were all walking the same way. I joined them, and thereby was led into the great meetinghouse of the Quakers near the market. I sat down among them, and, after looking around and hearing nothing said, being very drowsy through labor and want of rest the preceding night, I fell fast asleep, and continued so till the meeting broke up, when one was kind enough to rouse me. This was, therefore, the first house I was in, or slept in, in Philadelphia.

Walking down again toward the river and looking in the faces of people, I met a young Quaker man, whose countenance I liked, and accosting him, requested he would tell me where a stranger could get lodging. We were then near the sign of the Three Mariners. "Here," says he, "is one place that entertains strangers, but it is not a reputable house; if thee wilt walk with me, I'll show thee a better." He brought me to the

Crooked Billet in Water Street. Here I got a dinner; and while I was eating it several sly questions were asked me, as it seemed to be suspected from my youth and appearance that I might be some runaway.

After dinner my sleepiness returned, and, being shown to a bed, I lay down without undressing, and slept till six in the evening, was called to supper, went to bed again very early, and slept soundly till next morning. Then I made myself as tidy as I could and went to Andrew Bradford the printer's. I found in the shop the old man his father, whom I had seen at New York, and who, traveling on horseback, had got to Philadelphia before me. He introduced me to his son, who received me civilly, gave me a breakfast, but told me he did not at present want a hand, being lately supplied with one; but there was another printer in town, lately set up, one Keimer, who perhaps might employ me; if not, I should be welcome to lodge at his house, and he would give me a little work to do now and then till fuller business should offer.

The old gentleman said he would go with me to the new printer; and when we found him, "Neighbor," says Bradford, "I have brought to see you a young man of your business; perhaps you may want such a one." He asked me a few questions, put a composing stick in my hand to see how I worked, and then said he would employ me soon, though he had just then nothing for me to do; and, taking old Bradford, whom he had never seen before, to be one of the town's people that had a good will for him, entered into a conversation on his present undertaking and prospects, while Bradford, not discovering that he was the other printer's father, on Keimer's saying he expected soon to get the greatest part of the business into his own hands, drew him on by artful questions, and starting little doubts, to explain all his views, what interest he relied on, and in what manner he intended to proceed. I, who stood by and heard all, saw immediately that one of them was a crafty old sophister, and the other a mere novice. Bradford left me with Keimer, who was greatly surprised when I told him who the old man was.

Keimer's printing-house, I found, consisted of an old shattered press, and one small, worn-out font of English, which he was then using himself, composing an elegy on Aquila Rose, before mentioned, an ingenious young man, of excellent character, much respected in town, clerk of the Assembly, and a pretty poet. Keimer made verses too, but very indifferently. He could not be said to write them, for his manner was to compose them in the types directly out of his head. So there being no copy, but one pair of cases,* and the elegy likely to require all the letter, no one could help him. I endeavored to put his press (which he had not yet used, and of which he understood nothing) into order fit to be worked with; and, promising to come and print off his elegy as soon as he should have got it ready, I returned to Bradford's, who gave me

*Cases, meaning boxes of upper-case or lower-case letters, kept separate by printers.

a little job to do for the present, and there I lodged and dieted. A few days after, Keimer sent for me to print off the elegy. And now he had got another pair of cases, and a pamphlet to reprint, on which he set me to work.

COMING OF AGE

Early Struggles

ARTHUR RUBINSTEIN

from

MY YOUNG YEARS

This world-famous pianist recounts startling historical events as a backdrop to his childhood as a musical prodigy. **Arthur Rubinstein** (1887–1982) was born in Poland, became an American citizen in 1946, and continued to perform before adoring audiences into his nineties. Some critics consider his recorded interpretations of the piano literature, particularly the nineteenth-century romantics, unsurpassed.

My father bought a house and we occupied half of the second floor, while my grandparents Heyman took the other half. Being neighbors intensified greatly our contact with the rest of mother's large family, who were strict Orthodox Jews. Following the tradition that the children gather around the patriarch every Friday, we began to observe the Sabbath with great solemnity in our house.

My own life in these surroundings took a new turn with the appearance of a lovely and sweet

115

little girl, Noemi, a cousin who was exactly my age. The adopted child of Aunt Frandzia, one of my mother's three childless sisters, she lived right next door to us.

Noemi looked like an angel painted by Raphael with her round face, crowned by golden curls, her blue eyes shining with an unearthly expression, and her lovely, soft skin. She had a kind and sweet disposition, and we loved each other so passionately that we were inseparable. The fact that she had lost her own mother at birth and that her father, my Uncle Paul Heyman, had married again, made me feel that I had to look after her.

Aunt Frandzia adored the child, and since her husband was quite well off she made life very pleasant for Noemi, and indirectly for me, too. A beautiful nursery, consisting of two big sunny rooms filled with all sorts of toys, was our daily playground. A governess watched over our games and took us for walks; we had our meals together alternately at my aunt's or at my own house. Noemi — I called her Nemutka — particularly liked playing husband and wife with me. She would obey me blindly, leaving the choicest morsels of food for me, easily bursting into tears whenever she saw me in trouble. My piano playing made her gasp with admiration. I think we were probably the happiest children in the world.

The next two years were like a dream — the days of a completely happy, carefree childhood. When we grew tired of our games, Noemi and I would listen to fairy tales read to us by her governess, but soon we began to invent our own stories, and as this passion grew, life itself appeared to us as a continuous fairy tale. I am happy to say I have never changed this feeling toward life. . . .

Lodz was the most unhealthy and unhygienic city imaginable; there were no parks or squares, avenues or playgrounds for children. The air was so infected with gas from the chemical plants, and the black smoke from the chimneys which hid the sky was so thick, that our daily walks were, from a health standpoint, nothing but a ritual. At night Lodz was still worse. Lacking a modern system of sewage, the city had to remove its excrement in small iron tanks, driven by horses, which filled the streets with an unbearable odor.

But we saw all these flaws with quite different eyes, Noemi and I; we loved Lodz! The factories were castles with glorious towers, the Russian policemen were ogres, and people in the streets princes and princesses in disguise!

At home I used to illustrate on the piano our stories or little scenes from our daily lives. My greatest success was an imitation of grandmother's quarrels with cook. Tremolo in the bass would announce the coming storm, followed by the two voices fighting each other in a constant crescendo, and, finally, an abrupt chord brought the drama to an end.

One night my parents took me to the Opera, where *Aïda* was being played by an itinerant Italian company. I was much impressed by the singers and the scenery, but at the first forte of the trombones, I started to scream with terror and had to be taken home in a hurry. I could not bear the sound of trombones for a long time after that night. I had far better luck with the first concert I was taken to, and later I heard the Polish pianist Józef Śliwiński, but was too small to appreciate him.

About that time a little boy prodigy came to town for a concert and had a great success. He was the violinst Bronislaw Hubermann, then ten years old. I was delighted by his playing, and my parents invited him to visit us. At home, we played for each other, and he was charming to me. We were friends until he died.

The most important event for me in those days, however, was when a small symphony orchestra visited Lodz, conducted by a Dutchman, Julius Kwast. They performed the first suite of Grieg's *Peer Gynt*, which thrilled me so much that when we returned home I was able to play almost all of it — to the amazement of the family. Mr. Kwast was invited to our house, heard me play, and thought it was time for me to take piano lessons. His advice was promptly followed.

My first teacher was a Mrs. Pawlowska, a typical exponent of the old school, whose chief effort was to make me keep my elbows close to my body and to play scales without dropping the coin she placed on my hand. After three months of vain struggle, she had to admit her defeat, and my lessons were entrusted to Mr. Adolf Prechner, a strange, slightly demonic person with a pockmarked face and a thick yellowish mustache. He would always either speak too softly or shout at the top of his voice, but he knew his job. I made good progress in a short time, and was soon able to play pieces of Mozart, Mendelssohn, and Bach.

One morning my father entered my room with a terrifying expression on his face, waving a newspaper in his hand. He addressed me in a tragic voice, saying, "Arthur, do you know who has died?" I burst into tears, frightened by this question. "Anton Rubinstein," he murmured. "Now your future is ruined!" Apparently he had planned to send me to this great man, whose name I happened to share. He had been the director of the Imperial Conservatory in St. Peterburg — and now his premature death had shattered my father's plans and hopes. However, I failed to appreciate at that time the full impact of his loss. Only now can I realize how different my career might have been if Anton Rubinstein had lived a few years longer.

One day a committee from some institution came to see my parents asking if I could take part in a concert to raise money for their charities. This was a great decision for them to make. I was not yet eight, and Mr. Prechner had to be consulted. When he agreed to the idea, we started immediately to prepare a program for my debut as a concert pianist.

The date was fixed for December 14, 1894. The morning of that day the whole house was in a great state of excitement, but I remained calm and happy. I had just received a nice present from Noemi and had tried on my beautiful black velvet suit with a white lace collar, which made me feel very important. The concert went splendidly. A young lady played the Mendelssohn concerto for violin, a man sang a few songs, and then it was my turn. Having seen a huge box of chocolates in the artists' room, I performed my Mozart sonata and two pieces of Schubert and Mendelssohn in the happiest mood, and was rewarded with a warm ovation from an audience consisting mainly of my family, their friends, and the musical Jews and Germans of Lodz. Noemi was proud of me, and that filled me with joy.

A fortnight later I was sent to school — a Russian school it had to be, as no Polish schools were permitted. We were taught to rattle off the official titles of the Tsar and his family: "His Imperial Majesty, the Autocrat of all the Russias, King of Poland, Grand Duke of Finland, etc.," and then sing the Russian national anthem. I hated it, and resented the imposition of such a compely foreign element on me. We spoke Polish at home, I was a Pole. It is curious to note how much this alien atmosphere at school made me realize how I loved Poland. In the afternoon I had Polish lessons with my sister Frania which were a source of great pleasure to me.

My life went on for a year in a routine, monotonous way until, one evening, quite suddenly, I was taken to Jadwiga's home to spend the night. I had not seen Noemi for two days. She was ill, I was told. I had thought something was wrong, but my questions had been answered evasively: "You must keep away from her," they told me. "She is not well," and their faces were grave and tense. The next few days were an agony; people behaved strangely; they whispered in my presence, eluded me. I felt like a dog left behind by his master. Then, one afternoon, Jadwiga came home in tears. When she saw me, she broke down completely and I knew at once. I guessed everything: Nemutka was no more, my little Nemutka was dead!

Jadwiga said in a strange voice: "Noemi has left for a long journey," to which I nodded, with a silly, credulous smile. I could not bear to be told . . . I would not listen . . . I wanted to be left alone.

There is a Polish word, *zal*, a beautiful word, impossible to translate. It means sadness, nostalgia, regret, being hurt, and yet it is something else. It feels like a howling inside you, so unbearable that it breaks your heart.

Next morning, my father took me for a walk. At his first words, "You know, Arthur . . .," I cut him short, and said quickly, "Yes, I know, I know, Papa. She has left, but she will come back." My childhood was over; I was a boy now. Only years later could I talk about this and listen to the details of the abominable scarlet fever which took her away from me. My sweet little Nemutka — she is certainly an angel now if there are any!

I went through a bad time. I became irritable and disobedient, refusing food, avoiding people at home, and starting fights with boys at school. Nobody could persuade me to play the piano for pleasure. I would just practice my daily scales, but lazily, without conviction. The only thing I liked was to play cards with my sick grandfather, who distracted me by teaching me the most intricate games. I could not be reconciled to the loss of my little friend; there was a rage in me, a grudge, a resentment against something, or someone — I could not say what. One night, wide awake, I suddenly knew. Yes, it is God, this God of my grandfather, who prayed to Him so fervently, assuring me that God knows everything, is everywhere, perceives our most secret thoughts, protects us, and is never wrong. Well, then, I thought bitterly, how could He do such an unjust and terrible thing as this? He must have been distracted, or inattentive, but for God, they say, such a thing would be impossible. A frantic desire took hold of me. I had to find out if He really existed, if He knew my doubts — yes, I must risk that, even if it cost me my life. And the little boy I was, sitting upright in my bed, holding my breath in mortal fear, thought these horrible words: God is a Fool! I expected his immediate appearance, a deadly blow, or at least thunder, but nothing materialized. I repeated the dreadful insult aloud now, but still nothing! Night after night I went through the same scene, which was very hard on my nerves. In addition, I was unhappy at school, where we were made to absorb everything too mechanically, never putting our heart in our work. But I did succeed in learning Russian and German, which was spoken all around me. With my own Polish, it made three languages.

During those years the political situation in Russia was full of unrest and disorder. The discontented working classes listened eagerly to the socialistic theories explained to them by the so-called *inteligentzia,* mostly students of universities and high schools. As it became more and more difficult to cope with this propaganda, the revolutionary movement being well organized, the Russian secret police resorted to their famous system of "provocation." One of their men would mix with a crowd at some legal, peaceful meeting — a procession or a celebration. Whereupon the *agent provocateur* would shout something offensive about the Tsar and the government, or fire a shot — a signal for the police to intervene, beating up the people and arresting the leaders. These actions were the original "pogroms."

I had the misfortune to witness such a scene. After leaving school one day, some boys and I stopped to watch the funeral of a worker, a political agitator, I suppose. Hundreds of co-workers were following the hearse quietly, when suddenly a loud cry was heard. Masses of gendarmes, rushing up out of nowhere, entered the dense crowd with drawn sabers, slashing people. Terrified, we ran to the next portal for safety and from there continued to observe the scene. The mourners tried to disperse, picking up their wounded, but when the police attacked them again, they grew angry and turned against the aggressors. Then something dreadful happened. From a side street, waving their *nahajkas,* a detachment of Cossacks appeared. (We called them Cossacks, but they were really Mongols sent from Siberia.) Mounted on their small Arab horses, their caps pulled over one ear, they charged the crowd in a furious assault, beating everyone unmercifully, and when the victims, shrieking desperately, ran for their lives, the infuriated Cossacks attacked innocent bystanders, mostly old Jews in their long coats, trampling and hurting them cruelly. Then they started to break shop windows . . . there was blood all over the place . . . and we could see the heartbreaking expressions on the faces of the victims. We went home long after it was over, death in our hearts, our eyes filled forever with the horror of it all.

One night my dear old Grandfather Heyman died. He had been ill for a long time and passed quietly away in his sleep. I was roused by cries and laments. Next morning the whole family arrived, all in mourning, tears in their eyes, speaking in hushed voices, rushing in and out, making arrangements for the funeral. As for myself, I pretended once again not to understand what had happened, and would not let anyone explain. I hated death; in fact, I was so terribly afraid of it I used to inquire among my school friends who belonged to different creeds as to which religion seemed to offer the best care for dead bodies. I did not want to be buried. I wished to lie in a transparent coffin on a high catafalque in an airy mausoleum.

My parents became increasingly worried about my brooding and my aversion to the school. I even neglected the piano, and Mr. Prechner complained about my inattentiveness and laziness. The only thing I liked was reading, and I would consume anything I could put my hands on; the novels of Sienkiewicz, Jules Verne, fairy tales, history, and biographies of famous men were my favorites. But not poetry; to me poetry was sham music, a sort of "music's poor relation." I felt ashamed to hear its form, cadence, and rhythm used for exalted words instead of sounds. If one of the young girls in our family started declaiming poetry (a fashion in those days) I would have nervous laughing spells and would have to leave the room.

My parents decided I should go to Warsaw.

MARY McCARTHY

from

MEMORIES OF A CATHOLIC GIRLHOOD

Born in 1912, orphaned at age six, novelist and essayist **Mary McCarthy** describes here her early life under the harsh and miserly care of relatives Myles and Margaret and the unexplainable indifference of her wealthy grandmother to her plight, to both her material and emotional needs.

Mary McCarthy is a noted literary critic and drama reviewer as well as a short-story writer and novelist, with over twenty volumes to her credit to date; recent work includes essays on Vietnam and Watergate and another memoir, *How I Grew*.

———————

Whenever we children came to stay at my grandmother's house, we were put to sleep in the sewing room, a bleak, shabby, utilitarian rectangle, more office than bedroom, more attic than office, that played to the hierarchy of chambers the role of a poor relation. It was a room seldom entered by the other members of the family, seldom swept by the maid, a room without pride; the old sewing machine, some cast-off chairs, a shadeless lamp, rolls of wrapping paper, piles of cardboard boxes that might someday come in handy, papers of pins, and remnants of material united with the iron folding cots put out for our use and the bare floor boards to give an impression of intense and ruthless temporality. Thin white spreads, of the kind used in hospitals and charity institutions, and naked blinds at the windows reminded us of our orphaned condition and of the ephemeral character of our visit; there was nothing here to encourage us to consider this our home.

Poor Roy's children, as commiseration damply styled us, could not afford illusions, in the family opinion. Our father had put us beyond the pale by dying suddenly of influenza and taking our young mother with him, a defection that was remarked on with horror and grief commingled, as though our mother had been a pretty secretary with whom he had wantonly absconded into the irresponsible paradise of the hereafter. Our reputation was clouded by this misfortune. There was a prevailing sense, not only in the family but among storekeepers, servants, streetcar conductors, and other satellites of our circle, that my grandfather, a rich man, had behaved with extraordinary munificence in alloting a sum of money for our support and installing us with some disagreeable middle-aged relations in a dingy house two blocks distant from his own. What alternative he had was not mentioned; presumably he could have sent us to an orphan asylum and no one would have thought the worse of him. At any rate, it was felt, even by those who sympathized with us, that we led a priviledged existence, privileged because we had no rights, and the very fact that at the yearly Halloween or Christmas party given at the home of an uncle we appeared so dismal, ill clad, and unhealthy, in contrast to our rosy, exquisite cousins, confirmed the judgment that had been made on us — clearly, it was a generous impulse that kept us in the family at all. Thus, the meaner our circumstances, the greater seemed our grandfather's condescension, a view in which we ourselves shared, looking softly and shyly on this old man — with his rheumatism, his pink face and white hair, set off by the rosebuds in his Pierce-Arrow and in his buttonhole — as the font of goodness and philanthropy, and the nickel he occasionally gave us to drop into the collection plate on Sunday (two cents was our ordinary contribution) filled us not with envy but with simple admiration for his potency; this indeed was princely, *this* was the way to give. It did not occur to us to judge him for the disparity of our styles of living. Whatever bitterness we felt was kept for our actual guardians, who, we believed, must be embezzling the money set aside for us, since the standard of comfort achieved in our grandparents' house — the electric heaters, the gas logs, the lap robes, the shawls wrapped tenderly about the old knees, the white meat of chicken and red meat of beef, the silver, the white tablecloths, the maids, and the solicitous chauffeur — persuaded us that prunes and rice pudding, peeling paint and patched clothes were *hors concours* with these persons and therefore could not have been willed by them. Wealth, in our minds, was equivalent to bounty, and poverty but a sign of penuriousness of spirit.

Yet even if we had been convinced of the honesty of our guardians, we would still have clung to that beneficent image of our grandfather that the family myth proposed to us. We were too poor, spiritually speaking, to question his generosity, to ask why he allowed us to live in oppressed chill and deprivation at a long arm's length from himself and hooded his genial blue eye with a bluff, millionairish gray eyebrow whenever the evidence of our suffering presented itself at his knee. The official answer we knew: our benefactors were too old to put up with four wild young children; our grandfather was preoccupied with business matters and with his rheumatism, to which he devoted himself as though to a pious duty, taking it with him on pilgrimages to Ste. Anne de Beaupré and Miami, offering it with impartial reverence to the miracle of the Northern Mother and the Southern sun. This rheumatism hallowed my grandfather with the mark of a special vocation; he lived with it in the manner of an artist or a grizzled Galahad; it set him apart from all of us and even from my grandmother, who, lacking such an affliction, led a relatively unjustified existence and showed, in relation to us children, a sharper and more bellicose spirit. She felt, in spite of everything, that she was open to criticism, and, transposing this feeling with a practiced old hand, kept peering into our characters for symptoms of ingratitude.

We, as a matter of fact, were grateful to the point of servility. We made no demands, we had no hopes. We were content if we were permitted to enjoy the refracted rays of that solar prosperity and come sometimes in the summer afternoons to sit on the shady porch or idle through a winter morning on the wicker furniture of the sun parlor, to stare at the player piano in the music room and smell the odor of whisky in the mahogany cabinet in the library, or to climb about the dark living room examining the glassed-in paintings in their huge gilt frames, the fruits of European travel: dusky Italian devotional groupings, heavy and lustrous as grapes, Neapolitan women carrying baskets to market, views of Venetian canals, and Tuscan harvest scenes — secular themes that, to the Irish-American mind, had become tinged with Catholic feelings by a regional infusion from the Pope. We asked no more from this house than the pride of being connected with it, and this was fortunate for us, since my grandmother, a great adherent of the give-them-an-inch-and-they'll-take-a-yard theory of hospitality, never, so far as I can remember, offered any caller the slightest refreshment, regarding her own conversation as sufficiently wholesome and sustaining. An ugly, severe old woman with a monstrous balcony of a bosom, she officiated over certain set topics in a colorless singsong, like a priest intoning a Mass, topics to which repetition had lent a senseless solemnity: her audience with the Holy Father; how my own father had broken with family tradition and voted the Democratic ticket; a visit to Lourdes; the Sacred Stairs in Rome, bloodstained since the first Good Friday, which she had climbed on her knees; my crooked little fingers and how they meant I was a liar; a miracle-working bone; the importance of regular bowel movements; the wickedness of Protestants; the conversion of my mother to Catholicism; and the assertion that my other grandmother must certainly dye her hair. The most trivial reminiscences (my aunt's having hysterics in a haystack) received from her delivery and from the piety of the context a strongly monitory flavor; they inspired fear and guilt, and one searched uncomfortably for the moral in them, as in a dark and riddling fable.

Luckily, I am writing a memoir and not a work of fiction, and therefore I do not have to account for my grandmother's unpleasing character and look for the Oedipal fixation or the traumatic experience which would give her that clinical authenticity that is nowadays so desirable in portraiture. I do not know how my grandmother got the way she was; I assume, from family photographs and from the inflexibility of her habits, that she was always the same, and it seems as idle to inquire into her childhood as to ask what was ailing Iago or look for the error in toilet-training that was responsible for Lady Macbeth. My grandmother's sexual history, bristling with infant mortality in the usual style of her period, was robust and decisive: three tall, handsome sons grew up, and one attentive daughter. Her husband treated her kindly. She had money, many grandchildren, and religion to

131

sustain her. White hair, glasses, soft skin, wrinkles, needlework — all the paraphernalia of motherliness were hers; yet it was a cold, grudging, disputatious old woman who set all day in her sunroom making tapestries from a pattern, scanning religious periodicals, and setting her iron jaw against an infraction of her ways.

Combativeness was, I suppose, the dominant trait in my grandmother's nature. An aggressive churchgoer, she was quite without Christian feeling; the mercy of the Lord Jesus had never entered her heart. Her piety was an act of war against the Protestant ascendancy. The religious magazines on her table furnished her not with food for meditation but with fresh pretexts for anger; articles attacking birth control, divorce, mixed marriages, Darwin, and secular education were her favorite reading. The teachings of the Church did not interest her, except as they were a rebuke to others; "Honor thy father and thy mother," a commandment she was no longer called upon to practice, was the one most frequently on her lips. The extermination of Protestantism, rather than spiritual perfection, was the boon she prayed for. Her mind was preoccupied with conversion; the capture of a soul for God much diverted her fancy — it made one less Protestant in the world. Foreign missions, with their overtones of good will and social service, appealed to her less strongly; it was not a *harvest* of souls that my grandmother had in mind.

This pugnacity of my grandmother's did not confine itself to sectarian enthusiasm. There was the defense of her furniture and her house against the imagined encroachments of visitors. With her, this was not the gentle and tremulous protectiveness endemic in old ladies, who fear for the safety of their possessions with a truly touching anxiety, inferring the fragility of all things from the brittleness of their old bones and hearing the crash of mortality in the perilous tinkling of a tea cup. My grandmother's sentiment was more autocratic: she hated having her chairs sat in or her lawns stepped on or the water turned on in her basins, for no reason at all except pure officiousness; she even grudged the mailman his daily promenade up her sidewalk. Her home was a center of power, and she would not allow it to be derogated by easy or democratic usage. Under her jealous eye, its social properties had atrophied, and it functioned in the family structure simply as a political headquarters. Family conferences were held there, consultations with the doctor and the clergy; refractory children were brought there for a lecture or an interval of thought-taking; wills were read and loans negotiated and emissaries from the Protestant faction on state occasions received. The family had no friends, and entertaining was held to be a foolish and unnecessary courtesy as between blood relations. Holiday dinners fell, as a duty, on the lesser members of the organization: the daughters and daughters-in-law (converts from the false religion) offered up Baked Alaska on a platter, like the head of John the Baptist, while the old people sat enthroned at the table, and only their digestive processes acknowledged, with rumbling, enigmatic salvos, the festal day.

Yet on one terrible occasion my grandmother had kept open house. She had accommodated us all during those fatal weeks of the influenza epidemic, when no hospital beds were to be had and people went about with masks or stayed shut up in their houses, and the awful fear of contagion paralyzed all services and made each man an enemy to his neighbor. One by one, we had been carried off the train which had brought us from distant Puget Sound to make a new home in Minneapolis. Waving good-by in the Seattle depot, we had not known that we had carried the flu with us into our drawing rooms, along with the presents and the flowers, but, one after another, we had been struck down as the train proceeded eastward. We children did not understand whether the chattering of our teeth and Mama's lying torpid in the berth were not somehow a part of the trip (until then, serious illness, in our minds, had been associated with innovations — it had always brought home a new baby), and we began to be sure that it was all an adventure when we saw our father draw a revolver on the condutor who was trying to put us off the train at a small wooden station in the middle of the North Dakota prairie. On the platform at Minneapolis, there were stretches, a wheel chair, redcaps, distraught officials, and, beyond them, in the crowd, my grandfather's rosy face, cigar, and cane, my grandmother's feathered hat, imparting an air of festivity to this strange and confused picture, making us children certain that our illness was the beginning of a

134

delightful holiday.

We awoke to reality in the sewing room several weeks later, to an atmosphere of castor oil, rectal thermometers, cross nurses, and efficiency, and though we were shut out from the knowledge of what had happened so close to us, just out of our hearing — a scandal of the gravest character, a coming and going of priests and undertakers and coffins (Mama and Daddy, they assured us, had gone to get well in the hospital) — we became aware, even as we woke from our fevers, that everything, including ourselves, was different. We had shrunk, as it were, and faded, like the flannel pajamas we wore, which during these few weeks had grown, doubtless from the disinfectant they were washed in, wretchedly thin and shabby. The behavior of the people around us, abrupt, careless, and preoccupied apprised us without any ceremony of our diminished importance. Our value had paled, and a new image of ourselves — the image, if we had guessed it, of the orphan — was already forming in our minds. We had not known we were spoiled, but now this word, entering our vocabulary for the first time, served to define the change for us and to herald the new order. Before we got sick, we were spoiled; that was what was the matter now, and everything we could not understand, everything unfamiliar and displeasing, took on a certain plausibility when related to this fresh concept. We had not known what it was to have trays dumped summarily on our beds and no sugar and cream for our cereal, to take medicine in a gulp because someone could not be bothered to wait for us, to have our arms jerked into our sleeves and a comb ripped through our hair, to be bathed impatiently, to be told to sit up or lie down quick and no nonsense about it, to find our questions unanswered and our requests unheeded, to lie for hours alone and wait for the doctor's visit, but this, so it seemed, was an oversight in our training, and my grandmother and her household applied themselves with a will to remedying the deficiency.

Their motives were, no doubt, good; it was time indeed that we learned that the world was no longer our oyster. The happy life we had had — the May baskets and the valentines, the picnics in the yard, and the elaborate snowman — was a poor preparation, in truth, for the future that now opened up to us. Our new instructors could hardly be blamed for a certain impatience with our parents, who had been so lacking in foresight. It was to everyone's interest, decidedly, that we should forget the past — the quicker, the better — and a steady disparagement of our habits ("Tea and chocolate, can you imagine, and all those frosted cakes — no wonder poor Tess was always after the doctor") and praise that was rigorously comparative ("You have absolutely no idea of the improvement in those children") flattered the feelings of the speakers and prepared us to accept a loss that was, in any case, irreparable. Like all children, we wished to conform, and the notion that our former ways had been somehow ridiculous and unsuitable made the memory of them falter a little, like a child's recitation to strangers. We no longer demanded our due, and the wish to see our parents insensibly weakened. Soon we ceased to speak of it, and thus, without tears or tantrums, we came to know they were dead.

Why no one, least of all our grandmother, to whose repertory the subject seems so congenial, took the trouble to tell us, it is impossible now to know. It is easy to imagine her "breaking" the news to those of us who were old enough to listen in one of those official interviews in which her nature periodically tumefied, becoming heavy and turgid, like her portentous bosom, like peonies, her favorite flower, or like the dress-maker's dummy, that bombastic image of herself that, half swathed in a sheet for decorum's sake, lent a museumlike solemnity to the sewing room and aroused our first sexual curiosity. The mind's ear frames her sentences, but in reality she did not speak, whether from a hygenic motive (keep the mind ignorant and the bowels open), or from a mistaken kindness, it is difficult to guess. Perhaps really she feared our tears, which might rain on her like reproaches, since the family policy at the time was predicated on the axiom of our virtual insentience, an assumption that allowed them to proceed with us as if with pieces of furniture. Without explanations or coddling, as soon as they could safely get up, my three brothers were dispatched to the other house; they were much too young to "feel" it, I heard the grownups murmur, and would never know the difference "if Myers and Margaret were careful."

137

In my case, however, a doubt must have been experienced. I was six — old enough to "remember" — and this entitled me, in the family's eyes, to greater consideration, as if this memory of mine were a lawyer who represented me in court. In deference, therefore, to my age and my supposed powers of criticism and comparison, I was kept on for a time, to roam palely about my grandmother's living rooms, a dangling, transitional creature, a frog becoming a tadpole, while my brothers, poor little polyps, were already well embedded in the structure of the new life. I did not wonder what had become of them. I believe I thought they were dead, but their fate did not greatly concern me; my heart had grown numb. I considered myself clever to have guessed the truth about my parents, like a child who proudly discovers that there is no Santa Claus, but I would not speak of that knowledge or even react to it privately, for I wished to have nothing to do with it; I would not co-operate in this loss. Those weeks in my grandmother's house come back to me very obscurely, surrounded by blackness, like a mourning card: the dark well of the staircase, where I seem to have been endlessly loitering, waiting to see Mama when she would come home from the hospital, and the simply loitering with no purpose whatever; the winter-dim first-grade classroom of the strange academy I was sent to; the drab treatment room of the doctor's office, where every Saturday I screamed and begged on a table while electric shocks were sent through me, for what purpose I cannot conjecture. But this preferential treatment could not be accorded me forever; it was time that I found my niche. "There is someone here to see you" — the maid met me one afternoon with this announcement and a half-curious, half-knowledgeable smile. My heart bounded; I felt almost sick (who else, after all, could it be?), and she had to push me forward. But the man and woman surveying me in the sun parlor with my grandmother were strangers, two unprepossessing middle-aged people — a great-aunt and her husband, so it seemed — to whom I was now commanded to give a hand and a smile, for, as my grandmother remarked, Myers and Margaret had come to take me home that very afternoon to live with them, and I must not make a bad impression.

Once the new household was running, our parents' death was officially conceded and sentiment given its due. Concrete references to the lost ones, to their beauty, gaiety, and good manners, were naturally not welcomed by our guardians, who possessed none of these qualities themselves, but the veneration of our parents' *memory* was considered an admirable exercise. Our evening prayers were lengthened to include one for our parents' souls, and we were thought to make a pretty picture, all four of us in our pajamas with feet in them, kneeling in a neat line, our hands clasped before us, reciting the prayer for the dead. "Eternal rest grant unto them, oh Lord, and let the perpetual light shine upon them," our thin little voices cried, but this remembrancing, so pleasurable to our guardians, was only a chore to us. We connected it with lights out, washing, all the bedtime coercions, and particularly with the adhesive tape that, to prevent mouthbreathing, was clapped upon our lips the moment the prayer was finished, sealing us up for the night, and that was removed, very painfully, with the help of ether, in the morning. It embarrassed us to be reminded of our parents by these persons who had superseded them and who seemed to evoke their wraiths in an almost proprietary manner, as though death, the great leveler, had brought them within their province. In the same spirit, we were taken to the cemetery to view our parents' graves; this, in fact, being free of charge, was a regular Sunday pastime with us, which we grew to hate as we did all recreation enforced by our guardians — department-store demonstrations, band concerts, parades, trips to the Old Soldiers' Home, to the Botanical Gardens, to Minnehaha Park, where we watched other children ride on the ponies, to the Zoo, to the water tower — diversions that cost nothing, involved long streetcar trips or endless walking or waiting, and that had the peculiarly fatigued, dusty, proletarianized character of American municipal entertainment. The two mounds that now were our parents associated themselves in our minds with Civil War cannon balls and monuments to the doughboy dead; we contemplated them stolidly, waiting for a sensation, but these twin grass beds, with their junior-executive headstones, elicited nothing, whatever; tired of this interminable staring, we would beg to be allowed to go play in some collat-

140

eral mausoleum, where the dead at least were buried in drawers and offered some stimulus to fancy.

For my grandmother, the recollection of the dead became a mode of civility that she thought proper to exercise toward us whenever, for any reason, one of us came to stay at her house. The reason was almost always the same. We (that is, my brother Kevin or I) had run away from home. Independently of each other, this oldest of my brothers and I had evolved an identical project — to get ourselves placed in an orphan asylum. We had noticed the heightening of interest that mention of our parentless condition seemed always to produce in strangers, and this led us to interpret the word "asylum" in the old Greek sense and to look on a certain red brick building, seen once from a streetcar near the Mississippi River, as a haven of security. So, from time to time, when our lives became too painful, one of us would set forth, determined to find the red brick building and to press what we imagined was our legal claim to its protection. But sometimes we lost our way, and sometimes our courage, and after spending a day hanging about the streets peering into strange yards, trying to assess the kindheartedness of the owner (for we also thought of adoption), or a cold night hiding in a church confessional box or behind some statuary in the Art Institute, we would be brought by the police, by some well-meaning householder, or simply by fear and hunger, to my grandmother's door. There we would be silently received, and a family conclave would be summoned. We

141

would be put to sleep in the sewing room for a night, or sometimes more, until out feelings had subsided and we could be sent back, grateful, at any rate, for the promise that no reprisals would be taken and that the life we had run away from would go on "as if nothing had happened."

Since we were usually running away to escape some anticipated punishment, these flights at least gained us something, but in spite of the taunts of our guardians, who congratulated us bitterly on our "cleverness," we ourselves could not feel that we came home in triumph as long as we came home at all. The cramps and dreads of those long nights made a harrowing impression on us. Our failure to run away successfully put us, so we thought, at the absolute mercy of our guardians; our last weapon was gone, for it was plain to be seen that they could always bring us back and we never understood why they did not take advantage of this situation to thrash us, as they used to put it, within an inch of our lives. What intervened to save us, we could not guess — a miracle, perhaps; we were not acquainted with any *human* motive that would prompt Omnipotence to desist. We did not suspect that these escapes brought consternation to the family circle, which had acted, so it conceived, only in our best interests, and now saw itself in danger of unmerited obloquy. What would be the Protestant reaction if something still more dreadful were to happen? Child suicides were not unknown, and quiet, asthmatic little Kevin had been caught with matches under the house. The family would not acknowledge error, but it conceded a certain mismanagement on Myers' and Margaret's part. Clearly, we might become altogether intractable if our homecoming on these occasions were not mitigated with leniancy. Consequently, my grandmother kept us in a kind of neutral detention. She declined to be aware of our grievance and offered no words of comfort, but the comforts of her household acted upon us soothingly, like an automatic mother's hand. We ate and drank contentedly; with all her harsh views, my grandmother was a practical woman and would not have thought it worthwhile to unsettle her whole schedule, teach her cook to make a lumpy mush and watery boiled potatoes, and market for turnips and parsnips and all the other vegetables we hated, in order to approximate the conditions she considered suitable for our characters. Humble pie could be costly, especially when cooked to order.

Doubtless she did not guess how delightful these visits seemed to us once the fear of punishment had abated. Her knowledge of our own way of living was luxuriously remote. She did not visit our ménage or inquire into its practices, and though hypersensitive to a squint or a dental irregularity (for she was liberal indeed with glasses and braces for the teeth, disfiguring appliances that remained the sole token of our bourgeois origin and set us off from our parochial-school mates like the caste marks of some primitive tribe), she appeared not to notice the darns and patches of our clothing, our raw hands and scarecrow arms, our silence and our elderly faces. She imagined us as surrounded by certain playthings she had once bestowed on us — a sandbox, a wooden swing, a wagon, an ambulance, a toy fire engine. In my grandmother's consciousness, these objects remained always in pristine condition; years after the sand had spilled out of it and the roof had rotted away, she continued to ask tenderly after our lovely sand pile and to manifest displeasure if we declined to join in its praises. Like many egoistic people (I have noticed this trait in myself), she was capable of making a handsome outlay, but the act affected her so powerfully that her generosity was still lively in her memory when its practical effects had long vanished. In the case of a brown beaver hat, which she watched me wear for four years, she was clearly blinded to its matted nap, its shapeless brim, and ragged ribbon by the vision of the price tag it had worn when new. Yet, however her mind embroidered the bare tapestry of our lives, she could not fail to perceive that we felt, during these short stays with her, *some* difference between the two establishments, and to take our wonder and pleasure as a compliment to herself.

She smiled on us quite kindly when we exclaimed over the food and the nice, warm bathrooms, with their rugs and electric heaters. What funny little creatures, to be so impressed by things that were, after all, only the ordinary amenities of life! Seeing us content in her house, her emulative spirit warmed slowly to our admiration: she compared herself to our guardians, and though for expedient reasons she could not afford to deprecate them ("You children have been very ungrateful for all Myers and Margaret have done for you"), a sense of her own finer magnanimity disposed her subtly in our favor. In the flush of these emotions, a tenderness sprang up between us. She seemed half reluctant to part with whichever of us she had in her custody, almost as if she were experiencing a genuine pang of conscience. "Try and be good," she would advise us when the moment for leave-taking came, "and don't provoke your aunt and uncle. We might have made different arrangements if there had been only one of you to consider." These manifestations of concern, these tacit admissions of our true situation, did not make us, as one might have thought, bitter against our grandparents, for whom ignorance of the facts might have served as a justification, but, on the contrary, filled us with love for them and even a kind of sympathy — our sufferings were less terrible if someone acknowledged their existence, if someone were suffering for us, for whom we, in our turn, could suffer, and thereby absolve of guilt.

During these respites, the recollection of our parents formed a bond between us and our grandmother that deepened our mutual regard. Unlike our guardians or the whispering ladies who sometimes came to call on us, inspired, it seemed, by a pornographic curiosity as to the exact details of our feelings ("Do you suppose they remember their parents?" "Do they ever *say* anything?"), our grandmother was quite uninterested in arousing an emotion of grief in us. "She doesn't feel it at all," I used to hear her confide, of me, to visitors, but contentedly, without censure, as if I had been a spayed cat that, in her superior foresight, she had had "attended to." For my grandmother, the death of my parents had become, in retrospect, an eventful occasion upon which she looked back with pleasure and a certain self-satisfaction. Whenever we stayed with her, we were allowed, as a special treat, to look into the rooms they had died in, for the fact that, as she phrased it, "they died in separate rooms" had for her a significance both romantic and somehow self-gratulatory, as though the separation in death of two who had loved each other in life were beautiful in itself and also reflected credit on the chatelaine of the house, who had been able to furnish two master bedrooms for the emergency. The housekeeping details of the tragedy, in fact, were to her of paramount interest. "I turned my house into a hospital," she used to say, particuarly when visitors were present. "Nurses were as scarce as hen's teeth, and *high* — you can hardly imagine what those girls were charging an hour." The trays and the special cooking, the laundry and the disinfectants recalled themselves fondly to her thoughts, like items on the menu of some long-ago ball-supper, the memory of which recurred to her with a strong, possessive nostalgia.

My parents had, it seemed, by dying on her premises, become in a lively sense her property, and she dispensed them to us now, little by little, with a genuine sense of bounty, just as, later on, when I returned to her a grownup young lady, she conceded me a diamond lavaliere of my mother's as if the trinket were an inheritance to which she had the prior claim. But her generosity with her memories appeared to us as children, an act of the greatest indulgence. We begged her for more of these mortuary reminiscences as we might have begged for candy, and since ordinarily we not only had no candy but were permitted no friendships, no movies, and little reading beyond what our teachers prescribed for us, and were kept in quarantine, like carriers of social contagion, among the rhubarb plants of our neglected yard, these memories doled out by our grandmother became our secret treasures; we never spoke of them to each other but hoarded them, each against the rest, in the miserly fastnesses of our hearts. We returned, therefore, from our grandparents' house replenished in all our faculties; these crumbs from the rich man's table were a banquet indeed to us. We did not even mind going back to our guardians, for we now felt superior to them, and besides, as we well knew, we had no choice. It was only by accepting our situation as a just and unalterable arrangement that we could be allowed to transcend it and feel ourselves united to our grandparents in a love that was the more miraculous for breeding no practical results.

In this manner, our household was kept together, and my grandparents were spared the necessity of arriving at a fresh decision about it. Naturally, from time to time a new scandal would break out (for our guardians did not grow kinder

147

in response to being run away from), yet we had come, at bottom, to despair of making any real change in our circumstances, and ran away hopelessly, merely to postpone punishment. And when, after five years, our Protestant grandfather, informed at last of the facts, intervened to save us, his indignation at the family surprised us nearly as much as his action. We thought it only natural that grandparents should know and do nothing, for did not God in the mansions of Heaven look down upon human suffering and allow it to take its course?

MARGARET MEAD

from

BLACKBERRY WINTER

Born in Philadelphia into a family of academics, **Margaret Mead** (1901–78) entered the relatively new field of cultural anthropology in the 1920s. At graduate school at Columbia University, Mead became the protégé of Franz Boas and the close friend of his assistant, Ruth Benedict. Following Boas's suggestion that she study adolescent girls, she journeyed alone to the remote South Pacific and there developed her influential study, *The Coming of Age in Samoa,* the first of many works on the culture of tribal societies. On her many subsequent field studies to the South Pacific, she collected data on and took photographs of cultures soon to be changed forever by the encroachment of modern civilization.

In this excerpt, Mead speaks not of a distant society but of her own. She tells of her first exposure to prejudice — her exclusion from the all-pervasive sorority life at Depauw College. As an independent-minded outsider from the East, Mead did not conform to the rigid standards of a Midwestern college community and was not invited to join a single sorority. Here she describes the sharp stings of rejection, the first she had ever known.

College: DePauw

American families differ greatly in their expectations about what going to college will mean in their children's lives. In the intellectual community to which my parents belonged, college was as necessary as learning to read. It was an intellectual experience and the gateway to the rest of life. All my life I expected to go to college, and I was prepared to enjoy it.

My mother had included drawing lessons in the advantages she had wrested for me out of the various strange environments in which we lived, and I had enough talent to be encouraged to become a painter. However, when I was told by my artist cousins that in order to become a painter I should go to art school and skip college, I gave up the idea. For me, not to go to college was, in a sense, not to become a full human being.

This did not mean, of course, that all the children in the family felt as I did. My brother very dutifully went to college and took a Ph.D. But he never cared much for reading books. Instead, he fastened on the applied aspects of my father's essentially very intellectual but very concrete interests. What interested Richard primarily were the business aspects of the ongoing world — such matters as the relationship of

150

highway legislation to bus lines and trucking, or working out the best locations for chain stores, or the uses of coal. Had he come from a different kind of family, he might have gone very contentedly straight into business. As it was, he became for most of his life a college professor in schools of business concerned with the kinds of projects in which he himself did consulting. He exemplified in his own person one of the things that has happened in America as higher education has become instrumental in business, industry, and agriculture, as well as in professions like law and medicine which once had their own exclusive forms of preparation.

For my sister Elizabeth, college never was more than a background — and not a very relevant background at that — for the development of her gifts. She willingly left college to go to Italy with my mother and spent a happy year in Rome studying architecture. Afterward she continued to study architecture at the University of Pennsylvania and Columbia University and, still later, took courses both in fine arts and in education at New York University. When it was necessary to write papers, she wrote them. When it was necessary to read books, she read them and knew how to get a great deal out of them. Although her delight in painting and music and dancing made her seem to be a changeling in our midst, she too received the family intellectual imprint and she became a teacher and only secondarily — and sometimes and still with delight — a painter. And she married William Steig, an artist from a family of artists, who left college after one semester and made a name for himself as a cartoonist, one of the most ironic and compassionate of our time.

And there was my youngest sister, Priscilla, who was so responsive to the standards of the wider society. Having begun to read at five, she read what she chose, reached out for science fiction and formulas of dissent and assent, and used her reading as a weapon against the rest of the family. By the time she was ready for college, she was entrancingly beautiful; she was also competent and had a mind that could do anything asked of it. I decided, then, that if she were to resist the temptation to become a well-bred, well-dressed young woman who could talk intelligently about any subject but who cared really deeply about none, she would have to have an overdose of the kind of social life that at Vassar or Smith College would have been tempered by her relationships with fine women teachers who were using their own minds and hoped that some students would become intellectually active. So I helped her choose the University of Wisconsin, saw to it that she had the right introductions and the right clothes, made the right sorority, and was showered with the attentions to which her looks entitled her. She herself decided that she would make Phi Beta Kappa in three years. When she succeeded in this, she left the fraternity-sorority life of the Wisconsin campus behind, took what she had gained from the good teaching of professors who cared about their subject, and, in her own phrasing, went to the University of Chicago to learn something. In the same spirit, she resisted the attractions of young men with impeccable Ivy League backgrounds. Instead, she married Leo Rosten, a brilliant young political scientist who had worked his way through college by giving lectures on Great Literature to women's clubs and by teaching English to immigrants, an experience that he later utilized in *The Education of Hyman Kaplan*. Throughout her married life she restrained the exuberant imagination of her gifted husband by periodically advocating the kind of economies my mother had insisted on when she had made my father return the lapis lazuli necklace because the money should be given to a fellowship fund. In the last years of her life, she was studying to become a social worker.

So the overriding academic ethos shaped all our lives. This was tempered by my mother's sense of responsibility for society, by my father's greater interest in real processes than in theoretical abstractions, and by my grandmother's interest in real children, in chickens, and in how to season stewed tomatoes with toasted bread. But at the heart of their lives, the enjoyment of the intellect as mediated by words in books was central, and I was the child who could make the most of this — the child who was not asked to constrain or distort some other gift.

And so, even though it was decided that I was to go to DePauw rather than Bryn Mawr or Wellesley, I approached the idea of college with the expectation of taking part in an intellectual feast. I looked forward to studying fascinating subjects taught by people who understood what they were talking about. I imagined meeting brilliant students, students who would challenge me to stretch my mind and work instead of going skating with my lessons done well enough so that I led my classmates who hated what they were studying. In college, in some way that I devoutly believed in but could not explain, I expected to become a person.

At DePauw in 1919 I found students who were, for the most part, the first generation to go to college and whose parents appeared at Class Day poorly dressed while their daughters wore the raccoon or the muskrat coats that were appropriate to the sorority they had made. It was a college to which students had come for fraternity life, for football games, and for establishing the kind of rapport with other people that would make them good Rotarians in later life and their wives good members of the garden club.

I arrived with books of poetry, portraits of great personalities to hang on the wall, and the snobberies of the East, such as the expectation that one dressed in the evening for the members of one's own family. And I was confronted by the snobbery and cruelty of the sorority system at its worst, with rules against rushing that prevented the women who had gone to college with my father and who had married my father's fraternity brothers from ever speaking to me or inviting me to their homes — rules made by the Panhellenic Association in order to control competition that was so harsh and so unashamed that the very rules designed to control it made it even worse. This was my first and only real experience of discrimination — mild enough in all conscience.

It is very difficult to know how to evaluate how essential it is to have one's soul seared by the great injustices of one's own time — being born a serf or slave, a woman believed to have no mind or no soul, a black man or woman in a white man's world, a Jew among Christians who make a virtue of anti-Semitism, a miner among those who thought it good sport to hire Pinkertons to shoot down miners on strike. Such experiences sear the soul. They make their victims ache with bitterness and rage, with compassion for fellow sufferers or with blind determination to escape even on the backs of fellow sufferers. Such experiences can breed the desire to fight unrelentingly against the injustice that has let one's mother die because no doctor would attend her or let one's brother work in a mine because there was no school to recognize his talents — an injustice that substitutes arbitrary social categories for the recognition of humanity. Injustice experienced in the flesh, in deeply wounded flesh, is the stuff out of which change explodes. But the passionate fight for humanity — the fight to free slaves, free colonies, free women and children — also has been carried by those who have never experienced, and in the case of whites fighting for blacks or men for women, never could experience in their own persons the depth of injustice against which they have fought.

There is a great deal of talk today about the inexperience of the suburban children of affluent middle-class families, who have never seen an open wound, or a baby born, or anyone die, whose conceptions of humiliation, deprivation, and suffering are drawn wholly from films and television. But such discussions do not take into account the different kinds of fighters, all of whom are needed in any case — both those who know at first hand the searing effects of discrimination and those who are shocked to the core by their encounters with tragedies that are part of others' everyday experience.

The point of John Howard Griffin's book, *Black Like Me*, was precisely that he was not black. For a brief period he experienced the humiliation and hostility that a black man can expect to experience daily — and throughout his life in the United States. But Griffin experienced this *not* as a black man but as a white man with temporarily blackened skin, a white man who had been reared to expect something else and who suddenly drew back from his own image when he called his own wife — white and far away at the other end of a telephone line — by an endearing term. Out of his experience, Griffin was able to tell men and women in the white world things that no black individual had ever thought to tell them. And I think it is no accident that some of the most impassioned statements about woman's rights have been made by men, or that anti-imperialist movements in colonial countries have been inspired and even led by Europeans who were outraged by the consequences of social arrangements through which they, as members of a privileged group, had never suffered.

Yet it is very difficult to draw a line. Certainly, positions of privilege can breed a kind of hardened insensitivity, an utter inability to imagine what it is to be an outsider, an individual who is treated with contempt or repulsion for reasons of skin color, or sex, or religion, or nationality, or the occupation of his parents and grandparents. Some kind of experience is necessary to open one's eyes and so to loosen the ties of unimaginative conformity. It can come from a terrible shock — through the brutal experience of having a close companion ejected from a restaurant or even shot down in the street. But there is another kind of initiation into humiliation — through the experience of hardship in some petty caricature of the real world which, by its very pettiness, engages one's emotions and enlarges one's consciousness of the destructive effects of every kind of social injustice.

All my life I had been a leader in children's groups that were democratically constituted. In our family, my mother's idealistic altruism and egalitarian principles meant that the children of farm laborers were treated with no less — and perhaps even more — gentleness and consideration than were the children of educated, professional parents. From this position of security, I believed that I could dictate egalitarian behavior. I had been brought up to the American standard of good breeding, based on the assumption that a well-bred person never intentionally hurt anyone — an assumption that reverses the English conception of a well-bred person as someone who is never rude unintentionally. My father sometimes paraphrased Chesterfield's admonition to be considerate of one's inferiors, courteous to one's equals, and stiff with one's superiors. But no one suggested that we had any superiors, only people who had more money or who were more interested in validating their social position. My father refused to make social efforts and my mother's position was, therefore, related to her own associations with other women who were equally concerned with good works. My mother used to complain because my father would not make the effort, but no one suggested that he would not have succeeded had he wanted to.

In some ways I was in the position of a child who is brought up in a leading family in a sequestered minority group, in the position, for example, of the daughter of the rabbi in a Jewish community or of the pastor in a segregated black community, a girl who has never questioned her privileged status but who has absorbed an ethic that is deeply critical of injustice in the world. In *Ex-Prodigy*, Norbert Wiener describes how he was reared, in a setting of anti-Semitism, with an attributed superiority as a Russian. When he discovered that he himself was Jewish, he could not identify only with Jews but had to identify with all oppressed peoples. The stigmata of privilege remained.

When I arrived at DePauw, I found that I had two roommates. One was a girl who had come to college to join a sorority, and this had been arranged in advance; the other expected to be rushed by a sorority that had little prestige. I soon learned that no one belonging to a sorority

158

could speak to an unpledged freshman. This, of course, explained why I heard nothing from the effusive girl who had written me so many letters during the summer. When the invitations came out, I was invited to the Kappa rushing party. But when I arrived wearing my unusual and unfashionable dress that was designed to look like a wheat field with poppies blooming in it, my correspondent turned her back on me and never spoke to me again. I found the whole evening strangely confusing. I could not know, of course, that everyone had been given the signal that inviting me had been a mistake. Afterward, my two roommates got the bids they expected, but I did not get a bid.

It still took a little time for me to realize the full implications of what it meant to be an unpledged freshman in a college where everything was organized around the fraternities and sororities. For one thing, I had no dates; these were all arranged through commands to the freshman pledges of certain fraternities to date the freshman pledges of certain sororities. Although all freshmen had to live in dormitories, it meant also that there was a widening gulf between the pledges, who spent a lot of time at their sorority houses being disciplined and shaped up, and the unpledged freshmen and the few upperclassmen in the dormitories.

With a very few exceptions, these upperclassmen were pretty dismal. But there was Katharine Rothenberger, who became my lifelong friend; she had transferred from a college where she had turned down a sorority bid because it was too expensive. And there was an English girl, very tall and very serious, also a transfer, who in later life became a very well-known missionary. By and large, however, the girls who were, by sorority standards, ineligible were less attractive and less sparkling than their classmates who were among the chosen. Moreover, all those who still hoped had one characteristic in common — their fear of making friends with others of their own kind. Although I was experiencing the bitter injustice of being excluded, on grounds that I did not respect, I experienced also what I have come to regard as a principal reason for abolishing such exclusive institutions, that is, the damage done to the arbitrarily excluded who continue to believe that one day they still may enter the ranks of the chosen.

It also took some little time for me to discover that previously rejected students might nevertheless be accepted later if they displayed some special ability that would help a chapter keep up the kind of competitive records that were cherished by rival chapters on the campus or within the intrafraternity and sorority rivalries that were fostered by the national Greek-letter societies. So a student could continue to hope that the members of a chapter would eventually recognize in him — or her — some sign of high scholarship or an outstanding ability in some extracurricular field or a strong political potential and then, overlooking the initial disability, they would invite the girl or boy to join the chapter and perhaps even make some effort to like the person who once had been so harshly excluded.

It was many years before liberal white Americans came to realize that what they offered Negro Americans was not so very different from this. In the period between the two wars, Negro physicians, lawyers, scientists, and men with other recognized talents and outstanding abilities were admitted to the fraternal relationships of occupations that hitherto had been closed to them and they were treated almost as though they had been accepted by the group they had joined.

During the next forty years, before fraternities and clubs lost almost all their power on campuses in the general rejection of elitism that developed in the 1960s, various efforts were made to democratize an institution that was essentially incapable of democratization — for the only point of exclusiveness is that someone is excluded. But the main result of such efforts was that they strengthened the conviction of members of Greek-letter societies that students who were left out had not wanted to join or could not afford to do so. And the unchosen seldom talked.

The blandness with which the privileged accept their status was illustrated when the Panhellenic Association of Syracuse University, during World War II, invited me to be a dinner speaker on "Democracy," a topic that was particularly fashionable at that time. The organizers had not bothered to find out whether I had ever attended a college where there were Greek-letter societies. So they heard a lot of stories they had previously been protected from hearing.

During the year I studied at DePauw, I did not deny that I was hurt, nor did I pretend to

161

myself that I would have refused the chance to be accepted by a sorority. The truth is, I would not have known enough to refuse. And once inside, it is quite possible that I would have been as unseeing as the rest. As it was, what particularly offended me as the year wore on was the contrast between the vaunted democracy of the Middle West and the blatant, strident artificiality of the Greek-letter societies on that midwestern campus, the harshness of the rules that prevented my father's classmates from ever addressing a hospitable word to me, and, more than anything else, the lack of loyalty that rejection engendered among the unchosen.

I discovered, too, that simple rejection was not enough. It had to be rubbed in. At that time it was fashionable for girls to wear what were called Peter Thompson suits — tailored middy suits in dark-colored wool or pastel-colored linen. In the spring, when I too acquired a Peter Thompson suit, a prominent Theta, meeting me on the campus, roughly turned down my collar to look at the label, certainly expecting to find that my new dress was not authentic — as it was.

My unusual clothing was not all that was held against me. There was my room with its carefully planned color scheme, my books and pictures, and, above all, my tea set. And I did not chew gum. Then, as if these things were not enough, there was my accent. The big Freshman English Literature course was taught by a New Englander who conceived it to be his principal task to educate provincial Americans. The very first day he glared around the room and asked, "Does anyone in this class know how to pronounce c-a-l-f?" I volunteered, and when I used the broad *a* he commented, "Oh, you come from the East, don't you? Out here they say 'calf,' " and mockingly drew out the flat *a* sound. A third of the freshman class heard that doubtful compliment. There were two other students from the East. One was the daughter of a Methodist bishop who had formerly been the president of DePauw; the other was her close friend. That saved them. But I was branded. After a while some of my friends thought it was fun to get me to say, "I have been there," using the Bryn Mawr pronunciation, "bean," instead of the Middle Western "bin." This usually happened when mothers came to visit and the girls wanted to show off the local curiosities.

And, although the sorority rejection was the sharper blow, there was another. I found out that I was also ineligible to belong to the Y.W.C.A. because, as an Episcopalian, I did not belong to an Evangelical religion. There were five of us at DePauw who were religious rejects — myself, one Roman Catholic, one Greek Orthodox, one Lutheran, and one Jew. The Jew was David Lilienthal. On one occasion he was asked to give a talk to the Methodist Sunday School on the Jewish conception of Jesus. The rest of us were simply beyond the pale.

So I was confronted, for the first time in my life, with being thoroughly unacceptable to almost everyone and on grounds in which I had previously been taught to take pride. I responded by setting out to see what I could do within this

163

system, which I found sufficiently uncongenial so that I spent no time lamenting my exclusion.

I wrote a stunt that was performed by the freshman dormitory, Mansfield Hall, as part of a competition in which we challenged the senior dormitory and the sororities — the first time this was done. I set to work to make the English honors society, Tusitala, which was the Samoan name that had been given Robert Louis Stevenson. I wrote and directed the pageant that the entire feminine student body, under the direction of the Department of Physical Education, gave each year. I also designed the freshman float for this occasion. And finally, I went into the political arena and succeeded in getting Katharine Rothenberger elected vice-president of the class by setting the sororities against one another. I was satisfied that by the end of the year I would have received a bid to join a sorority — probably at least two. For although no sorority might want to have me, each one would be afraid that I might become the property of a rival.

The teaching at DePauw was far less disappointing than the college social organization. In my catalogue I had marked courses totaling over 200 hours, even though 120 hours was all that a student could take in four years. I thoroughly enjoyed the magnificent teaching given by men who were first and foremost teachers, interested in their students and unharassed by the demand that they "publish or perish," an attitude that later came to haunt even small colleges like DePauw. The training in writing given me by Professor Pence was never equaled by anyone else. At DePauw I was introduced to discussions of the Old Testament prophets and the Social Gospel, and this firmly established association between the Old and the New Testament and the demands of social justice provided me with an ethical background up to the time of the development of ecumenicism and Vatican II. These courses were taught by deeply religious men who regarded it a privilege to be teaching where they were.

At DePauw, too, I took a course in History as Past Ethics, to which I still refer. However, there were only two girls and a couple of dozen boys in that class, and the two girls received the highest marks. As long as I was in high school, the greater maturity of adolescent girls had not struck me. But in the setting of this coeducational college it became perfectly clear both that bright girls could do better than bright boys and that they would suffer for it.

This made me feel that coeducation was thoroughly unattractive. I neither wanted to do bad work in order to make myself attractive to boys nor did I want them to dislike me for doing good work. It seemed to me that it would be much simpler to go to a girl's college where one could work as hard as one pleased.

This preference foreshadowed, I suppose, my anthropological field choices — not to compete with men in male fields, but instead to concentrate on the kinds of work that are better done by women. Actually, there are two kinds of field work that women can do better than men. One is working with women and children in situations in which male investigators are likely to be suspected and resented by the men of a society. The other is working with both men and women as an older woman, using a woman's postmenopausal high status to achieve an understanding of the different parts of a culture, particularly in those cultures in which women past the reproductive period are free from the constraints and taboos that constrict the lives of younger women. The first choice can be effectively exercised only in a situation in which the culture is being studied by a male-female pair or a team. For when a woman explicitly classifies herself with excluded women and uninitiated children, she does not have access to the rest of the culture. The second role is very practical for an older woman who is working alone in a culture that has already been explored by a male and female pair.

Nevertheless, as long as I remained at DePauw, I felt I was an exile. I used to sit in the library and read the drama reviews in *The New York Times*. Like so many other aspiring American intellectuals and artists, I developed the feeling that American small towns were essentially unfriendly to the life of the mind and the senses. I believed that the center of life was in New York City, where Mencken and George Jean Nathan were publishing *Smart Set*, where *The Freeman, The New Republic*, and *The Nation* flourished, where F.P.A. and Heywood Broun were writing their diatribes, and where the theater was a living world of contending ideas.

And Luther Cressman was in New York. I had had enough of the consolation of knowing that I was engaged, so that all the nonsense about having dates — or not having dates — was irrelevant. I wanted a life that demonstrated in a more real and dramatic form that I was not among the rejected and unchosen. And so, at the end of the year, I persuaded my father to let me leave DePauw and enter Barnard College.

What did I learn from this essentially very mild experience of being treated as an outsider and a reject from my own society? Just enough to know more clearly than ever that this is not the way to organize society — that those who reject or those who are rejected, and usually both, suffer irreversible character damage. It is true that sometimes one or the other may show magnificent character traits. I believe that the ideal of the English gentleman, embodied in the belief that he alone — and no one else — can destroy his position, is valuable. Equally, the position of the Jews, steadily persecuted but sustained by their conception of themselves as a chosen people, has produced an enormous number of highly intelligent, humanly sensitized, valuable men and women. But the reciprocal, the belief of the Nazis that they were the proper heirs of European civilization, from which all whom they regarded as lesser men should be excluded, was an evil that the world cannot face again. Whatever advantages may have arisen, in the past, out of the existence of a specially favored and highly privileged aristocracy, it is clear to me that today no argument can stand that supports unequal opportunity or any intrinsic disqualification for sharing in the whole of life.

By the very contrast that it provided, DePauw clarified my picture of the kind of college at which I wanted to be a student — a place where people were intellectually stirred and excited by ideas, where people stayed up all night talking about things that mattered, where one would meet one's peers and, still more important, people with different and superior minds, and, not least, where one would find out what one could do in life.

I left DePauw, sorry only to leave Katharine Rothenberger. At the time, I hardly realized how lasting some of my impressions would be. I never again went to a football game as a partisan, but more than twenty-five years later, when I was asked to lecture at Wabash College, the college that was DePauw's football rival, I felt a little like a traitor.

Even now, when I lecture in the Middle West, if I want my voice to be free of a carping note, I have to think myself back into the world of my grandmother and my mother — the Middle West as they presented it to me — and will myself to omit my own experience of DePauw in 1920. The dream glowed; the reality had been more than disappointing.

GLORIA VANDERBILT

from

ONCE UPON A TIME

Born in 1924 into one of the wealthiest families in America, **Gloria Vanderbilt** tells of searching for a loving relationship with her rather distant grandmother and, even more urgently, searching for a closeness to her mother. She was the center of a traumatic and sensational custody case at the age of ten, the result of which removed her from the custody of her mother and awarded her to the care of her formidable Aunt Gertrude. Despite all the wrenchings of her childhood, she subsequently emerged as a gifted artist, designer, and highly successful business woman, and is, according to the title of a recent biography, "happy at last."

We are to go, Paddy, twins Anne and Elsie, and I to have tea with Grandmother Vanderbilt. But we cannot stay too long as it may tire her. Twins Anne and Elsie wear the same dresses, with blobs of roseate flowers all over and bibs of smocking at the top. The bows of fat silk in their curls are

169

pinky color too. Paddy's dress and my dress also have smocking, only our dresses are not exactly alike. Paddy's ringlets have all been cut off and now she has bangs like mine, so there's no place on our heads for bows, but we look our best anyway.

We drive along past the so tall oak trees, waving good-bye good-bye to Oakland Farm — away away we go singing Merrily merrily all the way. Big Elephant and Paddy's Dumpling Nanny, Deedee, sit squeezed in the back singing along too. After a while we reach gates which are enormous. A giant wearing a tall hat chooses a key from a long chain and opens the gates just for us. We drive through, right up to the doors of the Castle, and by magic they open for us. Twin giants in penguin suits stand by the portals as we enter. They are very solemn and pretend they don't see us. Big Elephant and Dumpling Deedee tell us to run on ahead into the Great Hall to find Grandma. I haven't seen her in a long time, but I remember her because she is a Fairy Queen and loves me a lot. But she is nowhere in sight.

Then we see her far, far away, high up on the long, long staircase of red that reaches right up to the sky. But as she comes closer, Grandma looks even tinier — why, even tinier than the Little Countess. A little soft cloud of dove-grey — is it fur? — rests over the lace of her dress, although the day is hot. Pearls are garlanded around her tiny neck, but they don't weigh her down or jiggle as she walks, for she carries herself so straight I think she is wearing a crown. As we run to her, coming closer, I see that this is not so, yet still I see the crown as if it were there. We are close close now . . . Grandma sees us and stops. We stop too. She stares at us and we wait for her to speak. But she doesn't, she just keeps looking at us. Why doesn't someone say something? What is the matter? Please, please, someone think of something to say! Grandma, Grandma, I want to call out — I love you, Grandma, I love you. But I am silent. Years go by, hundreds of them, and all the time she looks into our faces, looking into one and then into another, back and forth. And then she says, very curious —

Who are these children?

She does not know Paddy. She does not know twins Anne and Elsie — unknown children, unknown. She does not know me. She is my grandmother, but she doesn't know me, and if she doesn't know me, who am I? who am I? who am I? Someone comes and my Grandma turns and goes back up the long stairs of red, away away away away, back up into the sky.

Come, children, someone else says. It's time to go home. Grandma is tired.

My mother is going to a costume ball and she and Aunt Toto go on and on about it all the livelong day. They're in a real dither trying to decide what to wear. It's ages away, this fancy-dress ball, but to hear them go on about it makes it seem as if it's happening tomorrow night and they've been caught without a stitch to wear. Now the pace has eased up a little as they come to a unanimous decision. A Miss Yvonne has come into our lives and she feverishly sews and snips away at bolts of creamy white velvet which have been spread out on a table in that room on the top floor.

It was in this top-floor room — in fact on the very spot where Miss Yvonne's sacred table now stands — that a weekend ago a settee had been placed, and on this settee my mother had sat, with me placed close beside her. We had been so placed by Aunt Toto for photographs she was to take. It was all part of a game that I wasn't supposed to know about — but, good sport that I am, I went along with it. Actually, I went along with it because I was thrilled to be with my mother in this just-we-two situation, not to mention the niftiness of being the center not only of her attention but of Aunt Toto's as well. Aunt Toto, in her artful way, had draped a silk scarf over a Brownie camera. This scarf had tiny toy wooden soldiers printed on it, rows and rows of them, and they bobbed around the room over the Brownie in a casual way, as Aunt Toto tried to pretend the camera wasn't pointed in our direction and hopped around, chatting up a storm. The scarf was one I had seen my mother wear, but I knew that Aunt Toto had one exactly like it, so who's to say which scarf was which. There was a moment at the start when I could have pulled away and said, The jig is up! But I didn't — and then it was too late. So there we all were, caught up in and accepting the rules of this particular little game. Only sometimes Aunt Toto was naughty and would cheat and lapse

172

into Spanish, and in between the Spanish the name Hearst popped in rather a lot — and from that I guessed that these pictures were being taken especially for Mr. Hearst and that they would end up in his newspapers. Oh, well . . . But would I ever get to see them?

But by the next weekend the settee my mother and I had sat on had disappeared, and this room was now dedicated to Miss Yvonne and her comings and goings. She would arrive early, this Miss Yvonne, long before my mother and Aunt Toto were awake, entering the house with a singular energy, intent upon the task at hand. She spoke not at all, nor did she look to the right or to the left as she entered, and if the lift didn't happen to be on the ground floor in readiness, she would disdain the wait and race through the air in her garb of puce, up the stairs to her aerie on the top floor.

Not only was there the rippling cream of white velvet in this sanctuary on the top floor, there were laces, soft as my mother's skin, to be made into jabots, and tendrils, curling into the feathered white of plumes, to be placed on the velvet black richness of hats to be worn with this fancy dress, for my mother and Aunt Toto would make their appearance at the ball dressed as ladies of the court of Marie Antoinette. Elsewhere across the city, at M. Antoine's, there were also serious doings — for to complete the costumes, wigs were to be fashioned. Yes, and not only that — it was deemed necessary that they be of real hair curled into white ringlets. But whose curling white hair would be cut to cover the beauty of my mother's tresses? It would never be known, because M. Antoine never divulged important secrets.

Every weekend I would arrive expecting the costumes to be finished, but they were not. And each time I would glimpse Miss Yvonne coming in or going out. And that's all I saw, for no one except my mother and Aunt Toto (and of course Wannsie) was allowed to enter the room on the top floor, for to do so would be to disturb the concentration of Miss Yvonne.

But all things come to an end, and here I am at my mother's and there is no sign of Miss Yvonne or her snippets anywhere in sight. Not only that, but my mother and Aunt Toto say they have a surprise for me — which must mean that the costumes are finished and that I will see them.

And now I have not only seen the costumes but seen my mother and Aunt Toto *in* the costumes. *Sans gêne,* as the Twins so often say. And it is a sight to behold, for my mother pirouettes back and forth in the long mirror of her boudoir, entranced by the double image of her luscious magnolia self . . . only it is not her double image at all — it is the image of Aunt Toto as well, swinging to and fro so pleasingly beside her. Together they waltz around the room, with white flower bell skirts swinging, for there are petticoats of hooped steel beneath the skirts, making the velvety waves fall just right. And next to my mother's skin are the jabots of lace, frothy as the white of egg in a bowl of floating island, and on the hat a feather rests over the crown reaching forward over the brim, as if hoping to touch the beauty of my mother's face.

But this is *not* the surprise. The surprise is that at my mother's request, stitch by stitch, Miss Yvonne has also made a costume for me, identical in every way to my mother's — and it's just awful. Rooted to the spot, I stand in this ridiculous getup as the Twins in their Dresden way cavort in the background, and I want to run run from the room so that my fatness is no longer reflected in my mother's boudoir in this hideous way.

But this is not the end of it. No — I have been told that a special occasion has been arranged for me to wear this fancy dress. Not a party, because it's obvious that my fatness is too much of a muchness to accompany my mother and Aunt Toto to the ball — not to mention my babyishness, which is much too babyish to boot. No, its' something else that has been cooked up — a real treat. There's to be another photograph session, only this time it's no nonsense. Mr. Hal Phyfe himself is coming right here to this house, and traipsing behind him will be assistants bearing lights and cameras, and I am to squeeze my fatness into the fatfulness of this steel hoop of a skirt, don this feathered hat, and sit next to my mother, right here in the living room. And I know, I just know, that this time I will not be able to pretend it isn't happening, because it is, it is! And I wish I could die!

But no such luck, for here I am all rigged up and standing around waiting for the assistants to get the lights bright bright bright so that no

175

detail of my mother's beauty will be missed and no detail of my hooped-up fatness will slip by either. Mr. Hal Phyfe is thin thin and tall tallest and winsome as can be — why not, because he is a most famous photographer who photographs my mother every year, to make certain her beauty is properly recorded.

Slowly down the stairs my mother now is making her descent. The cherubim and seraphim herald her arrival — all turn towards her as, drawn out of our lowly selves, we stand in awe and wonder at this apparition. On her head even the hated wig of white sits in beauty, and I dare not imagine the preposterous apparition of mine which has been pulled down to cover my fat hair, for, yes, M. Antoine has created a wig of white, from who-knows-whose hair, for me to wear. It is identical to my mother's, right down to each strand. I am indeed, piece by piece, a dressed replica of my mother — and more's the pity.

But now Mr. Phyfe has unfrozen himself and is no longer a statue, and there is much hugging and kissing as he and my mother exchange foolish banter, while around her all the minions ooh and aah. Soon surely the floor will open and I will make a merciful descent into realms unknown. But no, it is another descent I make, for unknown hands are pushing me into the sun which circles my mother, as she sits in perfection, while the lowly ones adjust the oceans of velvet around the hoops. Yes, I am to sit on the arm of her chair and lean in close to her just as though we belonged together. Oh, the cruelty of it! From this pool of white light I peer out through the blaze into caves of darkness as voices echo through caverns, for our every gesture is directed into attitudes of tenderness, while other voices flicker in and out mumbling about fuses blowing and more light on Mrs. Vanderbilt's right cheek — and all I want to do is to shrink into a tiny ball and hurl myself off the face of this earth forever.

Smile, Little Gloria, smile. It is the voice of the dragon from somewhere far at the distant end of the cave. And I try I try I try, but instead my face turns into a pumpkin with no candle inside and a mouth going down instead of up. Beside me my mother remains valiant, but I can sense that her endurance is waning. What will happen if she too collapses into a miserable pumpkin?

Little Gloria, lean closer lean closer to Big Gloria.

Now my eyes have grown used to sunbursts, and if I squint, I can make out the shadow of the dragon bending over a pillar of stone as it stands immovable and silent, and I can see it is not a dragon at all, nor is it a pillar of stone. It is Mr. Hal Phyfe calling from the cave's hollow darkness, while others, in mysterious ways, drift silently around the cave, still fiddling around, adjusting things.

That's better that's better, Little Gloria — only smile, please, smile smile smile smile!

In rage I lean over to take my mother's hand, but it is spread out just so, and her fingers, all five, placed just so — the long nails of mahogany red presented just so. How heartless to disturb such symmetry. So I pull back.

Little Gloria, put your arm around Big Gloria — arm around her arm around her.

And I do, without hesitation. And now I reach over and, without disturbing her hand, my hand circles her wrist, lightly and gently, so gently, I will her towards me — but it is for nought. She gazes out through the blaze of sun into the abyss, hooked to the image she projects, and I know that she is not aware of my intent at all. And the dragon's teeth click away, and I see how it will look, this picture Mr. Hal Phyfe is conjuring up, when framed in silver and standing on a table somewhere in my mother's house, or on the piano maybe. Others will look at it and my mother will look at it, but no one will look at as I do, for to me it will always be a picture of a greedy little night-hunting rabbit, in pursuit of something . . . but what? A mother perhaps? Yes, that's as good a name for it as any . . .

ANNE FRANK

from

THE DIARY OF A YOUNG GIRL

By confiding her thoughts in her diary, **Anne Frank** unwittingly left us a vivid account of a tragic historical episode — Jewish families in Holland hiding from the Nazis during World War II — as seen through the eyes of a sensitive and remarkably insightful and likable child. At age thirteen, Anne thought of her diary as a substitute for the close friend she had not yet found — someone in whom she could confide her most deeply felt thoughts. In these entries, we hear of the first days of adjusting to the tedious confinement of the hiding place, and the panic of the moments when the two families thought they were discovered.

They were indeed eventually found out by the Nazis, and Anne perished at Bergen-Belsen concentration camp at age sixteen. Of the seven hiding in the annex, only Anne's father survived the war. That life-loving Anne was not allowed to live out her full span of years is one of the countless wrongs of that bleak period of human history.

———

I haven't written for a few days, because I wanted first of all to think about my diary. It's an odd idea for someone like me to keep a diary; not only because I have never done so before, but because it seems to me that neither I — nor for that matter anyone else — will be interested in the unbosomings of a thirteen-year-old school-girl. Still, what does that matter? I want to write, but more than that, I want to bring out all kinds of things that lie buried deep in my heart.

There is a saying that "paper is more patient than man"; it came back to me on one of my slightly melancholy days, while I sat chin in hand, feeling too bored and limp even to make up my mind whether to go out or stay at home. Yes, there is no doubt that paper is patient and as I don't intend to show this cardboard-covered notebook, bearing the proud name of "diary," to anyone, unless I find a real friend, boy or girl, probably nobody cares. And now I come to the root of the matter, the reason for my starting a diary: it is that I have no such real friend.

Let me put it more clearly, since no one will believe that a girl of thirteen feels herself quite alone in the world, nor is it so. I have darling parents and a sister of sixteen. I know about thirty people whom one might call friends — I have strings of boy friends, anxious to catch a glimpse of me and who, failing that, peep at me through mirrors in class. I have relations, aunts and uncles, who are darlings too, a good home, no — I don't seem to lack anything. But it's the same with all my friends, just fun and joking, nothing more. I can never bring myself to talk of anything outside the common round. We don't seem to be able to get any closer, that is the root of the trouble. Perhaps I lack confidence, but anyway, there it is, a stubborn fact and I don't seem to be able to do anything about it.

Hence, this diary. In order to enhance in my mind's eye the picture of the friend for whom I have waited so long, I don't want to set down a series of bald facts in a diary like most people do, but I want this diary itself to be my friend, and I shall call my friend Kitty. No one will grasp what I'm talking about if I begin my letters to Kitty just out of the blue, so albeit unwillingly, I will start by sketching in brief the story of my life.

My father was thirty-six when he married my mother, who was then twenty-five. My sister Margot was born in 1926 in Frankfort-on-Main, I followed on June 12, 1929, and, as we are Jewish, we emigrated to Holland in 1933, where my father was appointed Managing Director of Travies N.V. This firm is in close relationship with the firm of Kolen & Co. in the same building, of which my father is a partner.

The rest of our family, however, felt the full impact of Hitler's anti-Jewish laws, so life was filled with anxiety. In 1938 after the pogroms, my two uncles (my mother's brothers) escaped to the U.S.A. My old grandmother came to us, she was then seventy-three. After May 1940 good

181

times rapidly fled: first the war, then the capitulation, followed by the arrival of the Germans, which is when the sufferings of us Jews really began. Anti-Jewish decrees followed each other in quick succession. Jews must wear a yellow star,* Jews must hand in their bicycles, Jews are banned from trains and are forbidden to drive, Jews are only allowed to do their shopping between three and five o'clock and then only in shops which bear the placard "Jewish shop." Jews must be indoors by eight o'clock and cannot even sit in their own gardens after that hour. Jews are forbidden to visit theaters, cinemas, and other places of entertainment. Jews may not take part in public sports. Swimming baths, tennis courts, hockey fields, and other sports grounds are all prohibited to them. Jews may not visit Christians. Jews must go to Jewish schools, and many more restrictions of a similar kind.

So we could not do this and were forbidden to do that. But life went on in spite of it all. Jopie used to say to me, "You're scared to do anything, because it may be forbidden." Our freedom was strictly limited. Yet things were still bearable.

Granny died in January 1942; no one will ever know how much she is present in my thoughts and how much I love her still.

In 1934 I went to school at the Montessori

*To distinguish them from others, all Jews were forced by the Germans to wear, prominently displayed, a yellow six-pointed star.

Kindergarten and continued there. It was at the end of the school year, I was in form 6B, when I had to say good-by to Mrs. K. We both wept, it was very sad. In 1941 I went, with my sister Margot, to the Jewish Secondary School, she into the fourth form and I into the first.

So far everything is all right with the four of us and here I come to the present day.

Saturday, 20 June, 1942

Dear Kitty,

I'll start straight away. It is so peaceful at the moment, Mummy and Daddy are out and Margot has gone to play ping-pong with some friends.

I've been playing ping-pong a lot myself lately. We ping-pongers are very partial to an ice cream, especially in summer, when one gets warm at the game, so we usually finish up with a visit to the nearest ice-cream shop, Delphi or Oasis, where Jews are allowed. We've given up scrounging for extra pocket money. Oasis is usually full and among our large circle of friends we always manage to find some kindhearted gentleman or boy friend, who presents us with more ice cream than we could devour in a week.

I expect you will be rather surprised at the fact that I should talk of boy friends at my age. Alas, one simply can't seem to avoid it at our school. As soon as a boy asks if he may bicycle home with me and we get into conversation, nine out of ten times I can be sure that he will fall head over heels in love immediately and simply won't allow me out of his sight. After a while it cools down of course, especially as I take little notice of ardent looks and pedal blithely on.

If it gets so far that they begin about "asking Father" I swerve slightly on my bicycle, my satchel falls, the young man is bound to get off and hand it to me, by which time I have introduced a new topic of conversation.

These are the most innocent types; you get some who blow kisses or try to get hold of your arm, but then they are definitely knocking at the wrong door. I get off my bicycle and refuse to go further in their company, or I pretend to be insulted and tell them in no uncertain terms to clear off.

There, the foundation of our friendship is laid, till tomorrow!

Yours, Anne

Sunday morning, 5 July, 1942

Dear Kitty,

Our examination results were announced in the Jewish Theater last Friday. I couldn't have hoped for better. My report is not at all bad, I had one *vix satis*, a five for alegbra, two sixes, and the rest were all sevens or eights. They were certainly pleased at home, although over the question of marks my parents are quite different from most. They don't care a bit whether my reports are good or bad as long as I'm well and happy, and not too cheeky: then the rest will come by itself. I am just the opposite. I don't want to be a bad pupil; I should really have stayed in the seventh form in the Montessori

School, but was accepted for the Jewish Secondary. When all the Jewish children had to go to Jewish schools, the headmaster took Lies and me conditionally after a bit of persuasion. He relied on us to do our best and I don't want to let him down. My sister Margot has her report too, brilliant as usual. She would move up with *cum laude* if that existed at school, she is so brainy. Daddy has been at home a lot lately, as there is nothing for him to do at business; it must be rotten to feel so superfluous. Mr. Koophuis has taken over Travies and Mr. Kraler the firm Kolen & Co. When we walked across our little square together a few days ago, Daddy began to talk of us going into hiding. I asked him why on earth he was beginning to talk of that already. "Yes, Anne," he said, "you know that we have been taking food, clothes, furniture to other people for more than a year now. We don't want our belongings to be seized by the Germans, but we certainly don't want to fall into their clutches ourselves. So we shall disappear of our own accord and not wait until they come and fetch us."

"But, Daddy, when would it be?" He spoke so seriously that I grew very anxious.

"Don't you worry about it, we shall arrange everything. Make the most of your carefree young life while you can." That was all. Oh, may the fulfillment of these somber words remain far distant yet!

Yours, Anne

Dear Kitty,

Years seem to have passed between Sunday and now. So much has happened, it is just as if the whole world had turned upside down. But I am still alive, Kitty, and that is the main thing, Daddy says.

Yes, I'm still alive, indeed, but don't ask where or how. You wouldn't understand a word, so I will begin by telling you what happened on Sunday afternoon.

At three o'clock (Harry had just gone, but was coming back later) someone rang the front doorbell. I was lying lazily reading a book on the veranda in the sunshine, so I didn't hear it. A bit later, Margot appeared at the kitchen door looking very excited. "The S.S. have sent a call-up notice for Daddy," she whispered. "Mummy has gone to see Mr. Van Daan already." (Van Daan is a friend who works with Daddy in the business.) It was a great shock to me, a call-up; everyone knows what that means. I picture concentration camps and lonely cells — should we allow him to be doomed to this? "Of course he won't go," declared Margot, while we waited together. "Mummy has gone to the Van Daans to discuss whether we should move into our hiding place tomorrow. The Van Daans are going with us, so we shall be seven in all." Silence. We couldn't talk any more, thinking about Daddy, who, little knowing what was going on, was visiting some old people in the Joodse Invalide; waiting for Mummy, the heat and suspense, all made us very overawed and silent.

Suddenly the bell rang again. "That is Harry," I said. "Don't open the door." Margot held me back, but it was not necessary as we heard Mummy and Mr. Van Daan downstairs, talking to Harry, then they came in and closed the door behind them. Each time the bell went, Margot or I had to creep softly down to see if it was Daddy, not opening the door to anyone else.

Margot and I were sent out of the room. Van Daan wanted to talk to Mummy alone. When we were alone together in our bedroom, Margot told me that the call-up was not for Daddy, but for her. I was more frightened than ever and began to cry. Margot is sixteen; would they really take girls of that age away alone? But thank goodness she won't go, Mummy said so herself; that must be what Daddy meant when he talked about us going into hiding.

Into hiding — where would we go, in a town or the country, in a house or a cottage, when, how, where . . . ?

These were questions I was not allowed to ask, but I couldn't get them out of my mind. Margot and I began to pack some of our most vital belongings into a school satchel. The first thing I put in was this diary, then hair curlers, handkerchiefs, schoolbooks, a comb, old letters; I put in the craziest things with the idea that we were going into hiding. But I'm not sorry, memories mean more to me than dresses.

At five o'clock Daddy finally arrived, and we phoned Mr. Koophuis to ask if he could come around in the evening. Van Daan went and fetched Miep. Miep has been in the business with Daddy since 1933 and has become a close friend, likewise her brand-new husband, Henk. Miep came and took some shoes, dresses, coats, underwear, and stockings away in her bag, promising to return in the evening. Then silence fell on the house; not one of us felt like eating anything, it was still hot and everything was very strange. We let our large upstairs room to a certain Mr. Goudsmit, a divorced man in his thirties, who appeared to have nothing to do on this particular evening; we simply could not get rid of him without being rude; he hung about until ten o'clock. At eleven o'clock Miep and Henk Van Santen arrived. Once again, shoes, stockings, books, and underclothes disappeared into Miep's bag and Henk's deep pockets, and at eleven-thirty they too disappeared. I was dog-tired and although I knew that it would be my last night in my own bed, I fell asleep immediately and didn't wake up until Mummy called me at five-thirty the next morning. Luckily it was not so hot as Sunday; warm rain fell steadily all day. We put on heaps of clothes as if we were going to the North Pole, the sole reason being to take clothes with us. No Jew in our situation would have dreamed of going out with a suitcase full of clothing. I had on two vests, three pairs of pants, a dress, on top of that a skirt, jacket, summer coat, two pairs of stockings, lace-up shoes, woolly cap, scarf, and still more; I was nearly stifled before we started, but no one inquired about that.

Margot filled her satchel with schoolbooks, fetched her bicycle, and rode off behind Miep into the unknown, as far as I was concerned. You see I still didn't know where our secret hiding place was to be. At seven-thirty the door closed behind us. Moortje, my little cat, was the only creature to whom I said farewell. She would have a good home with the neighbors. This was all written in a letter addressed to Mr. Goudsmit.

There was one pound of meat in the kitchen for the cat, breakfast things lying on the table, stripped beds, all giving the impression that we had left helter-skelter. But we didn't care about impressions, we only wanted to get away, only escape and arrive safely, nothing else. Continued tomorrow.

Yours, Anne

Thursday, 9 July, 1942

Dear Kitty,

So we walked in the pouring rain, Daddy, Mummy, and I, each with a school satchel and shopping bag filled to the brim with all kinds of things thrown together anyhow.

We got sympathetic looks from people on their way to work. You could see by their faces how sorry they were they couldn't offer us a lift; the gaudy yellow star spoke for itself.

Only when we were on the road did Mummy and Daddy begin to tell me bits and pieces about the plan. For months as many of our goods and chattels and necessities of life as possible had been sent away and they were sufficiently ready for us to have gone into hiding of our own accord on July 16. The plan had had to be speeded up ten days because of the call-up, so our quarters would not be so well organized, but we had to make the best of it. The hiding place itself would be in the building where Daddy has his office. It will be hard for outsiders to understand, but I shall explain that later on. Daddy didn't have many people working for him: Mr. Karler, Koophuis, Miep, and Elli Vossen, a twenty-three-year-old typist who all knew of our arrival. Mr. Vossen, Elli's father, and two boys worked in the warehouse; they had not been told.

I will describe the building: there is a large warehouse on the ground floor which is used as a store. The front door to the house is next to the warehouse door, and inside the front door is a second doorway which leads to a staircase. There is another door at the top of the stairs, with a frosted glass window in it, which has "Office" written in black letters across it. That is the large main office, very big, very light, and very full. Elli, Miep, and Mr. Koophuis work there in the daytime. A small dark room containing the safe, a wardrobe, and a large cupboard leads to a small somewhat dark second office. Mr. Kraler and Mr. Van Daan used to sit here, now it is only Mr. Kraler. One can reach Kraler's office from the passage, but only via a glass door which can be opened from the inside, but not easily from the outside.

From Kraler's office a long passage goes past the coal store, up four steps and leads to the showroom of the whole building: the private office. Dark, dignified furniture, linoleum and carpets on the floor, radio, smart lamp, everything first-class. Next door there is a roomy kitchen with a hot-water faucet and a gas stove. Next door the W.C. That is the first floor.

A wooden staircase leads from the downstairs passage to the next floor. There is a small landing at the top. There is a door at each end of the landing, the left one leading to a storeroom at the front of the house and to the attics. One of those really steep Dutch staircases runs from the side to the other door opening on to the street.

The right-hand door leads to our "Secret Annexe." No one would ever guess that there would be so many rooms hidden behind that plain gray door. There's a little step in front of the door and then you are inside.

There is a steep staircase immediately opposite the entrance. On the left a tiny passage brings you into a room which was to become the Frank family's bed-sitting-room, next door a smaller room, study and bedroom for the two young ladies of the family. On the right a little room without windows containing the washbasin and a small W.C. compartment, with another door leading to Margot's and my room. If you go up the next flight of stairs and open the door, you are simply amazed that there could be such a big light room in such an old house by the canal. There is a gas stove in this room (thanks to the fact that it was used as a laboratory) and a sink. This is now the kitchen for the Van Daan couple, besides being general living room, dining room, and scullery.

A tiny little corridor room will become Peter Van Daan's apartment. Then, just as on the lower landing, there is a large attic. So there you are, I've introduced you to the whole of our beautiful "Secret Annexe."

Yours, Anne

Friday, 10 July, 1942

Dear Kitty,

I expect I have thoroughly bored you with my long-winded descriptions of our dwelling. But still I think you should know where we've landed.

But to continue my story — you see, I've not finished yet — when we arrived at the Prinsengracht, Miep took us quickly upstairs and into the "Secret Annexe." She closed the door behind us and we were alone. Margot was already waiting for us, having come much faster on her bicycle. Our living room and all the other rooms were chock-full of rubbish, indescribably so. All the cardboard boxes which had been sent to the office in the previous months lay piled on the floor and the beds. The little room was filled to the ceiling with bedclothes. We had to start clearing up immediately, if we wished to sleep in decent beds that night. Mummy and Margot were not in a fit state to take part; they were tired and lay down on their beds, they were miserable, and lots more besides. But the two "clearers-up" of the family — Daddy and myself — wanted to start at once.

The whole day long we unpacked boxes, filled cupboards, hammered and tidied, until we were dead beat. We sank into clean beds that night. We hadn't had a bit of anything warm the whole day, but we didn't care; Mummy and Margot were too tired and keyed up to eat, and Daddy and I were too busy.

On Tuesday morning we went on where we left off the day before. Elli and Miep collected our rations for us, Daddy improved the poor blackout, we scrubbed the kitchen floor, and were on the go the whole day long again. I hardly had time to think about the great change in my life until Wednesday. Then I had a chance, for the first time since our arrival, to tell you all about it, and at the same time to realize myself what had actually happened to me and what was still going to happen.

Yours, Anne

Tuesday, 11 April, 1944

Dear Kitty,

My head throbs, I honestly don't know where to begin.

On Friday (Good Friday) we played Monopoly, Saturday afternoon too. These days passed quickly and uneventfully. On Sunday afternoon, on my invitation, Peter came to my room at half past four; at a quarter past five we went to the front attic, where we remained until six o'clock. There was a beautiful Mozart concert on the radio from six o'clock until a quarter past seven. I enjoyed it all very much, but especially the "Kleine Nachtmusik." I can hardly listen in the room because I'm always so inwardly stirred when I hear lovely music.

On Sunday evening Peter and I went to the

front attic together and, in order to sit comfortably, we took with us a few divan cushions that we were able to lay our hands on. We seated ourselves on one packing case. Both the case and the cushions were very narrow, so we sat absolutely squashed together, leaning against other cases. Mouschi kept us company too, so we weren't unchaperoned.

Suddenly at a quarter to nine, Mr. Van Daan whistled and asked if we had one of Dussel's cushions. We both jumped up and went downstairs with cushion, cat, and Van Daan.

A lot of trouble arose out of this cushion, because Dussel was annoyed that we had one of his cushions, one that he used as a pillow. He was afraid that there might be fleas in it and made a great commotion about his beloved cushion! Peter and I put two hard brushes in his bed as a revenge. We had a good laugh over this little interlude!

Our fun didn't last long. At half past nine Peter knocked softly on the door and asked Daddy if he would just help him upstairs over a difficult English sentence. "That's a blind," I said to Margot, "anyone could see through that one!" I was right. They were in the act of breaking into the warehouse. Daddy, Van Daan, Dussel, and Peter were downstairs in a flash. Margot, Mummy, Mrs. Van Daan, and I stayed upstairs and waited.

Four frightened women just have to talk, so talk we did, until we heard a bang downstairs. After that all was quiet, the clock struck a quarter to ten. The color had vanished from our faces, we were still quiet, although we were afraid. Where could the men be? What was that bang? Would they be fighting the burglars? Ten o'clock, footsteps on the stairs: Daddy, white and nervous, entered, followed by Mr. Van Daan. "Lights out, creep upstairs, we expect the police in the house!"

There was no time to be frightened: the lights went out, I quickly grabbed a jacket, and we were upstairs. "What has happened? Tell us quickly!" There was no one to tell us, the men having disappeared downstairs again. Only at ten past ten did they reappear; two kept watch at Peter's open window, the door to the landing was closed, the swinging cupboard shut. We hung a jersey round the night light, and after that they told us:

Peter heard two loud bangs on the landing, ran downstairs, and saw there was a large plank out of the left half of the door. He dashed upstairs, warned the "Home Guard" of the family, and the four of them proceeded downstairs. When they entered the warehouse, the burglars were in the act of enlarging the hole. Without further thought Van Daan shouted: "Police!"

A few hurried steps outside, and the burglars had fled. In order to avoid the hole being noticed by the police, a plank was put against it, but a good hard kick from outside sent it flying to the ground. The men were perplexed at such impudence, and both Van Daan and Peter felt murder welling up within them; Van Daan beat on the ground with a chopper, and all was quiet again. Once more they wanted to put the plank in front of the hole. Disturbance! A married couple outside shone a torch through the opening, lighting up the whole warehouse. "Hell!" muttered one of the men, and now they switched over from their role of police to that of burglars. The four of them sneaked upstairs, Peter quickly opened the doors and windows of the kitchen and private office, flung the telephone onto the floor, and finally the four of them landed behind the swinging cupboard.

END OF PART ONE

The married couple with the torch would probably have warned the police: it was Sunday evening, Easter Sunday, no one at the office on Easter Monday, so none of us could budge until Tuesday morning. Think of it, waiting in such fear for two nights and a day! No one had anything to suggest, so we simply sat there in pitch-darkness, because Mrs. Van Daan in her fright had unintentionally turned the lamp right out; talked in whispers, and at every creak one heard "Sh! sh!"

It turned half past ten, eleven, but not a sound; Daddy and Van Daan joined us in turns. Then a quarter past eleven, a bustle and noise downstairs. Everyone's breath was audible, otherwise no one moved. Footsteps in the house, in the private office, kitchen, then . . . on our staircase. No one breathed audibly now, footsteps on our staircase, then a rattling of the swinging cupboard. This moment is indescribable. "Now we are lost!" I said, and could see us all being taken away by the Gestapo that very night. Twice they rattled at the cupboard, then there was nothing, the footsteps withdrew, we were saved so far. A shiver seemed to pass from one to another, I heard someone's teeth chattering, no one said a word.

There was not another sound in the house, but a light was burning on our landing, right in front of the cupboard. Could that be because it was a secret cupboard? Perhaps the police had forgotten the light? would someone come back to put it out? Tongues loosened, there was no one in the house any longer, perhaps there was someone on guard outside.

Next we did three things: we went over again what we supposed had happened, we trembled with fear, and we had to go to the lavatory. The buckets were in the attic, so all we had was Peter's tin wastepaper basket. Van Daan went first, then Daddy, but Mummy was too shy to face it. Daddy brought the wastepaper basket into the room, where Margot, Mrs. Van Daan, and I gladly made use of it. Finally Mummy decided to do so too. People kept on asking for paper — fortunately I had some in my pocket!

The tin smelled ghastly, everything went on in a whisper, we were tired, it was twelve o'clock. "Lie down on the floor then and sleep." Margot and I were each given a pillow and one blanket; Margot lying just near the store cupboard and I between the table legs. The smell wasn't quite so bad when one was on the floor, but still Mrs. Van Daan quietly brought some chlorine, a tea towel over the pot serving as a second expedient.

Talk, whispers, fear, stink, flatulation, and always someone on the pot; then try to go to sleep! However, by half past two I was so tired that I knew no more until half past three. I awoke when Mrs. Van Daan laid her head on my foot.

"For heaven's sake, give me something to put on!" I asked. I was given something, but don't ask what — a pair of woolen knickers over my pajamas, a red jumper, and a black skirt, white oversocks and a part of sports stockings full of holes. Then Mrs. Van Daan sat in the chair and her husband came and lay on my feet. I lay thinking till half past three, shivering the whole time, which prevented Van Daan from sleeping. I prepared myself for the return of the police, then we'd have to say that we were in hiding; they would either be good Dutch people, then we'd be saved, or N.S.B-ers,* then we'd have to bribe them!

"In that case, destroy the radio," sighed Mrs. Van Daan. "Yes, in the stove!" replied her husband. "If they find us, then let them find the radio as well!"

"Then they will find Anne's diary," added Daddy. "Burn it then," suggested the most terrified member of the party. This, and when the police rattled the cupboard door, were my worst moments. "Not my diary; if my diary goes, I go with it!" But luckily Daddy didn't answer.

*The Dutch National Socialist Movement.

There is no object in recounting all the conversations that I can still remember; so much was said. I comforted Mrs. Van Daan, who was very scared. We talked about escaping and being questioned by the Gestapo, about ringing up, and being brave.

"We must behave like soldiers, Mrs. Van Daan. If all is up now, then let's go for Queen and Country, for freedom, truth, and the right, as they always say on the Dutch News from England. Thee only thing that is really rotten is that we get a lot of other people into trouble too."

Mr. Van Daan changed places with his wife after an hour, and Daddy came and sat beside me. The men smoked non-stop, now and then there was a deep sigh, then someone went on the pot and everything began all over again.

Four o'clock, five o'clock, half past five. Then I went and sat with Peter by his window and listened, so close together that we could feel each other's bodies quivering; we spoke a word or two now and then, and listened attentively. In the room next door they took down the blackout. They wanted to call up Koophuis at seven o'clock and get him to send someone around. Then they wrote down everything they wanted to tell Koophuis over the phone. The risk that the police on guard at the door, or in the warehouse, might hear the telephone was very great, but the danger of the police returning was even greater.

The points were these:

Burglars broken in: police have been in the

house, as far as the swinging cupboard, but no further.

Burglars apparently disturbed, forced open the door in the warehouse and escaped through the garden.

Main entrance bolted, Kraler must have used the second door when he left. The typewriters and adding machines are safe in the black case in the private office.

Try to warn Henk and fetch the key from Elli, then go and look around the office — on the pretext of feeding the cat.

Everything went according to plan. Koophuis was phoned, the typewriters which we had upstairs were put in the case. Then we sat around the table again and waited for Henk or the police.

Peter had fallen asleep and Van Daan and I were lying on the floor, when we heard loud footsteps downstairs. I got up quietly: "That's Henk."

"No, no, it's the police," some of the others said.

Someone knocked at the door, Miep whistled. This was too much for Mrs. Van Daan, she turned as white as a sheet and sank limply into a chair, had the tension lasted one minute longer she would have fainted.

Our room was a perfect picture when Miep and Henk entered, the table alone would have been worth photographing! A copy of *Cinema and Theater*, covered with jam and a remedy for diarrhea, opened at a page of dancing girls, two jam pots, two started loaves of bread, a mirror, comb, matches, ash, cigarettes, tobacco, ash tray, books, a pair of pants, a torch, toilet paper, etc., etc., lay jumbled together in variegated splendor.

Of course Henk and Miep were greeted with shouts and tears. Henk mended the hole in the door with some planks, and soon went off again to inform the police of the burglary. Meip had also found a letter under the warehouse door from the night watchman Slagter, who had noticed the hole and warned the police, whom he would also visit.

So we had half an hour to tidy ourselves. I've never seen such a change take place in half an hour. Margot and I took the bedclothes downstairs, went to the W.C., washed, and did our teeth and hair. After that I tidied the room a bit and went upstairs again. The table there was already cleared, so we ran off some water and made coffee and tea, boiled the milk, and laid the table for lunch. Daddy and Peter emptied the potties and cleaned them with warm water and chlorine.

At eleven o'clock we sat round the table with Henk, who was back by that time, and slowly things began to be more normal and cozy again. Henk's story was as follows:

Mr. Slagter was asleep, but his wife told Henk that her husband had found the hole in our door when he was doing his tour round the canals, and that he had called a policeman, who had gone through the building with him. He would be coming to see Kraler on Tuesday and would tell him more then. At the police station they knew nothing of the burglary yet, but the

201

policeman had made a note of it at once and would come and look round on Tuesday. On the way back Henk happened to meet our greengrocer at the corner, and told him that the house had been broken into. "I know that," he said quite coolly. "I was passing last evening with my wife and saw the hole in the door. My wife wanted to walk on, but I just had a look in with my torch; then the thieves cleared at once. To be on the safe side, I didn't ring up the police, as with you I didn't think it was the thing to do. I don't know anything, but I guess a lot."

Henk thanked him and went on. The man obviously guesses that we're here, because he always brings the potatoes during the lunch hour. Such a nice man!

It was one by the time Henk had gone and we'd finished doing the dishes. We all went for a sleep. I awoke at a quarter to three and saw that Mr. Dussel had already disappeared. Quite by chance, and with my sleepy eyes, I ran into Peter in the bathroom; he had just come down. We arranged to meet downstairs.

I tidied myself and went down. "Do you still dare to go to the front attic?" he asked. I nodded, fetched my pillow, and we went up to the attic. It was glorious weather, and soon the sirens were wailing; we stayed where we were. Peter put his arm around my shoulder, and I put mine around his and so we remained, our arms around each other, quietly waiting until Margot came to fetch us for coffee at four o'clock.

We finished our bread, drank lemonade and joked (we were able to again), otherwise everything went normally. In the evening I thanked Peter because he was the bravest of us all.

None of us has ever been in such danger as that night. God truly protected us; just think of it — the police at our secret cupboard, the light on right in front of it, and still we remained undiscovered.

If the invasion comes, and bombs with it, then it is each man for himself, but in this case the fear was also for our good, innocent protectors. "We are saved, go on saving us!" That is all we can say.

This affair has brought quite a number of changes with it. Mr. Dussel no longer sits downstairs in Kraler's office in the evenings, but in the bathroom instead. Peter goes round the house for a checkup at half past eight and half past nine. Peter isn't allowed to have his window open at nights any more. No one is allowed to pull the plug after half past nine. This evening there's a carpenter coming to make the warehouse doors even stronger.

Now there are debates going on all the time in the "Secret Annexe." Kraler reproached us for our carelessness. Henk, too, said that in a case like that we must never go downstairs. We have been pointedly reminded that we are in hiding, that we are Jews in chains, chained to one spot, without any rights, but with a thousand duties. We Jews mustn't show our feelings, must be brave and strong, must accept all inconveniences and not grumble, must do what is within our power and trust in God. Sometime this terrible war will be over. Surely the time will come when we are people again, and not just Jews.

Who has inflicted this upon us? Who has made us Jews different from all other people? Who has allowed us to suffer so terribly up till now? It is God that has made us as we are, but it will be God, too, who will raise us up again. If we bear all this suffering and if there are still Jews left, when it is over, then Jews, instead of being doomed, will be held up as an example. Who knows, it might even be our religion from which the world and all peoples learn good, and for that reason and that reason only do we have to suffer now. We can never become just Netherlanders, or just English, or representatives of any country for that matter, we will always remain Jews, but we want to, too.

Be brave! Let us remain aware of our task and not grumble, a solution will come, God has never deserted our people. Right through the ages there have been Jews, through all the ages they have had to suffer, but it has made them strong too; the weak fall, but the strong will remain and never go under!

During that night I really felt that I had to die, I waited for the police, I was prepared, as the soldier is on the battlefield. I was eager to lay down my life for the country, but now, now I've been saved again, now my first wish after the war is that I may become Dutch! I love the Dutch, I love this country, I love the language and want to work here. And even if I have to write to the Queen myself, I will not give up until I have reached my goal.

I am becoming still more independent of my

parents, young as I am, I face life with more courage than Mummy; my feeling for justice is immovable, and truer than hers. I know what I want, I have a goal, an opinion, I have a religion and love. Let me be myself and then I am satisfied. I know that I'm a woman, a woman with inward strength and plenty of courage.

If God lets me live, I shall attain more than Mummy ever has done, I shall not remain insignificant, I shall work in the world and for mankind!

And now I know that first and foremost I shall require courage and cheerfulness!

Yours, Anne

INFLUENCES

Parents and Background

N. SCOTT MOMADAY

from

THE WAY TO RAINY MOUNTAIN

Born in 1934, raised on an Indian reservation in Oklahoma, **N. Scott Momaday** remembers his grandmother, a Kiowa Indian, and describes the devastation of an entire way of life, of an entire people — the total annihilation of her tribe. In about 1890 when his grandmother was ten, the Kiowan tribe gathered for its last sun dance near Rainy Mountain Creek: "My grandmother had a reverence for the sun, a holy regard that now is all but gone out of mankind."

Momaday, a writer and teacher, was awarded the Pulitzer Prize for his first novel, *House Made of Dawn,* and the following excerpt is from the autobiographical preface to *The Way to Rainy Mountain,* a collection of Indian legends.

———

A single knoll rises out of the plain in Oklahoma, north and west of the Wichita Range. For my people, the Kiowas, it is an old landmark, and they gave it the name Rainy Mountain. The hardest weather in the world is there. Winter brings blizzards, hot tornadic winds arise in the spring, and in summer the prairie is an anvil's edge. The grass turns brittle and brown, and it cracks beneath your feet. There are green belts along the rivers and creeks, linear groves of hickory and pecan, willow and witch hazel. At a distance in July or August the steaming foliage seems almost to writhe in fire. Great green and yellow grasshoppers are everywhere in the tall grass, popping up like corn to sting the flesh, and tortoises crawl about on the red earth, going nowhere in the plenty of time. Loneliness is an aspect of the land. All things in the plain are isolate; there is no confusion of objects in the eye, but *one* hill or *one* tree or *one* man. To look upon that landscape in the early morning, with the sun at your back, is to lose the sense of proportion. Your imagination comes to life, and this, you think, is where Creation was begun.

I returned to Rainy Mountain in July. My grandmother had died in the spring, and I wanted to be at her grave. She had lived to be very old and at last infirm. Her only living daughter was with her when she died, and I was told that in death her face was that of a child.

I like to think of her as a child. When she was born, the Kiowas were living the last great moments of their history. For more than a hundred years they had controlled the open range from the Smoky Hill River to the Red, from the headwaters of the Canadian to the fork of the Arkansas and Cimarron. In alliance with the Comanches, they had ruled the whole of the southern Plains. War was their sacred business, and they were among the finest horsemen the world has ever known. But warfare for the Kiowas was preeminently a matter of disposition rather than of survival, and they never understood the grim, unrelenting advance of the U.S. Cavalry. When at last, divided and ill-provisioned, they were driven onto the Staked Plains in the cold rains of autumn, they fell into panic. In Palo Duro Canyon they abandoned their crucial stores to pillage and had nothing then but their lives. In order to save themselves, they surrendered to the soldiers at Fort Sill and were imprisoned in the old stone corral that now stands as a military museum. My grandmother was spared the humiliation of those high gray walls by eight or ten years, but she must have known from birth the affliction of defeat, the dark brooding of old warriors.

Her name was Aho, and she belonged to the last culture to evolve in North America. Her forebears came down from the high country in western Montana nearly three centuries ago. They were a mountain people, a mysterious tribe of hunters whose language has never been positively classified in any major group. In the late seventeenth century they began a long migration to the south and east. It was a journey toward the dawn, and it led to a golden age. Along the way the Kiowas were befriended by the Crows, who gave them the culture and religion of the Plains. They acquired horses, and their ancient nomadic spirit was suddenly free of the ground. They acquired Tai-me, the sacred Sun Dance

211

doll, from that moment the object and symbol of their worship, and so shared in the divinity of the sun. Not least, they acquired the sense of destiny, therefore courage and pride. When they entered upon the southern Plains they had been transformed. No longer were they slaves to the simple necessity of survival; they were a lordly and dangerous society of fighters and thieves, hunters and priests of the sun. According to their origin myth, they entered the world through a hollow log. From one point of view, their migration was the fruit of an old prophecy, for indeed they emerged from a sunless world.

Although my grandmother lived out her long life in the shadow of Rainy Mountain, the immense landscape of the continental interior lay like memory in her blood. She could tell of the Crows, whom she had never seen, and of the Black Hills, where she had never been. I wanted to see in reality what she had seen more perfectly in the mind's eye, and traveled fifteen hundred miles to begin my pilgrimage.

Yellowstone, it seemed to me, was the top of the world, a region of deep lakes and dark timber, canyons and waterfalls. But, beautiful as it is, one might have the sense of confinement there. The skyline in all directions is close at hand, the high wall of the woods and deep cleavages of shade. There is a perfect freedom in the mountains, but it belongs to the eagle and the elk, the badger and the bear. The Kiowas reckoned their stature by the distance they could see, and they were bent and blind in the wilderness.

Descending eastward, the highland meadows are a stairway to the plain. In July the inland slope of the Rockies is luxuriant with flax and buckwheat, stonecrop and larkspur. The earth unfolds and the limit of the land recedes. Clusters of trees, and animals grazing far in the distance, cause the vision to reach away and wonder to build upon the mind. The sun follows a longer course in the day, and the sky is immense beyond all comparison. The great billowing clouds that sail upon it are shadows that move upon the grain like water, dividing light. Farther down, in the land of the Crows and Blackfeet, the plain is yellow. Sweet clover takes hold of the hills and bends upon itself to cover and seal the soil. There the Kiowas paused on their way; they had come to the place where they must change their lives. The sun is at home on the plains. Precisely there does it have the certain character of a god. When the Kiowas came to the land of the Crows, they could see the dark lees of the hills at dawn across the Bighorn River, the profusion of light on the grain shelves, the oldest deity ranging after the solstices. Not yet would they veer southward to the caldron of the land that lay below; they must wean their blood from the northern winter and hold the mountains a while longer in their view. They bore Tai-me in procession to the east.

A dark mist lay over the Black Hills, and the land was like iron. At the top of a ridge I caught sight of Devil's Tower upthrust against the gray sky as if in the birth of time the core of the earth had broken through its crust and the motion of the world was begun. There are things in nature that engender an awful quiet in the heart of man; Devil's Tower is one of them. Two centuries ago, because they could not do otherwise, the Kiowas made a legend at the base of the rock. My grandmother said:

Eight children were there at play, seven sisters and their brother. Suddenly the boy was struck dumb; he trembled and began to run upon his hands and feet. His fingers became claws, and his body was covered with fur. Directly there was a bear where the boy had been. The sisters were terrified; they ran, and the bear after them. They came to the stump of a great tree, and the tree spoke to them. It bade them climb upon it, and as they did so it began to rise into the air. The bear came to kill them, but they were just beyond its reach. It reared against the tree and scored the bark all around with its claws. The seven sisters were borne into the sky, and they became the stars of the Big Dipper.

From that moment, and so long as the legend lives, the Kiowas have kinsmen in the night sky. Whatever they were in the mountains, they could be no more. However tenuous their well-being, however much they had suffered and would suffer again, they had found a way out of the wilderness.

My grandmother had a reverence for the sun, a holy regard that now is all but gone out of mankind. There was a wariness in her, and an ancient awe. She was a Christian in her later years, but she had come a long way about, and she never forgot her birthright. As a child she had been to the Sun Dances; she had taken part in those annual rites, and by then she had learned the restoration of her people in the presence of Tai-me. She was about seven when the last Kiowa Sun Dance was held in 1887 on the Washita River above Rainy Mountain Creek. The buffalo were gone. In order to consummate the ancient sacrifice — to impale the head of a buffalo bull upon the medicine tree — a delegation of old men journeyed into Texas, there to beg and barter for an animal from the Goodnight herd. She was ten when the Kiowas came together for the last time as a living Sun Dance culture. They could find no buffalo; they had to hang an old hide from the sacred tree. Before the dance could begin, a company of soliders rode out from Fort Sill under orders to disperse the tribe. Forbidden without cause the essential act of their faith, having seen the wild herds slaughtered and left to rot upon the ground, the Kiowas backed away forever from the medicine tree. That was July 20, 1890, at the great bend of the Washita. My grandmother was there. Without bitterness, and for as long as she lived, she bore a vision of deicide.

Now that I can have her only in memory, I see my grandmother in the several postures that were peculiar to her: standing at the wood stove on a winter morning and turning meat in a great iron skillet; sitting at the south window, bent above her beadwork, and afterwards, when her vision failed, looking down for a long time into the fold of her hands; going out upon a cane, very slowly as she did when the weight of age came upon her; praying. I remember her most often at prayer. She made long, rambling prayers out of suffering and hope, having seen many things. I was never sure that I had the right to hear, so exclusive were they of all mere custom and company. The last time I saw her she prayed standing by the side of her bed at night, naked to the waist, the light of a kerosene lamp moving upon her dark skin. Her long, black hair, always drawn and braided in the day, lay upon her shoulders and against her breasts like a shawl. I do not speak Kiowa, and I never understood her prayers, but there was something inherently sad in the sound, some merest hesitation upon the syllables of sorrow. She began in a high and descending pitch, exhausting her breath to silence; then again and again — and always the same intensity of effort, of something that is, and is not, like urgency in the human voice. Transported so in the dancing light among the shadows of her room, she seemed beyond the reach of time. But that was illusion; I think I knew then that I should not see her again.

Houses are like sentinels in the plain, old keepers of the weather watch. There, in a very little while, wood takes on the appearance of great age. All colors wear soon away in the wind and rain, and then the wood is burned gray and the grain appears and the nails turn red with rust. The windowpanes are black and opaque; you imagine there is nothing within, and indeed there are many ghosts, bones given up to the land. They stand here and there against the sky, and you approach them for a longer time than you expect. They belong in the distance; it is their domain.

Once there was a lot of sound in my grandmother's house, a lot of coming and going, feasting and talk. The summers there were full of excitement and reunion. The Kiowas are a summer people; they abide the cold and keep to themselves, but when the season turns and the land becomes warm and vital they cannot hold still; an old love of going returns upon them. The aged visitors who came to my grandmother's house when I was a child were made of lean and leather, and they bore themselves upright. They wore great black hats and bright ample shirts that shook in the wind. They rubbed fat upon their hair and wound their braids with strips of colored cloth. Some of them painted their faces and carried the scars of old and cherished enmities. They were an old council of warlords, come to remind and be reminded of who they were. Their wives and daughters served them well. The women might indulge themselves; gossip was at once the mark and compensation of their servitude. They made loud and elaborate talk among themselves, full of jest and gesture, fright and false alarm. They went abroad in fringed and flowered shawls, bright beadwork and German silver. They were at home in the kitchen, and they prepared meals that were banquets.

There were frequent prayer meetings, and great nocturnal feasts. When I was a child I played with my cousins outside, where the lamplight fell upon the ground and the singing of the old people rose up around us and carried away into the darkness. There were a lot of good things to eat, a lot of laughter and surprise. And afterwards, when the quiet returned, I lay down with my grandmother and could hear the frogs away by the river and feel the motion of the airs.

Now there is a funeral silence in the rooms, the endless wake of some final word. The walls have closed in upon my grandmother's house. When I returned to it in mourning, I saw for the first time in my life how small it was. It was late at night, and there was a white moon, nearly full. I sat for a long time on the stone steps by the kitchen door. From there I could see out across the land; I could see the long row of trees by the creek, the low light upon the rolling plains, and the stars of the Big Dipper. Once I looked at the moon and caught sight of a strange thing. A cricket had perched upon the handrail, only a few inches away from me. My line of vision was such that the creature filled the moon like a fossil. It had gone there, I thought, to live and die, for there, of all places, was its small definition made whole and eternal. A warm wind rose up and purled like the longing within me.

The next morning I awoke at dawn and went out on the dirt road to Rainy Mountain. It was already hot, and the grasshoppers began to fill the air. Still, it was early in the morning, and the birds sang out of the shadows. The long yellow grass on the mountain shone in the bright light, and a scissortail hied above the land. There,

218

where it ought to be, at the end of a long and legendary way, was my grandmother's grave. Here and there on the dark stones were ancestral names. Looking back once, I saw the mountain and came away.

PATRICIA HAMPL

from

A ROMANTIC EDUCATION

Born in 1946 in St. Paul, Minnesota, **Patricia Hampl** proceeded to write her memoirs at a comparatively early age — while still in her thirties. In *A Romantic Education*, she explores the relationship between her Czech family background and her American upbringing and education.

In this excerpt she evokes her father's strong sense of doing meaningful work as a florist, as he defines with great vehemence the spiritual and aesthetic "uses of a red rose."

In our family it was my father who, everyone agreed, was the beauty. "Handsome as a movie star," my mother's friends would sigh. For a while in the first grade I was under the impression that he was president of the United States (he was president of the church Men's Altar Guild that year, I believe). It seemed natural that someone so handsome should run the country.

My father was not only handsome. As a florist

he was, to me, somehow in charge of beauty. A man "handsome as a movie star" whose business was beauty. In second grade, when we were given an assignment to find out how our fathers' work "helped the community," I went home with foreboding, sensing that my father's work did not help the community in any way, that in fact it was superfluous to the community. As I saw it, children whose fathers were doctors or house painters, for instance, were home free. But my father's occupation struck me as iffy, lightweight, positively extraneous and therefore (to my Catholic puritan logic) not useful to the community.

I felt this foreboding in spite of the fact that I loved the greenhouse and often played in the palmhouse (which was Africa). I once saw a rabbit give birth to her babies in the root cellar, and in the summer I trailed my finger teasingly across the low pool in the back lot where the goldfish — some of them alarmingly large — and the water plants were kept. In winter I wandered through the moist houses, as each glassy room was called, watching the exotic trick my father played on the Minnesota weather. I read the labels on the huge, ancient rose trees and great geranium plants in expensive pots, which wealthy matrons had left in the greenhouse to be cared for while they went to Florida or Arizona, or, the really ethereal ones, to Italy.

The odor of crushed evergreen, the intense little purple berries of juniper, the fans of cedar and the killing hard work of the Christmas rush *were* Christmas to me. I preferred this marketplace Christmas, full of overworked employees and

221

cross tempers and the endless parade of "gift plants" and boxed cut flowers, to our own family Christmas with its ordinary tree and turkey like everybody else's.

But was any of this of use to the community? Did it do any good? I did not want to put my father on the spot. Still, I had the assignment and I asked my question, beginning first with the innocuous part: what, exactly, was his job? He answered at great and technical length; he loved his work.

Then the real question: "Is your job of any use to the community?" I had decided to word it this way, rather than asking *how* it was useful, sensing as I did that it was of no use whatever. I thought that he could simply say, as painlessly as possible, no. And then we'd just drop the subject. My handsome father, who had been enjoying the interrogation, the opportunity to explain his place in the world, frowned. "What do you mean — is it of any use to the community?" he asked sharply.

"I mean, does it do any good — to the community?" I was flustered and was losing hold of what community meant. I was only eight and the whole thing was beginning to unravel as I saw my movie star father frowning at me.

"Who asked you to ask that?"

"Sister, Sister said," I practically cried, falling back on the Catholic school child's great authority.

"Sister," my father said. He was angry. It was as I had thought: he served no use to the community. He was silent for some time, not weighing his words, but apparently deciding whether to speak at all.

"You tell Sister," he finally said, coldly, as if he were talking to an adult, "I do the most important thing for the community. Do you think people can live without beauty? Flowers — do they kill anybody? Do they hurt anyone? Flowers are beautiful — that's all. That's enough. So they're sending you home to find out what's the *use!* You tell her they're beautiful. Tell her I bring beauty to the community." He said the final word with regal contempt, as if he only used the grimy jargon of Sister and her band of philistines for purposes of argument.

It was less than ten years after the Second World War; the Korean "conflict" was just ended. My father wasn't talking to me, not to an eight-year-old, and probably not to a nun with a "unit on work" in her social studies class. He spoke, I think, to himself, in a cry for values, dismayed that the use of a red rose had to be explained, as if my question were proof that the world had been more brutalized than he had known.

MAXINE HONG KINGSTON

from

CHINA MEN

Maxine Hong Kingston was born of Chinese parents in California in 1940 and currently lives in Hawaii where she writes and teaches at the University of Hawaii. In this selection, she describes her parents by letting us pore over old family photographs with her. She once wrote about her own need to write: "I have no idea how people who don't write endure their lives."

Once in a long while, four times so far for me, my mother brings out the metal tube that holds her medical diploma. On the tube are gold circles crossed with seven red lines each — "joy" ideographs in abstract. There are also little flowers that look like gears for a gold machine. According to the scraps of labels with Chinese and American addresses, stamps, and postmarks, the family airmailed the can from Hong Kong in 1950. It got crushed in the middle, and whoever tried to peel the labels off stopped because the red and gold paint came off too, leaving silver scratches that rust. Somebody tried to pry the end off before discovering that the tube pulls apart. When I open it, the smell of China flies out, a thousand-year-old bat flying heavy-headed out of the Chinese caverns where bats are as white as dust, a smell that comes from long ago, far back in the brain. Crates from Canton, Hong Kong, Singapore, and Taiwan have that smell too, only stronger because they are more recently come from the Chinese.

Inside the can are three scrolls, one inside another. The largest says that in the twenty-third year of the National Republic, the To Keung School of Midwifery, where she has had two years of instruction and Hospital Practice, awards its Diploma to my mother, who has shown through oral and written examination her Proficiency in Midwifery, Pediatrics, Gynecology, "Medecine," "Surgary," Therapeutics, Ophthalmology, Bacteriology, Dermatology, Nursing, and Bandage. . . .

The school seal has been pressed over a photograph of my mother at the age of thirty-seven. The diploma gives her age as twenty-seven. She looks younger than I do, her eyebrows are thicker, her lips fuller. Her naturally curly hair is parted on the left, one wavy wisp tendrilling off to the right. She wears a scholar's white gown, and she is not thinking about her appearance. She stares straight ahead as if she could see me and past me to her grandchildren and grandchildren's grandchildren. She has spacy eyes, as all people recently from Asia have. Her eyes do not focus on the camera. My mother is

225

not smiling; Chinese do not smile for photographs. Their faces command relatives in foreign lands — "Send money" — and posterity forever — "Put food in front of this picture." My mother does not understand Chinese-American snapshots. "What are you laughing at?" she asks.

The second scroll is a long narrow photograph of the graduating class with the school officials seated in front. I picked out my mother immediately. Her face is exactly her own, though forty years younger. She is so familiar, I can only tell whether or not she is pretty or happy or smart by comparing her to the other women. For this formal group picture she straightened her hair with oil to make a chin-length bob like the others'. On the other women, strangers, I can recognize a curled lip, a sidelong glance, pinched shoulders. My mother is not soft; the girl with the small nose and dimpled underlip is soft. My mother is not humorous, not like the girl at the end who lifts her mocking chin to pose like Girl Graduate. My mother does not have smiling eyes; the old woman teacher (Dean Woo?) in front crinkles happily, and the one faculty member in the western suit smiles westernly. Most of the graduates are girls whose faces have not yet formed; my mother's face will not change anymore, except to age. She is intelligent, alert, pretty. I can't tell if she's happy.

The graduates seem to have been looking elsewhere when they pinned the rose, zinnia, or chrysanthemum on their precise black dresses. One thin girl wears hers in the middle of her chest. A few have a flower over a left or a right nipple. My mother put hers, a chrysanthemum, below her left breast. Chinese dresses at that time were dartless, cut as if women did not have breasts; these young doctors, unaccustomed to decorations, may have seen their chests as black expanses with no reference points for flowers. Perhaps they couldn't shorten that far gaze that lasts only a few years after a Chinese emigrates. In this picture too my mother's eyes are big with what they held — reaches of oceans beyond China, land beyond oceans. Most emigrants learn the barbarians' directness — how to gather themselves and stare rudely into talking faces as if trying to catch lies. In America my mother has eyes as strong as boulders, never once skittering off a face, but she has not learned to place decorations and phonograph needles, nor has she stopped seeing land on the other side of the oceans. Now her eyes include the relatives in China, as they once included my father smiling and smiling in his many western outfits, a different one for each photograph that he sent from America.

He and his friends took pictures of one another in bathing suits at Coney Island beach, the salt wind from the Atlantic blowing their hair. He's the one in the middle with his arms about the necks of his buddies. They pose in the cockpit of a biplane, on a motorcycle, and on a lawn beside the "Keep Off the Grass" sign. They are always laughing. My father, white shirt sleeves rolled up, smiles in front of a wall of clean laundry. In the spring he wears a new straw hat, cocked at a Fred Astaire angle. He steps out, dancing down the stairs, one foot forward, one back, a hand in his pocket. He wrote to her about the American custom of stomping on straw hats come fall. "If you want to save your hat for next year," he said, "you have to put it away early, or else when you're riding the subway or walking along Fifth Avenue, any stranger can snatch it off your head and put his foot through it. That's the way they celebrate the change of seasons here." In the winter he wears a gray felt hat with his gray overcoat. He is sitting on a rock in Central Park. In one snapshot he is not smiling; someone took it when he was studying, blurred in the glare of the desk lamp.

JOHN WATERS

from

SHOCK VALUE

Filmmaker **John Waters** understands that, although his parents never cared for his experimental and X-rated movies, they always cared for him. Waters lives in Baltimore, Maryland, where he was born in 1946.

The oddest question I ever get from college students is "Do you have parents?" The first time I heard this, I was shocked. Did they think somebody found me under a rock and dragged me home? What person in his right mind would clone me, I wonder. "Everyone has parents," I tell them. "Even Lee Harvey Oswald had a great mother." I guess by this question they are tactfully trying to ask, "What on earth could your parents think of you?" and this I can see, because whenever I read about some lunatic I admire, this question is the first thing that pops into my mind. I especially delight in imagining the reactions of punk rockers' parents to their children's startling look. I can see some kid running down the steps in the family home wearing a "Hang the Hostages" button, a blue crew cut, and a safety pin through his nose, and a stern-faced father coming out of the TV room to demand, "Just where do you think you're going in that getup, young man?"

Yes, I have parents and I love them very much. When I'm in Baltimore, I see them about once a week, and even though there certainly have been major disagreements over the years, I think we've managed to get along astonishingly well, considering all they've had to go through. I think their attitude about my career can best be summed up by my mother's comment after seeing a favorable editorial about me in the Baltimore *Sun* entitled "The Prince of Puke." "Well," she said, "being the 'Prince of Puke' is hardly what we had in mind for you when you were a child."

My parents are very straight, thank God. I've always felt extremely embarrassed for friends with parents who try to be hip. I'm proud that my mother and father have never smoked pot, gone to Plato's Retreat, or disco-danced. I can't think of anything more humiliating than being in a nightclub or at a crazy party and seeing your parents walk in, all decked out in trendy clothes, ready to go wild for the evening. I think it's healthy to see your parents often (sort of like a tuneup), but I think it's neurotic to actually hang around with them.

No matter how hard you rebel against your parents, you always end up being exactly like them. There can be millions of surface differences on how you live your life, but underneath it all, you will always share their basic beliefs. You could become a drug addict, a necrophiliac, or the President of the United States, but if your parents taught you that it was slothful not to make your bed, you'd end up making it faithfully every day or neurotically sleeping in a bunch of rags just to prove how wrong they really were. In turn, parents are indelibly influenced by their own children, no matter how weird they may become. The less financial aid parents are asked for, the more they will grow to accept whatever they think aberrant about their child's behavior. As the years pass, parents soften and begin to realize that the *Leave It to Beaver*-type family atmosphere they expected is just impossible to achieve. My parents are quite conservative, yet my father will clip me news articles about especially grisly murders when I'm out of town, and my mother spent many months needlepointing me an "X" to hang in my office — symbolizing a homey reproduction of my films' ratings. I, in turn, always dress conservatively when I visit my parents and astonish them by admitting I realize they were right all along.

It took many years, however, to achieve this fragile peace. I was born two months premature, so I guess I shocked them right from the beginning. From the first sign of my childhood obsessions, they realized I was not likely to turn out to be the all-American boy. I remember sitting at the top of the steps as a child, eavesdropping on my parents' conversation and hearing my mother confide to my father: "I don't know what to do. He's just an odd duck." Thrilled that they could see the future, I plotted how to further my "odd-duckism." My early rock 'n' roll mania was the first concrete thing that drove them crazy. For some reason my father was especially offended that I hung a picture of Annette Funicello over my bed. They both seemed mortified when I graduated from a good private grade school (the only school where I ever learned anything) and the "class jingles" were read. Most of the other kids had little verses about their athletic prowess, but mine started off with "Johnny Waters is the rock 'n' roll king/He likes to hear Elvis Presley sing."

All I wanted to do was jitterbug, but they enrolled me in a proper dancing class and expected me to attend predeb parties for all my girl classmates. After a few of those horrors, I sought out another circuit. As soon as I entered public school for the two years before beginning Catholic high school, I used to delight in asking the cheapest girls for dates, since I knew my parents would have to drive us, and they always seemed appalled at my taste. One girl, Sherry, really got to them. Sherry was about twelve, was missing teeth, and wore her hair in a huge ratted, one-sided bouffant wing. I invited her to my parents' home for dinner. My mother, who idolizes Queen Elizabeth, spent many hours preparing the family meal, and my father, as always, was dressed in suit and tie to meet the little lady he had heard so much about. When the front door swung open and a gum-chewing Sherry entered, looked my mother straight in the eye, and said, "Hi, hon," I thought both parents would collapse.

During the sixties I really got a chance to practice my shock-value tactics on my parents. Today my mother looks back on this period and still can't laugh about it: "We thought we'd come home and find that you had hung yourself in your bedroom," she remembers. No matter how hard I try, I can't convince her that I look back to those years with incredible fondness, since being rotten can be tremendously fulfilling.

My long hair practically made my father have a nervous breakdown. If I really wanted to see him gag, all I had to do was wear it in a ponytail. The family meal was usually traumatic. My father would eat silently, trying to avoid hair-eye contact. Out of the corner of his eye he'd catch a glimpse of my locks and you could see him start uncomfortably shifting in his chair. This would enrage me, so I'd bait him into a political discussion:

Me: I'm going to New Haven for a Black Panther rally. We're going to burn that town down.
Dad: They ought to take every one of you bums and lock you up for life.
Me: I am for the total destruction of this government. I want communism and we get our orders from Russia.
Dad: [Shaking] In Communist countries they'd cut off your hands if they caught you stealing!! That's what we ought to do here! Or just shoot rioters on sight!

Politics was an especially touchy subject around the house, since my mother's brother, John Whitaker, was undersecretary of the interior for Nixon. I loved the irony of the whole situation. Some of my relatives would show up for Agnew's inauguration dinner, and I'd be outside with the rioters throwing horseshit at the arriving dignitaries. During Watergate, my uncle was one of the few Nixon men who was never even accused of any wrongdoing. Unscathed by the scandal, he moved on to better things, but to this day remains loyal enough to attend Nixon administration reunions, and I'm secretly jealous. Think how fascinating these get-togethers must be — all the biggest villains of our time avoiding the press, sneaking behind closed doors to have a secret party. I can only hope they give a big toast to Rosemary Woods, surely the Secretary of the Century, because her loyalty really impresses me. No matter what these onetime fat cats pulled, it would *have* to be more interesting than spending the evening with Jerry Rubin or Ralph Nader.

My parents always pleaded with me never to lie to them, but I think they eventually regretted this demand and began to fear the truth: "Yes, I'm on LSD right this minute," I'd tell them, and they finally stopped asking. But no matter how much trouble I got into, they never threw me out of the house. Despite all the hassles, I knew I could count on them if *real* traumas arose and I think this kept me from taking the final plunge to the deep end.

EUDORA WELTY

from

ONE WRITER'S BEGINNINGS

Eudora Welty, born in 1909 in Jackson, Mississippi, is a well-known Southern writer of novels, short stories, and essays, including *The Optimist's Daughter*, which won a Pulitzer Prize in fiction. In a recent book, *One Writer's Beginnings*, in which she examines how she became a writer, Eudora Welty remembers an exchange of intimacies with her mother.

It was when my mother came out onto the sleeping porch to tell me goodnight that her trial came. The sudden silence in the double bed meant my younger brothers had both keeled over in sleep, and I in the single bed at my end of the porch would be lying electrified, waiting for this to be the night when she'd tell me what she'd promised for so long. Just as she bent to kiss me I grabbed her and asked: "Where do babies come from?"

My poor mother! But something saved her every time. Almost any night I put the baby question to her, suddenly, as if the whole outdoors exploded, Professor Holt would start to sing. The Holts lived next door; he taught penmanship (the Palmer Method), typing, bookkeeping and shorthand at the high school. His excitable voice traveled out of their dining room windows across the two driveways between our houses, and up to our upstairs sleeping porch. His wife, usually so quiet and gentle, was his uncannily spirited accompanist at the piano. "High-ho! Come to the Fair!" he'd sing, unless he sang "Oho ye oho ye, who's bound for the ferry, the briar's in bud and the sun's going down!"

"Dear, this isn't a very good time for you to hear Mother, is it?"

She couldn't get started. As soon as she'd whisper something, Professor Holt galloped into the chorus, "And 'tis but a penny to Twickenham town!" "Isn't that enough?" she'd ask me. She'd told me that the mother and the father had to both *want* the baby. This couldn't be enough. I knew she was not trying to fib to me, for she never did fib, but also I could not help but know she was not really *telling* me. And more than that, I was afraid of what I was going to hear next. This was partly because she wanted to tell me in the dark. I thought *she* might be afraid. In something like childish hopelessness I thought she probably *couldn't* tell, just as she *couldn't* lie.

On the night we came the closest to having it over with, she started to tell me without being asked, and I ruined it by yelling, "Mother, look at the lightning bugs!"

In those days, the dark was dark. And all the

dark out there was filled with the soft, near lights of lightning bugs. They were everywhere, flashing on the slow, horizontal move, on the upswings, rising and subsiding in the soundless dark. Lightning bugs signaled and answered back without a stop, from down below all the way to the top of our sycamore tree. My mother just gave me a businesslike kiss and went on back to Daddy in their room at the front of the house. Distracted by lightning bugs, I had missed my chance. The fact is she never did tell me.

I doubt that any child I knew ever was told by her mother any more than I was about babies. In fact, I doubt that her own mother ever told her any more than she told me, though there were five brothers who were born after Mother, one after the other, and she was taking care of babies all her childhood.

Not being able to bring herself to open that door to reveal its secret, one of those days, she opened another door.

In my mother's bottom bureau drawer in her bedroom she kept treasures of hers in boxes, and had given me permission to play with one of them — a switch of her now chestnut-colored hair, kept in a heavy bright braid that coiled around like a snake inside a cardboard box. I hung it from her doorknob and unplaited it; it fell in ripples nearly to the floor, and it satisfied the Rapunzel in me to comb it out. But one day I noticed in the same drawer a small white cardboard box such as her engraved calling cards came in from the printing house. It was tightly closed, but I opened it, to find to my puzzlement

237

and covetousness two polished buffalo nickels, embedded in white cotton. I rushed with this opened box to my mother and asked if I could run out and spend the nickels.

"No!" she exclaimed in a most passionate way. She seized the box into her own hands. I begged her; somehow I had started to cry. Then she sat down, drew me to her, and told me that I had had a little brother who had come before I did, and who had died as a baby before I was born. And these two nickels that I'd wanted to claim as my find were his. They had lain on his eyelids, for a purpose untold and unimaginable. "He was a fine little baby, my first baby, and he shouldn't have died. But he did. It was because your mother almost died at the same time," she told me. "In looking after me, they too nearly forgot about the little baby."

She'd told me the wrong secret — not how babies could come but how they could die, how they could be forgotten about.

I wondered in after years: how could my mother have kept those two coins? Yet how could someone like herself have disposed of them in any way at all? She suffered from a morbid streak which in all the life of the family reached out on occasions — the worse occasions — and touched us, clung around us, making it worse for her; her unbearable moments could find nowhere to go.

The future story writer in the child I was must have taken unconscious note and stored it away then: one secret is liable to be revealed in the place of another that is harder to tell, and the substitute secret when nakedly exposed is often the more appalling.

Perhaps telling me what she did was made easier for my mother by the two secrets, told and still not told, being connected in her deepest feeling, more intimately than anyone ever knew, perhaps even herself. So far as I remember now, this is the only time this baby was ever mentioned in my presence. So far as I can remember, and I've tried, he was never mentioned in the presence of my father, for whom he had been named. I am only certain that my father, who could never bear pain very well, would not have been able to bear it.

It was my father (my mother told me at some later date) who saved her own life, after that baby was born. She had in fact been given up by the doctor, as she had long been unable to take any nourishment. (That was the illness when they'd cut her hair, which formed the switch in the same bureau drawer.) What had struck her was septicemia, in those days nearly always fatal. What my father did was to try champagne.

I once wondered where he, who'd come not very long before from an Ohio farm, had ever heard of such a remedy, such a measure. Or perhaps as far as he was concerned he invented it, out of the strength of desperation. It would have been desperation augmented because champagne couldn't be bought in Jackson. But somehow he knew what to do about that too. He telephoned to Canton, forty miles north, to an Italian orchard grower, Mr. Trolio, told him the necessity, and asked, begged, that he put a bottle of his wine on Number 3, which was due in a few minutes to stop in Canton to "take on water" (my father knew everything about train schedules). My father would be waiting to meet the train in Jackson. Mr. Trolio did — he sent the bottle in a bucket of ice and my father snatched it off the baggage car. He offered my mother a glass of chilled champagne and she drank it and kept it down. She was to live, after all.

Now, her hair was long again, it would reach in a braid down her back, and now I was her child. She hadn't died. And when I came, I hadn't died either. Would she ever? Would I ever? I couldn't face *ever*. I must have rushed into her lap, demanding her like a baby. And she had to put her first-born aside again, for me.

HENRY ADAMS

from

THE AUTOBIOGRAPHY OF HENRY ADAMS

Almost all other writers of autobiographies use the first-person "I," but **Henry Adams** wrote his autobiography in the third person, as if objectively describing someone else.

The grandson of President John Quincy Adams and the great-grandson of President John Adams, Henry had a background of greatness to measure himself against. Even as a youngster, he felt this pressure and comments upon it here in the first chapter of his autobiography, in which he contrasts his two families, his mother's fashionable Boston family and his father's political Quincy family.

In this excerpt he describes a firm and important lesson given to him by his grandfather, the former president John Quincy Adams. (Also included in this anthology is a youthful piece of writing by his wife-to-be, Clover Hooper.)

Under the shadow of Boston State House, turning its back on the house of John Hancock, the little passage called Hancock Avenue runs, or ran, from Beacon Street, skirting the State House grounds, to Mount Vernon Street, on the summit of Beacon Hill; and there, in the third house below Mount Vernon Place, February 16, 1838, a child was born, and christened later by his uncle, the minister of the First Church after the tenets of Boston Unitarianism, as Henry Brooks Adams.

Had he been born in Jerusalem under the shadow of the Temple and circumcised in the Synagogue by his uncle the high priest, under the name of Israel Cohen, he would scarcely have been more distinctly branded, and not much more heavily handicapped in the races of the coming century, in running for such stakes as the century was to offer; but, on the other hand, the ordinary traveller, who does not enter the field of racing, finds advantages in being, so to speak, ticketed through life, with the safeguards of an old established traffic. Safeguards are often irksome, but sometimes convenient, and if one needs them at all, one is apt to need them badly. A hundred years earlier, such safeguards as his would have secured any young man's success; and although in 1838 their value was not very great compared with what they would have had in 1738, yet the mere accident of starting a twentieth-century career from a nest of associations so colonial — so troglo-

242

dytic★ — as the First Church, the Boston State House, Beacon Hill, John Hancock and John Adams, Mount Vernon Street and Quincy, all crowding on ten pounds of unconscious babyhood, was so queer as to offer a subject of curious speculation to the baby long after he had witnessed the solution. What could become of such a child of the seventeenth and eighteenth centuries, when he should wake up to find himself required to play the game of the twentieth? Had he been consulted, would he have cared to play the game at all, holding such cards as he held, and suspecting that the game was to be one of which neither he nor any one else back to the beginning of time knew the rules or the risks or the stakes? He was not consulted and was not responsible, but had he been taken into the confidence of his parents, he would certainly have told them to change nothing as far as concerned him. He would have been astounded by his own luck. Probably no child, born in the year, held better cards then he. Whether life was an honest game of chance, or whether the cards were marked and forced, he could not refuse to play his excellent hand. He could never make the usual plea of irresponsibility. He accepted the situation as though he had been a party to it, and under the same circumstances would do it again, the more readily for knowing the exact values. To his life as a whole he was a consenting, contracting party and partner from the moment he was born to the moment he died. Only with that under-

★Like a prehistoric cave dweller.

standing — as a consciously assenting member in full partnership with the society of his age — had his education an interest to himself or to others.

As it happened, he never got to the point of playing the game at all; he lost himself in the study of it, watching the errors of the players; but this is the only interest in the story, which otherwise has no moral and little incident. A story of education — seventy years of it — the practical value remains to the end in doubt, like other values about which men have disputed since the birth of Cain and Abel; but the practical value of the universe has never been stated in dollars. Although every one cannot be a Gargantua-Napoleon-Bismarck and walk off with the great bells of Notre Dame, every one must bear his own universe, and most persons are moderately interested in learning how their neighbors have managed to carry theirs.

This problem of education, started in 1838, went on for three years, while the baby grew, like other babies, unconsciously, as a vegetable, the outside world working as it never had worked before, to get his new universe ready for him. Often in old age he puzzled over the question whether, on the doctrine of chances, he was at liberty to accept himself or his world as an accident. No such accident had ever happened before in human experience. For him, alone, the old universe was thrown into the ash-heap and a new one created. He and his eighteenth-century, troglodytic Boston were suddenly cut apart — separated forever — in act if not in sentiment, by the opening of the Boston and Albany Railroad; the appearance of the first Cunard steamers in the bay; and the telegraphic messages which carried from Baltimore to Washington the news that Henry Clay and James K. Polk were nominated for the Presidency. This was in May, 1844; he was six years old; his new world was ready for use, and only fragments of the old met his eyes.

Of all this that was being done to complicate his education, he knew only the color of yellow. He first found himself sitting on a yellow kitchen floor in strong sunlight. He was three years old when he took this earliest step in education; a lesson of color. The second followed soon; a lesson of taste. On December 3, 1841, he developed scarlet fever. For several days he was as good as dead, reviving only under the careful nursing of his family. When he began to recover strength, about January 1, 1842, his hunger must have been stronger than any other pleasure or pain, for while in after life he retained not the faintest recollection of his illness, he remembered quite clearly his aunt entering the sick-room bearing in her hand a saucer with a baked apple.

The order of impressions retained by memory might naturally be that of color and taste, although one would rather suppose that the sense of pain would be first to educate. In fact, the third recollection of the child was that of discomfort. The moment he could be removed, he was bundled up in blankets and carried from the little house in Hancock Avenue to a larger one which his parents were to occupy for the rest of their lives in the neighboring Mount Vernon Street. The season was midwinter, January 10, 1842, and he never forgot his acute distress for want of air under his blankets, or the noises of moving furniture.

As a means of variation from a normal type, sickness in childhood ought to have a certain value not to be classed under any fitness or unfitness of natural selection; and especially scarlet fever affected boys seriously, both physically and in character, though they might through life puzzle themselves to decide whether it had fitted or unfitted them for success; but this fever of Henry Adams took greater and greater importance in his eyes, from the point of view of education, the longer he lived. At first, the effect was physical. He fell behind his brothers two or three inches in height, and proportionally in bone and weight. His character and processes of mind seemed to share in this fining-down process of scale. He was not good in a fight, and his nerves were more delicate than boys' nerves ought to be. He exaggerated these weaknesses as he grew older. The habit of doubt; of distrusting his own judgment and of totally rejecting the judgment of the world; the tendency to regard every question as open; the hesitation to act except as a choice of evils; the shirking of responsibility; the love of line, form, quality; the horror of ennui; the passion for companionship and the antipathy to society — all these are well-known qualities of New England character in no way peculiar to individuals but in this instance they seemed to be stimulated by the fever, and

Henry Adams could never make up his mind whether, on the whole, the change of character was morbid or healthy, good or bad for his purpose. His brothers were the type; he was the variation. . . .

Boys are wild animals, rich in the treasures of sense, but the New England boy had a wider range of emotions than boys of more equable climates. He felt his nature crudely, as it was meant. To the boy Henry Adams, summer was drunken. Among senses, smell was the strongest — smell of hot pine-woods and sweet-fern in the scorching summer noon; of new-mown hay; of ploughed earth; of box hedges; of peaches, lilacs, syringas; of stables, barns, cow-yards; of salt water and low tide on the marshes; nothing came amiss. Next to smell came taste, and the children knew the taste of everything they saw or touched, from pennyroyal and flagroot to the shell of a pignut and the letters of a spelling-book — the taste of A-B, AB, suddenly revived on the boy's tongue sixty years afterwards. Light, line, and color as sensual pleasures, came later and were as crude as the rest. The New England light is glare, and the atmosphere harshens color. The boy was a full man before he ever knew what was meant by atmosphere; his idea of pleasure in light was the blaze of a New England sun. His idea of color was a peony, with the dew of early morning on its petals. The intense blue of the sea, as he saw it a mile or two away, from the Quincy hills; the cumuli in a June afternoon sky; the strong reds and greens and purples of colored prints and children's picture-books, as the American colors then ran; these were ideals. The opposites or antipathies, were the cold grays of November evenings, and the thick, muddy thaws of Boston winter. With such standards, the Bostonian could not but develop a double nature. Life was a double thing. After a January blizzard, the boy who could look with pleasure into the violent snow-glare of the cold white sunshine, with its intense light and shade, scarcely knew what was meant by tone. He could reach it only be education.

Winter and summer, then, were two hostile lives, and bred two separate natures. Winter was always the effort to live; summer was tropical license. Whether the children rolled in the grass, or waded in the brook, or swam in the salt ocean, or sailed in the bay, or fished for smelts in the creeks, or netted minnows in the salt-marshes, or took to the pine-woods and the granite quarries, or chased muskrats and hunted snapping-turtles in the swamps, or mushrooms or nuts on the autumn hills, summer and country were always sensual living, while winter was always compulsory learning. Summer was the multiplicity of nature; winter was school.

The bearing of the two seasons on the education of Henry Adams was no fancy; it was the most decisive force he ever knew: it ran through life, and made the division between its perplexing, warring, irreconcilable problems, irreducible opposites, with growing emphasis to the last year of study. From earliest childhood the boy was accustomed to feel that, for him, life was double. Winter and summer, town and country, law and liberty, were hostile, and the man who pretended they were not, was in his eyes a schoolmaster — that is, a man employed to tell lies to little boys. Though Quincy was but two hours' walk from Beacon Hill, it belonged in a different world. For two hundred years, every Adams, from father to son, had lived within sight of State Street, and sometimes had lived in it, yet none had ever taken kindly to the town, or been taken kindly by it. The boy inherited his double nature. He knew as yet nothing about his great-grandfather, who had died a dozen years before his own birth: he took for granted that any great-grandfather of his must have always been good, and his enemies wicked; but he divined his great-grandfather's character from his own. Never for a moment did he connect the two ideas of Boston and John Adams; they were separate and antagonistic; the idea of John Adams went with Quincy. He knew his grandfather John Quincy Adams only as an old man of seventy-five or eighty who was friendly and gentle with him, but except that he heard his grandfather always called "the President," and his grandmother "the Madam," he had no reason to suppose that his Adams grandfather differed in character from his Brooks grandfather* who was equally kind and benevolent. He liked the Adams side best, but for no other reason than that it reminded him of the country, the summer, and the absence of restraint. Yet he felt also that Quincy was in a

---

*Adams's grandfather was one of the wealthiest citizens of Boston.

way inferior to Boston, and that socially Boston looked down on Quincy. The reason was clear enough even to a five-year old child. Quincy had no Boston style. Little enough style had either; a simpler manner of life and thought could hardly exist, short of cave-dwelling. The flint-and-steel with which his grandfather Adams used to light his own fires in the early morning was still on the mantelpiece of his study. The idea of a livery or even a dress for servants, or of an evening toilette, was next to blasphemy. Bathrooms, water-supplies, lighting, heating, and the whole array of domestic comforts, were unknown at Quincy. Boston had already a bathroom, a water-supply, a furnace, and gas. The superiority of Boston was evident, but a child liked it no better for that.

The magnificence of his grandfather Brooks's house in Pearl Street or South Street has long ago disappeared, but perhaps his country house at Medford may still remain to show what impressed the mind of a boy in 1845 with the idea of city splendor. The President's place at Quincy was the larger and older and far the more interesting of the two; but a boy felt at once its inferiority in fashion. It showed plainly enough its want of wealth. It smacked of colonial age, but not of Boston style or plush curtains. To the end of his life he never quite overcame the prejudice thus drawn in with his childish breath. He never could compel himself to care for nineteenth-century style. He was never able to adopt it, any more than his father or grandfather or great-grandfather had done. Not that he felt it as particularly hostile, for he reconciled himself to much that was worse; but because, for some remote reason, he was born an eighteenth-century child. The old house at Quincy was eighteenth century. What style it had was in its Queen Anne mahogany panels and its Louis Seize chairs and sofas. The panels belonged to an old colonial Vassall* who built the house; the furniture had been brought back from Paris in 1789 or 1801 or 1817, along with porcelain and books and much else of old diplomatic remnants; and neither of the two eighteenth-century styles — neither English Queen Anne nor French Louis Seize — was comfortable for a boy, or for any one else. The dark mahogany had been painted white to suit daily life in winter gloom. Nothing seemed to favor, for a child's objects, the older forms. On the contrary, most boys, as well as grown-up people, preferred the new, with good reason, and the child felt himself distinctly at a disadvantage for the taste.

Nor had personal preference any share in his bias. The Brooks grandfather was as amiable and as sympathetic as the Adams grandfather. Both were born in 1767, and both died in 1848. Both were kind to children, and both belonged rather to the eighteenth than to the nineteenth centuries. The child knew no difference between them except that one was associated with winter and the other with summer; one with Boston, the other with Quincy. Even with Medford, the

*Leonard Vassall, from whom John Adams bought the Quincy house in 1787.

251

association was hardly easier. Once as a very young boy he was taken to pass a few days with his grandfather Brooks under charge of his aunt, but became so violently homesick that within twenty-four hours he was brought back in disgrace. Yet he could not remember ever being seriously homesick again.

The attachment to Quincy was not altogether sentimental or wholly sympathetic. Quincy was not a bed of thornless roses. Even there the curse of Cain set its mark. There as elsewhere a cruel universe combined to crush a child. As though three or four vigorous brothers and sisters, with the best will, were not enough to crush any child, every one else conspired towards an education which he hated. From cradle to grave this problem of running order through chaos, direction through space, discipline through freedom, unity through multiplicity, has always been, and must always be, the task of education, as it is the moral of religion, philosophy, science, art, politics, and economy; but a boy's will is his life, and he dies when it is broken, as the colt dies in harness, taking a new nature in becoming tame. Rarely has the boy felt kindly towards his tamers. Between him and his master has always been war. Henry Adams never knew a boy of his generation to like a master, and the task of remaining on friendly terms with one's own family, in such a relation, was never easy.

All the more singular it seemed afterwards to him that his first serious contact with the President should have been a struggle of will, in which the old man almost necessarily defeated the boy, but instead of leaving, as usual in such defeats, a lifelong sting, left rather an impression of as fair treatment as could be expected from a natural enemy. The boy met seldom with such restraint. He could not have been much more than six years old at the time — seven at the utmost — and his mother had taken him to Quincy for a long stay with the President during the summer. What became of the rest of the family he quite forgot; but he distinctly remembered standing at the house door one summer morning in a passionate outburst of rebellion against going to school. Naturally his mother was the immediate victim of his rage; that is what mothers are for, and boys also; but in this case the boy had his mother at unfair disadvantage, for she was a guest, and had no means of enforcing obedience. Henry showed a certain tactical ability by refusing to start, and he met all efforts at compulsion by successful, though too vehement protest. He was in fair way to win, and was holding his own, with sufficient energy, at the bottom of the long staircase which led up to the door of the President's library, when the door opened, and the old man slowly came down. Putting on his hat, he took the boy's hand without a word, and walked with him, paralyzed by awe, up the road to the town. After the first moments of consternation at this interference in a domestic dispute, the boy reflected that an old gentleman close on eighty would never trouble himself to walk near a mile on a hot summer morning over a shadeless road to take a boy to school, and that it would be strange if a lad imbued with the passion of freedom could not find a corner to dodge around, somewhere before reaching the school door. Then and always, the boy insisted that this reasoning justified his apparent submission; but the old man did not stop, and the boy saw all his strategical points turned, one after another, until he found himself seated inside the school, and obviously the centre of curious if not malevolent criticism. Not till then did the President release his hand and depart.

The point was that this act, contrary to the inalienable rights of boys, and nullifying the social compact, ought to have made him dislike his grandfather for life. He could not recall that it had this effect even for a moment. With a certain maturity of mind, the child must have recognized that the President, though a tool of tyranny, had done his disreputable work with a certain intelligence. He had shown no temper, no irritation, no personal feeling, and had made no display of force. Above all, he had held his tongue. During their long walk he had said nothing; he had uttered no syllable of revolting cant about the duty of obedience and the wickedness of resistance to law; he had shown no concern in the matter; hardly even a consciousness of the boy's existence. Probably his mind at that moment was actually troubling itself little about his grandson's iniquities, and much about the iniquities of President Polk, but the boy could scarcely at that age feel the whole satisfaction of thinking that President Polk was to be the vicarious victim of his own sins, and he gave his grandfather credit for intelligent silence. For this forbearance he felt instinctive respect. He admitted force as a form of right; he admitted even temper, under protest; but the seeds of a moral education would at that moment have fallen on the stoniest soil in Quincy, which is, as every one knows, the stoniest glacial and tidal drift known in any Puritan land.

Neither party to this momentary disagreement can have felt rancor, for during these three or four summers the old President's relations with the boy were friendly and almost intimate. Whether his older brothers and sisters were still more favored he failed to remember, but he was himself admitted to a sort of familiarity which, when in his turn he had reached old age, rather shocked him, for it must have sometimes tried the President's patience. He hung about the library; handled the books; deranged the papers; ransacked the drawers; searched the old purses and pocket-books for foreign coins; drew the swordcane; snapped the travelling-pistols; upset everything in the corners, and penetrated the President's dressing-closet where a row of tumblers, inverted on the shelf, covered caterpillars which were supposed to become moths or butterflies, but never did. The Madam bore with fortitude the loss of the tumblers which her husband purloined for these hatcheries; but she made protest when he carried off her best cut-glass bowls to plant with acorns or peachstones that he might see the roots grow, but which, she said, he commonly forgot like the caterpillars.

At that time the President rode the hobby of tree-culture, and some fine old trees should still remain to witness it, unless they have been improved off the ground; but his was a restless mind, and although he took his hobbies seriously and would have been annoyed had his grandchild asked whether he was bored like an English duke, he probably cared more for the processes than for the results, so that his grandson was saddened by the sight and smell of peaches and pears, the best of their kind, which he brought up from the garden to rot on his shelves for seed. With the inherited virtues of his Puritan ancestors, the little boy Henry conscientiously brought up to him in his study the finest peaches he found in the garden, and ate only the less perfect. Naturally he ate more by way of compensation, but the act showed that he bore no grudge. As for his grandfather, it is even possible that he may have felt a certain self-reproach for his temporary role of schoolmaster — seeing that his own career did not offer proof of the wordly advantages of docile obedience — for there still exists somewhere a little volume of critically edited Nursery Rhymes with the boy's name in full written in the President's trembling hand on the fly-leaf. Of course there was also the Bible, given to each child at birth, with the proper inscription in the President's hand on the fly-leaf; while their grandfather Brooks supplied the silver mugs.

So many Bibles and silver mugs had to be supplied, that a new house, or cottage, was built to hold them. It was "on the hill," five minutes' walk above "the old house," with a far view eastward over Quincy Bay, and northward over

Boston. Till his twelfth year, the child passed his summers there, and his pleasures of childhood mostly centered in it. Of education he had as yet little to complain. Country schools were not very serious. Nothing stuck to the mind except home impressions, and the sharpest were those of kindred children; but as influences that warped a mind, none compared with the mere effect of the back of the President's bald head, as he sat in his pew on Sundays, in line with that of President Quincy,* who, though some ten years younger, seemed to children about the same age. Before railways entered the New England town, every parish church showed half-a-dozen of these leading citizens, with gray hair, who sat on the main aisle in the best pews, and had sat there, or in some equivalent dignity, since the time of St. Augustine, if not since the glacial epoch. It was unusual for boys to sit behind a President grandfather, and to read over his head the tablet in memory of a President great-grandfather, who had "pledged his life, his fortune, and his sacred honor" to secure the independence of his country and so forth; but boys naturally supposed, without much reasoning, that other boys had the equivalent of President grandfathers, and that churches would always go on, with the bald-headed leading citizens on the main aisle, and Presidents or their equivalents on the walls. The Irish gardener once said to the child: "You'll be thinkin' you'll be President too!" The casualty of the remark made so strong an impression on his mind that he

*President of Harvard College, Josiah Quincy.

never forgot it. He could not remember ever to have thought on the subject; to him, that there should be a doubt of his being President was a new idea. What had been would continue to be. He doubted neither about Presidents nor about Churches, and no one suggested at that time a doubt whether a system of society which had lasted since Adam would outlast one Adams more.

The Madam was a little more remote than the President, but more decorative. She stayed much in her own room with the Dutch tiles, looking out on her garden with the box walks, and seemed a fragile creature to a boy who sometimes brought her a note or a message, and took distinct pleasure in looking at her delicate face under what seemed to him very becoming caps. He liked her refined figure; her gentle voice and manner; her vague effect of not belonging there, but to Washington or to Europe, like her furniture, and writing-desk with little glass doors above and little eighteenth-century volumes in old binding, labelled "Peregrine Pickle" or "Tom Jones" or "Hannah More." Try as she might, the Madam could never be Bostonian, and it was her cross in life, but to the boy it was her charm. Even at that age, he felt drawn to it. The Madam's life had been in truth far from Boston. She was born in London in 1775, daughter of Joshua Johnson, an American merchant, brother of Governor Thomas Johnson of Maryland; and Catherine Nuth, of an English family in London. Driven from England by the Revolutionary War, Joshua Johnson took his family to Nantes, where they remained till the peace. The girl Louisa Catherine was nearly ten years old when brought back to London, and her sense of nationality must have been confused; but the influence of the Johnsons and the services of Joshua obtained for him from President Washington the appointment of Consul in London on the organization of the Government in 1790. In 1794 President Washington appointed John Quincy Adams Minister to The Hague. He was twenty-seven years old when he returned to London, and found the Consul's house a very agreeable haunt. Louisa was then twenty.

At that time, and long afterwards, the Consul's house, far more than the Minister's, was the centre of contact for travelling Americans, either official or other. The Legation was a shifting point, between 1785 and 1815; but the Consulate, far down in the City, near the Tower, was convenient and inviting; so inviting that it proved fatal to young Adams. Louisa was charming, like a Romney portrait, but among her many charms that of being a New England woman was not one. The defect was serious. Her future mother-in-law, Abigail, a famous New England woman whose authority over her turbulent husband, the second President, was hardly so great as that which she exercised over her son, the sixth to be, was troubled by the fear that Louisa might not be made of stuff stern enough, or brought up in conditions severe enough, to suit a New England climate, or to make an efficient wife for her paragon son, and Abigail was right on that point, as on most others where sound judgment was involved; but sound judgment is sometimes a source of weakness rather than of force, and John Quincy already had reason to think that his mother held sound judgments on the subject of daughters-in-law which human nature, since the fall of Eve, made Adams helpless to realize. Being three thousand miles away from his mother, and equally far in love, he married Louisa in London, July 26, 1797, and took her to Berlin to be the head of the United States Legation. During three or four exciting years, the young bride lived in Berlin; whether she was happy or not, whether she was content or not, whether she was socially successful or not, her descendants did not surely know; but in any case she could by no chance have become educated there for a life in Quincy or Boston. In 1801 the overthrow of the Federalist Party drove her and her husband to America, and she became at last a member of the Quincy household, but by that time her children needed all her attention, and she remained there with occasional winters in Boston and Washington, till 1809. Her husband was made Senator in 1803, and in 1809 was appointed Minister to Russia. She went with him to St. Petersburg, taking her baby, Charles Francis, born in 1807; but broken-hearted at having to leave her two older boys behind. The life at St. Petersburg was hardly gay for her; they were far too poor to shine in that extravagant society; but she survived it, though her little girl baby did not, and in the winter of 1814–15, alone with the boy of seven years old, crossed Europe from St. Petersburg to Paris, in her travelling-carriage, passing through the armies, and reaching Paris in the *Cent Jours* after Napoleon's return from Elba. Her husband next went to England as Minister, and she was for two years at the Court of the Regent. In 1817 her husband came home to be Secretary of State, and she lived for eight years in F Street, doing her work of entertainer for President Monroe's administration. Next she lived four miserable years in the White House. When that chapter was closed in 1829, she had earned the right to be tired and delicate, but she still had fifteen years to serve as wife of a Member of the House, after her husband went back to Congress in 1833. Then it was that her little Henry, her grandson, first remembered her, from 1845 to 1848, sitting in her panelled room, at breakfast, with her heavy silver teapot and sugar-bowl and cream-jug, which still exist somewhere as an heirloom of the modern safety-vault. By that time she was seventy years old or more, and thoroughly weary of being beaten about a stormy world. To the boy she seemed singularly peaceful, a vision of silver gray, presiding over her old President and her Queen Anne mahogany; an exotic, like her Sèvres china; an object of deference to every one, and of great affection to her son Charles; but hardly more Bostonian than she had been fifty years before, on her wedding-day, in the shadow of the Tower of London.

Such a figure was even less fitted than that of her old husband, the President, to impress on a boy's mind, the standards of the coming century. She was Louis Seize, like the furniture. The boy knew nothing of her interior life, which had been, as the venerable Abigail, long since at peace, foresaw, one of severe stress and little pure satisfaction. He never dreamed that from her might come some of those doubts and self-questionings, those hesitations, those rebellions against law and discipline, which marked more than one of her descendants; but he might even then have felt some vague instinctive suspicion that he was to inherit from her the seeds of the primal sin, the fall from grace, the curse of Abel, that he was not of pure New England stock, but half exotic. As a child of Quincy he was not a true Bostonian, but even as a child of Quincy he inherited a quarter taint of Maryland blood. Charles Francis, half Marylander by birth, had hardly seen Boston till he was ten years old, when his parents left him there at school in 1817, and he never forgot the experience. He was to be nearly as old as his mother had been in 1845, before he quite accepted Boston, or Boston quite accepted him.

A boy who began his education in these surroundings, with physical strength inferior to that of his brothers, and with a certain delicacy of mind and bone, ought rightly to have felt at home in the eighteenth century and should, in proper self-respect, have rebelled against the standards of the nineteenth. The atmosphere of his first ten years must have been very like that of his grandfather at the same age, from 1767 till 1776, barring the battle of Bunker Hill, and even as late as 1846, the battle of Bunker Hill remained actual. The tone of Boston society was colonial. The true Bostonian always knelt in self-abasement before the majesty of English standards; far from concealing it as a weakness, he was proud of it as his strength. The eighteenth century ruled society long after 1850. Perhaps the boy began to shake it off rather earlier than most of his mates.

Indeed this prehistoric stage of education ended rather abruptly with his tenth year. One winter morning he was conscious of a certain confusion in the house in Mount Vernon Street, and gathered, from such words as he could catch, that the President, who happened to be then staying there, on his way to Washington, had fallen and hurt himself. Then he heard the word paralysis. After that day he came to associate the word with the figure of his grandfather, in a tall-backed, invalid armchair, on one side of the spare bedroom fireplace, and one of his old friends, Dr. Parkman or P.P.F. Degrand, on the other side, both dozing.

The end of this first, or ancestral and Revolutionary, chapter came on February 21, 1848 — and the month of February brought life and death as a family habit — when the eighteenth century, as an actual and living companion, vanished. If the scene on the floor of the House, when the old President fell, struck the still simple-minded American public with a sensation unusually dramatic, its effect on a ten-year-old boy, whose boy-life was fading away with the life of his grandfather, could not be slight. One had to pay for Revolutionary patriots; grandfathers and grandmothers; Presidents; diplomats; Queen Anne mahogany and Louis Seize chairs, as well as for Stuart portraits. Such things warp young life. Americans commonly believed that they ruined it, and perhaps the common-sense of the American mind judged right. Many a boy might be ruined by much less than the emotions of the funeral service in the Quincy church, with its surroundings of national respect and family pride. By another dramatic chance it happened that the clergyman of the parish, Dr. Lunt, was an unusual pulpit orator, the ideal of a somewhat austere intellectual type, such as the school of Buckminster and Channing inherited from the old Congregational clergy. His extraordinarily refined appearance, his dignity of manner, his deeply cadenced voice, his remarkable English and his fine appreciation, gave to the funeral service a character that left an overwhelming impression on the boy's mind. He was to see many great functions — funerals and festivals — in after-life, till his only thought was to see no more, but he never again witnessed anything nearly so impressive to him as the last services at Quincy over the body of one President and the ashes of another.

The effect of the Quincy service was deepened by the official ceremony which afterwards took place in Faneuil Hall, when the boy was taken to hear his uncle, Edward Everett, deliver a Eulogy. Like all Mr. Everett's orations, it was an admirable piece of oratory, such as only an admirable orator and scholar could create; too good for a ten-year-old boy to appreciate at its value; but already the boy knew that the dead President could not be in it, and had even learned why he would have been out of place there; for knowledge was beginning to come fast. The shadow of the War of 1812 still hung over State Street; the shadow of the Civil War to come had already begun to darken Faneuil Hall. No rhetoric could have reconciled Mr. Everett's audience to his subject. How could he say there, to an assemblage of Bostonians in the heart of mercantile Boston, that the only distinctive mark of all the Adamses, since old Sam Adams's father a hundred and fifty years before, had been their inherited quarrel with State Street, which had again and again broken out into riot, bloodshed, personal feuds, foreign and civil war, wholesale banishments and confiscations, until the history of Florence was hardly more turbulent than that of Boston? How could he whisper the word Hartford Convention before the men who had made it? What would have been said had he suggested the chance of Secession and Civil War?

Thus already, at ten years old, the boy found himself standing face to face with a dilemma that might have puzzled an early Christian. What was he? — where was he going? Even then he felt that something was wrong, but he concluded that it must be Boston. Quincy had always been right, for Quincy represented a moral principle — the principle of resistance to Boston. His Adams ancestors must have been right, since they were always hostile to State Street. If State Street was wrong, Quincy must be right! Turn the dilemma as he pleased, he still came back on the eighteenth century and the law of Resistance; of Truth; of Duty, and of Freedom. He was a ten-year-old

265

priest and politician. He could under no circumstances have guessed what the next fifty years had in store, and no one could teach him; but sometimes, in his old age, he wondered — and could never decide — whether the most clear and certain knowledge would have helped him. Supposing he had seen a New York stock-list of 1900, and had studied the statistics of railways, telegraphs, coal, and steel — would he have quitted his eighteenth-century, his ancestral prejudices, his abstract ideals, his semi-clerical training, and the rest, in order to perform an expiatory pilgrimage to State Street, and ask for the fatted calf of his grandfather Brooks and a clerkship in the Suffolk Bank?

Sixty years afterwards he was still unable to make up his mind. Each course had its advantages, but the material advantages, looking back, seemed to lie wholly in State Street.

HIGH SPIRITS

Taking on the World

WILLIAM A. NOLEN

from

THE MAKING OF A SURGEON

William Nolen, writer and surgeon, was born in 1928 and practices surgery in Minnesota. In this description of his first solo surgical procedure, almost everything goes wrong that possibly can, but patient and doctor manage to pull through.

Nolen was eventually able to look back on his first appendectomy and see the humor of it, but at the time of the operation, he was terrified and humiliated. And when the operating nurse laughed when the assistant surgeon said "Nice job" after the surgery, Nolen reached a low point in his self-esteem. He admits that if the patient had died, he probably would have given up surgery forever.

———————

The patient, or better, victim, of my first major surgical venture was a man I'll call Mr. Polansky. He was fat, he weighed one hundred and ninety pounds and was five feet eight inches tall. He spoke only broken English. He had had a sore abdomen with all the classical signs and symptoms of appendicitis for twenty-four hours before he came to Bellevue.

After two months of my internship, though I had yet to do anything that could be decently called an "operation," I had had what I thought was a fair amount of operating time. I'd watched the assistant residents work, I'd tied knots, cut sutures and even, in order to remove a skin lesion, made an occasional incision. Frankly, I didn't think that surgery was going to be too damn difficult. I figured I was ready, and I was chomping at the bit to go, so when Mr. Polansky arrived I greeted him like a long-lost friend. He was overwhelmed at the interest I showed in his case. He probably couldn't understand why any doctor should be so fascinated by a case of appendicitis: wasn't it a common disease? It was just as well that he didn't realize my interest in him was so personal. He might have been frightened, and with good reason.

At any rate, I set some sort of record in preparing Mr. Polansky for surgery. He had arrived on the ward at four o'clock. By six I had examined him, checked his blood and urine, taken his chest x-ray and had him ready for the operating room.

George Walters, the senior resident on call that night, was to "assist" me during the operation. George was older than the rest of us. I was twenty-five at this time and he was thirty-two. He had taken his surgical training in Europe and was spending one year as a senior resident in an American hospital to establish eligibility for the American College of Surgeons. He had had more experience than the other residents and it took a lot to disturb his equanimity in the operating room. As it turned out, this made him the ideal assistant for me.

It was ten o'clock when we wheeled Mr. Polansky to the operating room. At Bellevue, at night, only two operating rooms were kept open — there were six or more going all day — so we had to wait our turn. In the time I had to myself before the operation I had reread the section on appendectomy in the *Atlas of Operative Technique* in our surgical library, and had spent half an hour tying knots on the bedpost in my room. I was, I felt, "ready."

I delivered Mr. Polansky to the operating room and started an intravenous going in his arm. Then I left him to the care of the anesthetist. I had ordered a sedative prior to surgery, so Mr. Polansky was drowsy. The anesthetist, after checking his chart, soon had him sleeping.

Once he was asleep I scrubbed the enormous expanse of Mr. Polansky's abdomen for ten minutes. Then, while George placed the sterile drapes, I scrubbed my own hands for another five, mentally reviewing each step of the operation as I did so. Donning gown and gloves I took my place on the right side of the operating-room table. The nurse handed me the scalpel. I was ready to begin.

Suddenly my entire attitude changed. A split second earlier I had been supremely confident; now, with the knife finally in my hand, I stared down at Mr. Polansky's abdomen and for the life of me could not decide where to make the incision. The "landmarks" had disappeared. There was too much belly.

George waited a few seconds, then looked up at me and said, "Go ahead."

"What?" I asked.

"Make the incision," said George.

"Where?" I asked.

"Where?"

"Yes," I answered, "where?"

"Why, here, of course," said George and drew an imaginary line on the abdomen with his fingers.

I took the scalpel and followed where he had directed. I barely scratched Mr. Polansky.

"Press a little harder," George directed. I did. The blade went through the skin to a depth of perhaps one sixteenth of an inch.

"Deeper," said George.

There are five layers of tissue in the abdominal wall: skin, fat, fascia (a tough membranous tissue), muscle and peritoneum (the smooth, glistening, transparent inner lining of the abdomen). I cut down into the fat. Another sixteenth of an inch.

"Bill," said George, looking up at me, "this patient is big. There's at least three inches of fat to get through before we even reach the fascia. At the rate you're going we won't be into the abdomen for another four hours. For God's sake, will you cut?"

I made up my mind not to be hesitant. I pressed down hard on the knife, and suddenly we were not only through the fat but through the fascia as well.

272

"Not that hard," George shouted, grabbing my right wrist with his left hand while with his other hand he plunged a gauze pack into the wound to stop the bleeding. "Start clamping," he told me.

The nurse handed us hemostats and we applied them to the numerous vessels I had so hastily opened. "All right," George said, "start tying."

I took the ligature material from the nurse and began to tie off the vessels. Or rather, I tried to tie off the vessels, because suddenly my knot-tying proficiency had melted away. The casual dexterity I had displayed on the bedpost a short hour ago was nowhere in evidence. My fingers, greasy with fat, simply would not perform. My ties slipped off the vessels, the sutures snapped in my fingers, at one point I even managed to tie the end of my rubber glove into the wound. It was, to put it bluntly, a performance in fumbling that would have made Robert Benchley blush.

Here I must give my first paean of praise to George. His patience during the entire performance was nothing short of miraculous. The temptation to pick up the catgut and do the tying himself must have been strong. He could have tied off all the vessels in two minutes. It took me twenty.

Finally we were ready to proceed. "Now," George directed, "split the muscle. But gently, please."

I reverted to my earlier tack. Fiber by fiber I spread the muscle which was the last layer but one that kept us from the inside of the abdomen.

Each time I separated the fibers and withdrew my clamp, the fibers rolled together again. After five minutes I was no nearer the appendix than I had been at the start.

George could stand it no longer. But he was apparently afraid to suggest I take a more aggressive approach, fearing I would stick the clamp into, or possibly through, the entire abdomen. Instead he suggested that he help me by spreading the muscle in one direction while I spread it in the other. I made my usual infinitesimal attack on the muscle. In one fell swoop George spread the rest.

"Very well done," he complimented me. "Now let's get in."

We each took a clamp and picked up the tissue-paper-thin peritoneum. After two or three hesitant attacks with the scalpel I finally opened it. We were in the abdomen.

"Now," said George, "put your fingers in, feel the cecum (the portion of the bowel to which the appendix is attached) and bring it into the wound."

I stuck my right hand into the abdomen. I felt around — but what was I feeling? I had no idea.

It had always looked so simple when the senior resident did it. Open the abdomen, reach inside, pull up the appendix. Nothing to it. But apparently there was.

Everything felt the same to me. The small intestine, the large intestine, the cecum — how did one tell them apart without seeing them? I grabbed something and pulled it into the wound. Small intestine. No good. Put it back. I grabbed again. This time it was the sigmoid colon. Put it back. On my third try I had the small intestine again.

"The appendix must be in an abnormal position," I said to George. "I can't seem to find it."

"Mind if I try?" he asked.

"Not at all," I answered. "I wish you would."

Two of his fingers disappeared into the wound. Five seconds later they emerged, cecum between them, with the appendix flopping from it.

"Stuck down a little," he said kindly. "That's probably why you didn't feel it. It's a hot one," he added. "Let's get at it."

The nurse handed me the hemostats, and one by one I applied them to the mesentery of the appendix — the veil of tissue in which the blood vessels run. With George holding the veil between his fingers I had no trouble; I took the ligatures and tied the vessels without a single error. My confidence was coming back.

"Now," George directed, "put in your purse string." (The cecum is a portion of the bowel which has the shape of half a hemisphere. The appendix projects from its surface like a finger. In an appendectomy the routine procedure is to tie the appendix at its base and cut it off a little beyond the tie. Then the remaining stump is inverted into the cecum and kept there by tying the purse-string stitch. This was the stitch I was now going to sew.)

It went horribly. The wall of the cecum is not very thick — perhaps one eighth of an inch. The suture must be placed deeply enough in the wall so that it won't cut through when tied, but not so deep as to pass all the way through the wall. My sutures were alternately too superficial or too deep, but eventually I got the job done.

"All right," said George, "let's get the appendix out of here. Tie off the base."

I did.

"Now cut off the appendix."

At least in this, the definitive act of the operation, I would be decisive. I took the knife and with one quick slash cut through the appendix — too close to the ligature.

"Oh oh, watch it," said George. "That tie is going to slip."

It did. The appendiceal stump lay there, open. I felt faint.

"Don't panic," said George. "We've still got the purse string. I'll push the stump in — you pull up the stitch and tie. That will take care of it."

I picked up the two ends of the suture and put in the first stitch. George shoved the open stump into the cecum. It disappeared as I snugged my tie. Beautiful.

"Two more knots," said George. "Just to be safe."

I tied the first knot and breathed a sigh of relief. The appendiceal stump remained out of sight. On the third knot — for the sake of security — I pulled a little tighter. The stitch broke; the open stump popped up; the cecum disappeared into the abdomen. I broke out in a cold sweat and my knees started to crumble.

Even George momentarily lost his composure.

"For Chirst's sake, Bill," he said, grasping desperately for the bowel, "what did you have to do that for?" The low point of the operation had been reached.

By the time we had retrieved the cecum, Mr. Polansky's peritoneal cavity had been contaminated. My self-confidence was shattered. And still George let me continue. True, he all but held my hand as we retied and resutured, but the instruments were in my hand.

The closure was anticlimactic. Once I had the peritoneum sutured, things went reasonably smoothly. Two hours after we began, the operation was over. "Nice job," George said, doing his best to sound sincere.

"Thanks," I answered, lamely.

The scrub nurse laughed.

Mr. Polansky recovered, I am happy to report, though not without a long and complicated convalescence. His bowel refused to function normally for two weeks and he became enormously distended. He was referred to at our nightly conferences as "Dr. Nolen's pregnant man." Each time the reference was made, it elicited a shudder from me.

During his convalescence I spent every spare moment I could at Mr. Polansky's bedside. My feelings of guilt and responsibility were overwhelming. If he had died I think I would have given up surgery for good.

RICHARD P. FEYNMAN

from

SURELY YOU'RE JOKING, MR. FEYNMAN!

These excerpts from Nobel-Prize winner and physicist **Richard Feynman's** recent book of recollections suggest an exuberant and idiosyncratic personality — someone willing to take risks in his daily encounters. Born in 1918, Dr. Feynman is a professor of physics at the California Institute of Technology at Pasadena and served on the government commission to investigate the Challenger disaster.

In the first piece, Feynman describes the hazards of taking on an army psychiatrist (he finds himself almost rejected from the army as a questionable mental case). In the second piece, he tells of his special facility for languages — his imitation Italian that almost passes for the real thing.

———

After the war the army was scraping the bottom of the barrel to get the guys for the occupation forces in Germany. Up until then the army deferred people for some reason *other* than physical first (I was deferred because I was working on the bomb), but now they reversed that and gave everybody a physical first.

That summer I was working for Hans Bethe at General Electric in Schenectady, New York, and I remember that I had to go some distance — I think it was to Albany — to take the physical.

I get to the draft place, and I'm handed a lot of forms to fill out, and then I start going around to all these different booths. They check your vision at one, your hearing at another, they take your blood sample at another, and so forth.

Anyway, finally you come to booth number thirteen: psychiatrist. There you wait, sitting on one of the benches, and while I'm waiting I can see what is happening. There are three desks, with a psychiatrist behind each one, and the "culprit" sits across from the psychiatrist in his BVDs and answers various questions.

At that time there were a lot of movies about psychiatrists. For example, there was *Spellbound*, in which a woman who used to be a great piano player has her hands stuck in some awkward position and she can't move them, and her family calls in a psychiatrist to try to help her, and the psychiatrist goes upstairs into a room with her, and you see the door close behind them, and downstairs the family is discussing what's going to happen, and then she comes out of the room, hands still stuck in the horrible position, walks dramatically down the stairs over to the piano and sits down, lifts her hands over the keyboard, and suddenly — *dum diddle dum diddle dum, dum, dum* — she can play again. Well, I can't stand this kind of baloney, and I had decided that psychiatrists are fakers, and I'll have nothing to do with them. So that was the mood I was in when it was my turn to talk to the psychiatrist.

I sit down at the desk, and the psychiatrist starts looking through my papers. "Hello, Dick!" he says in a cheerful voice. "Where do you work?"

I'm thinking, "Who does he think he is, calling me by my first name?" and I say coldly, "Schenectady."

"Who do you work for, Dick?" says the psychiatrist, smiling again.

"General Electric."

"Do you like your work, Dick?" he says, with that same big smile on his face.

"So-so." I just wasn't going to have anything to do with him.

Three nice questions, and then the fourth one is completely different. "Do you think people talk about you?" he asks, in a low, serious tone.

I light up and say, "Sure! When I go home, my mother often tells me how she was telling her friends about me." He isn't listening to the explanation; instead, he's writing something down on my paper.

Then again, in a low, serious tone, he says, "Do you think people *stare* at you?"

I'm all ready to say no, when he says, "For instance, do you think any of the boys waiting on the benches are staring at you now?"

While I had been waiting to talk to the

psychiatrist, I had noticed there were about twelve guys on the benches waiting for the three psychiatrists, and they've got nothing else to look at, so I divide twelve by three — that makes four each — but I'm conservative, so I say, "Yeah, maybe two of them are looking at us."

He says, "Well just turn around and look" — and *he's* not even bothering to look himself!

So I turn around, and sure enough, two guys are looking. So I point to them and I say, "Yeah — there's *that* guy, and that guy over *there* looking at us." Of course, when I'm turned around and pointing like that, other guys start to look at us, so I say, "Now him, and those two over there — and now the whole bunch." He still doesn't look up to check. He's busy writing more things on my paper.

Then he says, "Do you ever hear voices in your head?"

"Very rarely," and I'm about to describe the two occasions on which it happened when he says, "Do you talk to yourself?"

"Yeah, sometimes when I'm shaving, or thinking: once in a while." He's writing down more stuff.

"I see you have a deceased wife — do you talk to *her?*"

This question really annoyed me, but I contained myself and said, "Sometimes, when I go up on a mountain and I'm thinking about her."

More writing. Then he asks, "Is anyone in your family in a mental institution?"

"Yeah, I have an aunt in an insane asylum."

"Why do you call it an insane asylum?" he says, resentfully. "Why don't you call it a mental institution?"

"I thought it was the same thing."

"Just what do you think insanity is?" he says, angrily.

"It's a strange and peculiar disease in human beings," I say honestly.

"There's nothing any more strange or peculiar about it than appendicitis!" he retorts.

"I don't think so. In appendicitis we understand the causes better, and something about the mechanism of it, whereas with insanity it's much more complicated and mysterious." I won't go through the whole debate; the point is that I meant insanity is *physiologically* peculiar, and he thought I meant it was *socially* peculiar.

Up until this time, although I had been unfriendly to the psychiatrist, I had nevertheless been honest in everything I said. But when he asked me to put out my hands, I couldn't resist pulling a trick a guy in the "bloodsucking line" had told me about. I figured nobody was ever going to get a chance to do this, and as long as I was halfway under water, I would do it. So I put out my hands when one palm up and the other one down.

The psychiatrist doesn't notice. He says, "Turn them over."

I turn them over. The one that was up goes down, and the one that was down goes up, and he *still* doesn't notice, because he's always looking very closely at one hand to see if it is shaking. So the trick had no effect.

Finally, at the end of all these questions, he becomes friendly again. He lights up and says, "I see you have a Ph.D., Dick. Where did you study?"

"MIT and Princeton. And where did *you* study!"

"Yale and London. And what did you study, Dick?"

"Physics. And what did *you* study?"

"Medicine."

"And *this* is *medicine?*"

"Well, yes. What do you *think* it is? You go and sit down over there and wait a few minutes!"

So I sit on the bench again, and one of the other guys waiting sidles up to me and says, "Gee! You were in there twenty-five minutes! The other guys were in there only five minutes!"

"Yeah."

"Hey," he says. "You wanna know how to fool the psychiatrist? All you have to do is pick your nails, like this."

"Then why don't *you* pick *your* nails like that?"

"Oh," he says, "I wanna get in the army!"

"You wanna fool the psychiatrist?" I say. "You just tell him that!"

After a while I was called over to a different desk to see another psychiatrist. While the first psychiatrist had been rather young and innocent-looking, this one was gray-haired and distinguished-looking — obviously the superior psychiarist. I figure all of this is now going to get straightened out, but no matter what happens, I'm not going to become friendly.

The new psychiatrist looks at my papers, and

283

puts a big smile on his face, and says, "Hello, Dick. I see you worked at Los Alamos during the war."

"Yeah."

"There used to be a boys' school there, didn't there?"

"That's right."

"Were there a lot of buildings in the school?"

"Only a few."

Three questions — same technique–and the next question is completely different. "You said you hear voices in your head. Describe that, please."

"It happens very rarely, when I've been paying attention to a person with a foreign accent. As I'm falling asleep I can hear his voice very clearly. The first time it happened was while I was a student at MIT, I could hear old professor Vallarta say, 'Dee-a-dee-a electric field-a.' And the other time I was in Chicago during the war, when Professor Teller was explaining to me how the bomb worked. Since I'm interested in all kinds of phenomena, I wondered how I could hear these voices with accents so precisely, when I couldn't imitate them that well . . . Doesn't everybody have something like that happen once in a while?"

The psychiatrist put his hand over his face, and I could see through his fingers a little smile (he wouldn't answer the question).

Then the psychiatrist checked into something else. "You said that you talk to your deceased wife. What do you say to her?"

I got angry. I figured it's none of his damned

business, and I say, "I tell her I love her, if it's all right with you!"

After some more bitter exchanges he says, "Do you believe in the supernormal?"

I say, "I don't know what the 'supernormal' is."

"What? You, a Ph.D. in physics, don't know what the supernormal is?"

"That's right."

"It's what Sir Oliver Lodge and his school believe in."

That's not much of a clue, but I knew it. "You mean the *supernatural*."

"You can call it that if you want."

"All right, I will."

"Do you believe in mental telepathy?"

"No. Do you?"

"Well, I'm keeping an open mind."

"What? You, a psychiatrist, keeping an *open mind?* Ha!" It went on like this for quite a while.

Then at some point near the end he says, "How much do you value life?"

"Sixty-four."

"Why did you say 'sixty-four'?"

"How are you *supposed* to measure the value of life?"

"No! I mean, why did you say 'sixty-four,' and not 'seventy-three,' for instance?"

"If I had said 'seventy-three,' you would have asked me the same question!"

The psychiatrist finished with three friendly questions, just as the other psychiatrist had done, handed me the papers, and I went off to the next booth.

While I'm waiting in the line, I look at the paper which has the summary of all the tests I've taken so far. And just for the hell of it I show my paper to the guy next to me, and I ask him in a rather stupid-sounding voice, "Hey! What did you get in 'Psychiatric?' Oh! You got an 'N.' I got an 'N' in everything else, but I got a 'D' in 'Psychiatric.' What does *that* mean?" I knew what it meant: "N" is normal, and "D" is deficient.

The guy pats me on the shoulder and says, "Buddy, it's perfectly all right. It doesn't mean anything. Don't worry about it!" Then he walks way over to the other corner of the room, frightened: It's a lunatic!

I started looking at the papers the psychiatrist had written, and it looked pretty serious! The first guy wrote:

Thinks people talk about him.
Thinks people stare at him.
Auditory hypnogogic hallucinations.
Talks to self.
Talks to deceased wife.
Maternal aunt in mental institution.
Very peculiar stare. (I knew what *that* was — that was when I said, "And *this* is *medicine?*")

The second psychiatrist was obviously more important, because his scribble was harder to read. His notes said things like "auditory hypnogogic hallucinations confirmed." ("Hypnogogic" means you get them while you're falling asleep.)

He wrote a lot of other technical-sounding notes, and I looked them over, and they looked pretty bad. I figured I'd have to get all of this straightened out with the army somehow.

At the end of the whole physical examination there's an army officer who decides whether you're in or you're out. For instance, if there's something the matter with your hearing, *he* has to decide if it's serious enough to keep you out of the army. And because the army was scraping the bottom of the barrel for new recruits, this officer wasn't going to take anything from anybody. He was tough as nails. For instance, the fellow ahead of me had two bones sticking out from the back of his neck — some kind of displaced vertebra, or something — and this army officer had to get up from his desk and *feel* them — he had to make sure they were real!

I figure *this* is the place I'll get this whole misunderstanding straightened out. When it's my turn, I hand my papers to the officer, and I'm ready to explain everything, but the officer doesn't look up. He sees the "D" next to "Psychiatric," immediately reaches for the rejection stamp, doesn't ask me any questions, doesn't say anything; he just stamps my papers "RE-JECTED," and hands me my 4-F paper, still looking at his desk.

So I went out and got on the bus for Schenectady, and while I was riding on the bus I thought about the crazy thing that had happened, and I started to laugh — out loud — and I said to myself, "My God! If they saw me now, they would be *sure!*"

When I finally got back to Schenectady I went in to see Hans Bethe. He was still sitting behind his desk, and he said to me in a joking voice, "Well, Dick, did you pass?"

I made a long face and shook my head slowly. "No."

Then he suddenly felt terrible, thinking that they had discovered some serious medical problem with me, so he said in a concerned voice, "What's the matter, Dick?"

I touched my finger to my forehead.

He said, "No!"

"Yes!"

He cried, "No-o-o-o-o-o-o!!!" and he laughed so hard that the roof of the General Electric Company nearly came off.

I told the story to many other people, and everybody laughed, with a few exceptions.

When I got back to New York, my father, mother, and sister called for me at the airport, and on the way home in the car I told them all the story. At the end of it my mother said, "Well, what should we do, Mel?"

My father said, "Don't be ridiculous, Lucille. It's absurd!"

So that was that, but my sister told me later that when we got home and they were alone, my father said, "Now, Lucille, you shouldn't have said anything in front of him. Now what *should* we do?"

By that time my mother had sobered up, and she said, "Don't be ridiculous, Mel!"

One other person was bothered by the story. It was at a Physical Society meeting dinner, and Professor Slater, my old professor at MIT, said, "Hey, Feynman! Tell us that story about the

288

draft I heard."

I told the whole story to all these physicists — I didn't know any of them except Slater — and they were all laughing throughout, but at the end one guy said, "Well, maybe the psychiatrist had something in mind."

I said resolutely, "And what profession are *you*, sir?" Of course, that was a dumb question, because they were all physicists at a professional meeting. But I was surprised that a physicist would say something like that.

He said, "Well, uh, I'm really not supposed to be here, but I came as the guest of my brother, who's a physicist. I'm a psychiatrist." I smoked him right out!

After a while I began to worry. Here's a guy who's been deferred all during the war because he's working on the bomb, and the draft board gets letters saying he's important, and now he gets a "D" in "Psychiatric" — it turns out he's a nut! Obviously he *isn't* a nut; he's just trying to make us *believe* he's a nut — we'll get him!

The situation didn't look good to me, so I had to find a way out. After a few days, I figured out a solution. I wrote a letter to the draft board that went something like this:

Dear Sirs:
    I do not think I should be drafted because I am teaching science students, and it is partly in the strength of our future scientists that the national welfare lies. Nevertheless, you may decide that I should be deferred because of the result of my medical report,

namely, that I am psychiatrically unfit. I feel that no weight whatsoever should be attached to this report because I consider it to be a gross error.

I am calling this error to your attention because I am insane enough not to wish to take advantage of it.

Sincerely,
R. P. Feynman

Result: "Deferred. 4F. Medical Reasons."

There was an Italian radio station in Brooklyn, and as a boy I used to listen to it all the time. I LOVed the ROLLing SOUNds going over me, as if I was in the ocean, and the waves weren't very high. I used to sit there and have the water come over me, in this BEAUtiful iTALian. In the Italian programs there was always some kind of family situation where there were discussions and arguments between the mother and father:

High voice: *"Nio teco TIEto capeto TUtto . . ."*

Loud, low voice: *"DRO tone pala TUtto!!"* (with hand slapping).

It was great! So I learned to make all these emotions: I could cry; I could laugh; all this stuff. Italian is a lovely language.

There were a number of Italian people living near us in New York. Once while I was riding my bicycle, some Italian truck driver got upset at me, leaned out of his truck, and, gesturing, yelled something like, *"Me aRRUcha LAMpe etta TIche!"*

290

I felt like a crapper. What did he say to me? What should I yell back?

So I asked an Italian friend of mine at school, and he said, "Just say, '*A te! A te!*' — which means 'The same to you! The same to you!' "

I thought it was a great idea. I would say "*A te! A te!*" back — gesturing, of course. Then, as I gained confidence, I developed my abilities further. I would be riding my bicycle, and some lady would be driving in her car and get in the way, and I'd say, "*PUzzia a la maLOche!*" — and she'd shrink! Some terrible Italian boy had cursed a terrible curse at her!

It was not so easy to recognize it as fake Italian. Once, when I was at Princeton, as I was going into the parking lot at Palmer Laboratory on my bicycle, somebody got in the way. My habit was always the same: I gesture to the guy, "*oREzze caBONca MIche!*" slapping the back of one hand against the other.

And way up on the other side of a long area of grass, there's an Italian gardner putting in some plants. He stops, waves, and shouts happily, "*REzza ma LIa!*"

I call back, "*RONte BALta!*", returning the greeting. He didn't know I didn't know, and I didn't know what he said, and he didn't know what I said. But it was OK! It was great! It works! After all, when they hear the intonation, they recognize it immediately as Italian — maybe it's Milano instead of Romano, what the hell. But he's an iTALian! So it's just great. But you have to have absolute confidence. Keep right on going, and nothing will happen.

One time I came home from college for a vacation, and my sister was sort of unhappy, almost crying: her Girl Scouts were having a father-daughter banquet, but our father was out on the road, selling uniforms. So I said I would take her, being the brother (I'm nine years older, so it wasn't so crazy).

When we got there, I sat among the fathers for a while, but soon became sick of them. All these fathers bring their daughters to this nice little banquet, and all they talked about was the stock market — they don't know how to talk to their own children, much less their children's friends.

During the banquet the girls entertained us by doing little skits, reciting poetry, and so on. Then all of a sudden they bring out this funny-looking, apron-like thing, with a hole at the top to put your head through. The girls announce that the fathers are now going to entertain *them*.

So each father has to get up and stick his head through and say something — one guy recites "Mary Had a Little Lamb" — and they don't know what to do. I didn't know what to do either, but by the time I got up there, I told them that I was going to recite a little poem, and I'm sorry that it's not in English, but I'm sure they will appreciate it anyway:

A TUZZO LANTO
— Poici di Pare

TANto SAca TULna TI, na PUta TUchi
PUti TI la.

292

RUNto CAta CHANto CHANta MANto CHI
la TI da.
YALta CAra SULda MI la CHAta PIcha
PIno TIto BRALda
pe te CHIna nana CHUNda lala CHINda
lala CHUNda!
RONto piti CA le, a TANto CHINto quinta
LALda
O la TINta dalla LALta, YENta PUcha lalla
TALta!

I do this for three or four stanzas, going through all the emotions that I heard on Italian radio, and the kids are unraveled, rolling in the aisles, laughing with happiness.

After the banquet was over, the scoutmaster and a schoolteacher came over and told me they had been discussing my poem. One of them thought it was Italian and the other thought it was Latin. The schoolteacher asks, "Which one of us is right?"

I said, "You have to go ask the girls — they understood what language it was right away."

CLYDE BEATTY

from

FACING THE BIG CATS

Born in 1905, **Clyde Beatty** was a world-famous animal trainer in the thirties and forties. In this excerpt, he recalls an animal trainer's nightmare — the night one of his tigers broke loose from his cage and was wandering about a large hotel. How to find the animal and return it to its cage required all of Beatty's skill and ingenuity.

Perhaps the spookiest of my experiences with escaped animals took place some years ago in the Shrine Temple in Detroit. I was to give a private show there for a convention of automobile salesmen, and had quartered my cats comfortably in the basement. One large room was filled with supplies, including a truckload of sawdust, a battery of water buckets, and a lot of extra pedestals and other equipment. This room was also used as a "pantry," where my men cut up the meat for the lions and tigers. Beyond, in dimly lighted corridors, the cages were ranged along the concrete walls.

The building above was only partly finished at the time. The upper floors that were completed were cut up into hotel rooms, about half of them occupied. As I remember it, about one hundred guests were sleeping there that night.

A little before midnight I made the rounds of my pets, and gave a few words of advice to the watchman, an experienced man I had brought with me. For some reason I felt uneasy, but I laid this to the fact that the cellar was still somewhat damp, probably because the concrete was not yet perfectly dry. I went over all the cages again and inspected the bars and fastenings carefully. One of my lions had a slight infection from a scratch on the foot. I treated this foot before leaving and instructed the watchman to telephone me at my hotel if the animal didn't quiet down.

I was somehow reluctant to leave. I tried out the telephone, which connected with a switchboard on the main floor of the building. Learning that the board was manned all night, I gave the operator the number of my hotel. While I was talking to him over the phone, I noticed a stairway leading upward from the basement, and idly speculated on where it went. Evidently it was just a flight of service stairs leading to the hotel floors above, and to the big swimming pool, still uncompleted, which was to be an important feature of the building. I envied the hotel guests snoring comfortably in their rooms above.

Bidding my watchman a hasty goodnight, I hurried over to my nearby hotel to crowd in as much sleep as I could.

From a dream about the old days in the Chillicothe High School, I was suddenly awakened by a ring that had something peremptory about it, like a fire alarm. My watch, lying on the table beside the telephone, registered three o'clock as I switched on the light.

It was the night clerk downstairs. His voice was shrill and excited.

"Hell's broke loose at the Shrine!" he shouted, almost wrecking a perfectly good eardrum. "Your watchman's here at the desk. . . . Says your tigers are out. . . . What's that? . . . All of them, I guess."

It's odd how a fellow can be amused even when an emergency like this suddenly arises. I recall a curious desire to laugh as I quickly pulled on my trousers. There was no more likelihood of my tigers *all* being loose than of the Shrine Temple disappearing into a hole in the ground. Probably just one, I reflected, and not much danger of that one getting any farther than the pantry, where the smell of meat would probably hold him bewitched for a while. But this was a contingency I couldn't count on. It was too pat — the kind of wishful thinking a guy does when he's still half asleep.

My watchman was waiting for me down at the desk. He was pale, his voice had taken on a nervous stammer and there was a frightened look in his eyes. He was too panicky to be very coherent, but I gathered from a few hasty questions, as I nudged him toward the door that led to the street, that he had been sitting in his corner of the basement when suddenly Gracie, my largest tigress, bounded past him and rushed off up the service stairs.

The watchman was still so shattered by fear that I left him behind me and raced down the street to the Shrine Temple. I dashed through the entrance and down the cellar stairs, into the corridor where the cages were lined up. I took a hasty look at Gracie's cage. It was one of my ordinary "shifting dens," consisting of a stout timber frame, with iron bars set firmly into the wood. Gracie had worked one of the bars loose, and then had bent the adjoining ones enough so that she could wriggle through.

Oh, for a flashlight! I remembered, ironically, an old resolve to keep one handy at all times. . . .

Quickly satisfying myself that the tigress had not stopped in the pantry, I grabbed the watchman's chair. It was a folding camp chair and would not be much good in a battle with Gracie, but I couldn't find anything better. Gracie had been upstairs for at least ten minutes, and I shuddered to think what might have happened in one of those guest rooms.

I dashed up the service stairs three steps at a time. Two flights up a hall door was open, and I saw flickering light at the other end of the long corridor.

"Who's there?" I called.

"Night watchman!" came the answer. It was one of the hotel patrols. I called out again to him, asking him if he had seen anything of a stray tiger. (What a question to spring on a man suddenly in the middle of the night!) He gave me some befuddled reply. Not waiting to explain further, I hurried back and up another flight of stairs. On each floor I stopped and explored a little way down the corridor, calling Gracie by name. I have never yet seen an escaped animal that would not respond to its name — usually by turning and attacking. But there was no response from Gracie, not even a snarl.

I came to the top floor, the fifth. Here the door from the staircase was ajar. I pushed it wide open, holding my chair in front of me. The light from the electric bulb on the landing showed dimly a huge room, cluttered with a mass of timbers, scaffolding, bags of mortar and piles of building material. Only gradually did I begin to figure out that this was the uncompleted swimming pool, with half-finished partitions and cubicles that eventually would be towel rooms, shower baths, locker rooms and so on. Altogether it was a man-made jungle that offered as many treacherous hiding places for a tiger as any tangled forest or swamp that nature ever provided in India or Sumatra.

Although my calls to Gracie brought no response, I was fairly sure that the tigress was in this room. If that was the case, sooner or later she would respond when I called out her name. I closed the door and bolted it temporarily with a piece of timber across the doorknob, then went back downstairs and closed every door, so that when I found Gracie I could drive her down to the cellar without danger to the sleeping guests.

As I raced back up the stairs to the bolted door of the fifth floor, I had a feeling of relief. Things were not as bad as they might have been. It was unlikely that the tigress had taken any human victims, unless she had dragged some sleeper to the shelter of the unfinished swimming pool; and I couldn't convince myself that she could have done this without leaving quickly recognizable signs of her passing.

I opened the door to the swimming pool. Within, it was so dark that the little pinpoint of light on the landing merely accented the blackness. I'd have felt a bit safer if I could have known exactly what that room looked like, and what was going to be underfoot at my next step forward. If Gracie was here, near the door, she had probably taken refuge under some of that scaffolding on the right. Holding my chair in front of me, I peered into that corner, seeking two little spots of green reflected light, which would be her eyes.

Very slowly I moved forward. Suddenly my ears caught a soft sound just behind me, where I remembered a pile of mortar bags. I wheeled toward the sound. "Gracie!" I called, sharply. She leaped at me with a snarl, almost before I was really sure she was there. Intuitively I stepped aside as I felt, rather than saw, her coming. She lashed out at the legs of my camp chair as she swept by, and disappeared beneath a mass of scaffolding.

For several minutes I pushed cautiously around the room, trying to locate her again. I tipped over a keg of nails that went clattering down a slanting pile of floor boards with a din that must have frightened the tigress a good deal more than it did me. I nearly lost my footing in a mess of wet paint. Finally I came to a swinging door that apparently led to a dressing room or office. Through the door I could see Gracie's eyes. The tigress had plunged through the door and couldn't get back, because a piece of two-by-four timber had slipped down and prevented it from moving outward.

I picked up the two-by-four and let the door swing free as I again called Gracie's name, tauntingly. She came out on the run, full of fight. I fended her off toward the hallway, first with the two-by-four and then with my chair. She turned on me halfway across the floor, but as she turned she touched a great mound of spilled nails and loosened a few hundred which made strange noises as her feet scattered them about. She hesitated and I gave her a shove with the timber, toward the door.

In the doorway she made a stand. I was in an awkward position, with a treacherous footing of littered tiles and mortar. As she came for me I realized that this was a time when I would have to suspend my philosophy that kindness to animals — the affectionate approach, in other words — is the one and only way to deal with them. What a rude reminder that there is an exception to every rule as I swung my two-by-four, with all my strength, down on Gracie's head. For after all, this was a matter of survival. Gracie reeled backward through the doorway, and immediately I began to force her down the stairs.

Two flights down she halted on a landing and showed her teeth. As she swung around, her weight against the door burst it open, and she disappeared into the corridor. This was a dangerous development, and I was after her with all possible speed. I was only a few feet behind as she turned into the open door of a bedroom. If there was anyone sleeping in there, he was going to have a few exciting moments.

But it happened that the room was unoccupied. I turned on the light with a button by the door, while Gracie retired, snarling and angry-eyed, into a corner near the bed. Retreating into the hall, I closed the door behind me. I needed a moment to plan my next move. I could get Gracie out of the room, but how was I going to prevent her bouncing back up to her hide-out on the fifth floor?

She was safely tucked away in that room for a while, so I began the task of lugging down from the swimming-pool floor a miscellaneous assortment of mortar bags, nail kegs, sawhorses, and timbers, to form a barricade across the stairs. Fortunately I found several broad strips of painters' canvas up there, and these I nailed across the hall, forming a frail cloth wall about ten feet high, blocking the way upward.

Now I must try again to drive Gracie down to the basement. As I entered the lighted bedroom, it was apparent that she had been enjoying a refreshing rest during my absence. She was ready to play in earnest now. For several minutes she charged me all over the room. My camp chair was smashed to splinters, and I replaced it with a red-plush chair that had been standing sedately before a small writing desk. The tigress quickly finished this new shield of mine and I armed myself next with the telphone table. All the time I was watching carefully for another chance to use my two-by-four. Finally Gracie gave me an opening and I swung for the top of her head, where I could stun her without inflicting any serious damage. She reacted by backing into the corridor.

On the landing I approached her with my two-by-four uplifted. She glowered and prepared to spring, but I rushed her before she could develop any momentum. To avoid my improvised club she rose on her hind legs and swung at me with both forepaws. Her aim was so accurate that she knocked the two-by-four from my right hand and the remnants of the telephone table from my left. I was completely disarmed and at her mercy, if she had but known it. But, not realizing her victory, she whirled off down the stairs to the cellar, leaping into her cage through the widened opening that had been hopefully prepared for her homecoming, and retiring to its farthest corner.

One of the Temple watchmen helped me nail some timbers across the cage opening. Later, when Gracie quieted down, we transferred her to another cage. We always carry a spare.

That night's encounter with Gracie was as tough a battle as I've ever fought with an animal. It was well after four o'clock when the watchman and I sat down with his dinner pail; the duel had lasted over an hour and I was exhausted.

MARION "CLOVER" ADAMS

from

THE LETTERS OF MRS. HENRY ADAMS

Marion Hooper Adams (1843–85), called "Clover" by her friends, was a member of a prominent Boston family and, as the wife of historian and writer Henry Adams, was a much-admired hostess in Washington, D.C., in the years after the Civil War. In this youthful and exuberant piece of reporting to a cousin (traveling in Europe), she describes the heady excitement of visiting Washington at the very end of the Civil War to see the grand two-day parade honoring the victorious Northern armies of Grant and Sherman. She also chronicles seeing the still blood-stained room where Lincoln was taken after shot and briefly attending the trial of the conspirators, including the one woman accomplice later executed.

The youthful joie de vivre displayed in this writing was somehow lost: Clover ended her own life in her early forties.

The Grand Review of Grant's and Sherman's Armies

Sunday, May 28, 1865

Dearest Lou

I can think of no better way of showing the deep sympathy I feel for you, in being away from this victorious country in these past two months, than by writing you a long letter telling you what I have seen.* To begin at the end instead of the beginning, I got home from Washington last week, having had one week of intense excitement and enjoyment — for one week I have had my eyes wide open and my ears and my mouth, and my pulse and heart going like race horses.

A week ago Thursday, Ellen, Pater, and I were coming home from Greenfield, where we had been making a visit at the Davises'. Reading the newspaper in the cars, I found there was to be a grand review of Grant's and Sherman's armies the next week. Then and there I vowed to myself that go I would. I begged Father to take me, but he hooted at the idea of such a thing. The next morning, I lay in wait for John Reed,† to attack him as he went down town. He came, and I seized him and begged him to take me. He scoffed and jeered, manlike, and left me momentarily quenched. I then stamped for an hour or

*This letter was written to her cousin, Mary Louise Shaw, in Europe.
†Her cousin.

304

two; said all the naughty words I could think of — then put on my most festive bonnet and went forth to seek a man. I went to Uncle Henry's. He wanted to go but could not possibly. I came home, and found Ellen had "tuke" the fever since morning, and found Mollie Felton also infected. Well, the day wore on, and never a man in the horizon. Ellen said, "Despair is a free man, hope a slave," and folded her hands. I said, "Ellen, you're craven-hearted, I *shall* go." I drove to Brookline in the rain, to find Alice Mason. She was out. I came home to find Annette Rogers, who, hearing at the Sanitary★ how we felt, had attacked her father — and he, heaven bless him, said that he would take her and Mollie and Ellen and me. He telegraphed for rooms. We waited. At noon Saturday came the answer, "I cannot engage you any rooms." We held a council of war, and decided to go.

We left Boston Saturday evening, and travelled all night and all the next night — got to Washington — no rooms — no place to see the review from, and no chance apparently. Ellen and I looked at each other blankly — then said that we would go to Uncle Sam's†. He was just home from the West. We came to his house, where President Johnson has been living since the assassination‡; soldiers pacing up and down, we passed in; guards in the entry, we asked for

★The Sanitary Commission distributed relief to soldiers during the Civil War.
†Her uncle lived on 15th and H streets.
‡Lincoln's assassination.

Uncle Sam. He fairly staggered at seeing us. His house was filled with the President's guests — he, himself, in that position. We told him we only wanted a corner to lie in; so up we went to the attic, and agreed to pass as the housekeeper's nieces — to take our meals with her. It was all he could do, not cheerful, but a little better than sleeping in the streets, which we thought might be our fate. Looking out of the attic window, whom should I spy ploughing through the mud but James Higginson with an orderly riding behind. I called, "Jim, Jim!" at the top of my voice. A sentry ran after him, and up he came booted and spurred. We told him we did not want to stay where we were if he could get us a room anywhere else. We then went to the Sanitary Headquarters, found our party, and that there was an attic room in a house near Willard's; we could sleep there and take our meals at the hotel. So we decided on that; wrote a note to Uncle Sam, and all four of us turned in to our welcome attic room. I only tell you all this to show you what fun we had in meeting one obstacle after another, and knocking them over as fast as they came up. Even the horse-cars were engaged to sleep in, and many people, it was said, passed the night in the street. Mollie and Annette and I drove to Georgetown to find an officer in an hospital, for whom I had some money. A lovely summer afternoon — blue sky overhead — roses everywhere all over the houses — regiment after regiment came marching past, bands playing — squads of contrabands looking on. We sang out as each regiment passed, "What regiment are you?" "Michigan!" "Wisconsin!" "Iowa!" And so on! It was so jolly, and they all looked at us as we passed, in a pleased sort of way — then home to dinner. Before night we had tickets to the Congressional platform — the best place from which to see the review — Uncle Sam got them for us. In the evening Uncle Sam brought a Major Knox to see us, a young fellow — officer of the guard — who knew a thing or two, having been through Sherman's campaign — Vicksburg and all. Ellen and I drove with them to the Forbeses' to make a call.

Tuesday A.M., up at five-thirty, the most perfect day I ever saw; a bad breakfast — so bad! and then off to our seats. Mr. Wolcott, Ellen, and I to the Congressional platform; the others, opposite us at Mr. Forbes's, which he put up by permission of General Augur to seat wounded soldiers from hospitals, who came, some in ambulances, some hobbling on crutches — and wasn't it just like Mr. Forbes with his kind heart. We were early and got nice seats, roofed over to keep off the sun; and eighty feet from us across the street sat the President, Generals Grant, Sherman, Howard, Hancock, Meade, and many others — Secretaries of War and Navy — diplomatic corps and ladies. The platform covered with Stars and Stripes, gay flags; between the pillars pots of flowers — azaleas, cactus, and all in full bloom; then Grant's victories in great letters laid over the flags between the pillars — Vicksburg, Shiloh, Richmond, Wilderness, Antietam, Gettysburg. Up drove Uncle Sam's carriage — Martin stately on the box — out got the President. He sat in the middle of the box, Stanton on his right — Grant on Stanton's right — Sherman in the corner on the left, opposite Grant; and then after each crack general had passed out of sight with his division, he came on foot and into the box, shaking hands all around, and then looked on with the rest.

About nine-thirty the band struck up "John Brown," and by came Meade with his staff, splendidly mounted. Almost all the officers in the army had their hands filled with roses, and many had wreaths around their horses' necks. After Meade passed there was a pause. Suddenly a horse dashed by with a hatless rider, whose long golden curls were streaming in the wind; his arms hung with a wreath, and his horse's neck with one, too. It was General Custer, who stands as a cavalry officer next to Sheridan. He soon got control of his horse and came back at a more sober pace, put himself at the head of his division, and they came riding by, 10,000 men. Sheridan's cavalry, Custer's Division, are called cutthroats, and each officer and man wears a scarlet scarf around his neck with ends hanging half a yard long. Among the cavalry came the dear old Second, Caspar Crowninshield looking splendidly on his war horse — then came artillery, pontoon bridges, ambulances, army wagons, negro and white pioneers with axes and spades, Zouave regiments, some so picturesque with red bag trousers, pale sea-green sashes, and dark blue jackets braided with red, red fezzes on their heads with yellow tassels. Other Zouave regiments with entirely different uniforms, gay and Arab-like. And so it came, this glorious old army of the Potomac, for six hours marching past, eighteen or twenty miles long, their colours telling their sad history. Some regiments with nothing but a bare pole, a little bit of rag only, hanging a few inches, to show where their flag had been. Others that had been Stars and Stripes, with one or two stripes hanging, all the rest shot away. It was a strange feeling to be so intensely happy and triumphant, and yet to feel like crying. As each corps commander and division general rode by, the President and secretaries and generals stood up, and down went the swords as salute, and the colours dipped. Between the different corps there was often a delay of five minutes or so. Then the crowd rushed to the front of the stand, cheering the different generals, who had to stand and acknowledge it. Grant looked so bashful and modest with his little boy sitting on his lap — it was touching to see him. Sherman was nervous and looked bored — talked fast all the time, his hands gesticulating. I like the President's face — it looked strong and manly.

About half past three the procession ended. We got separated from our party; met Jim and we [went] to the Forbeses'; found about thirty people there having luncheon-dinner, and fell in with them — General Barlow, Hallowell girls, stray officers, etc. About seven P.M. Annette Rogers and I went off to see Ford's Theatre. It is closed, but we went round to the back — saw the stable where Booth's horse was kept, and the back door by which he escaped — found a coloured woman who saw him lead his horse up to the theatre door (she lives in the alley, and said she went to the door, hearing a noise — saw, as he stood in the lighted doorway, that it was "Mr. Booth," as she called him. About an hour after, she heard a noise as of a rushing horse — ran to the door, but the horse and rider were out of sight). She had been one of the witnesses, as she heard Booth call "Ned" three or four times to a man in the theatre to come and hold his horse. From that we went to the house, where the President was carried and where he died. The room is a small one in an ell on the ground floor; the pillow is soaked with blood, and the pillow case; it is left just as it was on that night — a painful sight, and yet we wanted to see it, as it is an historical fact and it makes it so vivid to be in the place where such a tragedy has been enacted.

Wednesday, another glorious day — bright and cool, and we sit in the same place as before and see Sherman ride by at the head of 70,000 men, who, in physique and marching, surpass decidedly the Potomac Army. Regiments where the average height is six foot two or three — real Americans all, intelligent and brave-looking. Very little cavalry in this army — squads of negroes, picked up upon the march, with picks and shovels on their shoulders. At the end of one army corps come two very small white donkeys, each ridden by a small black boy; a black boy marching by the donkey lifts his cap and salutes the President's box, which is only done by generals in the procession, and the fun makes us all laugh. Sherman has come into the box, and today looks eager and happy, talking to his wife, whom he met yesterday for the first time for two years. They all shake hands with Sherman as he comes in — but when Stanton holds out his hand, Sherman looks at him as if he were a dog, and hardly vouchsafes a cool blow. It's a breach of military etiquette, if not worse, as the Secretary of War is his superior officer. Sherman is undoubtedly a genius, but not a man of half the character of Grant; he is furious at the way in which his disgraceful treaty with Joe Johnston has been received, and cannot control his temper. I make the acquaintance of a reporter of the *New York Herald,* who sits next to me. He's been through Sherman's campaign and tells me the names of the generals as they ride by. Howard looks finely with his one arm; and General Logan, with Indian blood in his veins — very little of anything else, I should think. By and by comes the dear old 2d Massachusetts Infantry, not an officer in it now that we know. General William Dwight from the sidewalk calls out, "Three cheers for the 2d Massachusetts!" and they come with a will. By four o'clock it is all over, leaving one stunned, almost, with all this excitement — then a hasty dinner; after which Ellen and Jim and I go to walk — come home starved. Jim is sent to buy us crackers and fruit, and we sit and eat and talk on the doorstep till bedtime, different people dropping in. Then we four girls hie to our loft, and chatter and laugh till Morpheus becomes inexorable.

Thursday morning, up early, and off to the trial of the conspirators — a long way off. Ellen and I stay about half an hour, and then come away, having an engagement to drive with Uncle Sam and Major Knox. We drive through a lovely wooded road, Sherman's army lying on each side of the road and under the trees; mules and horses tied to fences; army wagons in long succession filing by; batteries, etc. We go to General Logan's headquarters on a grassy hill. Major Knox introduces us to him and some of his staff. We stay there some time; then we drive off to find General Sherman's headquarters, which seems to be well-nigh impossible. When we find it, to our disgust the General has gone in town. So we drive back to Washington, get a dinner, and then we four girls go to Armory [Square] Hospital to tea. Ellen has written you about it, so I won't, except that I never had such an interesting evening in my life. Before tea I talked to some men in the ward — one bright little fellow, wounded at Cedar Creek, who was standing by Charley Lowell when he was shot. Another young fellow, sitting up near him, said he was in that fight, and after it was over he saw General Sheridan come up, throw his arms round Custer's neck, and kiss him, saying, "Well, old fellow, you've done a good work today."

Friday, a pouring rain, so we can't go over the river to Arlington and the camps, as we meant to — Jim and Ellen go to the hospital — Annette and I drag poor Mr. Rogers to the court again. It's crowded; but we squeeze in and get some reporters' chairs. Mr. Rogers waits outside and reads the paper. Being a woman has its advantages on this occasion. The evidence is not very interesting, but it is to see the prisoners. Mrs. Surratt* only shows her eyes, keeping her fan to her face. All the men except Paine have weak, low faces. Paine is handsome, but utterly brutal, and sits there a head higher than all the others, his great gray eyes rolling about restlessly, not fixing on anything, looking like a wild animal at bay. It is a sad impressive sight.

Friday night we leave Washington and get home in twenty-four hours. I am very tired. It's taken me three hours to write this letter and I haven't written it carefully at all. It is absurd to try and describe such a week — I know you will like it better than nothing and so send it, hoping that some words will be legible.

*The conspirators who planned Lincoln's assassination met at the house of Mary Surratt; she was hanged on July 7, 1865.

CHALLENGES AND CRISES

HELEN KELLER

from

THE STORY OF MY LIFE

Helen Keller (1880–1968) became blind and deaf through a disease that struck her at nineteen months, leaving her permanently handicapped and leaving her family with the dilemma of how best to raise and educate her. In her autobiography, written when she was only twenty-three, Helen tells of the arrival of her teacher Anne Sullivan, just before she turned seven, and how Sullivan was able to break through the barriers of silence and sightlessness and bring Helen Keller language — and connections to the world. So successful was her schooling by Anne Sullivan that Helen Keller was able to attend and graduate from Radcliffe College.

In a later excerpt from her autobiography, Helen gives her candid appraisal of college life at Radcliffe (now Harvard), which remains relevant and provocative. Her ultimately rich, profitable life has become a symbol of hope and perserverance to others who must overcome daunting handicaps.

———

317

The most important day I remember in all my life is the one on which my teacher, Anne Mansfield Sullivan, came to me. I am filled with wonder when I consider the immeasurable contrasts between the two lives which it connects. It was the third of March, 1887, three months before I was seven years old.

On the afternoon of that eventful day, I stood on the porch, dumb, expectant. I guessed vaguely from my mother's signs and from the hurrying to and fro in the house that something unusual was about to happen, so I went to the door and waited on the steps. The afternoon sun penetrated the mass of honeysuckle that covered the porch, and fell on my upturned face. My fingers lingered almost unconsciously on the familiar leaves and blossoms which had just come forth to greet the sweet southern spring. I did not know what the future held of marvel or surprise for me. Anger and bitterness had preyed upon me continually for weeks and a deep languor had succeeded this passionate struggle.

Have you ever been at sea in a dense fog, when it seemed as if a tangible white darkness shut you in, and the great ship, tense and anxious, groped her way toward the shore with plummet and sounding-line, and you waited with beating heart for something to happen? I was like that ship before my education began, only I was without compass or sounding-line, and had no way of knowing how near the harbour was. "Light! give me light!" was the wordless cry of my soul, and the light of love shone on me in that very hour.

I felt approaching footsteps. I stretched out my hand as I supposed to my mother. Some one took it, and I was caught up and held close in the arms of her who had come to reveal all things to me, and, more than all things else, to love me.

The morning after my teacher came she led me into her room and gave me a doll. The little blind children at the Perkins Institution had sent it and Laura Bridgman had dressed it; but I did not know this until afterward. When I had played with it a little while, Miss Sullivan slowly spelled into my hand the word "d-o-l-l." I was at once interested in this finger play and tried to imitate it. When I finally succeeded in making the letters correctly I was flushed with childish pleasure and pride. Running downstairs to my mother I held up my hand and made the letters for doll. I did not know that I was spelling a word or even that words existed; I was simply making my fingers go in monkey-like imitation. In the days that followed I learned to spell in this uncomprehending way a great many words, among them *pin*, *hat, cup* and a few verbs like *sit, stand* and *walk*. But my teacher had been with me several weeks before I understood that everything has a name.

One day, while I was playing with my new doll, Miss Sullivan put my big rag doll into my lap also, spelled "d-o-l-l" and tried to make me understand that "d-o-l-l" applied to both. Earlier in the day we had had a tussle over the words "m-u-g" and "w-a-t-e-r." Miss Sullivan had tried to impress it upon me that "m-u-g" is *mug* and that "w-a-t-e-r" is *water*, but I persisted in confounding the two. In despair she had dropped the subject for the time, only to renew it at the first opportunity. I became impatient at her repeated attempts and, seizing the new doll, I dashed it upon the floor. I was keenly delighted when I felt the fragments of the broken doll at my feet. Neither sorrow nor regret followed my passionate outburst. I had not loved the doll. In the still, dark world in which I lived there was no strong sentiment of tenderness. I felt my teacher sweep the fragments to one side of the hearth, and I had a sense of satisfaction that the cause of my discomfort was removed. She brought me my hat, and I knew I was going out into the warm sunshine. This thought, if a wordless sensation may be called a thought, made me hop and skip with pleasure.

We walked down the path to the well-house, attracted by the fragrance of the honeysuckle with which it was covered. Some one was drawing water and my teacher placed my hand under the spout. As the cool stream gushed over one hand she spelled into the other the word *water*, first slowly, then rapidly. I stood still, my whole attention fixed upon the motions of her fingers. Suddenly I felt a misty consciousness as of something forgotten — a thrill of returning thought; and somehow the mystery of language was revealed to me. I knew then that "w-a-t-e-r" meant the wonderful cool something that was flowing over my hand. That living word awakened my soul, gave it light, hope, joy, set it free!

There were barriers still, it is true, but barriers that could in time be swept away.

I left the well-house eager to learn. Everything had a name, and each name gave birth to a new thought. As we returned to the house every object which I touched seemed to quiver with life. That was because I saw everything with the strange, new sight that had come to me. On entering the door I remembered the doll I had broken. I felt my way to the hearth and picked up the pieces. I tried vainly to put them together. Then my eyes filled with tears; for I realized what I had done, and for the first time I felt repentance and sorrow.

I learned a great many new words that day. I do not remember what they all were; but I do know that *mother, father, sister, teacher* were among them — words like that were to make the world blossom for me, "like Aaron's rod, with flowers." It would have been difficult to find a happier child than I was as I lay in my crib at the close of that eventful day and lived over the joys it had brought me, and for the first time longed for a new day to come.

The struggle for admission to college was ended, and I could now enter Radcliffe whenever I pleased. Before I entered college, however, it was thought best that I should study another year under Mr. Keith. It was not, therefore, until the fall of 1900 that my dream of going to college was realized.

I remember my first day at Radcliffe. It was a day full of interest for me. I had looked forward to it for years. A potent force within me, stronger than the persuasion of my friends, stronger even than the pleadings of my heart, had impelled me to try my strength by the standards of those who see and hear. I knew that there were obstacles in the way; but I was eager to overcome them. I had taken to heart the words of the wise Roman who said, "To be banished from Rome is but to live outside of Rome." Debarred from the great highways of knowledge, I was compelled to make the journey across country by unfrequented roads — that was all; and I knew that in college there were many bypaths where I could touch hands with girls who were thinking, loving and struggling like me.

I began my studies with eagerness. Before me I saw a new world opening in beauty and light, and I felt within me the capacity to know all things. In the wonderland of Mind I should be as free as another. Its people, scenery, manners, joys, tragedies should be living, tangible interpreters of the real world. The lecture-halls seemed filled with the spirit of the great and the wise, and I thought the professors were the embodiment of wisdom. If I have since learned differently, I am not going to tell anybody.

But I soon discovered that college was not quite the romantic lyceum I had imagined. Many of the dreams that had delighted my young inexperience became beautifully less and "faded into the light of common day." Gradually I began to find that there were disadvantages in going to college.

The one I felt and still feel most is lack of

time. I used to have time to think, to reflect, my mind and I. We would sit together of an evening and listen to the inner melodies of the spirit, which one hears only in leisure moments when the words of some loved poet touch a deep, sweet chord in the soul that until then had been silent. But in college there is no time to commune with one's thoughts. One goes to college to learn, it seems, not to think. When one enters the portals of learning, one leaves the dearest pleasures — solitude, books and imagination — outside with the whispering pines. I suppose I ought to find some comfort in the thought that I am laying up treasures for future enjoyment, but I am improvident enough to prefer present joy to hoarding riches against a rainy day.

My studies the first year were French, German, history, English composition and English literature. In the French course I read some of the work of Corneille, Molière, Racine, Alfred de Musset and Sainte-Beuve, and in the German those of Goethe and Schiller. I reviewed rapidly the whole period of history from the fall of the Roman Empire to the eighteenth century, and in English literature studied critically Milton's poems and "Aeropagitica."

I am frequently asked how I overcome the peculiar conditions under which I work in college. In the classroom I am of course practically alone. The professor is as remote as if he were speaking through a telephone. The lectures are spelled into my hand as rapidly as possible, and much of the individuality of the lecturer is lost to me in the effort to keep in the race. The words rush through my hand like hounds in pursuit of a hare which they often miss. But in this respect I do not think I am much worse off than the girl who takes notes. If the mind is occupied with the mechanical process of hearing and putting words on paper at pellmell speed, I should not think one could pay much attention to the subject under consideration or the manner in which it is presented. I cannot take notes during the lectures, because my hands are busy listening. Usually I jot down what I can remember of them when I get home. I write the exercises, daily themes, criticisms and hour-tests, the mid-year and final examinations, on my typewriter, so that the professors have no difficulty in finding out how little I know. When I began the study of Latin prosody, I devised and explained to my professor a system of signs indicating the different meters and quantities.

I use the Hammond typewriter. I have tried many machines, and I find the Hammond is the best adapted to the peculiar needs of my work. With this machine movable type shuttles can be used, and one can have several shuttles, each with a different set of characters — Greek, French, or mathematical, according to the kind of writing one wishes to do on the typewriter. Without it, I doubt if I could go to college.

Very few of the books required in the various courses are printed for the blind, and I am obliged to have them spelled into my hand. Consequently I need more time to prepare my lessons than other girls. The manual part takes longer, and I have perplexities which they have not. There are days when the close attention I must give to details chafes my spirit, and the thought that I must spend hours reading a few chapters, while in the world without other girls are laughing and singing and dancing, makes me rebellious; but I soon recover my buoyancy and laugh the discontent out of my heart. For, after all, everyone who wishes to gain true knowledge must climb the Hill Difficulty alone, and since there is no royal road to the summit, I must zigzag it in my own way. I slip back many times, I fall, I stand still, I run against the edge of hidden obstacles, I lose my temper and find it again and keep it better, I trudge on. I gain a little, I feel encouraged, I get more eager and climb higher and begin to see the widening horizon. Every struggle is a victory. One more effort and I reach the luminous cloud, the blue depths of the sky, the uplands of my desire. I am not always alone, however, in these struggles. Mr. William Wade and Mr. E. E. Allen, Principal of the Pennsylvania Institution for the Instruction of the Blind, get for me many of the books I need in raised print. Their thoughtfulness has been more of a help and encouragement to me than they can ever know.

Last year, my second year at Radcliffe, I studied English composition, the Bible as English literature, the governments of America and Europe, the Odes of Horace, and Latin comedy. The class in composition was the pleasantest. It was very lively. The lectures were always interesting, vivacious, witty; for the instructor, Mr. Charles Townsend Copeland, more than any one else I have had until this year, brings before you literature in all its original freshness and power. For one short hour you are permitted to drink in the eternal beauty of the old masters without needless interpretation or exposition. You revel in their fine thoughts. You enjoy with all your soul the sweet thunder of the Old Testament, forgetting the existence of Jahweh and Elohim; and you go home feeling that you have had "a glimpse of that perfection in which spirit and form dwell in immortal harmony; truth and beauty bearing a new growth on the ancient stem of time."

This year is the happiest because I am studying subjects that especially interest me, economics, Elizabethan literature, Shakespeare under Professor George L. Kittredge, and the History of Philosophy under Professor Josiah Royce. Through philosophy one enters with sympathy of comprehension into the traditions of remote ages and other modes of thought, which erewhile seemed alien and without reason.

But college is not the universal Athens I thought it was. There one does not meet the great and the wise face to face; one does not even feel their living touch. They are there, it is true; but they seem mummified. We must extract them from the crannied wall of learning and dissect and analyze them before we can be sure that we have a Milton or an Isaiah, and not merely a clever imitation. Many scholars forget, it seems to me, that our enjoyment of the great works of literature depends more upon the depth of our sympathy than upon our understanding.

The trouble is that very few of their laborious explanations stick in the memory. The mind drops them as a branch drops its overripe fruit. It is possible to know a flower, root and stem and all, and all the processes of growth, and yet to have no appreciation of the flower fresh bathed in heaven's dew. Again and again I ask impatiently, "Why concern myself with these explanations and hypotheses?" They fly hither and thither in my thought like blind birds beating the air with ineffectual wings. I do not mean to object to a thorough knowledge of the famous works we read. I object only to the interminable comments and bewildering criticisms that teach but one thing: there are as many opinions as there are men. But when a great scholar like Professor Kittredge interprets what the master said, it is "as if new sight were given the blind." He brings back Shakespeare, the poet.

There are, however, times when I long to sweep away half the things I am expected to learn for the overtaxed mind cannot enjoy the treasure it has secured at the greatest cost. It is impossible, I think, to read in one day four or five different books in different languages and treating of widely different subjects, and not lose sight of the very ends for which one reads. When one reads hurriedly and nervously, having in mind written tests and examinations, one's brain becomes encumbered with a lot of choice bric-à-brac for which there seems to be little use. At the present time my mind is so full of heterogeneous matter that I almost despair of ever being able to put it in order. Whenever I enter the region that was the kingdom of my mind I feel like the proverbial bull in the china shop. A thousand odds and ends of knowledge come crashing about my head like hailstones, and when I try to escape them, theme-goblins and college nixies of all sorts pursue me, until I wish — oh, may I be forgiven the wicked wish! — that I might smash the idols I came to worship.

But the examinations are the chief bugbears of my college life. Although I have faced them many times and cast them down and made them bite the dust, yet they rise again and menace me with pale looks, until like Bob Acres I feel my courage oozing out at my finger ends. The days before these ordeals take place are spent in cramming your mind with mystic formulæ and indigestible dates — unpalatable diets, until you wish that books and science and you were buried in the depths of the sea.

At last the dreaded hour arrives, and you are a favoured being indeed if you feel prepared, and are able at the right time to call to your standard thoughts that will aid you in that supreme effort. It happens too often that your trumpet call is unheeded. It is most perplexing and exasperating that just at the moment when you need your memory and a nice sense of discrimination, these faculties take to themselves wings and fly away. The facts you have garnered with such infinite trouble invariably fail you at the pinch.

"Give a brief account of Huss and his work." Huss? Who was he and what did he do? The name looks strangely familiar. You ransack your budget of historic facts much as you would hunt for a bit of silk in a ragbag. You are sure it is somewhere in your mind near the top — you saw it there the other day when you were looking up the beginnings of the Reformation. But where is it now? You fish out all manner of odds and ends of knowledge — revolutions, schisms, massacres, systems of government; but Huss— where is he? You are amazed at all the things you know which are not on the examination paper. In desperation you seize the budget and dump everything out, and there in a corner is your man, serenely brooding on his own private thought, unconscious of the catastrophe which he has brought upon you.

Just then the proctor informs you that the time is up. With a feeling of intense disgust you kick the mass of rubbish into a corner and go home, your head full of revolutionary schemes to abolish the divine right of professors to ask questions without the consent of the questioned.

It comes over me that in the last two or three pages of this chapter I have used figures which will turn the laugh against me. Ah, here they are — the mixed metaphors mocking and strutting about before me, pointing to the bull in the china shop assailed by hailstones and the bugbears with pale looks, an unanalyzed species! Let them mock on. The words describe so exactly the atmosphere of jostling, tumbling ideas I live in that I will wink at them for once, and put on a deliberate air to say that my ideas of college have changed.

While my days at Radcliffe were still in the future, they were encircled with a halo of romance,

329

which they have lost; but in the transition from romantic to actual I have learned many things I should never have known had I not tried the experiment. One of them is the precious science of patience, which teaches us that we should take our education as we would take a walk in the country, leisurely, our minds hospitably open to impressions of every sort. Such knowledge floods the soul unseen with a soundless tidal wave of deepening thought. "Knowledge is power." Rather, knowledge is happiness, because to have knowledge — broad, deep knowledge — is to know true ends from false, and lofty things from low. To know the thoughts and deeds that have marked man's progress is to feel the great heart-throbs of humanity through the centuries; and if one does not feel in these pulsations a heavenward striving, one must indeed be deaf to the harmonies of life.

MALCOLM X

from

THE AUTOBIOGRAPHY OF MALCOLM X

In his autobiography, **Malcolm X** (1925–65) describes his transformation from an underworld street hustler to a political and spiritual leader of the Black Muslims. In this excerpt, he explains his motivation for and joy in discovering a "homemade" method of self-education while serving a ten-year prison sentence for burglary. He began by studying the dictionary in great detail, copying it page by page starting with letter A.

While in prison, Malcolm X became a convert to the Black Muslim faith led by Elijah Muhammed and, after his parole, became an outspoken leader of the sect, lecturing on black separatism. But after journeying to Mecca to continue his studies, he questioned whether its teachings were authentic and faithful to true Muslim beliefs and subsequently formed his own group, the Organization of African Unity. Conflicts over theological questions and over leadership of the Black Muslim sect probably resulted in his assassination in New York in 1965 at age forty.

———————

It was because of my letters that I happened to stumble upon starting to acquire some kind of a homemade education.

I became increasingly frustrated at not being able to express what I wanted to convey in letters that I wrote, especially those to Mr. Elijah Muhammad. In the street, I had been the most articulate hustler out there — I had commanded attention when I said something. But now, trying to write simple English, I not only wasn't articulate, I wasn't even functional. How would I sound writing in slang, the way I would *say* it, something such as, "Look, daddy, let me pull your coat about a cat, Elijah Muhammad —"

Many who today hear me somewhere in person, or on television, or those who read something I've said, will think I went to school far beyond the eighth grade. This impression is due entirely to my prison studies.

It had really begun back in the Charlestown Prison, when Bimbi first made me feel envy of his stock of knowledge. Bimbi had always taken charge of any conversation he was in, and I had tried to emulate him. But every book I picked up had few sentences which didn't contain anywhere from one to nearly all of the words that might as well have been in Chinese. When I just skipped those words, of course, I really ended up with little idea of what the book said.

So I had come to the Norfolk Prison Colony still going through only book-reading motions. Pretty soon, I would have quit even these motions, unless I had received the motivation that I did.

I saw that the best thing I could do was get hold of a dictionary — to study, to learn some words. I was lucky enough to reason also that I should try to improve my penmanship. It was sad. I couldn't even write in a straight line. It was both ideas together that moved me to request a dictionary along with some tablets and pencils from the Norfolk Prison Colony school.

I spent two days just riffling uncertainly through the dictionary's pages. I'd never realized so many words existed! I didn't know *which* words I needed to learn. Finally, just to start some kind of action, I began copying.

In my slow, painstaking, ragged handwriting, I copied into my tablet everything printed on that first page, down to the punctuation marks.

I believe it took me a day. Then, aloud, I read back, to myself, everything I'd written on the tablet. Over and over, aloud, to myself, I read my own handwriting.

I woke up the next morning, thinking about those words — immensely proud to realize that not only had I written so much at one time, but I'd written words that I never knew were in the world. Moreover, with a little effort, I also could remember what many of these words meant. I reviewed the words whose meanings I didn't remember. Funny thing, from the dictionary first page right now, that "aardvark" springs to my mind. The dictionary had a picture of it, a long-tailed, long-eared, burrowing African mammal, which lives off termites caught by sticking out its tongue as an anteater does for ants.

I was so fascinated that I went on — I copied the dictionary's next page. And the same experience came when I studied that. With every succeeding page, I also learned of people and places and events from history. Actually the dictionary is like a miniature encyclopedia. Finally the dictionary's A section had filled a whole table — and I went on into the B's. That was the way I started copying what eventually became the entire dictionary. It went a lot faster after so much practice helped me to pick up handwriting speed. Between what I wrote in my tablet, and writing letters, during the rest of my time in prison I would guess I wrote a million words.

I suppose it was inevitable that as my word-base broadened, I could for the first time pick up a book and read and now begin to understand what the book was saying. Anyone who has read a great deal can imagine the new world that opened. Let me tell you something: from then until I left that prison, in every free moment I had, if I was not reading in the library, I was reading on my bunk. You couldn't have gotten me out of books with a wedge. Between Mr. Muhammad's teachings, my correspondence, my visitors — usually Ella and Reginald — and my reading of books, months passed without my even thinking about being imprisoned. In fact, up to then, I never had been so truly free in my life.

The Norfolk Prison Colony's library was in

the school building. A variety of classes was taught there by instructors who came from such places as Harvard and Boston universities. The weekly debates between inmate teams were also held in the school building. You would be astonished to know how worked up convict debaters and audiences would get over subjects like "Should Babies Be Fed Milk?"

Available on the prison library's shelves were books on just about every general subject. Much of the big private collection that Parkhurst had willed to the prison was still in crates and boxes in the back of the library — thousands of old books. Some of them looked ancient: covers faded, old-time parchment-looking binding. Parkhurst, I've mentioned, seemed to have been principally interested in history and religion. He had the money and the special interest to have a lot of books that you wouldn't have in general circulation. Any college library would have been lucky to get that collection.

As you can imagine, especially in a prison where there was heavy emphasis on rehabilitation, an inmate was smiled upon if he demonstrated an unusually intense interest in books. There was a sizable number of well-read inmates, especially the popular debaters. Some were said by many to be practically walking encyclopedias. They were almost celebrities. No university would ask any student to devour literature as I did when this new world opened to me, of being able to read and *understand*.

I read more in my room than in the library itself. An inmate who was known to read a lot could check out more than the permitted maximum number of books. I preferred reading in the total isolation of my own room.

When I had progressed to really serious reading, every night at about ten P.M. I would be outraged with the "lights out." It always seemed to catch me right in the middle of something engrossing.

Fortunately, right outside my door was a corridor light that cast a glow into my room. The glow was enough to read by, once my eyes adjusted to it. So when "lights out" came, I would sit on the floor where I could continue reading in that glow.

At one-hour intervals the night guards paced past every room. Each time I heard the approaching footsteps, I jumped into bed and feigned sleep. And as soon as the guard passed, I got back out of bed onto the floor area of that light-glow, where I would read for another fifty-eight minutes — until the guard approached again. That went on until three or four every morning. Three or four hours of sleep a night was enough for me. Often in the years in the streets I had slept less than that.

THOMAS MERTON

from

THE SEVEN STOREY MOUNTAIN

After leading a seemingly full and unstinting life first as a student at Cambridge University, England, and at Columbia University, and later as a teacher and writer, **Thomas Merton** (1915–68) converted to the Catholic faith and eventually withdrew to a Trappist monastery in Kentucky at the age of twenty-six, the vows of which require total silence.

As a monk, Merton's need for solitude grew so insistent that he withdrew into his own cabin in the woods, visiting the main monastery only once a day for mass and for a single meal and receiving no visitors. In his state of complete solitude, he continued to study and write, and published thirty volumes of essays, poetry, and translations, some of which are inspirational in nature.

In this excerpt from his autobiography, he recalls the spiritual transformation that took place within him when, as an adult, he attended his first Catholic mass and felt the first joyous hint of his eventual vocation.

By the time I was ready to begin the actual writing of my thesis, that is, around the beginning of September 1938, the groundwork of conversion was more or less complete. And how easily and sweetly it had all been done, with all the external graces that had been arranged, along my path, by the kind Providence of God! It had taken little more than a year and a half, counting from the time I read Gilson's *The Spirit of Medieval Philosophy* to bring me up from an "atheist" — as I considered myself — to one who accepted all the full range and possibilities of religious experience right up to the highest degree of glory.

I not only accepted all this, intellectually, but now I began to desire it. And not only did I begin to desire it, but I began to do so efficaciously: I began to want to take the necessary means to achieve this union, this peace. I began to desire to dedicate my life to God, to His service. The notion was still vague and obscure, and it was ludicrously impractical in the sense that I was already dreaming of mystical union when I did not even keep the simplest rudiments of the moral law. But nevertheless I was convinced of the reality of the goal, and confident that it could be achieved: and whatever element of presumption was in this confidence I am sure God excused, in His mercy, because of my stupidity and helplessness, and because I was really beginning to be ready to do whatever I thought He wanted me to do to bring me to Him.

But, oh, how blind and weak and sick I was, although I thought I saw where I was going, and half understood the way! How deluded we sometimes are by the clear notions we get out of books. They make us think that we really understand things of which we have no practical knowledge at all. I remember how learnedly and enthusiastically I could talk for hours about mysticism and the experimental knowledge of God, and all the while I was stoking the fires of the argument with Scotch and soda.

That was the way it turned out that Labor Day, for instance. I went to Philadelphia with Joe Roberts, who had a room in the same house as I, and who had been through all the battles on the Fourth Floor of John Jay for the past four years. He had graduated and was working on some trade magazine about women's hats. All one night we sat, with a friend of his, in a big dark roadhouse outside of Philadelphia, arguing and arguing about mysticism, and smoking more and more cigarettes and gradually getting drunk. Eventually, filled with enthusiasm for the purity of heart which begets the vision of God, I went on with them into the city, after the closing of the bars, to a big speak-easy where we completed the work of getting plastered.

My internal contradictions were resolving themselves out, indeed, but still only on the plane of theory, not of practice: not for lack of goodwill, but because I was still so completely chained and fettered by my sins and my attachments.

I think that if there is one truth that people

need to learn, in the world, especially today, it is this: the intellect is only theoretically independent of desire and appetite in ordinary, actual practice. It is constantly being blinded and perverted by the ends and aims of passion, and the evidence it presents to us with such a show of impartiality and objectivity is fraught with interest and propaganda. We have become marvelous at self-delusion; all the more so, because we have gone to such trouble to convince ourselves of our own absolute infallibility. The desire of the flesh — and by that I mean not only sinful desires, but even the ordinary, normal appetites for comfort and ease and human respect, are fruitful sources of every kind of error and misjudgement, and because we have these yearnings in us, our intellects (which, if they operated all alone in a vacuum, would indeed register with pure impartiality what they saw) present to us everything distorted and accommodated to the norms of our desire.

And therefore, even when we are acting with the best of intentions, and imagine that we are doing a great good, we may be actually doing tremendous material harm and contradicting all our good intentions. There are ways that seem to men to be good, the end whereof is in the depths of hell.

The only answer to the probelm is grace, docility to grace. I was still in the precarious position of being my own guide and my own interpreter of grace. It is a wonder I ever got to the harbor at all!

Sometime in August, I finally answered an

impulsion that had been working on me for a long time. Every Sunday, I had been going out on Long Island to spend the day with the same girl who had brought me back in such a hurry from Lax's town Olean. But every week, as Sunday came around, I was filled with a growing desire to stay in the city and go to some kind of a church.

At first, I had vaguely thought I might try to find some Quakers, and go and sit with them. There still remained in me something of the favorable notion about Quakers that I had picked up as a child, and which the reading of William Penn had not been able to overcome.

But, naturally enough, with the work I was doing in the library, a stronger drive began to assert itself, and I was drawn much more imperatively to the Catholic Church. Finally the urge became so strong that I could not resist it. I called up my girl and told her that I was not coming out that week-end, and made up my mind to go to Mass for the first time in my life.

The first time in my life! That was true. I had lived for several years on the continent, I had been to Rome, I had been in and out of a thousand Catholic cathedrals and churches, and yet I had never heard Mass. If anything had ever been going on in the churches I visited, I had always fled, in wild Protestant panic.

I will not easily forget how I felt that day. First, there was this sweet, strong, gentle, clean urge in me which said: "Go to Mass! Go to Mass!" It was something quite new and strange, this voice that seemed to prompt me, this firm, growing interior conviction of what I needed to do. It had a suavity, a simplicity about it that I could not easily account for. And when I gave in to it, it did not exult over me, and trample me down in its raging haste to land on its prey, but it carried me forward serenely and with purposeful direction.

That does not mean that my emotions yielded to it altogether quietly. I was really still a little afraid to go to a Catholic church of set purpose, with all the other people, and dispose myself in a pew, and lay myself open to the mysterious perils of that strange and powerful thing they called their "Mass."

God made it a very beautiful Sunday. And since it was the first time I had ever really spent a sober Sunday in New York, I was surprised at the clean, quiet atmosphere of the empty streets uptown. The sun was blazing bright. At the end of the street, as I came out the front door, I could see a burst of green, and the blue river and the hills of Jersey on the other side.

Broadway was empty. A solitary trolley came speeding down in front of Barnard College and past the School of Journalism. Then, from the high, grey, expensive tower of the Rockefeller Church, huge bells began to boom. It served very well for the eleven o'clock Mass at the little brick Church of Corpus Christi, hidden behind Teachers College on 121st Street.

How bright the little building seemed. Indeed, it was quite new. The sun shone on the clean bricks. People were going in the wide open door, into the cool darkness and, all at once, all the churches of Italy and France came back to me. The richness and fulness of the atmosphere of Catholicism that I had not been able to avoid apprehending and loving as a child, came back to me with a rush: but now I was to enter into it fully for the first time. So far, I had known nothing but the outward surface.

It was a gay, clean church, with big plain windows and white columns and pilasters and a well-lighted, simple sanctuary. Its style was a trifle eclectic, but much less perverted with incongruities than the average Catholic church in America. It had a kind of a seventeenth-century, oratorian character about it, though with a sort of American colonial tinge of simplicity. The blend was effective and original: but although all this affected me, without my thinking about it, the thing that impressed me most was that the place was full, absolutely full. It was full not only of old ladies and broken-down gentlemen with one foot in the grave, but of men and women and children young and old — especially young: people of all classes, and all ranks on a solid foundation of workingmen and -women and their families.

I found a place that I hoped would be obscure, over on one side, in the back, and went to it without genuflecting, and knelt down. As I knelt, the first thing I noticed was a young girl, very pretty too, perhaps fifteen or sixteen, kneeling straight up and praying quite seriously. I was very much impressed to see that someone who was young and beautiful could with such simplicity make prayer the real and serious principal reason for going to church. She was clearly kneeling that way because she meant it, not in order to show off, and she was praying with an absorption which, though not the deep recollection of a saint, was serious enough to show that she was not thinking at all about the other people who were there.

What a revelation it was, to discover so many ordinary people in a place together, more conscious of God than of one another: not there to show off their hats or their clothes, but to pray, or at least to fulfil a religious obligation, not a human one. For even those who might have been there for no better motive than that they were obliged to be, were at least free from any of the self-conscious and human constraint which is never absent from a Protestant church where people are definitely gathered together as people, as neighbors, and always have at least half an eye for one another, if not all of both eyes.

Since it was summer time, the eleven o'clock Mass was a Low Mass: but I had not come expecting to hear music. Before I knew it, the priest was in the sanctuary with the two altar boys, and was busy at the altar with something or other which I could not see very well, but the people were praying by themselves, and I was engrossed and absorbed in the thing as a whole: the business at the altar and the presence of the people. And still I had not got rid of my fear. Seeing the late-comers hastily genuflecting before entering the pew, I realised my omission, and got the idea that people had spotted me for a pagan and were just waiting for me to miss a few more genuflections before throwing me out or, at least, giving me looks of reproof.

Soon we all stood up. I did not know what it was for. The priest was at the other end of the altar, and, as I afterwards learned, he was reading the Gospel. And then the next thing I knew there was someone in the pulpit.

It was a young priest, perhaps not much over thirty-three or -four years old. His face was rather ascetic and thin, and its asceticism was heightened with a note of intellectuality by his horn-rimmed glasses, although he was only one of the assistants, and he did not consider himself an intellectual, nor did anyone else apparently consider him so. But anyway, that was the impression he made on me: and his sermon, which was simple enough, did not belie it.

It was not long: but to me it was very interesting to hear this young man quietly telling the people in language that was plain, yet tinged with scholastic terminology, about a point in Catholic Doctrine. How clear and solid the doctrine was: for behind those words you felt the full force not only of Scripture but of centuries of a unified and continuous and consistent tradition. And above all, it was a vital tradition: there was nothing studied or antique about it. These words, this terminology, this doctrine, and these convictions fell from the lips of the young priest as something that were most intimately part of his own life. What was more, I sensed that the people were familiar with it all, and that it was also, in due proportion, part of their life

345

also: it was just as much integrated into their spiritual organism as the air they breathed or the food they ate worked in to their blood and flesh.

What was he saying? That Christ was the Son of God. That, in Him, the Second Person of the Holy Trinity, God, had assumed a Human Nature, a Human Body and Soul, and had taken Flesh and dwelt amongst us, full of grace and truth: and that this Man, Whom Men called the Christ, was God. He was both Man and God: two Natures hypostatically united in one Person or suppositum, one individual Who was a Divine Person, having assumed to Himself a Human Nature. And His works were the works of God: His acts were the acts of God. He loved us: God, and walked among us: God, and died for us on the Cross, God of God, Light of Light, True God of True God.

Jesus Christ was not simply a man, a good man, a great man, the greatest prophet, a wonderful healer, a saint: He was something that made all such trivial words pale into irrelevance. He was God. But nevertheless He was not merely a spirit without a true body, God hiding under a visionary body: he was also truly a Man, born of the Flesh of the Most Pure Virgin, formed of her Flesh by the Holy Spirit. And what He did, in that Flesh, on earth, He did not only as Man but as God. He loved us as God, He suffered and died for us, God.

And how did we know? Because it was revealed to us in the Scriptures and confirmed by the teaching of the Church and of the powerful unanimity of Catholic Tradition from the first

Apostles, from the first Popes and the early Fathers, on down through the Doctors of the Church and the great scholastics, to our own day. *De Fide Divina.* If you believed it, you would receive light to grasp it, to understand it in some measure. If you did not believe it, you would never understand it: it would never be anything but scandal or folly.

And no one can believe these things merely by wanting to, of his own volition. Unless he receive grace, an actual light and impulsion of the mind and will from God, he cannot even make an act of living faith. It is God Who gives us faith, and no one cometh to Christ unless the Father draweth him.

I wonder what would have happened in my life if I had been given this grace in the days when I had almost discovered the Divinity of Christ in the ancient mosaics of the churches of Rome. What scores of self-murdering and Christ-murdering sins would have been avoided — all the filth I had plastered upon His image in my soul during those last five years that I had been scourging and crucifying God within me?

It is easy to say, after it all, that God had probably foreseen my infidelities and had never given me the grace in those days because He saw how I would waste and despise it: and perhaps that rejection would have been my ruin. For there is no doubt that one of the reasons why grace is not given to souls is because they have so hardened their wills in greed and cruelty and selfishness that their refusal of it would only harden them more — But now I had been beaten

347

into the semblance of some kind of humility by misery and confusion and perplexity and secret, interior fear, and my ploughed soul was better ground for the reception of a good seed.

The sermon was what I most needed to hear that day. When the Mass of the Catechumens was over, I, who was not even a catechumen, but only a blind and deaf and dumb pagan as weak and dirty as anything that ever came out of the darkness of Imperial Rome or Corinth or Ephesus, was not able to understand anything else.

It all became completely mysterious when the attention was refocused on the altar. When the silence grew more and more profound, and little bells began to ring, I got scared again and, finally, genuflecting hastily on my left knee, I hurried out of the church in the middle of the most important part of the Mass. But it was just as well. In a way, I suppose I was responding to a kind of liturgical instinct that told me I did not belong there for the celebration of the Mysteries as such. I had no idea what took place in them: but the fact was that Christ, God, would be visibly present on the altar in the Sacred Species. And although He was there, yes, for love of me: yet He was there in His power and His might, and what was I? What was on my soul? What was I in His sight?

It was liturgically fitting that I should kick myself out at the end of the Mass of the Catechumens, when the ordained *ostiarri* should have been there to do it. Anyway, it was done.

Now I walked leisurely down Broadway in the

sun, and my eyes looked about me at a new world. I could not understand what it was that had happened to make me so happy, why I was so much at peace, so content with life for I was not yet used to the clean savor that comes with an actual grace — indeed, there was no impossibility in a person's hearing and believing such a sermon and being justified, that is, receiving sanctifying grace in his soul as a habit, and beginning, from that moment, to live the divine and supernatural life for good and all. But that is something I will not speculate about.

All I know is that I walked in a new world. Even the ugly buildings of Columbia were transfigured in it, and everywhere was peace in these streets designed for violence and noise. Sitting outside the gloomy little Childs restaurant at 111th Street, behind the dirty, boxed bushes, and eating breakfast, was like sitting in the Elysian Fields.

ANNE MORROW LINDBERGH

from

HOUR OF GOLD,
HOUR OF LEAD

An exciting and adventurous life as the wife of famous aviator Charles Lindbergh was shattered by the kidnapping of the couple's infant son. The following selections from **Anne Lindbergh's** letters to her mother-in-law and from her diary, later collected by her in *Hour of Gold, Hour of Lead,* chronicle that tormenting period just after the baby was kidnapped — those long weeks when hope still remained for his safe return.

The eventual discovery that the child had been dead for some time and the adjustment to the loss of her blonde first-born son change Anne forever: she will never again be the same young and lighthearted wife of a great national hero.

[Hopewell], Wednesday, March 2, 1932
TO E. L. L. L. [Anne's mother-in-law]
(Better destroy after reading.)
I am going to write you this first afternoon all

that I know and some you may discover in the newspapers; however, they are trying to keep *some* items from the press, so I know you will keep all this private, as you always do. I will write everything as I would like it told me and as I *cannot* tell you on the telephone. Oh, it was dreadful just giving you the bad news last night and nothing else. But C. thought immediately of you and wanted me to get you — he and the detectives were busy around the place.

At 7:30 Betty and I were putting the baby to bed. We closed and bolted all the shutters except on one window where the shutters were warped and won't close. Then I left and went downstairs and sat at the desk in the living room. Betty continued to clean the bathroom etc. until some time between 7:45 and 8:00, when she went in to the baby again to see he was covered. He was fast asleep and covered. Then she went downstairs to supper.

C. was late in coming home, not till 8:20. Then we went upstairs. He washed his hands in the bathroom next to the baby's — we heard nothing — perhaps because of the water. Then downstairs to supper at about 8:35 to 9:10 (at this time Betty was still eating her supper — we were all in the west wing of the house). At 9:10 C. and I went upstairs. C. ran a bath, then went down again. I ran a bath. No noise heard. From about 9:30 to 10 C. was in his study, right next to the window under the baby's; no ladder could have been put up *then*. Betty and Elsie were upstairs still in the west wing.

At ten Betty went in to the baby, shut the

window first, then lit the electric stove, then turned to the bed. It was empty and the sides still up. No blankets taken. She thought C. had taken him for a joke. I did, until I saw his face. Evidently they got about one and a half hours' start. You know the rest except the bits of evidence which have *not* been released.

1 — A well-made small pair of ladders, found to the left of the house, evidently built and planned for that exact height window;

2 — mud on the sill of the window with the shutters unbarred;

3 — and a letter on the sill telling us that the baby would be taken good care of, that they wanted several thousand dollars, divided into three divisions, that they would let us know in four days where to leave the money. Experts found the ladder, bedclothes, window, and letter had been handled *with gloved fingers*.

Also footsteps below the window. Their knowledge of our being in Hopewell on a weekday. (We have not done it since *last* year and only stayed down because the baby had a cold. However, Tuesday, and Monday too, he had *no* temperature and was *cured* Tuesday really. We planned to take him to Englewood Wednesday.) Their knowledge of the baby's room, the lack of fingerprints, the well-fitted ladder, all point to *professionals*, which is rather good, as it means they want only the money and will not maliciously hurt the baby.

I was afraid of a lunatic. But the well-made plan knocks *that* out. C., Col. Henry [Breckinridge], and the detectives are rather optimistic though they think it will take *time and patience*. In fact they think the kidnappers have gotten themselves into a terrible jam — so *much* pressure, such a close net over the country, such sympathy for us, and the widespread publicity, every police force on its mettle, that their one hope is to get the baby back unharmed.

That is all I know, I have written fast so someone can take this out. C. is *marvelous* — calm, clear, alert, and observing. It is dreadful not to be able to do *anything* to help. I want *so* to help. I know you do, C. knows it too. Thank you for all I understood over the telephone — what you couldn't say.

Forgive this brief account for I send much love to you.

[Hopewell], Thursday morning [March 3rd]
Dear Mrs. Lindbergh,

I wish I had more to tell you. We are waiting for the move of the kidnappers who said they'd let us know where to put the money in two to four days (all this private, of course). They think now that they are not *real* professionals, that real professionals would not walk into such a hornets' nest, that the phrasing of the letter is not hard-boiled enough for professionals. Also the amazing knowledge of the country around here, the house, situation, etc., points more to a local gang. They think that the terrific pressure may force them to give in very soon, i.e., work for negotiations, or else it may frighten them so they don't dare negotiate. But the general impression is that the longer they keep the baby, the worse posi-

353

tion they're in.

We've gotten several fake postcards etc. about the baby's position, but they got a telegram this morning that looks as if it might be genuine, (addressed) to me, saying that the baby was under the care of a trained nurse and in good condition. All the papers said he was "ill" when he left but he *wasn't*. He was just over a cold and was dressed extra-warmly that night, with an extra shirt on under his regular shirt and then the wool cover-all sleeping suit on top.

Charles got a short nap yesterday afternoon and a good sleep last night. But he is very tired. But marvelously contained, and acts with such swiftness and judgment. He was pleased to see in the newspapers that you were going on with the teaching.

Wahgoosh was in the opposite wing of the house that night and did not bark. He couldn't have heard through the howling wind all that distance. He has been barking ever since. This house is bedlam: hundreds of men stamping in and out, sitting everywhere, on the stairs, on the pantry sink. The telephone goes all day and night. People sleep all over the floors on newspapers and blankets. I have never seen such self-sacrifice and energy. The chief of Jersey police* has not been to bed or to rest since the thing started. Col. Henry looks gray — under a great emotional strain. The press have moved

*Colonel H. Norman Schwarzkopf, Commander of the New Jersey State Police, in whom Charles and Anne Lindbergh had complete confidence.

down to Hopewell [the town] and are not photographing around the place any more. Which allows us to go out and walk. That is a great help to me. Wahgoosh follows C. around the grounds and I think it distracts and pleases Charles. There are planes overhead now.

I wish I had more to tell you. It is so hard to wait and do nothing. I know it is a terrible strain on you. It is easier to be in the place where things are happening, even though you can't do anything. I am in that position.

[Hopewell], Thursday afternoon [March 3rd]
Dear Mrs. Lindbergh,

The newspapers are not at all indicative of the progress of this search. That is, I suspect that the detectives only give out the clues they have already proved false. Also while all this open and almost "stock" running down of clues is going on there are three or four other lines that are being followed privately. One of these lines last night suddenly opened up and things are *really beginning to move* on that line. Definite moves toward negotiations with the kidnappers and (as much as is ever possible) therefore definite assurance that the baby is safe, and so a much more hopeful outlook for a safe return. I can't tell you any more than this.

Perhaps I should not tell this much, but as long as I know it and know how you must wait for news, I can't help sending it to you. It is of course a very very delicate situation — may take much time and endurance and patience. But if you could see the difference in C. tonight, from last night. He is tense and worried still, but excited and buoyant; Col. Henry, also. They are definitely moving toward the goal of the safe return of the baby.

This must go off. But please don't be discouraged by the newspapers, for the most hopeful things are going on quietly.

C. looks better today, got a pretty good sleep last night and has thrown off the cold he had yesterday. I feel much better.

I hope you haven't written C. or me because there are 700 letters or more coming in every day — eventually we'll see them. But now detectives go over all. You could write, though, in an envelope addressed to Mother★ with your name plainly on the front.

[Hopewell], Saturday [March 5th]

Dear Mrs. Lindbergh,

I can only tell you that everything I wrote yesterday seems to be corroborated and strengthened. Even Charles (who will not give me *anything* that I might build false hopes on, he is so afraid that I will count too desperately on something that looks plausible but might fall though) talked to me with almost assurance today. We seem to have pretty tangible word that the baby is safe, and *well cared for*. "Of course," he said, "you must never count on anything until you actually *have* it but the news looks good." The progress is slow, but we *are* progressing toward recovery

★E. C. M. [Elizabeth Cutler Morrow — Anne's Mother] had moved to Hopewell to be with A. M. L.

of the child. We are all quite hopeful tonight, more than last night and *much* more so than during the first two days.

I can tell more from C's actions and manner than from his words. The first two days he looked like a desperate man — I could not speak to him. I was afraid to. But these last two days he is quite himself, only stimulated more than usual.

It is impossible to describe the confusion — a police station downstairs by day — detectives, police, secret service men swarming in and out — mattresses all over the dining room and other rooms at night. At any time I may be routed out of my bed so that a group of detectives may have a conference in the room. It is so terrifically unreal that I do not feel anything. Betty was terribly pleased by a note from you this morning. It came just at the right time, for she has had so much grilling and criticism and is such a loyal girl. C. got good sleep last night.

[Hopewell], Sunday [March 6th]
Dear Mrs. Lindbergh,

Yesterday I wrote you not to believe anything the newspapers said and this morning they came out with very accurate and hopeful news, much more fully than I could tell you by letter. So this letter only corroborates the fact that we have come to an understanding with two of the biggest men of the underworld — men who have tremendous power with all gangs, even though they are not in touch with them and are not responsible for their actions. We do not know where the baby is or who has him, but everyone is convinced it was the work of professionals and therefore can be reached through professionals, and they seem to be convinced that the baby is safe and well cared for. It may take a good time to get him back because they naturally are *not* going to run any risks of being caught and the police and press will *have* to quiet down — the headlines *must* go before they will move.

Charles is buoyant and had good rest last night. I met the two underworld kings last night. Charles, Col. Henry, and I feel convinced they are sincere and will help us. Isn't it strange, they showed more sincerity in their sympathy than a lot of politicians who've been here. Whateley and Elsie and Betty are working like dogs — we all are, but they have been so fine.

[Hopewell], Monday [March 7th]
Dear Mrs. Lindbergh,
This morning the newspapers say "go-betweens fail." That is an unfair statement. The newspapers would not know if they failed or not, perhaps will never know. It is too soon to tell now. But they are really anxious to succeed — we are convinced of that. As I said in the last letter, we do not expect any culmination of this until the publicity dies down a little but we continue to have corroboration of the baby being safe. But even feeling pretty sure of this, it does not make it less tiring to wait and wait. I feel as though it had been years and years — I feel old and tired and numb. But C. and Col. Henry continue very hopeful and active. Things are moving — we must be patient.

Please do not let the newspapers worry you about C. or my health. C. and I both had very bad colds, but C. has thrown his off almost entirely and has slept every night except for the first. He is tireless working, but he seems buoyant and alive. I am much better and otherwise all right. Everything is so unreal. I am glad it is unreal, I do not want to realize anything. I don't think there's any danger of a miscarriage or any complication about the other baby. I am past the time when there is danger of miscarriage and I'm eating and sleeping fairly regularly and have no unusual pain — have not even felt nausea — and things are quieter now.

[Hopewell], Tuesday [March 8th]
TO E. L. L. L.
I hardly see C. at all. All day he is locked up with detectives, by the telephone, at night talking late. Last night he slept in Col. Henry's room while Aida [Mrs. Henry Breckinridge] came in here. She has acted as general buffer to the outside world, sometimes acting for me over the telephone. I have never in my life seen such selfless devotion and energy as is being poured out here by every trooper, officer, and detective etc. working on this thing. Col. Henry has hardly slept for six days. I am worried about him and C. counts on his judgment. It is a very hard time right now; everyone is under a terrific strain, the first stimulus has worn off, and the men who have worked hardest are on the verge of breaking. C. has gotten more sleep than most by choosing his time, not wasting strength on petty things,

and is now a general managing his forces with terrific discipline (which is necessary in such an emergency) but great judgment.

Conditions are just as before. It is a slow hard game, but they all have faith in the ultimate success. They know what they are doing.

[Hopewell], Wednesday [March 9th]

Dear Mrs. Lindbergh,

I can only write you that we're all waiting. The newspapers are quieting down a little, there are many fewer police here, everything is holding off. We are just waiting. It is a very hard time because there is nothing to do, but the men do not feel less hopeful. We must wait till things are fairly quiet and rest on our assurances that the baby is safe. This lull is good in a way for the men, for they can get sleep and exercise. C. slept late this morning and went out for a walk. Our colds have vanished. The house is being tidied up a little. Elsie and Whateley and Betty have more time. The police force have sent up a chef. Wahgoosh is the pet of the New Jersey police force!

With this lull the papers, especially the tabs, bring out wild stories every hour — none of them true, as you know. I am so afraid you get false clues and hopes every hour. They say the New York tabs bring out an "extra" every night to say the baby is found. But here they think it will be a slow unspectacular regular business "deal" — the return of the child — and it will not happen till things are quieter and safer for the kidnappers. The sympathy and indignation of hundreds of people all over the country, as shown by the thousand of letters, the newspapers and the editorials, is very inspiring.

[Hopewell], Thursday [March 10th]
Dear Mrs. Lindbergh,

I think you'd better send the letters to Mother direct, that is, addressed to her, because apparently the post office (now) only reads my name and then sends it to Hopewell along with the other thousands.

But perhaps it isn't worth the trouble.

Nothing seems to be. I have been trying to make up the baby's record. I haven't kept it since November, partly because I felt so miserably in December and January. I know that I did write *some* letters to you. I don't know whether you keep any letters. I don't usually and I never can find them again. But if you happen to find any having facts about him during November, December, January, and February they might refresh my memory.

Everything here is going on as usual — nothing has changed.

[Hopewell], Thursday [March 10th]
Dear Mrs. Lindbergh,

There *really* is definite progress. I feel *much* happier today. It does seem to be going ahead. Yesterday things began to move again and it was a great relief to everyone.

C. is resting now and says I *must* come in. We seem to work most of the night and now are working out a system of sleeping by day.

But it is a slow long negotiation and takes such care and patience.

C. is in much better shape and handling things wonderfully.

[Hopewell], Sunday [April 10], 1932
TO E.L.L.L.

You know from the papers all I could not tell you: that we have been in communication with the kidnappers (properly identified as such), that after five weeks of bargaining we finally took the chance, on the best advice of criminologists, detectives, etc., of giving up the money *first*. If we had not done that — and we were urged to do it *immediately* — we would have blamed ourselves forever for not trying what works in most cases.

You know what happened. We were told a location — the baby was not found. We informed the kidnappers of this and waited for further communication and have gotten none. We then were attempting to trace the bills. It was of course criminal that this information should have leaked out: it makes a difficult thing (tracing the money back to the kidnappers) impossible. We tried to get the newspapers to "kill the story." One paper broke faith with us and with all the others, and it splurged the whole thing in headlines over the front page. Of course the publicity makes it almost impossible for them to get the baby to us. There will probably be terrific delay.

C. does not think (nor do the others) — though of course there is always that possibility — that the baby has been killed. They say it is harder

362

to dispose of a dead baby than a live one. There is the chance that he died, but he was over his cold and was a strong baby. C. doesn't think there is much chance of that. He tells me not to be discouraged. I have told you all that (which has all been in the papers) so you will know just how we stand. It has of course broken very badly for us. That we can't keep anything private is most discouraging. Although things are bad they are not hopeless.

I wish I could say more. Things are quiet here now and we are waiting. It looks as though we were starting all over again with a worse start than we had six weeks ago. But of course that does not mean that things are hopeless.

[Hopewell], Wednesday [April 13], 1932
TO E. L. L. L.

You must know now from the newspapers — I will just corroborate — that the negotiations have been hitherto carried on through letters and through the go-between who was chosen by the kidnappers, apparently chosen through his offer in a newspaper to act as go-between. While the kidnappers can write us (and we can identify the letters unmistakably by comparison with the original note left in the nursery) we have had only one way of communicating with them: through the newspapers. That is unfortunate as anything as obvious as that is almost sure to be suspected.

We are at a standstill now of course until the publicity dies down. It is still front-page headlines here.

TO E. L. L. L.

Yesterday I forgot to answer your question about the boat C. was searching for in Buzzards Bay a month ago. They had definite instructions as to where to find it and a definite description of it. They went to the spot assigned and also all over that region by air, two days in succession, and there was no sign of it. Also men have been up there since by boat all over the region.

About the Englewood rumor, Col. Schwarzkopf has been moving more and more men away from here as the base of operations has been chiefly New York and environment. Trenton is the usual headquarters so there are always men there. Everything that can be done around here has, as far as possible, been done. He tells me that C. is seriously considering moving to Englewood to be nearer the base of operations. However, C. has not told me anything about it yet. I can see how it might be a good idea but I rather dread doing it. There is more to do here in my own house and woods, even though just futile routine.

Apparently we have had no definite contact with the kidnappers for a month. If you had any letter or message, no matter how ignorant, demanding ransom and sounding like the work of a reasoning mind (if one can say that of criminals) you would send it on, wouldn't you? Or telephone. Of course I know you have reported several things like that before so it is silly to reiterate this, but I feel they *must* communicate before long.

DIARY
Englewood-Hopewell, Wednesday, May 11, 1932

Woke from a dream of the return of the baby and someone saying, "Why, she hasn't even kissed him yet!" I thought, "They don't understand — I don't want to kiss him but just put my hand over the top of his curls."

Call from Col. Henry. Nothing developed from number. Dead end again.

Break in the newspapers about Curtis* in boat off New York, also reasons for failure at Norfolk; no word of C.

Long ride down — very blue. The eternal quality of certain moments in one's life. The baby being lifted out of his crib forever and ever, like Dante's hell. C.'s set face, carved onto Time for always.

The peculiar ephemeral quality of this last development. The people in the stories (told second and third hand) change their characters and melt into one another like faces in a dream. "You thought I was a face? I'm just a doorknob!"

We try to test one story by another story to prove both true. But we do not know how much of each story is a lie, intentional or unintentional. We argue along quite nicely: "This checks with that, that checks with this," until you come across the inevitable "according *to their story,*" and all your ground falls from underneath you.

*John Hughes Curtis, who had come with the story of a gang involved in the kidnapping, supposedly operating from a boat, the *Mary B. Moss.*

Long talk with Schwarzkopf encouraged me. His word is of bad weather; must remain in harbor.

Hopewell, Thursday, May 12, 1932

The baby's body found and identified by skull, hair, teeth, etc., in woods on Hopewell-Mount Rose road. Killed by a blow on head. They think he was killed immediately with intention of hiding all evidence. They took the sleeping garment off him to use to extort money.

The hardest thing to bear — Mother's "The baby is with Daddy." Called Mrs. Lindbergh. She is much braver than I. C. not able to be reached for several hours. But the weight on Mother is unbearable — wanted Baby to come back on a Monday, wanted to take the sting out of *Monday*.*

Everything is telescoped now into one moment, one of those eternal moments — the moment when I realized the baby had been taken and I saw the baby dead, killed violently, in the first flash of horror. Everything since then has been unreal, it has all vanished like smoke. Only that eternal moment remains. It *was* then and it *is* now.

I look at it now as a police case, a murder case, and I am interested in it as such and can and *have* to ask and talk about it. Soon it will be personal, but I do not face it yet.

I feel strangely a sense of peace — not peace, but an end to restlessness, a finality, as though I

*The day on which D. W. M. died [Dwight Whitney Morrow — Anne's father].

366

were sleeping in a grave.

It is a relief to know definitely that he did not live beyond that night. I keep him intact somehow, by that. He was with me the last weekend and left loving me better than anyone, I know that. But all that is merely selfish and small.

But to know anything definitely is a relief. If you can say "then he was living," "then he was dead," it is final and finalities can be accepted.

[Hopewell, May 12]

TO E. L. L. L.
(After telephoning)

Dear M.,

I know you thought my voice meant good news — we seemed so near it — and it was doubly terrible for you. But I know how Charles and I feel about bad news: we feel we must tell each other immediately. The newspapers have it already, so I felt I must call you. I will tell you all I know now.

The baby's body was found in the woods near the road from Hopewell to Princeton. It was identified by the homemade shirt Betty and I put on it. Also the teeth and hair. There seems to be no possible doubt. The child was evidently killed by a blow on the head — killed instantly undoubtedly, and, from the state of the body and from its being so near here, a long time ago, perhaps in panic during the first blast of publicity.

Charles is off on a boat somewhere off the Jersey coast between Cape May and Atlantic City. He telephoned us as late as 7 o'clock this morning but then they evidently went off to try to effect this contact with the gang that Curtis has been working with. Oh, Charles felt *so* encouraged and hopeful. I cannot bear to think of the news coming to him. They have not reached him yet though they are sending planes, cruisers, etc., to try to get him. What that gang is doing I can't see; perhaps they have another baby on the boat.

This is all I know now. They have just told me — at least perhaps a half hour to an hour ago.

I have never known such courage as you and Charles have. It is a wall to lean upon. I am grateful for both of you. You have and always will help me in that. I wish I could help you. You know how I am feeling for you. And we must both help Charles.

Later — 7:30 P.M. C. has been reached and will be here in two or three hours.

DIARY
Hopewell, Friday, May 13, 1932

He has already been dead a hundred years.

A long sleepless night but calm with C. sitting beside me every hour, and I could see it all from a great distance. His terrible patience and sweetness and silence — terrifying. "We look on Death as . . ."

Then a long day when everything personal flooded back over me, a personal physical loss, my little boy — no control over tears, no control over the hundred little incidents I had jammed out of sight when I was bargaining for my control.

C. to Trenton — the cremation — the blanket. C. going through that — even in the brief news account — is unbearable.

I am glad that I spoiled him that last weekend when he was sick and I took him on my lap and rocked him and sang to him. And glad that he wanted me those last days. . . .

Impossible to talk without crying.

Immortality perhaps for the spark of life, but not for what made up my little boy.

[Hopewell], Friday [May 14th]

TO E. L. L. L.

Dear M.,

Charles got home last night about 2 A.M. and was, as you know he would be, wonderful. He spoke so beautifully and calmly about death that it gave me great courage. He asked about you when he came in and said he was glad I had telephoned.

In the conversation about the whole thing two or three things came up that are not exactly consoling but keep us from remorse. They think the baby was killed that first night. And so nothing we did could make any difference, not if we had tried to keep it secret (we couldn't have anyway), not if we could have kept the publicity down, not if the ransom bill list had not leaked out. From the blow on the head, the baby must have been killed immediately. C. said, "I don't think he knew anything about it."

Of course it makes the kidnappers of the lowest brutality — I cannot conceive of it. I think it is well they did not have the baby long.

I know this is not real comfort — nothing is — but it is something definite for one's mind to settle on, and that is a relief — I only write hoping it will be some to you.

C. did not even lie down last night. They are, of course, working on tracing down all evidence. But he says that he will sleep tonight.

My letter sounds strange and unfeeling. I can't express what I'm feeling. C. is inarticulate too. But very courageous, as you are.

HARRY TRUMAN

from

YEAR OF DECISION

Feisty **Harry Truman** (1884–1972) was cata-
pulted into the presidency upon the sudden death
of a debilitated Franklin Delano Roosevelt in
April 1945. He immediately faced urgent problems, both international and domestic, particularly negotiations with Stalin, and he was forced
to make the unprecedented decision of whether
or not to use the atomic bomb against the
Japanese in an attempt to speed the end of World
War II. The information he received from
scientists was, in retrospect, a mixed bag: one
expert doubted that the thing would explode at
all. As vice-president, Truman had been kept
remarkably uninformed about ongoing research
and development of the bomb.

Here Truman recounts the critical days immediately following FDR's death and his own
hasty swearing-in as the thirty-third president.
As he moved into the Oval Office, surrounded
by momentoes of Roosevelt, Truman was forced
to take command of an ongoing world war and
to follow in the footsteps of a very popular
president; he turned out to be a decisive and

371

responsible leader, doing his best to do what was right for the world, given the temper of the times. Truman's sturdy character emerges in his tactful consideration of Eleanor Roosevelt and his unshakable love for Margaret and Bess Truman — and for his country.

During the first few weeks of Franklin Delano Roosevelt's fourth administration, I saw what the long years in the presidency had done to him. He had occupied the White House during twelve fateful years — years of awful responsibility. He had borne the burdens of the reconstruction from the great depression of the 'thirties. He shouldered the heavier burdens of his wartime leadership. It is no wonder that the years had left their mark.

The very thought that something was happening to him left me troubled and worried. This was all the more difficult for me because I could not share such feelings with anyone, not even with the members of my family. I kept saying to myself that this man had often demonstrated amazing recuperative powers. Only a few months earlier, during the closing days of the 1944 presidential campaign, he had ridden for four hours in an open car through a driving rain in New York City and had seemed none the worse for it.

Knowing something of the great responsibilities he was forced to carry, I did not want to think about the possibility of his death as President. The rumors were widespread but not publicly discussed. But there had always been baseless rumors about Franklin D. Roosevelt.

We all hoped that victory against our enemies was near. Under Roosevelt's inspiring leadership the war was approaching its climax. The things he stood for and labored for were about to be realized. The world needed his guiding hand for the coming transition to peace.

On February 20, 1945, while I was presiding over the Senate, a rumor that the President was dead swept through the corridors and across the floor. I left my place at once and headed for the office of Les Biffle, Secretary of the Senate. As I entered, I said to Biffle, "I hear the President is dead. What will we do? Let's find out what happened."

Biffle called the White House and was informed that it was Major General Edwin M. Watson — "Pa" Watson, the appointment secretary to the President — who was dead. He had died at sea aboard the U.S.S. *Quincy* while returning with President Roosevelt from the Yalta conference. And later that same day I received a wireless message from the *Quincy*. In it President Roosevelt asked me for my opinion and advice about his appearing before a joint session of Congress to make a personal report on the results of his just completed conference with Churchill and Stalin.

I met with the President a week later and was shocked by his appearance. His eyes were sunken. His magnificent smile was missing from his careworn face. He seemed a spent man. I had a hollow feeling within me, for I saw that the journey to Yalta must have been a terrible ordeal.

I tried to think how I could help him conserve his strength. With Mrs. Roosevelt and their daughter Anna, who was the President's close confidante, I had already discussed the problem of the strain of appearing before Congress. I recalled the expressions of pain I had seen on the President's face as he delivered his inauguration speech on January 20 on the south portico of the White House. Apparently he could no longer endure with his usual fortitude the physical pain of the heavy braces pressing against him.

With that in mind, and in order to spare him any unnecessary pain, I urged that he address Congress seated in the well of the House, and I explained that I had already cleared this unusual arrangement with the congressional leaders. He had asked for no such consideration, but he appeared relieved and pleased to be accorded this courtesy.

I shall never forget that day. The President's appearance before a joint meeting of the Senate and the House was a momentous occasion both for him and for the country. He was to report directly to Congress on the outcome of the deliberations at Yalta — deliberations that were bound to have a profound effect on the future peace of the world. He was anxious for bi-partisan support and wanted the full and sympathetic backing of Congress on foreign policy.

The speech was arranged for Thursday, March 1, 1945, and Mrs. Roosevelt, as well as Anna and her husband, Colonel Boettiger, were with him as he drove from the White House. Princess

Martha and Crown Prince Olaf of Norway were also in the presidential party, which reached the Capitol just a little after noon.

The President was met in the same way he had always been met. Formerly, however, he had spoken from the rostrum of the House of Representatives, with the stenographers for the Congressional Record in their usual places before him, and with the presiding officers of the Senate and the House side by side behind. This time, however, the microphone-laden table that had been set up for his use stood in the well of the House chamber within little more than arm's length of the first curved row of seats.

The chamber was filled as he entered, and Speaker Rayburn and I, together with the others who had met him, followed him in and took our places on the rostrum. The justices of the Supreme Court were in the places they always occupy on such occasions. The rows of seats were solidly filled with senators and representatives. I vaguely caught a glimpse of the many members of the diplomatic corps. Here and there a uniform was visible, and I remember looking up into the gallery for Mrs. Roosevelt and daughter, and for Mrs. Truman and our daughter, while the audience, which had risen in honor of the President as he entered, resumed their seats. The President looked about him and at the papers that lay before him.

Even before Speaker Rayburn let the gavel fall and introduced "the President of the United States," it was plain that this appearance of the nation's leader before Congress was to have about it an unusual atmosphere.

"Mr. Vice-President, Mr. Speaker, and members of the Congress," he began. "I hope that you will pardon me for the unusual posture of sitting down during the presentation of what I want to say, but I know that you will realize it makes it a lot easier for me in not having to carry about ten pounds of steel around on the bottom of my legs, and also because of the fact that I have just completed a 14,000-mile trip."

Everyone present was intent on his words, but unhappily the famous Roosevelt manner and delivery were not there. And he knew it. He frequently departed from his prepared script. At one point he brought in a mention of "a great many prima donnas in the world who want to be heard," and he interrupted his text at another point to warn his listeners that "we haven't won the war." But these attempts to get away from his excellent script with lighthearted references and more thoughtful asides were not of much help.

Congress was stirred. Many members of both Houses were awed by his dramatic display of sheer will power and courage, and there were very few who were critical of what he said.

I saw the President immediately after his speech had been concluded. Plainly, he was a very weary man.

"As soon as I can," he said to me, "I will go to Warm Springs for a rest. I can be in trim again if I can stay there for two or three weeks."

He left Washington for the South on March 30, 1945.

I never saw or spoke with him again.

Shortly before five o'clock in the afternoon of Thursday, April 12, 1945, after the Senate adjourned, I went to the office of House Speaker Sam Rayburn. I went there to get an agreement between the Speaker and the Vice President on certain legislation and to discuss the domestic and world situation generally. As I entered, the Speaker told me that Steve Early, the President's press secretary, had just telephoned, requesting me to call the White House.

I returned the call and was immediately connected with Early.

"Please come right over," he told me in a strained voice, "and come in through the main Pennsylvania Avenue entrance."

I turned to Rayburn, explaining that I had been summoned to the White House and would be back shortly. I did not know why I had been called, but I asked that no mention be made of the matter. The President, I thought, must have returned to Washington for the funeral of his friend, Bishop Atwood, the former Episcopal Bishop of Arizona, and I imagined that he wanted me to go over some matters with him before his return to Warm Springs.

On previous occasions when the President had called me to the White House for private talks he had asked me to keep the visits confidential. At such times I had used the east entrance to the White House, and in this way the meetings were kept off the official caller list. Now, however, I told Tom Harty, my government chauffeur, to drive me to the main entrance.

We rode alone, without the usual guards. The Secret Service had assigned three men to work in shifts when I became Vice-President. However, this guard was reinforced, as a routine practice, during the time President Roosevelt was away on his trip to Yalta and again when he went to Warm Springs. A guard had been placed on duty at my Connecticut Avenue apartment, where I had lived as Senator and continued to live as Vice-President, and another accompanied me wherever I went. These three men were capable, efficient, self-effacing, and usually the guard who was on duty met me at my office after the Senate had adjourned. But on this one occasion I slipped away from all of them. Instead of returning from Speaker Rayburn's office to my own before going to the car that was waiting for me, I ran through the basement of the Capitol Building and lost them. This was the only time in eight years that I enjoyed the luxury of privacy by escaping from the ever-present vigil of official protection.

I reached the White House about 5:25 P.M. and was immediately taken in the elevator to the second floor and ushered into Mrs. Roosevelt's study. Mrs. Roosevelt herself, together with Colonel John and Mrs. Anna Roosevelt Boettiger and Mr. Early, were in the room as I entered, and I knew at once that something unusual had taken place. Mrs. Roosevelt seemed calm in her characteristic, graceful dignity. She stepped forward and placed her arm gently about my shoulder.

"Harry," she said quietly, "the President is dead."

For a moment I could not bring myself to speak.

The last news we had had from Warm Springs was that Mr. Roosevelt was recuperating nicely. In fact, he was apparently doing so well that no member of his immediate family, and not even his personal physician, was with him. All this flashed through my mind before I found my voice.

"Is there anything I can do for you?" I asked at last.

I shall never forget her deeply understanding reply.

"Is there anything *we* can do for *you*?" she asked. "For you are the one in trouble now."

The greatness and the goodness of this remarkable lady showed even in that moment of sorrow. I was fighting off tears. The overwhelming fact that faced me was hard to grasp. I had been afraid for many weeks that something might happen to this great leader, but now that the worst had happened I was unprepared for it. I did not allow myself to think about it after I became Vice-President. But I had done a lot of thinking about it at the Chicago convention. I recall wondering whether President Roosevelt himself had had any inkling of his own condition. The only indication I had ever had that he knew he was none too well was when he talked to me just before I set out on my campaign trip for the vice-presidency in the fall of 1944. He asked me how I was going to travel, and I told him I intended to cover the country by airplane.

"Don't do that, please," he told me. "Go by

train. It is necessary that you take care of yourself."

Sometime later, too, Mrs. Roosevelt had seemed uneasy about the President's loss of appetite. She remarked to me at a dinner shortly after the elections, "I can't get him to eat. He just won't eat."

She was very devoted to the President, as he was to her. Mrs. Roosevelt was also close to the President in his work. In a way, she was his eyes and ears. Her famous trips were taken at his direction and with his approval, and she went on these long, arduous journeys mainly in order to be able to inform and advise him.

It seems to me that for a few minutes we stood silent, and then there was a knock on the study door. Secretary of State Stettinius entered. He was in tears, his handsome face sad and drawn. He had been among the first to be notified, for as Secretary of State, who is the keeper of the Great Seal of the United States and all official state papers, it was his official duty to ascertain and to proclaim the passing of the President.

I asked Steve Early, Secretary Stettinius, and Les Biffle, who now had also joined us, to call all the members of the Cabinet to a meeting as quickly as possible. Then I turned to Mrs. Roosevelt and asked if there was anything she needed to have done. She replied that she would like to go to Warm Springs at once, and asked whether it would be proper for her to make use of a government plane. I assured her that the use of such a plane was right and proper, and I made certain that one would be placed at her disposal, knowing that a grateful nation would insist on it.

But now a whole series of arrangements had to be made. I went to the President's office at the west end of the White House. I asked Les Biffle to arrange to have a car sent for Mrs. Truman and Margaret, and I called them on the phone myself, telling them what had happened — telling them, too, to come to the White House. I also called Chief Justice Harlan Fiske Stone, and having given him the news, I asked him to come as soon as possible so that he might swear me in. He said that he would come at once. And that is what he did, for he arrived within hardly more than fifteen or twenty minutes.

Others were arriving by now. Speaker Rayburn, House Majority Leader John W. McCormack, and House Minority Leader Joseph W. Martin were among them. I tried personally to reach Senator Alben W. Barkley, Senate majority leader, but I could not locate him. I learned later that word of the President's death had reached him promptly and that he had gone at once to see Mrs. Roosevelt. In fact, he was with her in the White House while the group about me was gathering in the Cabinet Room.

There was no time for formalities and protocol. Among the people there were a score or so of officials and members of Congress. Only three women were present — Mrs. Truman and Margaret and Secretary Frances Perkins.

The Cabinet Room in the White House is not extensive. It is dominated by the huge and odd-shaped table, presented to the President by Jesse

Jones, at which the President and the members of the Cabinet sit, and by the leather-upholstered armchairs that are arranged around it.

Steve Early, Jonathan Daniels, and others of the President's secretarial staff were searching for a Bible for me to hold when Chief Justice Stone administered the oath of office.

We were in the final days of the greatest war in history — a war so vast that few corners of the world had been able to escape being engulfed by it. There were none who did not feel its effects. In that war the United States had created military forces so enormous as to defy description, yet now, when the nation's greatest leader in that war lay dead, and a simple ceremony was about to acknowledge the presence of his successor in the nation's greatest office, only two uniforms were present. These were worn by Fleet Admiral Leahy and General Fleming, who, as Public Works Administrator, had been given duties that were much more civilian in character than military.

So far as I know, this passed unnoticed at the time, and the very fact that no thought was given to it demonstrates convincingly how firmly the concept of the supremacy of the civil authority is accepted in our land.

By now a Bible had been found. It was placed near where I stood at the end of the great table. Mrs. Truman and Margaret had not joined me for over an hour after I had called them, having gone first to see Mrs. Roosevelt. They were standing side by side now, at my left, while Chief Justice Stone had taken his place before me at the end of the table. Clustered about me and behind were nine members of the Cabinet, while Speaker Rayburn and a few other members of Congress took positions behind Chief Justice Stone. There were others present, but not many.

I picked up the Bible and held it in my left hand. Chief Justice Stone raised his right hand and gave the oath as it is written in the Constitution.

With my right hand raised, I repeated it after him:

"I, Harry S. Truman, do solemnly swear that I will faithfully execute the office of President of the United States, and will to the best of my ability, preserve, protect and defend the Constitution of the United States."

I dropped my hand.

The clock beneath Woodrow Wilson's portrait marked the time at 7:09.

Less than two hours before, I had come to see the President of the United States, and now, having repeated that simply worded oath, I myself was President.

The ceremony at which I had taken the oath of office had lasted hardly more than a minute, but a delay followed while the inevitable official photographs were taken. Then, after most of those present had gripped my hand — often without a word, so great were their pent-up emotions — and after Mrs. Truman and Margaret had left, everyone else withdrew except the members of the Cabinet.

We took our places around the table, though

Postmaster General Walker's chair was vacant, for he was ill, and as we did so, Secretary Early entered. The press, he explained, wanted to know if the San Francisco conference on the United Nations would meet, as had been planned, on April 25.

I did not hesitate a second. I told Early that the conference would be held as President Roosevelt had directed. There was no question in my mind that the conference had to take place. It was of supreme importance that we build an organization to help keep the future peace of the world. It was the first decision I made as President.

When Early had left, I spoke to the Cabinet. I told them briefly, as I had already told some of them individually, that I would be pleased if all of them would remain in their posts. It was my intention, I said, to continue both the foreign and the domestic policies of the Roosevelt administration. I made it clear, however, that I would be President in my own right and that I would assume full responsibility for such decisions as had to be made. I told them that I hoped they would not hesitate to give me their advice — that I would be glad to listen to them. I left them in no doubt that they could differ with me if they felt it necessary, but that all final policy decisions would be mine. I added that once such decisions had been made I expected them to support me. When there is a change in administration, there are bound to be some changes in the Cabinet, but I knew how necessary it was for me to keep an open mind on all the members of the Cabinet until we had had an opportunity to work together. Their experience with President Roosevelt and their knowledge were necessary to me in this crisis.

I intended, also, to maintain a similar attitude toward the heads of all the federal agencies. But I had some mental reservations about the heads of certain temporary war agencies.

That first meeting of the Cabinet was short, and when it adjourned, the members rose and silently made their way from the room — except for Secretary Stimson.

He asked to speak to me about a most urgent matter. Stimson told me that he wanted me to know about an immense project that was under way — a project looking to the development of a new explosive of almost unbelievable destructive power. That was all he felt free to say at the time, and his statement left me puzzled. It was the first bit of information that had come to me about the atomic bomb, but he gave me no details. It was not until the next day that I was told enough to give me some understanding of the almost incredible developments that were under way and the awful power that might soon be placed in our hands.

That so vast an enterprise had been successfully kept secret even from the members of Congress was a miracle. I had known, and probably others had, that something that was unusually important was brewing in our war plants. Many months before, as part of the work of the Committee to Investigate the National Defense Program, of which I was chairman, I had had investigators going into war plants all over the country. I had even sent investigators into Tennessee and the state of Washington with instructions to find out what certain enormous constructions were and what their purpose was.

At that time, when these investigators were sent out, Secretary Stimson had phoned me to say that he wanted to have a private talk with me. I told him that I would come to his office at once, but he said he would rather come to see me.

As soon as he arrived, I learned that the subject he had in mind was connected with the immense installations I had sent the committee representatives to investigate in Tennessee and the state of Washington.

"Senator," the Secretary told me as he sat beside my desk, "I can't tell you what it is, but it is the greatest project in the history of the world. It is most top secret. Many of the people who are actually engaged in the work have no idea what it is, and we who do would appreciate your not going into those plants."

I had long known Henry L. Stimson to be a great American patriot and statesman.

"I'll take you at your word," I told him. "I'll order the investigations into those plants called off."

I did so at once, and I was not to learn anything whatever as to what that secret was until the Secretary spoke to me after that first Cabinet meeting. The next day Jimmy Byrnes, who until shortly before had been Director of War Mobilization for President Roosevelt, came to see me, and even he told me few details, though with great solemnity he said that we were perfecting an explosive great enough to destroy the whole world. It was later, when Vannevar Bush, head of the Office of Scientific Research and Development, came to the White House, that I was given a scientist's version of the atomic bomb.

Admiral Leahy was with me when Dr. Bush told me this astonishing fact.

"That is the biggest fool thing we have ever done," he observed in his sturdy, salty manner. "The bomb will never go off, and I speak as an expert in explosives."

But on my first evening as President my principal concern was about the San Francisco conference. After the Cabinet meeting Stettinius, Early, and Daniels suggested that something needed to be done further to reassure our allies and the world that the San Francisco conference would be held as planned. We went to the Oval Room of the executive office to discuss the matter.

I felt strongly about the idea on which the United Nations organization was based and had been supporting it in every way I could on the Hill. I wanted to scotch any rumors or fears in the United States and abroad that there would be any changes in the plans that had been made. It was with that in mind that I decided to issue a statement at once, reassuring our allies of my support of the coming conference.

Meanwhile the White House correspondents were asking for a press conference, since they were not present when I took the oath of office.

"For the time being," I told Steve Early to inform them, "I prefer not to hold a press conference. It will be my effort to carry on as I believe the President would have done, and to that end I have asked the Cabinet to stay on with me."

During those first few hours, painful as they were because of our tragic loss, my mind kept turning to the task I had inherited and to the grave responsibilities that confronted our nation at that critical moment in history. From my reading of American history I knew there was no cut-and-dried answer to the question of what obligations a President by inheritance had in regard to the program of his predecessor — especially a program on which a great President had recently been re-elected for the fourth time.

Fortunately that program was no problem for me. I had not only been elected on the platform in which it had been outlined and which I had helped write at the Chicago convention, but also I believed in it firmly and without reservation. Its principal objectives were to win the war through co-ordinated military and economic action with our allies; to win an organized peace, along lines already laid down during the war years, in close co-operation with our allies and other peace-loving nations; and at home to operate the government in the interest of all the people.

I always fully supported the Roosevelt program — both international and domestic — but I knew that certain major administrative weaknesses existed. President Roosevelt often said he was no administrator. He was a man of vision and ideas, and he preferred to delegate administration to others — sometimes to others who were not ideally suited to carry out what he had in mind. I was well aware of this, and even on that first day I knew that I would eventually have to make changes, both in the Cabinet and in administrative policy.

Many problems confronted me, and I was tired. Within half an hour of the time the Cabinet meeting adjourned, I left for our apartment at 4701 Connecticut Avenue.

When I arrived, I found Mrs. Truman, Margaret, and Mrs. Truman's mother, Mrs. Wallace, at the apartment of General Jeff Davis, our next door neighbor. The Davises had had a ham and turkey dinner that evening, and they gave us something to eat. I do not know when Mrs. Truman and Margaret had eaten last, but I had had nothing since noon. Shortly, we returned to our apartment, where I went to bed and to sleep.

On April 13 I began my first full day in office. I was up at six-thirty and at nine o'clock, after a walk and breakfast, I left for the White House with Hugh Fulton, who had served as my counsel on the Truman Committee and who had been waiting with the Secret Service men until I was ready to leave.

My first official business was with Secretary of

State Edward R. Stettinius, Jr., who reported to me on current diplomatic matters and discussed some of the plans for the coming United Nations Conference at San Francisco.

Stettinius informed me that at President Roosevelt's request the State Department prepared for the President each day a two-page summary of the important diplomatic developments, and he handed me the current report.* He asked whether I wished to have this daily summary continued, and he informed me that an up-to-date reference book on the major points of the foreign policies of the United States was being prepared for me.

I told Stettinius that I would welcome both the daily summary and the reference book, but I requested him to let me have that same day an outline of the background and the present status of the principal problems confronting this government in its relations with other countries. These written reports, along with material from other departments and from the Joint Chiefs of Staff, came to me regularly from then on and were immensely helpful in filling gaps in my information. In fact, they were indispensable as aids in dealing with many issues, and from the first I studied them with the greatest care. Night after night I went over them in detail and never went to bed until I had thoroughly digested the information they contained.

*This supplemented the verbal report of the Secretary to the President.

Only a little while after Secretary Stettinius left, I met with the military leaders for the first time. It was eleven o'clock when Secretary of War Stimson and Secretary of the Navy Forrestal came in with General George C. Marshall, Army Chief of Staff, Admiral Ernest J. King, Chief of Naval Operations, Lieutenant General Barney M. Giles of the Air Force, and Admiral William D. Leahy, Chief of Staff to the President. I knew and respected all these men, and it was comforting to know that I would be advised by leaders of such ability and distinction.

In their report to me they were brief and to the point. Germany, they told me, would not be finally overcome for another six months at least. Japan would not be conquered for another year and a half. Their summary covered our far-flung military operations, but there was little detailed examination of our various positions. Everywhere, it appeared, our forces and those of our allies were doing well.

It did not take them long to give me the latest war developments and prospects, and when they had finished, I told them that I considered it urgent to send some word to our armed forces as to what they could expect from me. I added, however, that before doing so I thought I should first address Congress. As the new Chief Executive, I wanted the support of the legislative arm of the government, as I wished to assure our people, our armed forces, and our allies that we would continue our efforts unabated.

The military leaders agreed, and as they were leaving I asked Admiral Leahy to remain with me.

Leahy had occupied a unique position in the White House under President Roosevelt. He was a man of wide experience and was well known for his directness of expression and independence of judgment. Direct in manner and blunt in expression, he typified the Navy at its best, and Roosevelt had appointed him to act in a highly confidential role as chief of staff to the Commander in Chief. Prior to World War II there had been no such position in our government, but in Leahy's hands it soon proved to be immensely useful.

When the others had left, I told him that I would like to have him continue in a similar capacity under me.

"Are you sure you want me, Mr. President?" he asked. "I always say what's on my mind."

"I want the truth," I told him, "and I want the facts at all times. I want you to stay with me and always to tell me what's on your mind. You may not always agree with my decisions, but I know you will carry them out faithfully."

With Admiral Leahy in the White House, I felt that, whether they were good or bad, all the information and communications bearing on the war would reach me promptly. Furthermore, I felt convinced that he would see that I got the facts without suppression or censorship from any source.

The admiral looked at me with a warm twinkle in his eyes.

"You have my pledge," he told me. "You can count on me."

When Leahy left, I reached for the telephone

and called Les Biffle again. During my years as senator I had worked closely with Biffle. He was always unusually well-informed on legislative matters and was a parliamentarian who intimately understood the shadings and opinions of the dominant figures on the Hill. When I had called him earlier, I had asked him to arrange a luncheon in his office that noon with the leaders of Congress. I was anxious to meet the policy-making heads of both parties so that I might tell them of my earnest desire and need for the fullest co-operation between the legislative and the executive branches of the government.

I drove to the Capitol, surrounded and followed, as I was to be from that time on, by my ever-present Secret Service guards, and shortly after noon we sat down to lunch in Biffle's office — thirteen senators, four members of the House of Representatives, Les Biffle, and the very new President of the United States.

I had come, I told them, in order to ask that a joint session of the Senate and the House be arranged so that I might address them in person. It would not be fitting, of course, to call such a meeting until the funeral of Franklin Roosevelt had been held, but I suggested that they make the necessary arrangements as soon as possible thereafter — Monday, April 16, three days hence.

Some of the group were opposed, and others were doubtful. Most, however, were in agreement. I asked each one for his opinion and listened carefully to what they had to say. I then outlined my reasons for considering it imperative to let the nation know through Congress that I proposed to continue the policies of the late President. I felt that it was important, too, to ask for continued bi-partisan support of the conduct of the war.

The points I made appeared convincing, for those who had been doubtful now expressed their agreement.

"Harry," remarked one senator with whom I had long worked closely, "you were planning to come whether we liked it or not."

"You know I would have," I replied, "but I would rather do it with your full and understanding support and welcome."

As I was leaving the Senate office, a long line of white-shirted page boys gathered outside to greet me. Reporters crowded in and joined the line as well, and I shook hands with every one of them.

"Boys," I said, "if you ever pray, pray for me now. I don't know whether you fellows ever had a load of hay fall on you, but when they told me yesterday what had happened, I felt like the moon, the stars, and all the planets had fallen on me. I've got the most terribly responsible job a man ever had."

"Good luck, Mr. President," said one of the reporters.

"I wish you didn't have to call me that," I told him.

I turned away from that long line of serious faces and entered the Senate cloakroom. I looked into the empty Senate Chamber and entered the silent vice-presidential office. These were the surroundings in which I had spent ten active, happy years. In a way, this had been my political home, and here I had experienced the most exciting adventure I had ever expected to have. Less than twenty-four hours before, I had been here presiding over the Senate. But now I was President of the United States and had to return to the White House, there to take over the job in which my great predecessor had only yesterday been stricken.

My real concern at the moment, however, was divided between the war situation on the one hand and the problems of the coming peace on the other. We were close to victory, but the situation that would follow was not so clear. Already I was coming to be more fully informed on the most important and pressing problems in this complicated field, for I had been reading many documents and diplomatic messages that were being brought to me. I could see that there were more difficulties ahead. Already we were at odds with the Soviet government over the question of setting up a truly representative Polish government, and there were troubles in other areas. Many of these seemed to indicate an ominous trend. The next few months, I knew, could well be decisive in our effort to achieve an orderly world, reasonably secure in peace.

My desk was piled with papers, and all through the day I had been alternately reading and conferring. I have always been a heavy reader, and it is easy for me to concentrate. Fortunately, too, my memory is retentive, and this helped me greatly as I conferred with advisers and experts or found it necessary to make decisions. Nevertheless, on that first full day as President I did more reading than I ever thought I could. I even selected some papers to take home so that I might study them before retiring and upon waking. This was the first step in a routine of nightly work that I found to be one of the most trying but also one of the necessary duties of a President.

It was now evening, and I was weary. I picked up the papers I had decided to take with me, and as I left my desk I heard a loud buzzing. It was the signal to the Secret Service, who now came through the corridors to escort me home. An automobile was waiting for me at the Executive Avenue entrance — a closed car that was followed by a long, open one which carried the Secret Service men, some of whom rode standing on the running board.

Kind and considerate as the Secret Service men were in the performance of their duty, I couldn't help feeling uncomfortable. There was no escaping the fact that my privacy and personal freedom were to be greatly restricted from now on. I even began to realize, as I rode toward my apartment that evening, that our neighbors were beginning to be imposed upon. They were no longer able to come and go as they pleased. To enter their own homes it was now necessary for them to be properly identified and cleared by the Secret Service men.

They were all very nice about it, but Mrs. Truman and I felt that the sooner we could move to an official residence the easier it would be on neighbors and friends, from many of whom we hated to part. Furthermore, it was now necessary for me to be available at all times for messages and official callers, and such business could not be adequately conducted in an apartment house on Connecticut Avenue.

I had told Mrs. Roosevelt that Mrs. Truman and I had no intention of moving into the White House until she had had all the time necessary in which to make other arrangements. In the meantime, Blair House, which stands across Pennsylvania Avenue from the White House and which serves as an official guest house for foreign dignitaries visiting Washington, was being made ready for us as our temporary official residence.

On Saturday morning, April 14, I arose at dawn. I have always been an early riser, but this was earlier than usual. The body of Franklin Roosevelt was to arrive that morning from Warm Springs, Georgia, and I was going to the Union Station to meet the funeral train.

I got to the White House at 8:30 A.M. and was met by Steve Early and Bill Simmons. When I reached my desk I found many telegrams and communications already there, and I read as many as I could before nine o'clock, when my first appointment was scheduled.

My first visitor that morning was John W. Snyder of St. Louis. He was one of my closest personal friends, and I already knew that I wanted him in my administration in a trusted capacity. There was an important post vacant — that of Federal Loan Administrator, from which, not long before, Fred Vinson had resigned to become Director of War Mobilization and Reconversion — and Snyder was ideally fitted for it. He was an experienced banker who had been executive assistant to RFC Administrator Jesse Jones and the director of the Defense Plants Corporation.

"I don't think you ought to appoint me to that job," he told me when I had explained what I had in mind. "I'm not sure I am the right man."

"I think you are the right man for the place," I replied. "I'm sending your name to the Senate."

Later I telephoned Jesse Jones and said "the President" had appointed Snyder as Federal Loan Administrator.

"Did he make that appointment before he died?" asked Jones.

"No," I answered. "He made it just now."

Everyone, including myself, still continued to think of Roosevelt as "the President."

When Snyder left, Secretary of the Treasury Morgenthau came in for a brief conference. He was with me only a few minutes, and I asked him to submit to me as soon as possible a comprehensive report on the state of the nation's finances. Secretary of Commerce Wallace and Justice Byrnes joined me, and presently the three of us left for the Union Station. Mrs. Truman and Margaret were making arrangements to leave with me that evening for Hyde Park in order to be present at the interment of President Roosevelt. For that reason they were unable to go with me to the station.

The train bearing the body of Franklin

Roosevelt arrived at Union Station at ten o'clock. I went aboard at once, accompanied by Wallace and Byrnes, and we paid our respects to Mrs. Roosevelt, who had accompanied the body from Warm Springs. Brigadier General Elliott Roosevelt and Anna Roosevelt Boettiger were with their mother, and present also were Colonel John Boettiger and some of the younger members of the Roosevelt family.

The body of the late President was to lie in state during the day in the East room of the White House, and as the funeral procession was formed I took the place that had been assigned to me. Slowly we moved through the streets that were massed with mourners all the way to the White House.

I shall never forget the sight of so many grief-stricken people. Some wept without restraint. Some shed their tears in silence. Others were grim and stoic, but all were genuine in their mourning. It was impossible now to tell who had been for him and who had not. Throughout that enormous throng all of them were expressing their sense of loss and sadness at the passing of a remarkable man.

I saw an old Negro woman with her apron to her eyes as she sat on the curb. She was crying as if she had lost her son, and when the cortege passed along Constitution Avenue, most of those who lined the street were in tears.

The procession reached the White House at eleven o'clock, and the flag-draped casket was borne into the East Room. It was placed before a french door, banked high with lilies, roses, and other flowers. Five members of the armed forces stood guard, with an American flag on a standard at one side of the coffin and the blue presidential banner at the other. Chairs were placed before the bier for members of the immediate family, members of the Cabinet, and other state dignitaries.

Again I paid my respects to Mrs. Roosevelt, and then returned to the executive offices of the White House.

I had been constantly busy since returning to the executive offices. And now, shortly before four o'clock, I was joined by Mrs. Truman and Margaret, who were to go with me to the Executive Mansion for the service that was to be conducted by the Right Reverend Angus Dun, Bishop of the Episcopal Diocese of Washington, before the flag-draped coffin in the East Room.

At Mrs. Roosevelt's request, there were no eulogies. The late President's favorite hymns were sung by all of us, the first being "Eternal Father, Strong to Save." Mrs. Roosevelt asked Bishop Dun to repeat, as part of the service, the expression of faith which President Roosevelt used in his first inaugural address in 1933 — "The only thing we have to fear is fear itself."

At the conclusion of the service, Mrs. Truman, Margaret, and I returned to our apartment, where I rested for a time before resuming the reading of documents and reports.

The body of President Roosevelt was removed from the White House shortly after 9:30 P.M. and, accompanied by Mrs. Roosevelt and her family, was borne to the Union Station and placed again aboard the funeral train.

Mrs. Truman, Margaret, and I boarded the train a little later for the night trip to Hyde Park. Cabinet officers, members of the Supreme Court, military leaders, high government officials, friends of the Roosevelts, and representatives of the press and radio also occupied many of the cars of the long special train that carried the body of Franklin Roosevelt on his last trip home.

We arrived at Hyde Park about nine-thirty on Sunday morning and soon thereafter went to the Roosevelt garden, where the final ceremony took place. There Franklin Delano Roosevelt was buried.

We left for Washington at noon. With us were Mrs. Roosevelt, Anna, Elliott, and other members of the Roosevelt family. Mrs. Roosevelt, wonderfully in command of herself, broke the tension by talking about some of the household problems of the White House which we would have to face. Elliott complained about having been starved by the menus of Mrs. Nesbitt, the White House housekeeper. To which Mrs. Roosevelt replied that Mrs. Nesbitt had been properly trying to keep within the food budget.

The schedule that lay ahead for me was so pressing that I spent a good part of the return journey working on the speech I was to make at the joint session of Congress on the following day. I went over some of the points in the speech with the legislative leaders who were on the train. I discussed others with members of the Roosevelt administration.

Almost every presidential message is a complicated business. Many individuals and departments of the government are called on to take some part in it in order to maintain full co-ordination of policy. Experts and researchers are assigned to check and compile data, because no President can or should rely entirely on his own memory. Careful consideration must be given to every element of a presidential speech because of the impact it may have on the nation or the world.

A speech by the President is one of the principal means of informing the public what the policy of the administration is. Because of this, presidential messages have to be written and rewritten many times.

All presidential messages must begin with the President himself. He must decide what he wants to say and how he wants to say it. Many drafts are usually drawn up, and this fact leads to the assumption that presidential speeches are "ghosted." The final version, however, is the final word of the President himself, expressing his own convictions and his policy. These he cannot delegate to any man if he would be President in his own right.

Back in Washington that evening, I felt that an epoch had come to an end. A great President, whose deeds and words had profoundly affected our times, was gone. Chance had chosen me to carry on his work, and in these three days I had already experienced some of the weight of its unbelieveable burdens.

As I went to bed that night I prayed I would be equal to the task.

ELEANOR ROOSEVELT

from

THE AUTOBIOGRAPHY OF ELEANOR ROOSEVELT

Eleanor Roosevelt (1884–1962) will probably be remembered by history for her early and vigorous support of human rights, speaking out at a time not so long ago when women did not play dominant roles in any major political arenas. She earned her right to speak out in behalf of this great social cause as the wife of Franklin Delano Roosevelt, making the most of her quasi-official position of "First Lady" from 1932 to 1945.

In these two pivotal sections of her autobiography, she recalls two of the most daunting crises of her life: her husband's bout with polio (an illness that prevented him from walking for the rest of his life without heavy iron braces), and the adjustments of her first days in the White House.

Trial by Fire

The summer of 1921 found us all going to Campobello again and various visitors coming up for short or long periods. There was a certain amount of infantile paralysis in some places again that summer, but it was not an epidemic, particularly among children, as it had been a few years before.

My husband did not go up with us, but came early in August, after we were settled, bringing quite a party with him. He did a great deal of navigating on Mr. Van Lear Black's boat, which he had joined on his way up the coast.

While Mr. Black and his party were with us, we were busy and spent days on the water, fishing and doing all we could to give them a pleasant time. My husband loved these waters and always wanted everybody who came up to appreciate the fact that they were ideal for sailing and fishing. The fishing is deep-sea fishing and rather uninteresting unless you go outside and into the Bay of Fundy or have the luck to do some casting into schools of fish as they came in.

Mr. Black had left and we were out sailing one afternoon in the little *Vireo* which my husband had bought after giving up the *Half Moon*, in order that the boys might learn to sail. On our return trip we spied a forest fire, and of course we had to make for shore at once and go fight the fire. We reached home around four o'clock and my husband, who had been complaining of feeling logy and tired for several days, decided it would do him good to go in for a dip in the landlocked lake called Lake Glen Severn, inside the beach on the other side of the island. The children were delighted and they started away. After their swim Franklin took a dip in the Bay of Fundy and ran home.

When they came in, a good deal of mail had arrived and my husband sat around in his bathing suit, which was completely dry, and looked at his mail. In a little while he began to complain that he felt a chill and decided he would not eat supper with us but would go to bed and get thoroughly warm. He wanted to avoid catching cold.

In retrospect I realize he had had no real rest since the war. A hunting trip after the campaign had been strenuous, and plunging back into business had not given him any opportunity to relax and he had been going on his nerves.

We had Mrs. Louis Howe and her small boy, Hartley, staying in the house with us. Mr. Howe arrived a little later. He had stayed in the Navy Department after my husband left, to look after his papers and be of any assistance he could to the incoming assistant secretary, who happened to be Colonel Theodore Roosevelt. When Louis finally left the Navy Department he was considering an offer to go into business on a rather lucrative salary, and decided to take his holiday at Campobello before he made up his mind.

The next day my husband felt less well. He had quite a temperature and I sent for our faithful friend, Dr. Bennett, in Lubec. Dr. Bennett thought my husband had just an ordinary cold and I decided that the best thing to do was to get everybody else off on a camping trip, though I was sufficiently worried not to consider going myself.

The trip lasted three days, and by the time the campers were back it was evident that my husband's legs were getting badly paralyzed. Dr. Bennett wanted a consultation and we found that Dr. Keen was in Bar Harbor, Maine. By now Mr. Howe had arrived and he went with Captain Calder to meet Dr. Keen. Dr. Keen decided that it was some form of paralysis but could not explain it. By this time my husband's lower legs were paralyzed.

For a little while he showed no improvement. The days dragged on and the doctors kept saying he must have a nurse, but it was hard to get one, so I kept on taking care of him and slept on a couch in his room at night. His temperature at times was very high. It required a certain amount of skilled nursing and I was thankful for every bit of training Miss Spring had given me.

Finally my husband's uncle, Frederic Delano, begged us to have the well-known infantile paralysis doctor, Dr. Lovett, come up from Newport. He examined my husband carefully and after consultation told me it was infantile paralysis.

I was in a panic because, besides my own children, we had Mr. Howe's little boy with us. I asked Dr. Lovett what the chances were that some of the children would come down with it. He said that probably none of them would do so since they had not already become ill.

After Dr. Lovett's visit, we finally got a nurse from New York, called Miss Rockey, but Dr. Lovett had been so flattering as to certain aspects of my husband's care, not knowing that I had been the only nurse on the case, that it was decided I should continue to do a certain amount of the nursing. This I did until we were finally able to move him back to New York.

My mother-in-law returned from abroad and came up to see my husband and then returned to New York to get things ready for us. When it was considered safe, we obtained a private car in which to move my husband. Dr. Bennett agreed to go down with us, and it was arranged that the car was to be switched around in Boston so we would be able to go straight into New York without any change. This move required a great deal of planning.

Mr. Howe had made up his mind to give up all idea of taking the position that was open to him and to come back to his old boss, because he saw quite plainly that his help was going to be needed. From that time on he put his whole heart into working for my husband's future. The handling of his mail and the newspapers all fell entirely into Louis's hands.

At first we tried to keep all news out of the papers, not wanting to say anything until we knew something definite about the future. Of course we were anxious to make the trip home as inconspicuous and unsensational as possible. We put Franklin on an improvised stretcher and took him down from the house over the rough ground and stony beach and put him into the small motorboat, chugged two miles across the bay, carried him up the steep gangway, and placed him on one of the drays used for luggage in that northern part of the country. Every jolt was painful, as we walked to the station and the stretcher went into his compartment through the window.

The strain of this trip must have been great for my husband. First of all, a sense of helplessness when you have always been able to look after yourself makes you conscious every minute of the ease with which someone may slip and you may be dropped overboard, in transferring from the dock to the boat. In addition, he had not wanted crowds to witness his departure, and of course there was not only kindly interest in Eastport but there was a certain amount of interest inspired by newspapers in other parts of the country that were trying to find out just what was the matter.

We finally reached New York, and here again my husband was taken out of the car through the window and then by ambulance to the Presbyterian Hospital.

There followed days and weeks at the hospital. Dr. Lovett came occasionally, but his young associate, Dr. George Draper, was in charge most of the time.

The children were all back at school and stopped in to see him every day, with the exception of James, who was in Groton. The time seemed endless but he actually came home before Christmas.

Franklin's mother was really remarkable about this entire illness. It must have been a terrific strain for her, and I am sure that, out of sight, she wept many hours, but with all of us she was very cheerful. She had, however, made up her mind that Franklin was going to be an invalid for the rest of his life and that he would retire to Hyde Park and live there. Her anxiety over his general health was so great that she dreaded his making any effort whatever.

Though Franklin was in bed most of the time, Miss Rockey took charge of him except in the afternoons. Then I had to be at home. He was tall and heavy to lift, but somehow both of us managed to learn to do whatever was necessary. For several weeks that winter his legs were placed in plaster casts in order to stretch the muscles, and every day a little of the cast was chipped out at the back, which stretched the muscles a little bit more. This was torture and he bore it without the slightest complaint, just as he bore his illness from the very beginning. I never but once heard him say anything bordering on discouragement or bitterness. That was some years later, when he was debating whether to do something which would cost considerable money, and he remarked that he supposed it was better to spend the money on the chance that he might not be such a helpless individual.

In many ways this was the most trying winter of my entire life. It was the small personal irritations, as I look back upon them now, that made life so difficult. My mother-in-law thought we were tiring my husband and that he should be kept completely quiet, which made the discussions about his care somewhat acrimonious on occasion. She always thought that she understood what was best, particularly where her child was concerned, regardless of what any doctor might say. I felt that if you placed a patient in a doctor's care you must at least follow out his suggestions and treatment. The house was not overlarge and we were very crowded.

My husband's bedroom was at the back of the house on the third floor, because it was quieter there. I had given my daughter, who was fifteen that winter, the choice of a large room at the front of the third floor, which she would be obliged to share with the nurse during the afternoon and early evening, or a small room on the fourth floor rear, next to Elliott's room. This she would have entirely to herself. She chose the latter.

Mr. Howe took the big room on the third floor, as he had come to live with us during the week, because his wife could find no apartment in New York which was suitable both to their needs and their purse. During the weekends he journeyed to Poughkeepsie, where his wife and little boy were installed in a house and his daughter was at Vassar College. He was downtown most of the day at my husband's office, so the nurse could use his room undisturbed.

We had a connecting door into a room in my mother-in-law's house on the fourth floor, so the two little boys and their nurse had those rooms. This accounted for all the bedrooms and left me with no room. I slept on a bed in one of the little boys' rooms. I dressed in my husband's bathroom. In the daytime I was too busy to need a room.

The boys soon became entirely oblivious of the fact that their father had been ill. By spring he would sit on the floor with the little boys in the library, and they would play with him without the slightest idea that he was not able to do anything he wished to do in the way of roughhousing with them.

Anna, however, felt the strain of the over-crowded house and the atmosphere of anxiety. I had put her in Miss Chapin's School. I canvassed several schools and decided that Miss Chapin had the kind of personality which would appeal to me. I hoped the same relationship would grow up between Anna and Miss Chapin as I had had with Mlle. Souvestre. I did not realize how set and rigid New York schools were and that a girl coming in from outside would be looked upon by all the children as an outsider and would hardly be noticed by the teachers. Anna was very unhappy, though I did not realize it. She felt lost, and the different methods of teaching bewildered her. She tried to hide her feelings by being rather devil-may-care about her marks and her association with the other girls.

Someone had suggested to her that it was unfair that she should have a little fourth-floor room and Mr. Howe should have the large room on the third-floor front. Because of constant outside influences, the situation grew in her mind to a point where she felt that I did not care for her and was not giving her any consideration. It never occurred to her that I had far less than she had. There were times at the dinner table when she would annoy her father so much that he would be severe with her and a scene would ensue, then she would burst into tears and go sobbing to her room.

I knew nothing, of course, of what had been said to her and went on rather blindly thinking that girls of fifteen were far more difficult to bring up than boys.

I realize now that my attitude toward her had been wrong. She was an adolescent girl and I still treated her like a child and thought of her as a child. It never occurred to me to take her into my confidence and consult with her about our difficulties or tell her just what her father was going through in getting his nerves back into condition.

I have always had a bad tendency to shut up like a clam, particularly when things are going badly; and that attitude was accentuated, I think, as regards my children. I had done so much for them and planned everything and managed everything, as far as the household was concerned, for so many years that it never occurred to me that the time comes, particularly with a girl, when it is important to make her your confidante. If I had realized this I might have saved Anna and myself several years of real unhappiness. I would have understood her a great deal better because she would have been able to talk to me freely, and she would have understood me and probably understood her father and all he was fighting against.

As it was, I am responsible for having given her a most unhappy time, and we can both be extremely grateful for the fact that finally the entire situation got on my nerves and one afternoon in the spring, when I was trying to read to the two youngest boys, I suddenly found myself sobbing as I read. I could not think why I was sobbing, nor could I stop. Elliott came in from school, dashed in to look at me and fled. Mr. Howe came in and tried to find out what the matter was, but he gave it up as a bad job. The two little boys went off to bed and I sat on the sofa in the sitting room and sobbed and sobbed. I could not go to dinner in this condition. Finally I found an empty room in my mother-in-law's house, as she had moved to the country. I locked the door and poured cold water on a towel and mopped my face. Eventually I pulled myself together, for it requires an audience, as a rule, to keep on these emotional jags. This is the one and only time I remember in my entire life having gone to pieces in this particular manner. From that time on I seemed to have got rid of nerves and uncontrollable tears, for never again has either of them bothered me.

The effect, however, was rather good on Anna, because she began to straighten out, and at last she poured out some of her troubles and told me she had been wrong and she knew that I loved her and from that day to this our mutual understanding has constantly improved.

Today no one could ask for a better friend than I have in Anna or she has in me. Perhaps because it grew slowly, the bond between us is

413

all the stronger. No one can tell either of us anything about the other; and though we may not always think alike or act alike, we always respect each other's motives, and there is a type of sympathetic understanding between us which would make a real misunderstanding quite impossible.

Dr. Draper felt strongly that it was better for Franklin to make the effort to take an active part in life again and lead, as far as possible, a normal life, with the interests that had always been his. Even if it tired him, it was better for his general condition.

The previous January Franklin had accepted an offer made by Mr. Van Lear Black to become vice-president of the Fidelity and Deposit Company of Baltimore, in charge of the New York office, and he had worked there until his illness. Mr. Black was a warm friend and kept his place for him until he was well enough to resume his work.

Mr. Howe felt that the one way to get my husband's interest aroused was to keep him as much as possible in contact with politics. This seemed to me an almost hopeless task. However, in order to accomplish his ends Mr. Howe began to urge me to do some political work again. I could think of nothing I could do but during the spring I was thrown on two or three occassions with a young woman who interested me considerably. Her name was Marion Dickerman. She was interested in working conditions for women and she taught in a school. I, too, was interested in working conditions for women, harking back to the interests of my girlhood. Mrs. James Lees Laidlaw asked me to attend a luncheon of the Women's Trade Union League and become an associate member. I joined the organization and have been a member ever since. This luncheon was my second contact with some of the women whom I had first met in Washington at the International Conference for Working Women and this resulted in a long association. I have never lost touch with this group. Many of them were interested in politics, and I soon found that Marion Dickerman also was interested.

Through my acquaintance with Miss Dickerman I met her friend Nancy Cook. Miss Cook invited me to preside at a luncheon to raise funds for the women's division of the Democratic State Committee. I had been carrying on to a limited extent my work for the League of Women Voters, but I had never done anything for a political organization before nor had I ever made a speech in any sizable gathering. Here I found myself presiding at a luncheon, without the faintest idea of what I was going to say or what work the organization was really doing. That was the beginning of a warm and lasting friendship with both Miss Dickerman and Miss Cook, and through them I met Miss Harriet May Mills and Mrs. Caroline O'Day and went to work with the Democratic women of New York State.

We moved to Hyde Park, bag and baggage, and spent the whole summer there except for a short time when I took the younger children to

Fairhaven for a change of air and some sea bathing. I did not even stay with them all the time, but there I became conscious of the fact that I had two young boys who had to learn to do the things that boys must do — swim and ride and camp. I had never done any of these things. I had ridden when I was a child, and up to the age of twenty, but that was far behind me. I had no confidence in my ability to do physical things at this time. I could go into the water with the boys but I could not swim. It began to dawn upon me that if these two youngest boys were going to have a normal existence without a father to do these things with them, I would have to become a good deal more companionable and more of an all-round person than I had ever been before.

All that summer at Hyde Park my husband struggled to do a great number of things which would make it possible for him to be more active. He learned to use crutches and walked every day to gain confidence. Each new thing he did took not only determination but great physical effort.

That autumn of 1922 I took Elliott to Groton School. I drove him up myself, unpacked for him and left a much more miserable little boy than even James had been. I felt that he would settle down as James had done. He was far better prepared in his work, for he had had one year at the Buckley School, where he had done very well. He passed his examinations without any conditions. My hopes were vain, however; he never really loved the school as James did.

When we went back to New York, and when

my husband was there, he followed an ordinary businessman's routine. He now had a chauffeur to take him back and forth between his office and our house every day.

Through my interest in the League of Women Voters, the Women's Trade Union League and the Democratic State Committee, where now I had become finance chairman, I was beginning to find the political contacts that Louis wanted. I drove a car on election day and brought people to the polls. I began to learn a good deal about party politics in a small place. It was rather sordid in spots. I worked with our county committee and our associate county chairwoman. I saw how people took money or its equivalent on election day for their votes and how much of the party machinery was geared to crooked business. On the other hand, I saw hard work and unselfish public service and fine people in unexpected places. I learned again that human beings are seldom all good or all bad and that few human beings are incapable of rising to the heights now and then.

We were rid of a trained nurse and we never treated my husband as an invalid. Anna had graduated to the large room and we were much less crowded with James and Elliott at school. In the holidays we usually went to Hyde Park. The whole family relationship was simpler. Anna continued to tell me about things which upset her, and her trials and tribulations away from home, and I was able more intelligently to manage the various elements of our existence.

The boys at school had on the average one

accident each autumn during the football season which would necessitate my bringing them home or taking them to a hospital for a short time. We had, of course, a certain amount of illness among the children at home, but my husband's general health was good and I had not been ill since John was born. There was really no time for me to think of being ill.

In winter my husband had to go south, so for two winters we had a houseboat and cruised around the Florida waters. I went down and spent short periods with him; this was my first glimpse of the South in winter. I had never considered holidays in winter or escape from cold weather an essential part of living, and I looked upon it now as a necessity and not a pleasure. I tried fishing but had no skill and no luck. When we anchored at night and the wind blew, it all seemed eerie and menacing to me. The beauty of the moon and the stars only added to the strangeness of the dark waters and the tropic vegetation, and on occasion it could be colder and more uncomfortable than tales of the sunny South led me to believe was possible. Key West was the one place I remember as having real charm.

In New York I had begun to do a fairly regular job for the women's division of the Democratic State Committee and was finding work very satisfactory and acquiring pride in doing a semiprofessional job. We started a small mimeographed paper with which Mr. Howe gave me considerable help. We finally had it printed, and in an effort to make it pay for itself I learned a great deal about advertising, circulation, and make-up. From Mr. Howe I learned how to make a dummy for the printer, and though he never considered I was really capable of writing the headlines, I became quite proficient in planning, pasting, and so on.

Miss Cook and Miss Dickerman and I had become friends in just the way that Miss Lape and Miss Read and I had been first drawn together through the work we were doing. This is one of the most satisfactory ways of making and keeping friends.

Many of my old friends I saw very little, because they led more or less social lives. I had dropped out of what is known as society entirely, as we never went out. Now and then I would go to the theater with a friend, but my free hours were few. Ever since the war my interest had been in doing real work, not in being a dilettante. I gradually found myself more and more interested in workers, less and less interested in my old associates, who were busy doing a variety of things but were doing no job in a professional way.

Slowly a friendship grew with a young couple who lived in Dutchess County, New York, not far from us — Mr. and Mrs. Henry Morgenthau, Jr. The were younger and perhaps for that reason we did not at first see so much of one another. We had many interests in common in the county, and Mr. Morgenthau and my husband were thrown more and more together. Mrs. Morgenthau came eventually to work in the women's division of the Democratic State Committee, and she and I grew gradually to have a warm affection for each other. Good things are all the better for ripening slowly, but today this friendship with Elinor and Henry Morgenthau is one of the things I prize most highly.

During these years I also came to know Mrs. Carrie Chapman Catt, Mrs. Raymond Brown, Mrs. Louis Slade, Mrs. Henry Goddard Leach, Lillian Wald, Mary Simkovitch and many other women who had a great influence on me. To all of them I shall be deeply grateful always for opening up so many new avenues of thought and work.

I was beginning to make occasional speeches and on various occasions Louis Howe went with me and sat at the back of the audience and gave me pointers on what I should say and how I should say it. I had a bad habit, because I was nervous, of laughing when there was nothing to laugh at. He broke me of that by showing me how inane it sounded. His advice was: "Have something you want to say, say it, and sit down."

Under Mrs. O'Day, who was vice-chairman of the Democratic State Committee, I did a certain amount of organization work each summer among the Democratic women of the state. I usually went with either Miss Dickerman or Miss Cook. I paid my own traveling expenses and so did Mrs. O'Day; because money-raising was hard for women we felt every expense must be kept down. Miss Cook did wonders of economical management. All the work among the women had been started by Miss Harriet May Mills, who for many years was the outstanding Democratic woman leader of New York State. Even after her retirement as vice-chairman of the state committee, she responded to every call for assistance. I was always glad of this experience because I came to know my state, the people who lived in it, and rural and urban conditions extremely well.

Since his illness my husband had undertaken the presidency of the Boy Scout Foundation, the presidency of the American Construction Council, the chairmanship of the American Legion campaign, and a number of other nonpolitical activities. His only political effort during those years was in the summer of 1922 when he helped to persuade Al Smith to run again for the governorship.

He wes entirely well and lived a normal life, restricted only by his inability to walk. On the whole, his general physical condition improved year by year, until he was stronger in some ways than before his illness. He always went away in the winter for a time and in summer for a long vacation, trying in each case either to take treatment or at least to keep up exercises which would improve his ability to get about. In the spring of 1924, before the National Democratic Convention met in New York, Al Smith, who was a candidate for the presidential nomination, asked him to manage his preconvention campaign. This was the first time that my husband was to be in the public eye since his illness. A thousand and one little arrangements had to be made and Louis carefully planned each step of the way.

I had been asked to take charge of the committee to present to the resolutions committee of the convention some of the planks of interest to women. This was to be a new step in my education. I knew a little now about local politics, a good deal through the League of Women Voters and, through my Democratic organization work, about my state legislature and state politics, and I was to see for the first time where women stood when it came to a national convention. They stood outside the door of all important meetings and waited. I did get my resolutions in, but how much consideration they got was veiled in mystery.

I heard rumors of all kinds of maneuvers and all the different things that the men were talking about drifted my way, but most of the time at the convention I sat and knitted, suffered with the heat, and wished it would end.

At this convention I caught my first glimpse of Will Rogers when he wandered by the box one day and asked, "Knitting in the names of the future victims of the guillotine?" I felt like saying that I was almost ready to call any punishment down on the heads of those who could not bring the convention to a close.

Finally, in spite of all that could be done, in spite of a really fine nominating speech by my husband and the persuasion and influence of many other people in the convention, Al Smith lost the nomination. My husband stepped gracefully out of the political picture, though he did make one or two speeches for John W. Davis.

And so ended the early phases of the education

of Eleanor Roosevelt, both in life and in politics.

The First Year: 1933

During the early White House days when I was busy with organizing my side of the household, my husband was meeting one problem after another. It had a most exhilarating effect on him. Decisions were being made, new ideas were being tried, people were going to work and businessmen who ordinarily would have scorned government assistance were begging the government to find solutions for their problems.

What was interesting to me about the administration of those days was the willingness of everyone to co-operate with everyone else. As conditions grew better, of course, people's attitudes changed, but fundamentally it was that spirit of co-operation that pulled us out of the depression. Congress, which traditionally never has a long honeymoon with a new president, even when the political majority is of his party, went along during those first few months, delegating powers to the President and passing legislation that it would never have passed except during a crisis.

Soon after the inauguration of 1933 we began to have a succession of visitors whom after dinner Franklin would take upstairs to his study. There were two reasons why these particular people were invited to the White House those first years. One was that the economic and political situation in the world made it necesary for him to establish contacts with the leaders of other countries; the other was his desire to build new contacts for better understanding on this continent and abroad.

For the heads of nations, Franklin worked out a reception which he thought made them feel that the United States recognized the importance of their governments. If the guests arrived in the afternoon we had tea for the entire party; afterwards, all but the most important guests went to a hotel or to their own embassy. Later Blair House, across Pennsylvania Avenue, was acquired by the government and arranged for the use of important visitors. The head of a government spent one night in the White House, accompanied by his wife if she was with him. There usually was a state dinner with conversation or music afterwards. The following morning Franklin and his guest would often have another talk before the guest went over to Blair House or to his embassy.

One of our first guests in 1933 was Ramsay MacDonald, who came with his daughter, Ishbel. We enjoyed meeting him, but even then we sensed in him a certain weariness. The loss of his wife had been a great blow to him. In many ways his daughter was a more vivid and vital person than he.

I think Franklin believed even then that it was important for the English-speaking nations of the world to understand one another, whether the crisis was economic or, as later, military. This did not mean that he always agreed with the policies of these other countries; but he recognized the importance to us and to them of good feeling and understanding and co-operation.

The prime minister of Canada also came to stay with us that first spring, so that he and my husband and the prime minister of Great Britain could more or less co-ordinate their common interests.

In the same period Edouard Herriot, the French statesman, also arrived in Washington. As I look over the lists of what seems to be an unbelievable number of guests that first year, I find that we received an Italian mission, a German mission, and a Chinese mission, and even a Japanese envoy who came to lunch. Other guests included the governor general of the Philippines, Frank Murphy, later on the Supreme Court, who brought with him Manuel Quezon; the prime minister of New Zealand, who came with his wife to lunch; and His Highness Prince Ras Desta Dember, special ambassador of the Emperor of Ethiopia.

The President of Panama also paid us a visit. He was not the only guest from our own hemisphere. There was a stag dinner for the Brazilian delegation; we received a special ambassador from the Argentine; the Mexican envoy came to lunch; and the Brazilian envoy returned, after a trip through the country, to report on his travels.

Franklin had a deep conviction that we must learn to understand and to get on with our neighbors in this hemisphere. He believed it was up to us, who had been to blame in many ways for a big brother attitude which was not acceptable to our neighbors, to make the first effort. So even at that early date he was beginning to lay down through personal contacts the policy of the Good Neighbor, which was to become of increasing importance.

From the time we moved to Washington in 1933, Louis Howe became more and more of an invalid. At first he was able to be in his office and to keep his finger on much that was going on, and the second bonus march on Washington by the veterans of World War I he handled personally.

The first march, which had taken place in Mr. Hoover's administration, was still fresh in everybody's mind. I shall never forget my feeling of horror when I learned that the Army had actually been ordered to evict the veterans from their encampment. In the chaos that followed, the veterans' camp on the Anacostia flats was burned and many people were injured, some of them seriously. This one incident shows what fear can make people do, for Mr. Hoover was a Quaker, who abhorred violence, and General MacArthur, his chief of staff, must have known how many veterans would resent the order and never forget it. They must have known, too, the effect it would have on public opinion.

When the second bonus march took place in March of 1933 I was greatly worried for fear nothing would be done to prevent a similar tragedy. However, after talking the situation over with Louis Howe, Franklin immediately decided that the veterans should be housed in an old camp and provided with food through the relief administration. Louis spent hours talking with the leaders. I think they held their meetings in a government auditorium and were heard by the proper people in Congress. As a result, everything was orderly.

Although Louis often asked me to take him for a drive in the afternoon, I was rather surprised one day when he insisted that I drive him out to the veterans' camp just off Potomac Drive. When we arrived he announced that he was going to sit in the car but that I was to walk around among the veterans and see just how things were. Hesitatingly I got out and walked over to where I saw a line-up of men waiting for food. They looked at me curiously and one of them asked my name and what I wanted. When I said I just wanted to see how they were getting on, they asked me to join them.

After their bowls were filled with food, I followed them into the big eating hall. I was invited to say a few words to them — I think I mentioned having gone over the battle fronts in 1919 — and then they sang for me some of the old army songs. After lunch I was asked to look into several other buildings, and finally we came to the hospital that had been set up for them.

I did not spend as much as an hour there; then I got into the car and drove away. Everyone waved and I called, "Good luck," and they answered, "Good-by and good luck to you." There had been no excitement, and my only protection had been a weary gentleman, Louis Howe, who had slept in the car during my entire visit.

Most of us who watched Louis could tell that he was failing. He sat a good deal of the time in his room, surrounded by newspapers, but up to the last few months his advice was still valuable. He died on April 18, 1936, at the naval hospital in Washington. He had lived in the White House until a short time before his death.

I always felt that the loss of Louis's influence and knowledge and companionship was a great blow to my husband. Louis had seemed to have an acute sense of the need for keeping a balance in Franklin's appointments, making sure that my husband saw a cross section of people and heard a variety of points of view. While Louis was alive, I had fewer complaints from various groups that they had been excluded than ever again. Considering how many people want to see the President and how hard it is to keep some semblance of balance, I think Louis did a remarkable job. He tried to see that all points of view reached Franklin so that he would make no decision without full consideration.

The President's wife does not go out informally except on rare occasions to old friends. Now and then, in the spring, Elinor Morgenthau and I stole away in my car or hers, and stopped in at some little place for lunch or tea. Driving my own car was one of the issues the Secret Service people and I had a battle about at the very start. The Secret Service prefers to have an agent go with the President's wife, but I did not want either a chauffeur or a Secret Service agent always with me; I never did consent to have a Secret Service agent.

After the head of the Secret Service found I was not going to allow an agent to accompany me everywhere, he went one day to Louis Howe, plunked a revolver down on the table and said, "Well all right, if Mrs. Roosevelt is going to drive around the country alone, at least ask her to carry this in the car." I carried it religiously and during the summer I asked a friend, a man who had been one of Franklin's bodyguards in New York State, to give me some practice in target shooting so that if the need arose I would know how to use the gun. After considerable practice, I finally learned to hit a target. I would never have used it on a human being, but I thought I ought to know how to handle a revolver if I had to have one in my posession.

Always, when my husband and I met after a trip that either of us had taken, we tried to arrange for an uninterrupted meal so that we could hear the whole story while it was fresh and not dulled by repetition. That I became, as the years went by, a better reporter and a better observer was largely owing to the fact that Franklin's questions covered such a wide range. I found myself obliged to notice everything. For instance, when I returned from a trip around the Gaspé, he wanted to know not only what kind of fishing and hunting was possible in that area but what the life of the fisherman was, what he had to eat, how he lived, what the farms were like, how the houses were built, what type of education was available, and whether it was completely church-controlled like the rest of the life in the village.

When I spoke of Maine, he wanted to know about everything I had seen on the farms I visited, the kinds of homes and the types of people, how the Indians seemed to be getting on and where they came from.

Franklin never told me I was a good reporter nor, in the early days, were any of my trips made at his request. I realized, however, that he would not question me so closely if he were not interested, and I decided this was the only way I could help him, outside of running the house, which was soon organized and running itself under Mrs. Nesbitt.

In the autumn I was invited by the Quakers to investigate the conditions that they were making an effort to remedy in the coal-mining areas of West Virginia. My husband agreed that it would be a good thing to do, so the visit was arranged. I had not been photographed often enough then to be recognized, so I was able to spend a whole day going about the area near Morgantown, West Virginia, without anyone's discovering who I was.

The conditions I saw convinced me that with a little leadership there could develop in the mining areas, if not a people's revolution, at least a people's party patterned after some of the previous parties born of bad economic conditions. There were men in that area who had been on relief for from three to five years and who had almost forgotten what it was like to have a job at which they could work for more than one or two days a week. There were children who did not know what it was to sit down at a table and eat a proper meal.

One story which I brought home from that trip I recounted at the dinner table one night. In a company house I visited, where the people had evidently seen better days, the man showed me his weekly pay slips. A small amount had been deducted toward his bill at the company store and for his rent and for oil for his mine lamp. These deductions left him less than a dollar in cash each week. There were six children in the family, and they acted as though they were afraid of strangers. I noticed a bowl on the table filled with scraps, the kind that you and I might give to a dog, and I saw children, evidently looking for their noonday meal, take a handful out of that bowl and go out munching. That was all they had to eat.

As I went out, two of the children had gathered enough courage to stand by the door, the little boy holding a white rabbit in his arms. It was evident that it was a most cherished pet. The little girl was thin and scrawny, and had a gleam in her eyes as she looked at her brother. She said, "He thinks we are not going to eat it, but we are," and at that the small boy fled down the road clutching the rabbit closer than ever.

It happened that William C. Bullitt was at dinner that night and I have always been grateful to him for the check he sent me the next day, saying he hoped it might help to keep the rabbit alive.

This trip to the mining areas was my first

contact with the work being done by the Quakers. I liked the theory of trying to put people to work to help themselves. The men were started on projects and taught to use their abilities to develop new skills. The women were encouraged to revive any household arts they might once have known but which they had neglected in the drab life of the mining village.

This was only the first of many trips into the mining districts but it was the one that started the homestead idea. The University of West Virginia, in Morgantown, had already created a committee to help the miners on the Quaker agricultural project. With that committee and its experience as a nucleus, the government obtained the loan of one of the university's people, Mr. Bushrod Grimes, and established the Resettlement Administration. Louis Howe created a small advisory committee on which I, Mr. Pickett, and others served. It was all experimental work, but it was designed to get people off relief, to put them to work building their own homes and to give them enough land to start growing food.

It was hoped that business would help by starting on each of these projects an industry in which some of the people could find regular work. A few small industries were started but they were not often successful. Only a few of the resettlement projects had any measure of success; nevertheless, I have always felt that the good they did was incalculable. Conditions were so nearly the kind that breed revolution that the men and women needed to be made to feel their government's interest and concern.

I began to hear very serious reports of conditions in Logan County, West Virginia, where for many years whole families had been living in tents because they had been evicted from company houses after a strike. All the men had been blacklisted and could not get work anywhere; they were existing on the meager allowance that the State of West Virginia provided for the unemployed. Now the tents were worn out, illness was rampant, and no one had any medical care. Finally Mrs. Leonard Elmhirst and I established a clinic to take care of the children. When I told my husband of the conditions there he said to talk to Harry Hopkins and to tell him that these families must be out of tents by Christmas. It was done, and for two years, out of my radio money and Mrs. Elmhirst's generosity, we tried to remedy among the children the effects of conditions which had existed for many years.

I came to know very well a stream near Morgantown called Scott's Run, or Bloody Run, because of the violent strikes that once occurred in the mines there. Some of the company houses, perched on hills on either side of the run, seemed scarcely fit for human habitation. The homestead project started near Morgantown was called Arthurdale and took in people from all of the nearby mining villages.

One of the first people to go to Arthurdale was Bernard M. Baruch, who helped me to establish the original school and always took a great interest in the project, even visiting it without me on some occasions. I have always hoped that he got as much satisfaction as I did out of the change in the children after they had been living on the project for six months.

The homestead projects were attacked in Congress, for the most part by men who had never seen for themselves the plight of the miners or what we were trying to do for them. There is no question that much money was spent, perhaps some of it unwisely. The projects were all experimental. In Arthurdale, for instance, though the University of West Virginia recommended the site, apparently nobody knew what was afterwards discovered — that there was a substratum of porous rock which finally caused great expense in making the water supply safe. Nevertheless, I have always felt that many human beings who might have cost us thousands of dollars in tuberculosis sanitariums, insane asylums, and jails were restored to usefulness and given confidence in themselves. Later, when during World War II, I met boys from that area I could not help thinking that a great many of them were able to serve their country only because of the things that had been done to help their parents through the depression period.

Nothing we learn in this world is ever wasted and I have come to the conclusion that practically nothing we do ever stands by itself. If it is good, it will serve some good purpose in the future. If it is evil, it may haunt us and handicap our efforts in unimagined ways.

Years later, after the Social Security Act was passed, I saw how it worked in individual cases in this area. There was a mine accident in which several men were killed, and my husband asked me to go down and find out what the people were saying. One man received the Carnegie medal posthumously because he had gone back into the mine to help rescue other men. His widow had several children, so her social security benefits would make her comfortable. In talking to another widow who had three children, and a fourth about to be born, I asked how she was going to manage. She seemed quite confident and told me: "My sister and her two children will come to live with us. I am going to get social benefits of nearly sixty-five dollars a month. I pay fifteen dollars a month on my house and land, and I shall raise vegetables and have chickens and with the money from the government I will get along very well. In the past probably the mine company might have given me a small check and often the other miners took up a collection if they could afford it, but this income from the government I can count on until my children are grown."

Two other events of that first autumn in Washington stand out in my mind. On November 17, 1933, Henry Morgenthau, Jr., was sworn in as undersecretary of the treasury in the Oval Room in the White House, thus starting on his long and arduous labors in the Treasury Department. When Secretary Woodin resigned, Henry Morgenthau succeeded him and held the office until shortly before my husband's death, when he also resigned and left Washington.

On that same day my husband and Mr. Litvinov held the final conversations on the recognition of the Soviet Union. There was considerable excitement over the first telephone conversation between the two countries which took place between Mr. Litvinov in the White House and his wife and son in Russia. The ushers noted it in their daily record book because, while there had been overseas conversations with many other European countries, this was the opening of diplomatic relations with Russia.

Needless to say, among some of my husband's old friends there was considerable opposition to the recogition of Russia. His mother came to him before the announcement was made to tell him she had heard rumors that he was about to recognize Russia, but that she felt this would be a disastrous move and widely misunderstood by the great majority of their old friends.

Not only his old friends but with various other people my husband had frequent run-ins over the new theory that government had a responsibility to the people. I remember that when Senator Carter Glass insisted that Virginia needed no relief, Franklin suggested that he take a drive with him to see some of the bad spots. The senator never accepted his invitation.

The opening of diplomatic relations with Russia and our relations in this hemisphere were the administration's first points of attack in our foreign policy, but the major emphasis in those early years was and had to be on questions of domestic policy and our internal economic recovery.

As I look back over the actual measures undertaken in this first year I realize that the one in which my husband took the greatest pleasure was the establishment on April 5, 1933, of the Civilian Conservation Corps camps. The teen-age youngster, the boy finishing high school, the boy who had struggled to get through college, were all at loose ends. There was no organization except the Army that had the tents and other supplies essential for a setup of this kind, which was why part of the program was promptly put under its jurisdiction.

Franklin realized that the boys should be given some other kind of education as well, but it had to be subordinate to the day's labor required of them. The Civilian Conservation Corps had a triple value: it gave the boys a chance to see different parts of their own country, and to learn to do a good day's work in the open, which benefited them physically; also it gave them a cash income, part of which went home to their families. This helped the morale both of the boys themselves and of the people at home. The idea was his own contribution to the vast scheme of relief rehabilitation planning.

This was followed on June 16 by the National Recovery Act, with General Hugh Johnson in charge. The basic importance of the NRA was that it made it easier for the industrialist who wanted to do the right thing. The chiseler and the man who was willing to profit by beating down his labor could no longer compete unfairly with the man who wanted to earn a decent profit but to treat his employees fairly. The NRA was declared unconstitutional almost two years later. I thought this was unfortunate, for it seemed a simple way to keep bad employers doing what was right.

The Public Works Administration, which came into being on the same day, made it possible for the government to plan and undertake public works during this period of depression. It helped to take up the slack of unemployment by lending money to the states for projects that they could not finance by themselves.

Five months later, in November, 1933, the Civil Works Administration was set up and in time put four million unemployed to work.

In my travels around the country I saw many things built both by PWA and by CWA. I also saw the results of the work done by CCC. The achievements of these agencies began to dot city and rural areas alike. Soil conservation and forestry work went forward, recreation areas were built, and innumerable bridges, schools, hospitals and sanitation projects were constructed — lasting monuments to the good work done under these agencies. It is true they cost the people of the country vast sums of money, but they did a collective good and left tangible results which are evident today. They pulled the country out of the depression and made it possible for us to fight the greatest and most expensive war in our history.

Perhaps the most far-reaching project was the Tennessee Valley Authority. That was Senator George Norris' greatest dream and no one who witnessed the development of the Authority will ever forget the fight he put up for something that many people ridiculed. The development had been begun during World War I, but at the end of that war most of the work was stopped. Nothing further was done until my husband, who understood Senator Norris' vision, supplied the impetus at a time when it could accomplish the maximum results for the country. With the demands of a possible war in mind, Franklin insisted on pushing work on the TVA as rapidly as possible. He believed even then that under certain circumstances war might come soon, and he knew if that happened we would need everything the TVA could make available.

In the campaign of 1932 my husband and I had gone through some of the TVA area, and he had been deeply impressed by the crowds at the stations. They were so poor; their houses were unpainted, their cars were dilapidated, and many grownups as well as children were without shoes or adequate garments. Scarcely eight years later, after the housing and educational and agricultural experiments had had time to take effect, I went through the same area, and a more prosperous region would have been hard to find. I have always wished that those who oppose authorities to create similar benefits in the valleys of other great rivers could have seen the contrast as I saw it. I realize that such changes must come gradually, but I hate to see nothing done. I wish, as my husband always wished, that year by year we might be making a start on the Missouri River and the headwaters of the Mississippi. Such experiments, changing for the better the life of the people, would be a mighty bulwark against attacks on our democracy.

FREDERICK DOUGLASS

from

THE LIFE OF FREDERICK DOUGLASS

Frederick Douglass (1817?–95) published the first of several versions of his autobiography, *Narrative of the Life of Frederick Douglass*, in 1845 — a work that eventually became a classic statement on the condition of American slavery. Douglass describes the typically dehumanizing treatment of someone born into slavery: his father (probably white) unknown; his date of birth unknown; his mother carelessly shipped away as a farmhand far from her own child; and the child left in the complete control of an indifferent at best, and hostile at worst, master. Douglass was briefly luckier than most because one kind mistress decided to teach him to read although it was against state law to do so.

After an earlier attempt to escape failed, Douglass successfully fled to Massachusetts in 1838 where he was engaged by the Massachusetts Anti-Slavery Society as a persuasive and articulate speaker. His mission was to expose slavery for what it was, and in his own person to debunk the Southern myth that slaves, incapable of surviving alone, required their masters as caretakers. He repeatedly withstood insults, threats, and even physical blows to speak out forcefully in behalf of abolition.

I was born in Tuckahoe, near Hillsborough, and about twelve miles from Easton, in Talbot county, Maryland. I have no accurate knowledge of my age, never having seen any authentic record containing it. By far the larger part of the slaves know as little of their ages as horses know of theirs, and it is the wish of most masters within my knowledge to keep their slaves thus ignorant. I do not remember to have ever met a slave who could tell of his birthday. They seldom come nearer to it than planting-time, harvest-time, cherry-time, spring-time, or fall-time. A want of information concerning my own was a source of unhappiness to me even during childhood. The white children could tell their ages. I could not tell why I ought to be deprived of the same privilege. I was not allowed to make any inquiries of my master concerning it. He deemed all such inquiries on the part of a slave improper and impertinent, and evidence of a restless spirit. The nearest estimate I can give makes me now between twenty-seven and twenty-eight years of age. I come to this, from hearing my master say, some time during 1835, I was about seventeen years old.

My mother was named Harriet Bailey. She was the daughter of Isaac and Betsey Bailey, both colored, and quite dark. My mother was of a darker complexion than either my grandmother or grandfather.

My father was a white man. He was admitted to be such by all I ever heard speak of my parentage. The opinion was also whispered that my master was my father; but of the correctness of this opinion, I know nothing; the means of knowing was withheld from me. My mother and I were separated when I was but an infant — before I knew her as my mother. It is a common custom, in the part of Maryland from which I ran away, to part children from their mothers at a very early age. Frequently, before the child has reached its twelfth month, its mother is taken from it, and hired out on some farm a considerable distance off, and the child is placed under the care of an old woman, too old for field labor. For what this separation is done, I do not know, unless it be to hinder the development of the child's affection toward its mother, and to blunt and destroy the natural affection of the mother for the child. This is the inevitable result.

I never saw my mother, to know her as such, more than four or five times in my life; and each of these times was very short in duration, and at night. She was hired by a Mr. Stewart, who lived about twelve miles from my home. She made her journeys to see me in the night, travelling the whole distance on foot, after the performance of her day's work. She was a field hand, and a whipping is the penalty of not being in the field at sunrise, unless a slave has special permission from his or her master to the contrary — a permission which they seldom get, and one that gives to him that gives it the proud name of being a kind master. I do not recollect of ever seeing my mother by the light of day. She was with me in the night. She would lie down with me, and get me to sleep, but long before I waked she was gone. Very little communication ever took place between us. Death soon ended what little we could have while she lived, and with it her hardships and suffering. She died when I was about seven years old, on one of my master's farms, near Lee's Mill. I was not allowed to be present during her illness, at her death, or burial. She was gone long before I knew anything about it. Never having enjoyed, to any considerable extent, her soothing presence, her tender and watchful care, I received the tidings of her death with much the same emotions I should have probably felt at the death of a stranger.

Called thus suddenly away, she left me without the slightest information of who my father was. The whisper that my master was my father, may or may not be true; and, true or false, it is of but little consequence to my purpose whilst the fact remains, in all its glaring odiousness, that slaveholders have ordained, and by law established, that the children of slave women shall in all cases follow the condition of their mothers; and this is done too obviously to administer to their own lusts, and make a gratification of their wicked desires profitable as well as pleasurable; for by this cunning arrangement, the slaveholder, in cases not a few, sustains to his slaves the double relation of master and father.

I know of such cases; and it is worthy of remark that such slaves invariably suffer greater hardships, and have more to contend with, than others. They are, in the first place, a constant offence to their mistress. She is ever disposed to find fault with them; they can seldom do any thing to please her; she is never better pleased than when she sees them under the lash, especially when she suspects her husband of showing to his mulatto children favors which he withholds from his black slaves. The master is frequently compelled to sell this class of his slaves, out of deference to the feelings of his white wife; and, cruel as the deed may strike any one to be, for a man to sell his own children to human flesh-mongers, it is often the dictate of humanity for him to do so; for, unless he does this, he must not only whip them himself, but must stand by and see one white son tie up his brother, of but a few shades darker complexion than himself, and ply the gory lash to his naked back; and if he lisp one word of disapproval, it is set down to his parental partiality, and only makes a bad matter worse, both for himself and the slave whom he would protect and defend.

Every year brings with it multitudes of this class of slaves. It was doubtless in consequence of a knowledge of this fact, that one great statesman of the south predicted the downfall of slavery by the inevitable laws of population. Whether this prophecy is ever fulfilled or not, it is nevertheless plain that a very different-looking class of people are springing up at the south, and are now held in slavery, from those originally brought to this country from Africa; and if their increase will do no other good, it will do away the force of the argument, that God cursed Ham, and therefore American slavery is right. If the lineal descendants of Ham are alone to be scripturally enslaved, it is certain that slavery at the south must soon become unscriptural; for thousands are ushered into the world, annually, who, like myself, owe their existence to white fathers, and those fathers most frequently their own masters.

I have had two masters. My first master's name was Anthony. I do not remember his first name. He was generally called Captain Anthony — a title which, I presume, he acquired by sailing a craft on the Chesapeake Bay. He was not considered a rich slaveholder. He owned two or three farms, and about thirty slaves. His farms and slaves were under the care of an overseer. The overseer's name was Plummer. Mr. Plummer was a miserable drunkard, a profane swearer, and a savage monster. He always went armed with a cowskin and a heavy cudgel. I have known him to cut and slash the women's heads so horribly, that even master would be enraged at his cruelty, and would threaten to whip him if he did not mind himself. Master, however, was not a humane slaveholder. It required extraordinary barbarity on the part of an overseer to affect him. He was a cruel man, hardened by a long life of slaveholding. He would at times seem to take great pleasure in whipping a slave. I have often been awakened at the dawn of day by the most heart-rending shrieks of an own aunt of mine, whom he used to tie up to a joist, and whip upon her naked back till she was literally covered with blood. No words, no tears, no prayers, from his gory victim, seemed to move his iron heart from its bloody purpose. The louder she screamed, the harder he whipped; and where the blood ran fastest, there he whipped longest. He would whip her to make her scream, and whip her to make her hush; and not until overcome by fatigue, would he cease to swing the blood-clotted cowskin. I remember the first time I ever witnessed this horrible exhibition. I was quite a child, but I well remember it. I never shall forget it whilst I remember any thing. It was the first of a long series of such outrages, of which I was doomed to be a witness and a participant. It struck me with awful force. It was the blood-stained gate, the entrance to the hell of slavery, through which I was about to pass. It was a most terrible spectacle. I wish I could commit to paper the feelings with which I beheld it.

This occurrence took place very soon after I went to live with my old master, and under the following circumstances. Aunt Hester went out one night, — where or for what I do not know, — and happened to be absent when my master desired her presence. He had ordered her not to go out evenings, and warned her that she must never let him catch her in company with a young man, who was paying attention to her belonging to Colonel Lloyd. The young man's name was Ned Roberts, generally called Lloyd's Ned. Why master was so careful of her, may be safely left to conjecture. She was a woman of noble form, and of graceful proportions, having very few equals, and fewer superiors, in personal appearance, among the colored or white women of our neighborhood.

Aunt Hester had not only disobeyed his orders in going out, but had been found in company with Lloyd's Ned; which circumstance, I found, from what he said while whipping her, was the chief offence. Had he been a man of pure morals himself, he might have been thought interested in protecting the innocence of my aunt; but those who knew him will not suspect him of any such virtue. Before he commenced whipping Aunt Hester, he took her into the kitchen, and stripped her from neck to waist, leaving her neck, shoulders, and back, entirely naked. He then told her to cross her hands, calling her at the same time a d——d b——h. After crossing her hands, he tied them with a strong rope, and led her to a stool under a large hook in the joist, put in for the purpose. He made her get upon the stool, and tied her hands to the hook. She now stood fair for his infernal purpose. Her arms were stretched up at their full length, so that she stood upon the ends of her toes. He then said to her, "Now, you d——d b——h, I'll learn you how to disobey my orders!" and after rolling up his sleeves, he commenced to lay on the heavy cowskin, and soon the warm, red blood (amid heart-rendering shrieks from her, and horrid oaths from him) came dripping to the floor. I was so terrified and horror-stricken at the sight, that I hid myself in a closet, and dared not to venture out till long after the bloody transaction was over. I expected it would be my turn next. It was all new to me. I had never seen any thing like it before. I had always lived with my grandmother on the outskirts of the plantation, where she was put to raise the children of the younger women. I had therefore been, until now, out of the way of the bloody scenes that often occurred on the plantation.

My master's family consisted of two sons, Andrew and Richard; one daughter, Lucretia, and her husband, Captain Thomas Auld. They lived in one house, upon the home plantation of Colonel Edward Lloyd. My master was Colonel Lloyd's clerk and superintendent. He was what might be called the overseer of the overseers. I spent two years of childhood on this plantation in my old master's family. It was here that I witnessed the bloody transaction recorded in the first chapter; and as I received my first impressions of slavery on this plantation, I will give some description of it, and of slavery as it there existed. The plantation is about twelve miles north of Easton, in Talbot county, and is situated on the border of the Miles River. The principal products raised upon it were tobacco, corn, and wheat. These were raised in great abundance; so that, with the products of this and the other farms belonging to him, he was able to keep in almost constant employment a large sloop, in carrying them to market at Baltimore. This sloop was named Sally Lloyd, in honor of one of the colonel's daughters. My master's son-in-law, Captain Auld, was master of the vessel; she was otherwise manned by the colonel's own slaves. Their names were Peter, Isaac, Rich, and Jake. These were esteemed very highly by the other slaves, and looked upon as the privileged ones of the plantation; for it was no small affair, in the eyes of the slaves, to be allowed to see Baltimore.

Colonel Lloyd kept from three to four hundred slaves on his home plantation, and owned a large number more on the neighboring farms belonging to him. The names of the farms nearest to the home plantation were Wye Town and New Design. "Wye Town" was under the overseership of a man named Noah Willis. New Design was under the overseership of a Mr. Townsend. The overseers of these, and all the rest of the farms, numbering over twenty, received advice and direction from the managers of the home plantation. This was the great business place. It was the seat of government for the whole twenty farms. All disputes among the overseers were settled here. If a slave was convicted of any high misdemeanor, became unmanageable, or evinced a determination to run away, he was brought immediately here, severely whipped, put on board the sloop, carried to Baltimore, and sold to Austin Woolfolk, or some other slave-trader, as a warning to the slaves remaining.

Here, too, the slaves of all the other farms received their monthly allowance of food, and their yearly clothing. The men and women slaves received, as their monthly allowance of food, eight pounds of pork, or its equivalent in fish, and one bushel of corn meal. Their yearly clothing consisted of two coarse linen shirts, one pair of linen trousers, like the shirts, one jacket, one pair of trousers for winter, made of coarse negro cloth, one pair of stockings, and one pair of shoes; the whole of which could not have cost more than seven dollars. The allowance of the slave children was given to their mothers, or the old women having the care of them. The children unable to work in the field had neither shoes, stockings, jackets, nor trousers, given to them; their clothing consisted of two coarse linen shirts per year. When these failed them, they went naked until the next allowance-day. Children from seven to ten years old, of both sexes, almost naked, might be seen at all seasons of the year.

There were no beds given the slaves, unless one coarse blanket be considered such, and none but the men and women had these. This, however, is not considered a very great privation. They find less difficulty from the want of beds, than from the want of time to sleep; for when their day's work in the field is done, the most of them having their washing, mending, and cooking to do, and having few or none of the ordinary facilities for doing either of these, very many of their sleeping hours are consumed in preparing for the field the coming day; and when this is done, old and young, male and female, married and single, drop down side by side, on one common bed, — the cold, damp floor, — each covering himself or herself with their miserable blankets; and here they sleep till they are summoned to the field by the driver's horn. At the sound of this, all must rise, and be off to the field. There must be no halting; every one must be at his or her post; and woe betides them who hear not this morning summons to the field; for if they are not awakened by the sense of hearing, they are by the sense of feeling; no age or sex finds any favor. Mr. Severe, the overseer, used to stand by the door of the quarter, armed with a large hickory stick and heavy cowskin, ready to whip any one who was so unfortunate as not to hear, or, from any other cause, was prevented from being ready to start for the field at the sound of the horn.

Mr. Severe was rightly named: he was a cruel man. I have seen him whip a woman, causing the blood to run half an hour at the time; and this, too, in the midst of her crying children, pleading for their mother's release. He seemed to take pleasure in manifesting his fiendish barbarity. Added to his cruelty, he was a profane swearer. It was enough to chill the blood and stiffen the hair of an ordinary man to hear him talk. Scarce a sentence escaped him but that was commenced or concluded by some horrid oath. The field was the place to witness his cruelty and profanity. His presence made it both the field of blood and of blasphemy. From the rising till the going down of the sun, he was cursing, raving, cutting, and slashing among the slaves of the field, in the most frightful manner. His career was short. He died very soon after I went to Colonel Lloyd's; and he died as he lived, uttering, with his dying groans, bitter curses and horrid oaths. His death was regarded by the slaves as the result of a merciful providence.

451

Mr. Severe's place was filled by a Mr. Hopkins. He was a very different man. He was less cruel, less profane, and made less noise, than Mr. Severe. His course was characterized by no extraordinary demonstations of cruelty. He whipped, but seemed to take no pleasure in it. He was called by the slaves a good overseer.

The home plantation of Colonel Lloyd wore the appearance of a country village. All the mechanical operations for the farms were performed here. The shoemaking and mending, the blacksmithing, cartwrighting, coopering, weaving, and grain-grinding, were all performed by the slaves on the home plantation. The whole place wore a business-like aspect very unlike the neighboring farms. The number of houses, too, conspired to give it advantage over the neighboring farms. It was called by the slaves the *Great House Farm*. Few privileges were esteemed higher, by the slaves of the out-farms, than that of being selected to do errands at the Great House Farm. It was associated in their minds with greatness. A representative could not be prouder of his election to a seat in the American Congress, than a slave on one of the out-farms would be of his election to do errands at the Great House Farm. They regarded it as evidence of great confidence reposed in them by their overseers; and it was on this account, as well as a constant desire to be out of the field from under the driver's lash, that they esteemed it a high privilege, one worth careful living for. He was called the smartest and most trusty fellow, who had this honor conferred upon him the most frequently. The competitors for this office sought as diligently to please their overseers, as the office-seekers in the political parties seek to please and deceive the people. The same traits of character might be seen in Colonel Lloyd's slaves, as are seen in the slaves of the political parties.

The slaves selected to go to the Great House Farm, for the monthly allowance for themselves and their fellow-slaves, were peculiarly enthusiastic. While on their way, they would make the dense old woods, for miles around, reverberate with their wild songs, revealing at once the highest joy and the deepest sadness. They would compose and sing as they went along, consulting neither time nor tune. The thought that came up, came out — if not in the word, in the sound; — and as frequently in the one as in the other. They would sometimes sing the most pathetic sentiment in the most rapturous tone, and the most rapturous sentiment in the most pathetic tone. Into all of their songs they would manage to weave something of the Great House Farm. Especially would they do this, when leaving home. They would then sing most exultingly the following words: —

"I am going away to the Great House Farm!
O, yea! O, yea! O!"

This they would sing, as a chorus, to words which to many would seem unmeaning jargon, but which, nevertheless, were full of meaning to themselves. I have sometimes thought that the mere hearing of those songs would do more to impress some minds with the horrible character of slavery, than the reading of whole volumes of philosophy on the subject could do.

I did not, when a slave, understand the deep meaning of those rude and apparently incoherent songs. I was myself within the circle; so that I neither saw nor heard as those without might see and hear. They told a tale of woe which was then altogether beyond my feeble comprehension; they were tones loud, long, and deep; they breathed the prayer and complaint of souls boiling over with the bitterest anguish. Every tone was a testimony against slavery, and a prayer to God for deliverance from chains. The hearing of those wild notes always depressed my spirit, and filled me with ineffable sadness. I have frequently found myself in tears while hearing them. The mere recurrence to those songs, even now, afflicts me; and while I am writing these lines, an expression of feeling has already found its way down my cheek. To those songs I trace my first glimmering conception of the dehumanizing character of slavery. I can never get rid of that conception. Those songs still follow me, to deepen my hatred of slavery, and quicken my sympathies for my brethren in bonds. If any one wishes to be impressed with the soul-killing effects of slavery, let him go to Colonel Lloyd's plantation, and, on allowance-day, place himself in the deep pine woods, and there let him, in silence, analyze the sounds that shall pass through the chambers of his soul, — and if he is not thus impressed, it will only be because "there is no flesh in his obdurate heart."

I have often been utterly astonished, since I came to the north, to find persons who could speak of the singing, among slaves, as evidence of their contentment and happiness. It is impossible to conceive of a greater mistake. Slaves sing most when they are most unhappy. The songs of the slave represent the sorrows of his heart; and he is relieved by them, only as an aching heart is relieved by its tears. At least, such is my experience. I have often sung to drown my sorrow, but seldom to express my happiness. Crying for joy, and singing for joy, were alike uncommon to me while in the jaws of slavery. The singing of a man cast away upon a desolate island might be as appropriately considered as evidence of contentment and happiness, as the singing of a slave; the songs of the one and of the other are prompted by the same emotion.

As to my own treatment while I lived on Colonel Lloyd's plantation, it was very similar to that of the other slave children. I was not old enough to work in the fields, and there being little else than field work to do, I had a great deal of leisure time. The most I had to do was to drive up the cows at evening, keep the fowls out of the garden, keep the front yard clean, and run of errands for my old master's daughter, Mrs. Lucretia Auld. The most of my leisure time I spent in helping Master Daniel Lloyd in finding his birds, after he had shot them. My connection with Master Daniel was of some advantage to me. He became quite attached to me, and was a sort of protector of me. He would not allow the older boys to impose upon me, and would divide his cakes with me.

I was seldom whipped by my old master, and suffered little from any thing else than hunger and cold. I suffered much from hunger, but much more from cold. In hottest summer and coldest winter, I was kept almost naked — no shoes, no stockings, no jacket, no trousers, nothing on but a coarse tow linen shirt, reaching only to my knees. I had no bed. I must have perished with cold, but that, the coldest nights, I used to steal a bag which was used for carrying corn to the mill. I would crawl into this bag, and there sleep on the cold, damp, clay floor, with my head in and feet out. My feet have been so cracked with the frost, that the pen with which I am writing might be laid in the gashes.

We were not regularly allowanced. Our food was coarse corn meal boiled. This was called *mush*. It was put into a large wooden tray or trough, and set down upon the ground. The children were then called, like so many pigs, and like so many pigs they would come and devour the mush; some with oyster-shells, other with pieces of shingle, some with naked hands, and some with spoons. He that ate fastest got most; he that was strongest secured the best place; and few left the trough satisfied.

I was probably between seven and eight years old when I left Colonel Lloyd's plantation. I left it with joy. I shall never forget the ecstasy with which I received the intelligence that my old master (Anthony) had determined to let me go to Baltimore, to live with Mr. Hugh Auld, brother to my old master's son-in-law, Captain Thomas Auld. I received this information about three days before my departure. They were three of the happiest days I ever enjoyed. I spent the most part of all these three days in the creek, washing off the plantation scurf, and preparing myself for my departure.

The pride of appearance which this would indicate was not my own. I spent the time in washing, not so much because I wished to, but because Mrs. Lucretia had told me I must get all the dead skin off my feet and knees before I could go to Baltimore; for the people in Baltimore were very cleanly, and would laugh at me if I looked dirty. Besides, she was going to give me a pair of trousers, which I should not put on unless I got all the dirt off me. The thought of owning a pair of trousers was great indeed! It was almost a sufficient motive, not only to make me take off what would be called by pig-drovers the mange, but the skin itself. I went at it in good earnest, working for the first time with the hope of reward.

The ties that ordinarily bind children to their homes were all suspended in my case. I found no severe trial in my departure. My home was charmless; it was not home to me; on parting from it, I could not feel that I was leaving any thing which I could have enjoyed by staying. My mother was dead, my grandmother lived far off, so that I seldom saw her. I had two sisters and one brother, that lived in the same house with me; but the early separation of us from our mother had well nigh blotted the fact of our relationship from our memories. I looked for home elsewhere, and was confident of finding none which I should relish less than the one which I was leaving. If, however, I found in my new home hardship, hunger, whipping, and nakedness, I had the consolation that I should not have escaped any one of them by staying. Having already had more than a taste of them in the house of my old master, and having endured them there, I very naturally inferred my ability to endure them elsewhere, and especially at Baltimore; for I had something of the feeling about Baltimore that is expressed in the proverb, that "being hanged in England is preferable to dying a natural death in Ireland." I had the strongest desire to see Baltimore. Cousin Tom, though not fluent in speech, had inspired me with that desire by his eloquent description of the place. I could never point out any thing at the Great House, no matter how beautiful or powerful, but that he had seen something at Baltimore far exceeding, both in beauty and strength, the object which I pointed out to him. Even the Great House itself, with all its pictures, was far inferior to many buildings in Baltimore. So strong was my desire, that I thought a gratification of it would fully compensate for whatever loss of comforts I should sustain by the exchange. I left without a regret, and with the highest hopes of future happiness.

We sailed out of Miles River for Baltimore on a Saturday morning. I remember only the day of the week, for at that time I had no knowledge of the days of the month, nor the months of the year. On setting sail, I walked aft, and gave to Colonel Lloyd's plantation what I hoped would be the last look. I then placed myself in the bows of the sloop, and there spent the remainder of the day in looking ahead, interesting myself in what was in the distance rather than in things near by or behind.

In the afternoon of that day, we reached Annapolis, the capital of the State. We stopped but a few moments, so that I had no time to go on shore. It was the first large town that I had ever seen, and though it would look small compared with some of our New England factory villages, I thought it a wonderful place for its size — more imposing even than the Great House Farm!

We arrived at Baltimore early on Sunday morning, landing at Smith's Wharf, not far from Bowley's Wharf. We had on board the sloop a large flock of sheep; and after aiding in driving them to the slaughterhouse of Mr. Curtis on Louden Slater's Hill, I was conducted by Rich, one of the hands belonging on board of the sloop, to my new home in Alliciana Street, near Mr. Gardner's ship-yard, on Fells Point.

Mr. and Mrs. Auld were both at home, and met me at the door with their little son Thomas, to take care of whom I had been given. And here I saw what I had never seen before; it was a white face beaming with the most kindly emotions; it was the face of my new mistress, Sophia Auld. I wish I could describe the rapture that flashed through my soul as I beheld it. It was a

459

new and strange sight to me, brightening up my pathway with the light of happiness. Little Thomas was told, there was his Freddy, — and I was told to take care of little Thomas; and thus I entered upon the duties of my new home with the most cheering prospect ahead.

I look upon my departure from Colonel Lloyd's plantation as one of the most interesting events of my life. It is possible, and even quite probable, that but for the mere circumstance of being removed from that plantation to Baltimore, I should have to-day, instead of being here seated by my own table, in the enjoyment of freedom and the happiness of home, writing this Narrative, been confined in the galling chains of slavery. Going to live at Baltimore laid the foundation, and opened the gateway, to all my subsequent prosperity. I have ever regarded it as the first plain manifestation of that kind providence which has ever since attended me, and marked my life with so many favors. I regarded the selection of myself as being somewhat remarkable. There were a number of slave children that might have been sent from the plantation to Baltimore. There were those younger, those older, and those of the same age. I was chosen from among them all, and was the first, last, and only choice.

I may be deemed superstitious, and even egotistical, in regarding this event as a special interposition of divine Providence in my favor. But I should be false to the earliest sentiments of my soul, if I suppressed the opinion. I prefer to be true to myself, even at the hazard of incurring the ridicule of others, rather than to be false, and incur my own abhorrence. From my earliest recollection, I date the entertainment of a deep conviction that slavery would not always be able to hold me within its foul embrace; and in the darkest of hours of my career in slavery, this living word of faith and spirit of hope departed not from me, but remained like ministering angels to cheer me through the gloom. This good spirit was from God, and to him I offer thanksgiving and praise.

A DIFFERENT LIFE

The Rich and the Celebrated

LILLIAN HELLMAN

from

AN UNFINISHED WOMAN, A MEMOIR

Lillian Hellman (1905–84) wrote many well-received and enduring plays, including *The Children's Hour*, *The Little Foxes*, and *Toys in the Attic*. In this excerpt from her autobiography, she talks about her thirty-year relationship with her equally celebrated companion Dashiell Hammett, writer of detective fiction, including *The Maltese Falcon*.

──────────

For years we made jokes about the day I would write about him. In the early years, I would say, "Tell me more about the girl in San Francisco. The silly one who lived across the hall in Pine Street."

And he would laugh and say, "She lived across the hall in Pine Street and was silly."

"Tell more than that. How much did you like her and how — ?"

He would yawn. "Finish your drink and go to sleep."

But days later, maybe even that night, if I was on the find-out kick, and I was, most of the years, I would say, "O.K., be stubborn about the girls. So tell me about your grandmother and what you looked like as a baby."

"I was a very fat baby. My grandmother went to the movies every afternoon. She was very fond of a movie star called Wallace Reid and I've told you all this before."

I would say I wanted to get everything straight for the days after his death when I would write his biography and he would say that I was not to bother writing his biography because it would turn out to be the history of Lillian Hellman with an occasional reference to a friend called Hammett.

The day of his death came on January 10, 1961. I will never write that biography because I cannot write about my closest, my most beloved friend. And maybe, too, because all those questions through all the thirty-one on and off years, and the sometime answers, got muddled, and life changed for both of us and the questions and answers became one in the end, flowing together from the days when I was young to the days when I was middle-aged. And so this will be no attempt at a biography of Samuel Dashiell Hammett, born in St. Mary's County, Maryland, on May 27, 1894. Nor will it be a critical appraisal of his work. In 1966 I edited and published a collection of his stories. There was a day when I thought all of them very good. But all of them are not good, though most of them, I think, are very good. It is only right to say immediately that by publishing them at all I did what Hammett did not want to do: he turned down all offers to republish the stories, although I never knew the reason and never asked. I did know, from what he said about "Tulip," the unfinished novel that I included in the book, that he meant to start a new literary life and maybe didn't want the old work to get in the way. But sometimes I think he was just too ill to care, too worn out to listen to plans or read contracts. The fact of breathing, just breathing, took up all the days and nights.

In the First World War, in camp, influenza led to tuberculosis and Hammett was to spend years after in army hospitals. He came out of the Second World War with emphysema, but how he ever got into the Second World War at the age of forty-eight still bewilders me. He telephoned me the day the army accepted him to say it was the happiest day of his life, and before I could finish saying it wasn't the happiest day of mine and what about the old scars on his lungs, he laughed and hung up. His death was caused by cancer of the lungs, discovered only two months before he died. It was not operable — I doubt that he would have agreed to an operation even if it had been — and so I decided not to tell him about the cancer. The doctor said that when the pain came, it would come in the right chest and arm, but that the pain might never come. The doctor was wrong: only a few hours after he told me, the pain did come. Hammett had had self-diagnosed rheumatism in the right arm and had always said that was why he had given up hunting. On the day I heard about the cancer, he said his gun shoulder hurt him again, would I rub it for him. I remember sitting behind him, rubbing the shoulder and hoping he would always think it was rheumatism and remember only the autumn hunting days. But the pain never came again, or if it did he never mentioned it, or maybe death was so close that the shoulder pain faded into other pains.

He did not wish to die and I like to think he didn't know he was dying. But I keep from myself even now the possible meaning of a night, very late, a short time before his death. I came into his room, and for the only time in the years I knew him there were tears in his eyes and the book was lying unread. I sat down beside him and waited a long time before I could say, "Do you want to talk about it?"

He said, almost with anger, "No. My only chance is not to talk about it."

And he never did. He had patience, courage, dignity in those last, awful months. It was as if all that makes a man's life had come together to prove itself: suffering was a private matter and there was to be no invasion of it. He would seldom even ask for anything he needed, and so the most we did — my secretary and Helen, who were devoted to him, as most women always had been — was to carry up the meals he barely touched, the books he now could hardly read, the afternoon coffee, and the martini that I insisted upon before the dinner that wasn't eaten.

One night of the last year, a bad night, I said,

"Have another martini. It will make you feel better."

"No," he said, "I don't want it."

I said, "O.K., but I bet you never thought I'd urge you to have another drink."

He laughed for the first time that day. "Nope. And I never thought I'd turn it down."

Because on the night we had first met he was getting over a five-day drunk and he was to drink heavily for the next eighteen years, and then one day, warned by a doctor, he said he would never have another drink and he kept his word except for the last year of the one martini, and that was my idea.

We met when I was twenty-four years old and he was thirty-six in a restaurant in Hollywood. The five-day drunk had left the wonderful face looking rumpled, and the very tall thin figure was tired and sagged. We talked of T.S. Eliot, although I no longer remember what we said, and then went and sat in his car and talked at each other and over each other until it was daylight. We were to meet again a few weeks later and, after that, on and sometimes off again for the rest of his life and thirty years of mine.

Thirty years is a long time, I guess, and yet as I come to write about them the memories skip about and make no pattern and I know only certain of them are to be trusted. I know about the first meeting and the next, and there are many other pictures and sounds, but they are out of order and out of time, and I don't seem to want to put them into place. (I could have done a research job, I have on other people, but

I didn't want to do one on Hammett, or to be a bookkeeper of my own life.) I don't want modesty for either of us, but I ask myself now if it can mean much to anybody but me that my second sharpest memory is of a day when we were living on a small island off the coast of Connecticut. It was six years after we had first met: six full, happy, unhappy years during which I had, with help from Hammett, writen *The Children's Hour*, which was a success, and *Days to Come*, which was not. I was returning from the mainland in a catboat filled with marketing and Hammett had come down to the dock to tie me up. He had been sick that summer — the first of the sicknesses — and he was even thinner than usual. The white hair, the white pants, the white shirt made a straight, flat surface in the late sun. I thought: Maybe that's the handsomest sight I ever saw, that line of a man, the knife of a nose, and the sheet went out of my hand and the wind went out of the sail. Hammett laughed as I struggled to get back the sail. I don't know why, but I yelled angrily, "So you're a Dostoevsky sinner-saint. So you are." The laughter stopped and when I finally came in to the dock we didn't speak as we carried up the packages and didn't speak through dinner.

Later that night, he said, "What did you say that for? What does it mean?"

I said I didn't know why I had said it and I didn't know what it meant.

Years later, when his life had changed, I did know what I had meant that day: I had seen the sinner — whatever is a sinner — and sensed the change before it came. When I told him that, Hammett said he didn't know what I was talking about, it was all too religious for him. But he did know what I was taking about and he was pleased.

But the fat, loose, wild years were over by the time we talked that way. When I first met Dash he had written four of the five novels and was the hottest thing in Hollywood and New York. It is not remarkable to be the hottest thing in either city — the hottest kid changes for each winter season — but in his case it was of extra interest to those who collect people that the ex-detective who had bad cuts on his legs and an indentation in his head from being scrappy with criminals was gentle in manner, well educated, elegant to look at, born of early settlers, was eccentric, witty, and spent so much money on women that they would have liked him even if he had been none of the good things. But as the years passed from 1930 to 1948, he wrote only one novel and a few short stories. By 1945, the drinking was no longer gay, the drinking bouts were longer and the moods darker. I was there off and on for most of those years, but in 1948 I didn't want to see the drinking anymore. I hadn't seen or spoken to Hammett for two months until the day when his devoted cleaning lady called to say she thought I had better come down to his apartment. I said I wouldn't, and then I did. She and I dressed a man who could barely lift an arm or a leg and brought him to my house, and that night I watched delirium tremens, although I didn't know what I was watching until the doctor told me the next day at the hospital. The doctor was an old friend. He said, "I'm going to tell Hammett that if he goes on drinking he'll be dead in a few months. It's my duty to say it, but it won't do any good." In a few minutes he came out of Dash's room and said, "I told him. Dash said O.K., he'd go on the wagon forever, but he can't and he won't."

But he could and he did. Five or six years later, I told Hammett that the doctor had said he wouldn't stay on the wagon.

Dash looked puzzled. "But I gave my word that day."

I said, "Have you always kept your word?"

"Most of the time," he said, "maybe because I've so seldom given it."

He had made up honor early in his life and stuck with his rules, fierce in the protection of them. In 1951 he went to jail because he and two other trustees of the bail bond fund of the Civil Rights Congress refused to reveal the names of the contributors to the fund. The truth was that Hammett had never been in the office of the Congress, did not know the name of a single contributor.

The night before he was to appear in court, I said, "Why don't you say that you don't know the names?"

"No," he said, "I can't say that."

"Why?"

"I don't know why. I guess it has something to do with keeping my word, but I don't want to talk about that. Nothing much will happen, although I think we'll go to jail for a while, but you're not to worry because" — and then suddenly I couldn't understand him because the voice had dropped and the words were coming in a most untypical nervous rush. I said I couldn't hear him, and he raised his voice and dropped his head. "I hate this damn kind of talk, but maybe I better tell you that if it were more than jail, if it were my life, I would give it for what I think democracy is, and I don't let cops or judges tell me what I think democracy is." Then he went home to bed, and the next day he went to jail.

CANDICE BERGEN

from

KNOCK WOOD

Daughter of ventriloquist Edgar Bergen, one of the most popular entertainers of his day, **Candice Bergen** had the unusual experience of having to compete with sidekick dummy Charlie McCarthy for her father's attention. Now a successful movie star in her own right and noted as a great beauty, she tells in this excerpt of the phantasmagorical quality of parties and entertainments provided for the wealthy Hollywood children with whom she grew up, including the children of Ronald Reagan, Arthur Rubinstein, and David Selznick.

Little milestones were given majesty in Hollywood, the everyday made extraordinary. Family backyards were often studio backlots: mothers' movie sets, fathers' sound stages; and sometimes the backyards themselves were even better.

One of my playmates was Carla Kirkeby, the daughter of a hotel magnate. She lived alone with her mother in Bel Air in a small Versailles — a sugar-cube chateau that spread across acres.

There you flipped the switch to start the electric waterfall tumbling down boulders into the pool far below, danced across gleaming parquet in the vast gilded ballroom, took the elevator, ran through the tunnel, and jumped on the trampoline on the lower lawn, then hiked up the rocks of the rumbling waterfall and raced through the French gardens to reach the garage, which was nearly as palatial as the house itself — a hotel for cars, discreet and distinguished, giving onto a cobblestone courtyard enclosed by high walls. The automobiles were sleek and shining, always in a state of readiness — a Rolls-Royce coupe, a Bentley convertible, a Jaguar roadster and a station wagon; assorted others belonged to the staff. In the very last stall shone the smallest automotive models: three miniature convertibles that were electrically powered. These were for the children, and we stampeded toward them, clambered inside and hurried down the drive. Whirring along, feet clamped down on the pedals, we whizzed by boxwood hedges and long rows of topiary trees — like two Mister Toads in mad dashes, gangsters making our getaway.

Walt Disney had a miniature train built in *his* vast backyard; a perfect knee-high working replica of a steam engine with four cars and a caboose. It puffed along narrow graveled tracks and across a tiny trestle bridge while "Uncle Walt," in engineer's cap and kerchief sat happily astride the engine, shoveling coal and tooting the shrill steam whistle as he took us for rides.

For parents so expert at larger than life, they seemed mesmerized by the miniscule as well, fascinated with inflating the scale or reducing it. It was the life-size that failed to hold their interest.

Even in a landscape so completely at odds with it, Christmas took on fabled proportions as well. For here climate was given no quarter; here parents could create their own. You had only to dream of a white Christmas and white was what you got — boughs of massive fir trees sagging with snow. It was no accident that "sno-flocking," a costly process in which Christmas trees are sprayed with a sticky white substance flecked with silica for a realistic sparkle, found its way onto Hollywood trees — invented, perhaps, by a prop man at the request of a producer for his family's fir.

Snow fell, too, on the nighttime Christmas parade down Hollywood Boulevard, blown in swirling gusts by giant studio fans spaced along the route. This I remember particularly because as my parents, Charlie, Mortimer, and I chugged along in my father's antique Stanley Steamer — one of the many celebrity-filled convertibles — waving to the line of crowds, I got a fair dose of snow in the eyes. By then I knew that public display of tears was unacceptable so, eyes squeezed shut and furiously tearing, I kept waving and smiling crazily, like a child blind and bereft, pluckily bidding goodbye.

There were many children's parties at Christmas with assorted Santas giving gifts. One time, the man ho-hoing behind the spun-silver beard was David Niven — an elegant, urbane Father

Christmas, a soigné Saint Nick. Another year, Charlton Heston played him differently — a man of unearthly substance and stature, his ho-hos booming from a great height, somewhere between Santa Claus and God; when *he* asked if you'd been good all year, it caused a real crisis of conscience.

Come December, Hollywood living rooms became Nutcracker Suites. Towering trees seemed to shed presents like pine needles, thickly covering the floor. Gifts tumbled in all directions, piling up like snowdrifts and eclipsing the carpet. The rooms were impassable before December 26th.

At Christmas, Hollywood children grew giddy and greedy, buried under offerings. It was a child's dream come true, but I wonder if we children really believed it; there was a sense, somehow, that ours were weirdly bountiful harvests, that living rooms shouldn't swell so with loot.

Like the snowfall, the number of presents varied from year to year, depending on ratings, grosses and the well-wrapped gratitude of studio heads and sponsors. These gifts of grandeur — indications of the corporate value of the receiver — were often given to the children to impress the parents on whose shelves they usually ended up: Georgian silver porringers, carved ivory animals, tiny feathered mechanical birds that, when wound, twittered in fine-ribbed gold cages. Impeccably wrapped, lavish and useless to anyone four feet high.

It was Uncle Walt Disney's gift we looked forward to most and we began to wait for it in

October. A monolith in Micky Mouse paper, instantly spotted by size and wrapping, it was the only gift bigger than the receiver, for here was a man who shared our souls. His presents stood three feet high and three feet wide and were filled with every Disney treasure: a Snow White gramophone, Tinker Bell dolls and Pixie Dust, pirate swords and porcelain Peter Pans. We were dizzy with delight to get them. But as we grew taller, the presents grew smaller, until, by adolescence, they disappeared completely — a metaphor for our early youth.

Our birthdays, too, assumed the scope and shimmer of a studio production. A treasure hunt was held for Timothy Getty's seventh birthday, and the countless children invited were asked to come as pirates and buccaneers. Golden earrings in ears and noses, sashed in satin, wearing long blue beards, the children fanned out in short, greedy squadrons assisted by butlers in breeches and big black hats adorned with skulls and crossbones. The Getty estate — now the Getty Museum — sloped almost to the sea and, as legend has it, was once the site of true pirate booty and buried doubloons. But in Timothy's time the great lawn swarmed with bands of smaller brigands feverishly in search of tiny treasure chests stuffed with chocolate gold coins.

Our parties were true extravaganzas — lavish competitions in professional skill, loving displays of parental pride. It was innocent one-upsmanship, well-intentioned, yet tough to top. Most seemed to agree that the Oscar for Best Birthday Given by a Parent went to Vincent Minnelli for

Liza's sixth given at Ira Gershwin's house in Beverly Hills. That was the party parents spoke of with reverence, shaking their heads, smiling, Now *that* was a time. I don't think the children remembered but the grownups certainly did; my mother described it to me just recently, amazed I'd forgotten a day so splendid, so fresh was it still in her mind.

The Gershwin lawn rolled on forever, and in the center, children spun slowly on a many-colored carousel, while others clustered round the Magic Lady — a woman in a long blue gown sprinkled with stars who pulled doves from her sleeves and rabbits from hats. There were hot-dog stands and ice-cream cones and clouds of cotton candy. Clowns clowned and jugglers juggled and sleek, shining ponies circled the lawn at a tiny, clipped canter for any child who wanted a ride. It was a fairy-tale gift to a daughter from a father who was a master at making fairy tales come true.

If I don't remember her party, I do remember Liza: shy and soft-spoken, quick to smile. She peered with huge eyes though thick, long lashes, kind and gentle, generous and unspoiled. I remember always liking her for that because most of us were none of those things.

Parties, for me, were a source of terror; I was led in reluctantly, often tearfully, then hung by the edge. The day usually ended in tentative enjoyment as, party hat in hand, I curtsied goodbye at the door. Frightened and self-conscious with other, bolder children, I headed home relieved and happy, eager to hike the hills with my dogs. I remember being pleased to find Liza at these parties, often hovering at the edge as well — surprised at her shyness, grateful for her friendliness.

And I remember always asking to go to Liza's to play dress-up because in her closet hung little girls' dreams. Vincent Minelli had seen to that, too. In her dress-up closet, on low racks at child's-eye level, glowed tiny satin ball gowns embroidered with seed pearls, wispy white tutus, flowered pink crinolines. You could choose between Vivian Leigh's riding habit from *Gone With the Wind* or Leslie Caron's ballerina costume from *An American in Paris;* my favorite was Deborah Kerr's champagne satin ball gown from *The King and I*. Each one fit as if it were made for us. And each one was. Liza's father had had the most famous leading women's costumes from MGM movies copied by the designers themselves — all scaled down to perfect six-year-old sizes.

When I turned six, in the merry month of May, I wore a party dress of yellow organdy appliquéd with French lace and stood nervously with my mother at the gate of Bella Vista, ready to receive my guests. Little girls fluttered in like pastel puffs, the palest springtime flowers, and clustered together like a bouquet. The boys stumbled in — reluctant Princes of the Blood — hair slicked fast, sheepish in their navy knee socks, squirming in their gray wool flannel shorts. Shoving each other and giggling, they kept a ritual distance from the shy smiles of the girls as if anything in organdy might contaminate their budding manhood.

Parties were held in the patio, and that year my mother had had a maypole made that streamed with brightly colored ribbons. The girls skipped in a dainty circle, weaving the ribbons into tight stripes around the pole — delicately, demurely — till the boys took a turn and it became a tug of war. Quickly tearing the ribbons from the pole, waving them proudly like trophies of war, they soon used them as lassoes and bridles for the girls, who were delighted with the attention. After ice-cream animals and cake, two white police dogs precisely executed their tricks in the patio; our governesses hovered nearby in crisp, crackling uniforms while our parents — the Dick Powells, Ray Millands, Jimmy Stewarts, Arthur Rubinsteins, Randolph Scotts, David Selznicks and Ronald Reagans — gathered over cocktails inside.

Then — organdy wilted, hair ribbons undone, knee socks sagging and ties askew — we raced to the Rumpus Room, wound tighter than clocks, and scrambled for a place on the sofas. I wedged myself between Jimmy Stewart's son Ronnie and Dorothy Lamour's son Ridgeley. I had crushes on both of them. The lights went out, and in the darkness, giggling and whispering, we waited for *Snow White and the Seven Dwarfs* to begin.

Here was a story about *another* princess who lived far away in *another* Magic Kingdom, in love with a prince, surrounded by odd, tiny men. At long last, her prince finds her, gathers her gently onto his horse, and, with the creatures of the forest weeping and cheering, they ride together into the sunset.

The queen and the dwarfs stay home.

Our fantasy lives were shaped by movies like those of other kids of our generation, but it was our parents who *made* the fantasies, who cherished childhood more than we. Hollywood, for them, was the Sea of Dreams where they set their silver sails and filled their nets with magic. Our parents were Ivanhoe and Moses, Spartacus and Shane. They fought lions, roped stallions, slew dragons, rescued maidens; they healed the sick, sang in the rain, woke up in Oz and got back to Kansas. Snapped their fingers — it snowed in summer. Sent a memo — it rained indoors.

And we were the children of Paradise, where nothing seemed beyond our reach. Fantasy was, for us, familiar. The extraordinary, everyday. But reality remained a stranger, and most were pleased to leave it that way.

IRENE MAYER SELZNICK

from

A PRIVATE VIEW

Irene Selznick's father, Louis B. Mayer, was a commanding figure as the head of the most powerful studio in Hollywood, Metro-Goldwyn-Mayer, and she presents an insider's view of the very early days of the movie industry. Irene subsequently married another extremely powerful Hollywood producer, David Selznick, and was a witness to the gestation of *Gone with the Wind*, Selznick's astoundingly successful film. The night of the film's opening, instead of being a joyous occasion, turned into a nightmare of intense personal pain for Irene, as she recalls the events of the evening in the following excerpt.

In her later years, Irene Selznick became a producer in her own right, producing as one of her earliest and most well-received plays *A Streetcar Named Desire* by Tennessee Williams.

The company was less than a year old when David asked me if I wanted to see a movie of a Civil War story. Of course I didn't. *He* didn't.

No one did, not conceivably. David's story department in New York was headed by Kay Brown, who was putting pressure on him about a book that wasn't even published yet. He complained that she was giving him the rush act, and he was full of resistance. It was a first novel, carrying a stiff price and a terrible title. All that and the Civil War besides.

The first synopsis only convinced David that it would be expensive to make. And the price was foolish to pay if the book didn't turn out to be really big. On the other hand, if it were to be a huge success, he couldn't afford to pass it up, but then again he would have to be faithful to a wide readership. It was so long he said it would make twenty movies, not one. For a fellow who himself was over-length, he particularly dreaded the job of having to compress it. He stalled by asking for a long, detailed synopsis. Jock had the edge because he had read the book. He didn't push David the way Kay did, he just said he was going to buy it if David didn't. That clinched it.

David read *Gone With the Wind* some weeks later, on the way to Honolulu and back, as did half the passengers on the boat. The only difference was that he was reading it more slowly and he owned the picture rights. He decided that if he edited, omitted, and telescoped chunks of the book, he might get it down to gargantuan proportions. But its size and the challenge were about equal and they suited his temperament.

What usually held films up was the shooting script, so David started far in advance on *GWTW*. To counteract his own tendencies, he chose as writer an eminent playwright, Sidney Howard, who was a figure of considerable authority as well as strict about time and methods. But no amount of time would have sufficed. Later there were other writers, and in the end the script often came hot from the typewriter to the set, sometimes from David. But the script was essentially Sidney Howard's.

At first it was exciting to have an important property lined up, instead of being caught short without material. But there sprang up a nostalgia for the wonderful little company that had been and which was now threatened by the good forture of owning the book. Everything escalated: interest, scope, expectation. David had a tiger by the tail. Failure would mean the end of his company and his career.

My father used to say everyone had two businesses: his own and show business. Everyone in America was a casting expert on *GWTW*. It was not a national pastime, it was an obsession. David was assailed about the casting in print and inundated by mail as though it was all to be settled by public vote. Had there been a contest for Rhett Butler, Gable would have won unanimously, but there was no logical choice for Scarlett O'Hara. As is already too well documented elsewhere, David undertook to find a new girl.

The search for Scarlett made Russell Birdwell, the publicity director, look good, but even he couldn't engender the kind of publicity that project created; nobody is *that* good. When Birdwell could no longer control it, he quite sensibly took credit for it. As the book caught fire, anything about the film became news. David was beside himself trying to contain the ballyhoo because it could boomerang against the picture, himself, and Scarlett, whoever she turned out to be.

The role of Scarlett inspired many a young woman with the conviction that she had been born to play the part. Liz Whitney, of all people, pretended she was among them and even managed to have a test of herself made. One young hopeful went to extreme lengths: she arrived in our courtyard one Sunday morning on the open back of a truck which carried a very tall volume with a *GWTW* cover. In its open pages stood the would-be heroine, dressed in a Scarlett costume, ready to step into the house and the role. She only landed in the papers.

After a couple of years and still no Scarlett, discouragement set in. For protection David began to consider certain well-known actresses. The press jumped on him and cited fraud; the search had been a stunt! By the time the final tests were being scheduled, it had to be faced that there still was no girl.

Oddly enough, one of the finalists turned out to be our nearest neighbor, Paulette Goddard. She and Charlie Chaplin lived right across the road, in fact our driveways faced each other, so naturally we became friends — though not close friends, since David and Charlie were not a match made in heaven. The real link was Paulette, of whom I grew fond — a woman of considerable looks, charm, and resourcefulness, who was giving Charlie a rather happy life. I had noticed her when she was a dashing blonde in New York during the more adventurous days of her first marriage, and it was hard to believe that she could ever have turned into this ever-so-studious young woman, however playful.

Somehow I never put anything past Paulette. For instance: I had a hand-knit bathing suit, the color of lightly tanned skin — my favorite suit — which Paulette greatly admired; to be blunt, she coveted it. When that suit was missing one day, I called up Paulette and said not a word except, "Send it back, girl!" Back it came, only to disappear again shortly thereafter, right out of the pool house. She offered me certain swaps: no dice. We negotiated. Finally we compromised: Paulette was permitted to borrow it for very special occasions provided she returned it on her own. That would be the day!

Meanwhile, she had been acquiring professional skill though the coaching of the wise Constance Collier, and was beginning to achieve a place for herself as an actress. Now, quite unexpectedly, she was being considered as a possible Scarlett. At first we treated it as a joke. But her tests were good, and she was still in the running when the ranks had sifted down to the last half-dozen.

David called her in one day and told her it was no longer a joke. "My God, I may really be stuck with you!" (They were rather inclined to bait each other.) But he said he had to clarify her legal status; was she actually married to Charlie? She turned quite haughty: how dare David ask her a question like that? He said he had to, because he couldn't afford to jeopardize an investment like *GWTW* because of an irregularity in someone's personal life. She said she had been married on a boat off the China coast. He said that was clearly nonsense, although he had read it somewhere too. Then she declared that no one else had ever dared to talk to her that way. But David had the perfect answer: no one else had ever almost offered her a part like Scarlett O'Hara. Then, bursting into tears, Paulette told him he was about to hear something that she had sworn never to reveal: actually, she and Charlie had been married by the mayor of Catalina.

Eventually it emerged from an attempt to check the records that Catalina was an unincorporated part of Los Angeles. No mayor. No soap . . .

Sugar (as I called her) was a handful, but I never saw her in a difficult mood. Extraordinary that when she and Charlie split up, this number-one gimme girl parted from that number-one non-giver without a ripple. And years later, when she next got married (to Burgess Meredith), there could be no doubts — Jeff and Danny were witnesses.

Alas, Paulette or no Paulette, not one of the candidates was exactly right; if you have a half dozen, it means you don't have one. David still had hope, not because it would be humiliating to back down, but because his need was so great. He declared that his luck wouldn't desert him and pleaded with me to share his belief. At deadline, Vivien appeared. There had been magical intervention. David said, "See, I told you."

It seems so far-fetched that a dark horse could show up at the last moment that occasional tales still surface to challenge this fact. Vivien Leigh, a relatively minor actress under contract to Alexander Korda in England, came to town apparently to see her sweetheart, Laurence Olivier, who was making *Wuthering Heights*. Ten years later in London I learned that her timing was not coincidental. Vivien was as determined as she was beautiful. What she desperately wanted was Larry and Scarlett, in that order: they were both in California, and each made the other more possible. Moreover, Larry's agent was Myron. Myron was so rocked by her looks that he invited them both to watch the burning of Atlanta, which was being filmed some weeks before the rest of the picture was to start. As has oft been told, Myron brought Vivien to the back lot, and with the light of the flames reflected on her face, said to David, "Meet Scarlett O'Hara." David was flabbergasted.

The conclusive tests were a week off. David turned superstitious and told me to try not to think too much about Vivien. "The others are still in contention." That was technically true, and as much trouble was taken with the other actresses as though there were no Vivien. We watched the tests at home on successive evenings. The suspense was killing. Vivien was last and incomparable.

Now David had the perfect Scarlett and obviously an important star for his company, even though he would have to share her with Korda; half a new star is better than none. But none is what he got. Ironically, Vivien never made another picture for David.

The anticipation about *Gone With the Wind* was, not to bandy the word, colossal. A vast, ready-made audience is always desirable, but this one was also demanding, and exasperated by what it considered unwarranted delay. It was not the publicity which was damaging, but the scrutiny it brought. David's decisions and procedures were analyzed and criticized in print, the picture's faults were lamented before anything had been shot. No one but Margaret Mitchell, who cared the most, was prepared to wait and see.

It was not surprising that George Cukor joined up with SIP, just as he had come along to MGM with David. (Actually, I can't think of anyone, except perhaps Ingrid Bergman, on whose career David had more influence.) He was part of *GWTW* practically from the time the book was bought until he was fired a couple of weeks after shooting began.

I've never before or since felt as bad about anyone losing a job as I did about George and *GWTW*. His association with the movie had gone on so long that he and it seemed to me indivisible. He hadn't been particularly useful on the script, but then David had never found him so. He compensated in other ways. I feel he made a real contribution to the picture by his influence on casting and on the total visual conception. But from the start of shooting David was disappointed

490

in the results he was getting.

I couldn't accept the fact that he was actually going to change directors. His dissatisfaction was born with the first rushes, and his dissatisfaction grew. I pleaded George's case and won him a couple of days' respite at a time — I thought things would get better when everyone got less nervous. They didn't. Finally David called it quits. George was coming to the house that evening after dinner and David was going to have to break the news.

It was awful. David and I sat upstairs waiting in loud silence. When I heard the bell, then a voice in the downstairs hall, I flew down to greet him. (I thought of the stairs as "the last mile.") As George came around the bend halfway up the staircase, he guessed from the look on my face (as he later told me) that the verdict was in. I ran down and flung myself on him, weeping. He comforted me as far as David's room and I disappeared until I heard his car leave. I ached for them both.

The truth was, George's work was simply not up to David's expectations, and he said he had to trust his instincts, right or wrong. Everything was riding on him; he told George that if he was going to fail, it had to be on his own mistakes. At least he had already arranged an MGM contract for George and the much-desired opportunity to direct *The Women*.

A few years ago George phoned me to ask if I knew why he had been fired from *Gone With the Wind*. He had just told a man writing a book about him that *he* didn't know. Did I? I said I did. He didn't press me for the reason, so perhaps he didn't really want to know it. It pained him through the years, I am sure, because he appeared to be taking increasing credit for the film. He had such a distinguished record, he didn't need it.

The success of *Gone With the Wind* was not luck, just slogging. Apart from securing Clark and Vivien, the good luck of the picture was in not having bad luck. When the stakes are unbearably high, one thinks of the possiblity of illness or accident. It was important not to let David know that I shared that suspense, most seriously about whether *he* would last. If not, the intricately wrought edifice would come tumbling down. *GWTW* had become so complex that from the time it started shooting, there wasn't a prayer for anyone to pull it out but him.

David never drove anyone as he drove himself. His was a superhuman task, almost an endurance test. He would work all out to the last ounce, then home for repairs, and he needed support in proportion to the demands made upon him. "Pressure" was the key word and it was contagious. There was no way of sparing me.

The hours were the most punishing. They were insane and only made possible by Benzedrine, in increasing amounts. If he left a note at four A.M. for Farr to wake him at seven-thirty, he would add: "Regardless of what I may say." Several nights he did without sleep. We so adjusted to each stage that without our realizing it the new stress became the norm, but the strain was cumulative. I wondered whether anything was worth it. Perhaps it was only a movie, but on the home front it was more real than life. It was hard to keep a perspective — that movie had priority.

Contractually, he started on time and he got through on time. In the last month of production, five units were shooting simultaneously. David must have read my thoughts. "I assure you I haven't gone crazy. I know what I'm doing." Speed it up . . . get it done before an essential element conks out.

After shooting began, it was like being under seige. We were in a war and we were in it together. I had the house organized "for the duration." Breakfast was earlier, dinner was later, and the children were neglected. So were the amenities. His burden was formidable. He had to lay it off on someone; it would have been intolerable to carry it alone. I didn't know what a beating I was taking until David told me what guilt he felt when he looked at me.

He promised to make it up to me and the children, the poor children. For relief, he painted a picture of the most glorious trip ever under-taken, a year at least and around the world, children included. If he survived the picture — if, if, if the picture was a success — we'd sail away and to hell with it all. Perhaps he wouldn't work again for years. Perhaps he'd never again do movies. Perhaps he'd write. Better still, he would go to Oxford and study. It was "Hold out, hold out!" I could, by clinging to the belief that someday the filming would end. Someday people would be coming into a theatre to see it. That image helped too.

Life was not as grim as it sounds, not for the likes of David. If there was added work and strain, there was all the more need for fun. Perhaps less fun, but better; it was up to me to be choosy. Party-going was rarer and in snatches. I had to find something special for Saturday nights, and our Sunday gatherings were not entirely abandoned. Benzedrine was bad enough for work, but I found it appalling to use it just because a good time missed was lost forever.

The picture took over five months to film and an equal period of hard work until its premiere. In the interim there had to be a preview. That fact led people in Southern California to go to the movies uncommonly often that summer. Previews had always been "sneak," revealed by a modest warning posted outside the theatre. For a couple of months, theatres in adjacent towns, even counties, had taken to advertising a major preview. The more mysterious the signals, the longer the lines and the more resentment from the frustrated movie-goers.

For us, the preview which had been a goal for so long now loomed as a threat. It could spell the end of everything in a few hours. The postponements were many and maddening. Jock was on standby and, finally given the signal, arrived. This was it.

David decided when, but not where — you can't tell if you don't know. That is how the secret of the preview was kept. What a scoop it would have been.

Late one afternoon David, Jock, and I set forth, starting from the house the better to throw "them" off the scent. We pointed ourselves in the general direction of Orange County to find a theatre with the right kind of audience, which depended solely on the kind of film being shown that night. We were trailed by a studio car with Hal Kern, the cutter, and Bobby Keon, the production secretary, and mountains of film cans. The heat was searing, and the further we went, the hotter it became. There was either a dead silence or we were all talking at once. We couldn't sit back properly in the car; one or the other of us was always edging forward until reminded and then pulling back. Eventually we realized that all three of us were sitting on the very edge of the seat. That was the only laugh we had on the way out. Here we were, after more than three years. It was the longest-running emergency on record.

David was afraid we were being followed. I was worried as we passed town after town that it would get too late.

We finally pulled up at a theatre in Riverside, and David, standing on the pavement, sent for the manager. As David introduced himself, the manager obviously jumped to the right conclusion, because he threw out his arms, clearly promising anything, anything. The terms were laid down: he must interrupt the current film, put on a slide announcing the preview of a very long fim and stating that after a five-minute intermission the doors would be locked. Anyone could leave, but no one could enter.

Then there was trouble from the least-expected

495

source. Me. What a scene I made! I was unmanageable. Standing in the lobby with David and Jock, I looked into the house. There were a lot of strangers in there — what had they done to deserve to see this picture? I burst into tears and refused to go in. There was no reasoning with me. I wanted them out. When I finally grew calm, David and Jock took me firmly, one on each side, to our seats and sat me down. The three of us solemnly crossed arms and clasped hands. The lights darkened and the studio trademark appeared on the screen. The audience's hopes soared. When the main title came on, the house went mad. I fell apart again and sobbed as though my heart would break. I couldn't bear to see the first scenes. I was crouched down in my seat, protesting wildly. David and Jock took off their jackets and tried to bury me as though they were putting out a fire. I gradually subsided, daring a look now and then. For ten minutes I was the biggest nuisance I have ever been in my life.

The film took over and the hours sped by. The applause was enormous, and when the lights came on, everyone stood up, but most of them didn't move. It was as though something wonderful or terrible had happened. Half an hour later there were still people standing outside. They simply lingered on and on.

There wasn't a bar in sight. We settled for a soda at the corner drugstore while we went through the unusually large batch of preview cards. They were glorious.

We were reluctant to leave, but at last we

drove home in what seemed fifteen minutes. I apologized and David said, "It's all right, darling. You have it out of your system." Calm, controlled Irene. It was not so. Another episode of madness erupted in Atlanta, where I barricaded myself in our suite by moving heavy furniture against the door when David went out. It was all catching up with me.

That was mighty peculiar. At least I gave a decent account of myself at the opening itself; I had hysterics only in the intermission, quite privately. I did better in New York, where I sensibly didn't watch the first scenes. Los Angeles was the easiest and I sat there knowing I need never see the picture again. Several years later, however, I saw a tiny bit in New York. Walking past the Astor Theatre one evening, David had an impulse to pop in. "You're all right by now, aren't you?" We stood in the back. For ten minutes I became part of the rapt audience. Then, without warning, the old familiar pattern returned, and out we went. I hadn't completely healed, and never would.

The hottest ticket in memory was for the opening of *Gone With the Wind* in Atlanta. Private planes converged. There was press from all over the world — it had become an international event. A state holiday was declared. It was the biggest thing in the south since the Civil War. The crowds and the hospitality were overwhelming. There were processions, receptions, and balls. The good people of Atlanta were celebrating their history, paying tribute to Margaret Mitchell, and honoring their guests, but implicit in all this was the assumption that the film did justice to their book and their past. We had made it thus far, but were all too aware that the results weren't in. The verdict of Atlanta was crucial.

People had come for a good time. Good time? To me, it was momentous, portentous, and a workout. Our suite needed a switchboard. "Darling, I wouldn't dream of bothering David, but would you mind . . .?" We also needed an administrative staff. I couldn't cope and also attend the festivities, and I wasn't really needed out there. Besides, I didn't want to go, and David said I didn't have to. I did go briefly to something. I felt beset. I needed breathing space. I had to shore myself up for the main event. I had also to brace myself, "in case."

Margaret Mitchell proved to be modest, gentle, but unshakable. She had refused to be involved in any way at all with the film. No money could tempt her. Her restraint was admirable, her behavior impeccable. She had sold the rights and she had agreed to go to the premiere. She and her husband drove with us. The cars inched for miles along streets jam-packed with people. We might have been going to a coronation or a guillotine. Uppermost in David's mind was the hope of her approval.

GWTW opened on December 15, 1939. The response that night was enormous and blessed by Margaret Mitchell's glowing tribute from the stage. We arrived in New York more confident; it was one down and two to go. The film opened at both the Astor and the Capitol, lest there not be sufficient good seats available for those who felt entitled. Names had to be balanced so there was no Class A or Class B theatre.

Things had reached such a pitch that Jock threw open his mother's home, where he lived too, at 972 Fifth Avenue, that lovely Stanford White house, the contents of the main rooms dust-covered since his father's death ten years before. Jock went all out, as well he might, because he had done himself proud. He had withstood derision and taunts, and had dug himself in even deeper. It was a fine victory for him that night in his own home town.

There was no hurdle left but Hollywood, the following week. By this time we dared them to differ. A few days before the opening Jock called to ask whether I would mind taking over Mocambo for opening night and inviting the guests in his behalf. At that point, with the finish line in sight, it was a trifle. However, it was no minor matter to take care of the Hollywood audience. It was a question of getting them all in. For once they cared more about admission than location. It was the last lap and all exhilaration. Hollywood seemed to rejoice with us. It was their movie too, and they were the better for it.

Celebrate I did that night. The film was a triumph and my relief equal to the victory. David was bathed in glory, and I thought only of the wonderful peace ahead for us. Our exhaustion was bone-deep. I didn't know how we had survived. Not only the three years but the three openings in less than two weeks, with Christmas thrown in. David awarded me a medal. That year under the tree was a small gold disc, which I attached to my watch bracelet. It was engraved "To the real heroine of GWTW from her Four-Eyed Rhett." I was enchanted. David said, "Heroine, yes, but, alas, the victim." It turned out we were both victims, but David paid a heavier price.

The war in Europe and plans for our future were all secondary to Academy Award night, which was looming, a topic we superstitiously avoided. Despite many nominations, David had never won an Oscar. He had promised me one "someday." This year was surely it.

The build-up to that night was tremendous. We had several tables in the Cocoanut Grove; our guests were the *GWTW* nominees and those who accompanied them. Everyone met at our house first for drinks. When it was time to leave, we spread out in the courtyard. In a flash I saw David get into the first limousine with Clark and Vivien and their escorts and drive away, with nary a look behind. I'd been forgotten. I was dumbfounded. Perhaps "the real heroine" of *GWTW* had better go upstairs and go to bed. I didn't, assuming he'd be back for me any moment. I got the others organized into their respective limousines. David didn't come back for me. After they all had left, I went alone in the remaining car. I could think it over on the way.

When I arrived at the hotel, there was no repentant David at the entrance. I felt numb, but went in, still improvising. At the head of the stairs whoever had been alerted to spot me showed me the room near the Cocoanut Grove which SIP had engaged and where all our nominees and David were happily being photographed. I didn't go in. My only impulse was to flee. If we ever spoke again, he could tell me about it.

I must have changed the seating, because we sat at separate tables.

I couldn't look at David. Denial set in. It hasn't happened. Be reasonable. At least don't leave — see it through and be upset later. Don't think, don't feel; pretend he's not here. It was just a damn shame I couldn't put on an act, exult, and then raise hell when I got home and throw something at him. Too bad for him and too bad for me.

I acted as though it were some other Oscar evening and concentrated on my guests. Not David. He kept reminding me throughout the meal by sending emissaries, who didn't know what was going on, except that I was angry at him. It was hardly an occasion for a wife to be temperamental. He was making me the heavy and broadcasting it besides. But I had made my gesture: I was there and I was behaving. That was not enough. David needed solace. He sent Jock to plead his case. "You're ruining David's evening. For God's sake, nod, smile, anything. He's in misery." "So am I."

The only time I looked at him that evening was when he was on the rostrum. When he spoke, it was directly at me. His glance never wavered, hoping for some sign. I was punishing

501

myself as well as him — it was sick-making. I simply had not been able to rise above my hurt.

He won not only the Oscar, but also the Irving Thalberg Memorial Award for "the most consistent high quality of production," a prize he had dreamed of. He had hit the jackpot.

When we got home, I said, "David, how could you?" The only one who would understand, on whose shoulder I might have sobbed out my misery, was the villain of the piece. It was frightful for both of us. We were robbed of the dream of rejoicing with each other. He thought his behavior was rotten and couldn't forgive himself. I could forgive him only when I pitied him more than I did myself. I had no way to rationalize this one. It hadn't happened for the best. It was five years before David ever spoke of it again. It even cast a pall when the next year he won his second Oscar for *Rebecca*.

SHIRLEY MacLAINE

from

DON'T FALL OFF THE MOUNTAIN

With contagious joie de vivre, **Shirley MacLaine** describes her quick rise from underpaid chorus line to well-paid star, from being totally overlooked to being courted and hounded mercilessly by Hollywood agents. She starred in many major film roles, including *Apartment, Can-Can, Irma La Douce,* and *Some Came Running.* In addition to her highly successful career in films, MacLaine is an observant and spirited world traveler, deeply interested in the cultures of Japan, India, Bhutan, and Africa.

To write her own autobiography, Shirley MacLaine took some typing lessons, removed her shoes, and set to work. These first efforts became a best-seller, and thus encouraged, she went on to write several other popular books about her life and times.

503

I was born into a cliché-loving, middle-class Virginia family. To be consistent with my background, I should have married an upstanding member of the community and had two or three strong-bodied children who ate Wonder Bread eight ways. I should have settled down on a clean, tree-lined street in a suburb of Richmond, Virginia, had a maid once a week, a bridge game every Wednesday, and every three years or so a temptation — I would feel guilty about it — to have an affair.

We were taught to respect all material possessions, because it took long, hard years of work to be able to afford such things. Their value was something we should always be aware and proud of. We owned the very table that John Adams (or maybe it was George Mason) ate his wedding breakfast from, and it was our responsibility to uphold cultural tradition and keep the table in perfect condition for our children's children by never putting wet glasses on it. The Chippendale mirror in the dining room was never to be touched (even though it was a fake, as I found out later). The three Wedgewood bowls and the reproduction of "Blue Boy" in the goldplated frame always made me think twice before I invited someone to the house. I was afraid something would get knocked over.

The walls of the house seemed to remind us that we were a fine Virginia family, and anyone graced with an invitation should conduct himself accordingly. But it was such a plain house, really a plain, modest, middle-class, red-brick house — mortgaged and everything. The big tree in the front yard had to be cut down because one of the branches got sick. I asked, "Why, because a tree's arm got sick, did they have to cut down the whole body?" And they told me the tree doctor had said it was the right thing to do.

So I believed that almost everything that went on around me was the right thing to do. I certainly had loving parents and, it seemed, everything I wanted — I mean up to a point. There were lots of things I wanted, but they weren't "things"; they were feelings.

My father was the autocratic head of the family, well educated, with a portly build moving toward rotundity whenever there were peanuts around. He was a stern man with light blue eyes full of suspicion, the censor of all he surveyed, and the guardian of our safety. He sat in judgment on our actions and behavior. He was sometimes terrifying, because he had always acted as though he knew not only about the "bad" things we *had* done, but also those "bad" things we were *going* to do. Then there were times when he was so moved with pride for us that his chest puffed out even further than his stomach. His sensitivity was bottomless, but the fear of his own feelings was sometimes too painful to witness.

Mother was a tall, thin, almost ethereal creature with a romantic nature, who found even the most insignificant unpleasantness difficult to accept. In fact, it didn't exist — nothing unpleasant existed; it was a mistake or a misinterpretation.

While one of my father's primary motivations

seemed to be to ferret out a harsh truth, expose it, and gloat over his correct suspicion that it had indeed been there, Mother's was to say, "Ira, you're just tired; you'll feel different in the morning." So many nights and so many mornings rolled around with my trying to fathom the opposing natures of Mr. and Mrs. Ira O. Beaty, and at the same time condition myself to the best approach for survival and level-headedness. I wanted to believe Mother, that nothing bad existed, but it got to be so I knew it wasn't true. On the other hand, living wasn't always as suspect as Dad said either.

Thank goodness, when I was three, a companion in adjustment and rebellion entered my life. Wrapped in a blanket, he was handed to me to hold. He spent most of his time yelling, and with growing finesse and sometimes astounding precision, he has been doing so ever since. The grownups called him Little Henry, because he looked like the character in the comic strip. Looking on him today, I can't remember when he stopped looking like Little Henry and started looking like Superman. His real name is Warren.

He was my kid brother and we were friends, in fact allies. We had to be, because otherwise we found ourselves battling each other, vying for favor as a result of the competition unconsciously imposed on us by our parents. They probably didn't even know they were doing it, but Warren and I felt it. We would fight each other until an outside force intruded; then we stuck together. Sometimes my allegiance to him would go too far. If some bigger boy on the block started a fight with Warren, I would rush in like Rocky Graziano and finish him off. Warren would look grateful but bewildered, because he really wanted to take the risk himself; and I would lose boy friend after boy friend because I was too "powerhouse" (my nickname after hitting fifteen home runs in a row as the only girl on the team).

Conformity was the rule of behavior in our neighborhood. We were all Baptists. Every single last modest tree-lined person on the block was a white Southern American middle-class Baptist. Oh, maybe there were a few Methodists but not enough to hurt. We lived according to what our neighbors thought, and I guess they were living according to what we thought (which was wishing they would stop thinking what we were thinking).

Mother loved to garden, but someone gossiped over the back fence about the big picture sunhat and the shorts she wore. Warren and I loved to see her out there looking like a walking umbrella, but Dad agreed with the neighbors that she was too conspicuous, so she didn't go out very much after that.

Sometimes I felt I couldn't find Mother. She was under there somewhere, but Warren and I could never really find her.

When I finally quit the ball team and got a steady boy friend, Dad suggested that he (Dick, age fourteen) take a job painting someone else's house instead of ours, because across the street they said it took him six hours to paint my bedroom shutters. So, instead of coming to the house, Dick used to meet me by the creek. It was more fun anyway, and soon I discovered I

507

didn't have to ask my parents one single question about the birds and the bees. I didn't know my mother and father well enough anyway.

Warren used to love model cars, and he could name every car made since the invention of the wheel. Whenever he played with them and forgot to collect them at the end of the day, Dad would come home, feign tripping over one, fall down, and then warn Warren sternly that it was O.K. for that to happen to his own father, but could he imagine how much we could be sued for it if it happened to a stranger on our property? So Warren took his toy cars to his room and finally just didn't play with them any more.

So, because of Dad's sometimes distorted discipline and Mother's insistence that "we were lucky to have such a lovely life really," and the neighbors' twisted frustrations, which permeated even the good times, Warren and I breathed the breath of rebellion into each other. A kind of conniving rebellion to beat the system. It wasn't easy, because the principal of the school we attended was our father, so we were expected to set a good example. How could we set a good example and still enjoy life? It took teamwork. Together we shared the responsibility of being model children. Warren never tracked mud into the house or ate cookies in the living room. I always made beds, did the breakfast dishes, and shut the windows when it rained. In the house we were exemplary citizens, never too exemplary though, or they would suspect. And our parents were proud of us.

Outside we really lived. We emptied garbage

cans on other people's front porches, punched holes in tires, set off fire alarms, rang doorbells and ran, stole Twinkies cupcakes and Luden's cough drops from the corner grocery, and crossed busy boulevards with fake limps, sometimes pretending to drop dead in the middle until someone called a cop — and then we beelined it for shelter.

All this was somehow unknown to the stern figure who presided at the head of the dinner table. At the end of the day, we would sit nodding in agreement as he complained earnestly that delinquent kids were ruining the neighborhood. At the other end of the table Mother listened with a sad sparkle in her eyes, saying nothing.

After dinner Dad would light his brierwood pipe, the smoke curling about his head and drifting in blue layers up to the fake Chippendale mirror, blending with smells of roast beef and gravy. Presently he would pick up the thread again, expounding on his theory that all kids should be put on ice until they were twenty-one.

Enthusiastically willing to prove him right, Warren and I would retreat to our homework — and blueprint the plan of action for the next day — our new plan of action against the establishment. A small plan and a small establishment, but a promise of things to come.

I was born with very weak bone structure in my ankles. Soon after I learned to walk I began having problems. My ankles turned in so far and were so weak that with the slightest misstep I would fall. So, about age three, for therapeutic reasons, Mother took me to a ballet class. There my imagination took anchor, my energy found a channel. What started as therapy became my life. And I had an outlet for expression.

For the next fifteen years the long lines of girls in sweaty black leotards, straining in unison at the steel practice bar to the beat of the tinny piano, became my challenge, my competition. I needed no urging to join them; I loved it from the beginning. Some of the young ladies were there to lose weight, some to pass the awkward years of adolescence, others to give their mothers an extra two hours at the bridge table. But a few fragile, iron-willed youngsters truly wanted to dance, and dedicated themselves to endless hours of toil, sweat, sore muscles, and repetition. I became one of these — not fragile, but iron-willed.

We moved to Arlington, Virginia, and I went to classes in a big house built on a grassy knoll across the Potomac River in Washington, D. C. The house was renovated into a dance studio and became the Washington School of the Ballet.

Every afternoon during the school week, I spent an hour and a half on the bus going to and from the school. It was run by two expert lady teachers, and it was they who molded my professional attitudes toward my work. The elder was Lisa Gardiner, who had danced with Anna Pavlova. A dignified woman with silver hair, she moved with a stately gait and bearing that reminded me somehow of Cinderella's horses. She would sit for hours telling me of her travels with the ballet, and as she talked her graceful hands floated through the air, her slender pink nails accenting her words. "If you choose to do something, be sure to do it with your utmost," she would say to me. "And remember, expect nothing and life will be velvet."

Her partner, Mary Day, was fifteen years younger and had tiny feet that could turn out so far they made a straight line, piercing black eyes, and a temperament that would have frightened a Cossack. She was an excellent teacher, whose demanding, harsh, and sometimes irrational perfectionism made each class an event.

These were the women I strove to please, five days a week, year after year. We were not a professional group, because none of us was paid for our performances, but no greater precision could have been asked of professionals. By the time I was twelve, I was part of what I'm sure was the best amateur ballet company in the United States. At various times during the year, we performed ballets with the National Symphony at Constitution Hall, and for these occasions we rehearsed far into the night, after our regular classes. *Cinderella, The Nutcracker, The Wizard of Oz, Hansel and Gretel.* I always played Hansel — and every other boy's role, for that matter — because I was always the tallest in the class.

Rehearsals ended at midnight. I would rush for the bus, which, it seemed, was always either late or early, but never on schedule. I'd stumble groggily from the bus an hour and a half later, and make my way down the quiet street to a dark and silent house. My dinner usually was

511

saltine crackers smothered in ketchup and Tabasco, and with them a quart of ginger ale. I always ate standing up, and then I'd stagger to bed, rarely before two o'clock. Not surprisingly, my snacks produced nightmares, and the nightmares were always the same: night after night I missed the bus.

At six-thirty I was up again for school, ready to start over — day . . . after day . . . after day, until I was about seventeen. Rebellious, mischievous days with Warren were over. I had found a way out, a destiny I could follow, a life I could make for myself so I wouldn't end up like every other petty, comfortable Baptist in the community. I seldom saw my parents, and I didn't see Warren much after that, either. They were asleep when I left for school in the morning, because Washington-Lee was so crowded half the students went on early-morning shifts (six-thirty bus pickup), and generally asleep when I returned at night, because the bus trip home took 1½ hours from the time midnight rehearsals ended.

It was a lonely life, for a teenager especially, but I had a purpose — a good reason for being. And I learned something about myself that still holds true: I cannot enjoy anything unless I work hard at it.

An incident occurred when I was about sixteen that still blazes in my memory. I came home from a dancing-school rehearsal distraught because they had taken the role of Cinderella away from me for our Chirstmas production. Miss Day and Miss Gardiner said I had simply grown too tall, and that I looked clumsy.

I remember blurting it out in tears as I climbed the stairs to go to my room to be alone. Dad was coming down the stairs. He stopped, and with finger wagging told me that that should teach me to stop trying to do things I wasn't capable of. Wasn't this episode proof enough for me that, if I attempted to go beyond my range, I would only be crushed? Hadn't he told me many times during my life? When would I believe him? When would I understand that if I tried I would only be hurt?

It was like the time I sang "I Can't Say No" a few years before, at the entertainment assembly program. I had seen *Oklahoma* and fallen in love with the comedy character Ado Annie. I somehow felt I understood the level of her comedy. I put on a silly perky hat with a huge flower square on top and big clodhopper shoes, and when I did it at school everybody laughed — they really laughed. But Dad said I shouldn't be lulled into thinking that theirs was reliable laughter, that a high-school assembly wasn't the world, that I didn't know how to sing, and knew nothing about performing, and just because I had been tickled and moved by Celeste Holm didn't give me the right to take such a standard example of American musical comedy and desecrate it on the stage of Washington-Lee High School. . . . I never sang after that, not even "The Star-Spangled Banner" at assembly. I was too self-conscious. I thought he must be right. He said only people who had been taught things well and had been classically trained had the background to perform and be accepted. Naïve, raw instinct

513

was one thing, but it couldn't compare with traditional education. Only a fool would dare spread his arms wide, exposing his heart, and say — without training — "Here I am, World, I've got something to say." Only a deadhead would believe he could get away with that, because he'd get hurt — and hurt badly. And someone who might realize the pitfalls but say, "Up yours, World, I'm going to say it anyway," would have to be put away. Not only would he be insane — he'd be dangerous. He'd be dangerous because he was willing to be hurt.

I fell on the stairs, that December evening after rehearsal, with my father over me, berating me not only for trying to perform, but for thinking that I could dance Cinderella, and for making a conspicuous ass out of myself as a result. And I cried hard — I cried so hard that I vomited. But the vomit on the stairs didn't stop him; he went right on driving home his point, that I would only be hurt if I dared to dare. I couldn't move. I looked over at Mother in the living room. Warren wasn't home. Mother sat quietly until finally she said, "All right, Ira, that's enough." But Ira knew that wasn't going to be the end of it. He could see, even though I had dissolved into a little pile of protoplasm, that I would never stop daring. And he seemed to understand that ironically he, in effect, was teaching me to dare because I saw that he was such a spectacular disappointment to himself for having never tried it. A strange clear look of understanding came into his eyes as he realized I didn't want to be like him. He stepped over the vomit and went to the kitchen to fix himself a drink. It was then that I determined to make the most of whatever equipment I had been born with, and part of that equipment was to dare. But mostly I didn't want to be a disappointment to myself.

It was the evening of the *Cinderella* performance. I was dancing the Fairy Godmother, and I stood in the wings after completing my *pliés* and warming-up exercises. The orchestra tuned up, the house lights dimmed, and the audience quieted. The overture began and the curtain was about to open. Before it did, I took a few practice *grands jetés* across the stage. *Snap* — I went down. A sharp pain pierced my right ankle as it doubled under me. Terrified, I looked quickly around to see if anyone had noticed. No one had. Dancers fall down all the time. I looked at the ankle. It was already swollen. I tightened my toe-shoe ribbon to a death grip, and stood up. The curtain went up.

I climbed on point and began to dance. With each movement I seemed to step further out of myself. The pain left me. I began to feel a sense of triumph that gave me strength — not an anesthetized strength as though I had dulled the pain, but more as though my mind had risen above me and was looking down. The dance movements came in an easy flow, and I felt that I was soaring above myself. I knew the pain was there, but I was on top of it somehow. It was probably my first experience in mind over matter. And the feeling was exquisite. On a ballet stage in Washington, D.C., I first came in contact with my potential talent for becoming a mystic!

Two and a half hours later the ballet and curtain calls were over. I asked for an ambulance, and then the pain hit me. I didn't walk for four months.

While I was laid up with my broken ankle I asked mother to have a talk with me. There had never been many significant talks between us, because I always felt that "significant" subjects would be painful for her. But this talk was necessary, and I would have to stumble in the dark a bit, hoping that I could find part of her that I wouldn't hurt.

I remember sitting with my foot up on pillows on the edge of my bed in my room, gazing at my freckled face in a hand mirror. My face embarrassed me most of the time and I couldn't get a comb through my mass of unruly, tangled red hair.

Mother paused in front of the door. With a glance toward the back yard where my father sat, she entered the room and sat down beside me on the bed.

"What's wrong?" she asked, bracing herself as though anticipating disaster.

"I guess I want to be too many things, too many people," I began, gesturing at the walls covered with the symbols of my restlessness. She looked at the maps, the photographs of famous ballerinas, at the books filled with other people and other places, and at the high-powered telescope I wished would take me to the moon. The familiar sad sparkle filled her eyes.

"But I have to go away from here — away from the schedule, the rigid discipline, the conformity. Perhaps it's been good, and useful, and necessary, but there's so much out there I have to see, and have to do, and have to be a part of."

My words were cutting straight through to her heart, I could see that, and her expression was more than I could bear. She understood only too well. It was something she had wanted to do herself once, a long time ago when her spirit was independent, before she succumbed to being what she thought she *should* be. Her friends told me she had been "delightfully carefree" and that her gaiety had infected everyone she met. I never remembered her that way. I wondered what had happened, and I guess I didn't want it to happen to me.

She changed her position on the bed. "The ballet is stifling you, too, isn't it?"

"Yes," I answered. "I don't know how it started or why, but ballet seems so limited. Miss Gardiner and Miss Day are always telling me not to move my face so much, but I can't help it, and I don't *want* to help it. If the music means laughter to me, my face smiles, naturally. They told me that if I can't control it I should go into movies or something."

"What do *you* want to do to express yourself?" she asked.

"I want to interpret people and what they think and feel. I think I love people, but I don't know very much about them. And I want to be more specific about the way I express myself. I

517

don't want to be a mechancial doll in a mechanical art, and I'm not even sure I want to dance it."

"Have you thought about how you would do it?"

"Well, yes, but I never get very far because I'm afraid."

"Afraid of what?"

"Well, I don't know how to explain it. It's something about being stuck with being me."

"What do you mean?"

"Well, you know how much I love the Spanish dance, for instance."

"Yes."

"And you know that at ballet school it's my favorite class, and you know that I've worked hard at the castanets and the heel beats, and you know that Miss Gardiner and Miss Day think that I'm the best one in the class since Liane left."

"Yes," she agreed. "I think so, too."

"Well, even though it's something I really love doing, I'm self-conscious about it."

"Why?"

"Because how can I expect the audience to believe that I'm a Spanish dancer if I'm really an American girl from Virginia? How can I ever be anything more if that's what I really am?"

Mother folded her hands in her lap, sat up straighter than she had in years.

"Above all, you must know emotions. Study how people *feel*. I believe that is one thing we are all capable of understanding in others. We may not always be able to understand how they live, or accept what they eat, who they pray to, or why they die, but we can all, with a little effort, understand how another *feels*. How does a Spanish dancer feel? She dances to the same music we hear. What does she feel when she hears it? When you can convey what she feels, then anyone would believe you're a Spanish dancer, too, in spite of your red hair and freckles."

I hugged her. She didn't seem trampled on any more.

"May I go to New York? May I go as soon as I graduate?"

All her years of frustration came alive in one moment. The sad sparkle vanished from her eyes. She answered with unflinching certainty. "Yes, it's time. Your father won't like the idea, he'll think you'll get hurt or taken, but then isn't that always the risk? I think you're prepared."

So I was free to try my wings. I remember the morning I left home. Warren had skipped football practice. He sat down at the piano to beat the hell out of it. He used to work everything out on the piano, and this particular morning he was working it out on "Manhattan Towers." He was tall and handsome by now and didn't need me any more to finish his battles. I wondered when I'd see him again. I wondered when he'd decide what he would do with his life. He still had three years of high school to go, three years to be fending for himself. I didn't know then (because he was as shy about his inside self as all of us) that every afternoon while Mom and Dad were grocery shopping and I was at dancing class,

Warren was in the basement acting out his soul to every Al Jolson record ever made, and memorizing in detail every play Eugene O'Neill ever wrote. It wouldn't be long before we'd meet again; it would be only a matter of a few years, really — just long enough for us both to get established.

I don't think either of us ever seriously considered that we *wouldn't* be able to make something of ourselves. We *had* to; it was the only way we'd have any respect for ourselves. We *wanted* to live up to whatever our potentials might be. The frustrating spectacle of people who hadn't, who had been afraid to, and were bitterly disappointed in themselves as a result, had been crippling to us in many ways as we grew up; but, on the other hand, their failures and frustrations had been so clear that Warren and I had a precise blueprint of how *not* to be.

And one of the lessons we learned was to judge ourselves, to conduct ourselves according to what *we* thought was best for us, not by what others might think. In the final analysis, we would have only ourselves to answer to; to live inside of. It was *he* whom he didn't want to disappoint. And it was *I* whom I wanted to be proud of.

So I thought, as I left Virginia that day, "He'll do something. And it will be his way, just as I am going off to do something my way." But I knew then that, whatever it was, somehow it would continue to be a joint plan against the established way of doing things. And in a way I secretly thanked Mom and Dad for inadvertently channeling us on such a course.

I arrived in New York at eighteen, wide-eyed, optimistic, brave, and certain I would crash the world of show business overnight. Naïveté is a necessary personality trait in order to endure New York, and a masochistic sense of humor an indispensable quirk.

I took an apartment at 116th Street and Broadway with the money I had saved from babysitting in Arlington. It was a sub-sub-sublet, a fifth-floor walkup in an old brownstone building, where for sixty-four dollars a month I had two tiny bedrooms, a bath, a kitchen, and a view of the Hudson. To release the bathtub drain, I had to take up two of the floor boards and unplug it from underneath. To see the Hudson, I had to line myself up with a half-inch slit between two brick buildings. One of the bedrooms had no closet, the other no windows, and the kitchen was a hot plate and a small, filthy sink.

But the shabbiness wasn't the only reason for the low rent. At night people lurked in the dark shadows of doorways, and doors opened an inch or two as eyes followed me while I made my way up the four flights. The building was crawling with dope addicts.

The first year I had twelve different roommates. They bombed out on half the rent for reasons ranging from unemployment to out-of-wedlock motherhood. One of their problems I shared, the other I didn't.

One roommate departed regularly every night at midnight for cookies and milk. I never saw anyone so fond of cookies and milk. It took her all night to eat them. One morning she showed up wearing a mink coat, and that afternoon she moved out.

My first few weeks in New York were an initiation into the kingdom of bugs. Sleep was impossible. I complained to the absentee landlord about my six-legged companions. He told me to plug my ears and keep my mouth closed.

The exterminator I called was more sympathetic, but he was a thirty-year-old Italian with an appetite for other things. He squirted the bed bugs. He saved the cockroaches until I called him again.

At first I lived principally on whole-wheat English muffins, graham crackers, and honey (for energy). It all tasted of garlic, because the superintendent's wife cooked with so much garlic that nobody else in the building ever had to buy any. Every night, before going to bed, I'd sit watching the cockroach army as it marched across the living room toward the kitchen. I could almost hear them groan as, night after night, they found the same old graham-cracker and muffin crumbs.

Summer was stifling and the apartment a tomb. I would climb up the fire escape to the street roof, where I'd cling precariously, hoping to hang on long enough to get some sun. Instead I'd be covered with soot.

Winter was a different nightmare. The double window in the bedroom was minus several panes, which were never replaced. The snow filtered down between the buildings and piled up on the floor in patterns that matched the missing panes as I lay shivering in bed.

Jobs were unheard of, especially for dancers. I had been lucky in the summer, having gotten a job at a "summer theatre in the round" in New Jersey, but for the fall season the competition was too severe. Every penny I owned went into dance lessons, which were essential if I was ever to get a job. Food was less important. I always ate at an Automat, where I learned to stretch a dime in a manner that might have won the approval of Horatio Alger himself — a manner that was standard among ballet dancers in New York. Lined up on the iced-tea counter were rows of glasses, each containing a wedge of lemon. I took several glasses, proceeded to the water fountain, filled them with water, carried them to a table, and poured in the sugar. At no cost I filled myself to the bloating point with delicious lemonade before spending the precious dime for a peanut-butter sandwich on raisin bread. This went on for nearly a year, and it took me another ten before I could face lemonade or peanut butter again.

Even though they couldn't really afford it, my parents were willing to help me, but I never asked. I didn't want them to. I had chosen this life and I would handle it in the best way I knew how.

My funds were completely gone and the landlord had posted an eviction notice on the door, when Fate led me to an audition for the Servel Ice Box trade show, which, though not in my fantasized life plan, would enable me to eat.

The show was auditioning for the road — the

southern circuit — with one-night stands in every major city in the South, playing before conventions of traveling salesmen who worked for Servel. Normally only a deadbeat would take such a job, but at that time even solo dancers begged for chorus jobs.

I was standing in line with the other applicants, staring into the darkness of the theater and waiting for the audition to begin, when suddenly a harsh voice called from the back row, "Hey, you with the legs."

Everyone stood stock-still.

"You with the red hair and the legs that start at your shoulders — step forward."

I looked right and then left. There were short girls on either side of me.

"You mean me, sir?" I asked timidly.

"Yeah. What's your name?"

"Shirley Beaty, sir."

"Shirley Batty? That's a funny name."

"Not Batty. Beaty."

"Yeah, that's what I said: Beauty."

"Not Beauty, Bay-tee."

"Okay, so it's BAY-TEE. Don't you have a middle name or something?"

"Yes, sir — MacLaine."

"Okay, Shirley MacLaine, you're hired."

"But I haven't danced a step yet."

"Who asked you? You've got legs, haven't you?"

"Yes, sir."

"Well, go over and sign in with the stage manager if you want to be in this show."

"Yes, sir."

"Wait a minute. Can you do fouetté turns — you know — the ones where you keep going around on the same foot?"

"Yes sir. Would you like to see them?"

"Why, do you lie?"

"Of course not, sir."

"Well, never mind then. Your job is to do those fouetté turns around the Servel ice-maker machine until the ice is made. And if the machine gets stuck you keep going — understand?"

"Yes, sir."

I walked across the stage, thinking of the small life-time of hard work, the iron discipline of ballet, the money poured into the lessons, the grueling schedule I'd kept — and here all I'd had to do was put on a pair of mesh tights and stand up.

"Wait a minute, kid. How old are you?"

"Just twenty-one, sir."

"I thought you said you didn't lie."

"Well, I . . ."

"Forget it — you're the liar. I'm not."

In Raleigh, North Carolina, the ice maker got stuck. I fouettéed and fouettéd until I nearly turned into whipped cream, while the salesmen, turning dizzy at the sight, whistled and clapped for me to stop.

In most of the cities we played in defunct movie houses with stages to match, and dancing on them was like dancing on the Burma Road. A piano player and conductor traveled with the company, and to round out the band we used pickup musicians along the way.

The musicians had orders to stop playing as

soon as the curtain closed, and the signal that we were ready to go on to the next number was when the curtain reopened. The musicians took their instructions very literally. Sometimes the men hired to close the curtain took a longer smoke than usual and missed a cue. Seeing the curtain still open, the musicians wouldn't stop, going right on into the next number. In order to catch up with the runaway music we changed our costumes in full view of the audience, dancing the next number as we dressed. Whenever that happened, the Servel salesmen brought us back for encores.

Swan Lake was the *pièce de résistance* of the show, and the fact that it was performed around a Servel washing machine added spice to the choreographer's conception. As Queen of the Swans, I decided to spice the spice.

Dressed in a beautiful white tutu, I adjusted my toe shoes and made ready for the rigorous workout ahead. The classical strains of *Swan Lake* rose to the rafters of the abandoned movie house that would soon be a bowling alley. Neatly sidestepping the rusty nails that protruded every few feet, I made my entrance.

I had blacked out my two front teeth and did the whole number with a saintly smile. After the show I was fired, and sent back to New York.

My husband and I met in a bar on West Forty-fifth Street in New York City. The year was 1952.

Securely trapped in the chorus line of *Me and Juliet,* my insubordinate spirit was rapidly becoming subordinate. The rut was unbearable. The security of the weekly paycheck, meager but constant, lulled me into a state of habitual nonproductivity. There seemed no challenge to anything.

I looked up. He was standing beside our table.

"Shirley," my girl friend from the chorus said, "this is Steve Parker."

He was of medium height, about five feet nine, and as I stood to make room for him, I quickly slipped off my high heels. He noticed and smiled. Our eyes met. They were the bluest truth I had ever seen. I nearly climbed into them. His nose and cheekbones were perfectly chiseled, and his jawline was so firm I thought he must know exactly where he was going. He was about twelve years older than I. My mouth must have dropped open.

"How do you do," he said. "Why don't you shut your mouth and sit down? Aren't you drinking?"

"No, I don't drink," I answered as I shoved the whole top of my ginger-ale glass into my mouth in an effort to be intriguing. I was nineteen.

"That's cute," he said, "What do you do for an encore?"

"I try to get it out," I mumbled, realizing that it was stuck. He reached over and pried the glass from my mouth before it cracked.

I fell in love with him immediately.

"You need taking care of," he said, laughing. "Don't do any more of those tricks, or I may fall in love with you."

Four hours later he asked me to marry him. Because I was a respectable lady from Virginia, I made him wait until morning for my answer.

He was not surprised. "Fine, then it's settled," he said. "It was only a question of time, anyway."

He was right then, and he has always been the only person in my life to be unfailingly right about me. He knows me better than I know myself. He knows what gives me life and what drives it from me. And when I met him my life began.

The world came alive. Frustration became courage, and hard work became inspired concentration. We read books together — books I had never known existed. He had traveled all over the world, and even though his own wanderlust had been partially satisfied, he recognized the same restlessness in me. If I was to know myself, he said, I must know others. He encouraged me to resurrect my collection of maps, and we pored over them, claiming the faraway lands for our own, and vowing to touch the soul of every one of them. We promised to devote ourselves to trying to understand people and ideas beyond our local experience.

He seemed to be an extension of what I wanted to be myself, and the more dependent I became on him, the more independent I seemed to become in my own life.

An enigmatic man with an air of sophistication, Steve was assertive, but he was shy among the profiteering rodents of theatrical society. An actor by trade, Shakespearean by choice, he often directed off-Broadway plays containing "some meaning," but his background propelled him in other directions, making it impossible for him to accept the competitive battleground of show business as a way of life.

His formative years had been spent aboard a cargo ship. When he was nine years old the Depression hit, putting his father, a ship's engineer, out of work. In the same year his mother contracted tuberculosis. The family was destitute. His mother was placed in a welfare hospital in New England, and his father, desperate for a job, finally found one on a cargo ship bound for the Orient — not as a ship's engineer, but as a stoker.

With no other living relatives to care for him, Steve shipped out with his father, and a small bunk in a cramped stateroom became his home. The world and its ports became his boyhood neighborhood and their inhabitants his playmates. Mr. Parker taught him everything there was to know about ships, including how to shovel coal, and at night they talked of the world and the places they would see together.

From childhood, Steve's favorite land was Japan. Sometimes his father allowed him to stay with old family friends, the Hasagawas. During those times he went to school in the port of Yokohama while the cargo ship continued its run to Kobe, Osaka, Nagasaki, Niigata, Shanghai, Hong Kong, Taipei, and finally back to Yokohama. Whenever the ship went back to the United States, Steve returned to New England to visit his mother.

The ruggedly good-looking blue-eyed boy with

the securely independent nature became more Asian than Occidental. He learned his schoolwork in Japanese, and by the time he was twelve years old he could speak, read, and write several other Asian languages as well. Except for the separation from his mother, he enjoyed the wandering life, which lasted for five years, until he returned to America in 1936. Slowly the Depression came to an end, and the family enjoyed one year together before his mother died. Within a year, his despondent father died too, and Steve was left alone. After teenage years of odd jobs and a meager existence, he managed to complete his high-school education not long before his beloved boyhood land bombed Pearl Harbor.

He joined the paratroops and later found himself fighting in hand-to-hand combat with people he had actually gone to school with. He was invaluable to his outfit because of his knowledge of the Japanese — their language and customs. He continued to fight until he was separated from his outfit during a mission in the jungles of New Guinea, where he survived by making friends with headhunters.

Steve was with the first troops that went to Hiroshima after the bomb. He surveyed the remains of the land he had once loved. Lost and numb, he cursed his partnership with both worlds.

He stayed in the army because he had no other path to follow. He was highly decorated and discharged with honors — a captain at twenty-two. He would return to his other world, of that he was certain. The question was when — and how.

Steve and I met in 1952, but so intense was our involvement, we forgot to get married until 1954. In fact, 1954 was a landmark for two reasons.

The Pajama Game was a musical based on Richard Bissel's novel *7½ Cents*, and it was all about life in an Iowa pajama factory. Early in 1954, when the show was forming, Steve encouraged me to audition for a place in the chorus. Director George Abbott said he hired me because whenever I opened my mouth on stage they could hear every breath in the peanut gallery.

Even while the show was still on the road, it was obvious that it would be a hit, and equally obvious that it would give Broadway a new star, the late Carol Haney. The out-of-town critics couldn't find words sufficient to express their delight in her sense of comedy and in her songs and dances.

The night before the New York opening, I was made Carol's understudy. I had never had a rehearsal, but as the producer, Hal Prince, said, "It doesn't really matter. Carol is one person who would go on with a broken neck."

On May 9, 1954, *The Pajama Game* opened in New York to rave reviews both for the show and for Carol. She had been a choreographer's assistant for years, but now the public thronged to the stage door, clamoring for a glimpse of the brilliant performer they had discovered "overnight." She was singled out as the musical-comedy find of the decade.

It looked very much as though I, on the other hand, would be chorus girl of the century. Four nights passed. I still hadn't had an understudy rehearsal, but whenever I wasn't onstage I watched Carol from the wings, trying to learn the part even though I doubted I would ever need to know it. Only four days after the opening and already I was deeply depressed. I was in another hit! More weekly paychecks, enervating security, and monotony.

After the first Wednesday matinee I went back to the apartment to fix dinner for Steve. While we were eating I had a phone call from one of the producers of *Can-Can*, which had been running about two years. He offered me a job as understudy to his lead dancer.

"We know you must realize," he said, "that nothing will ever keep Haney from going on in *Pajama Game*, and our girl is out every now and then."

I asked him to let me think it over.

While we finished eating, I discussed it with Steve, who felt that if being in another long run was more than I could take, then I should leave *Pajama Game* immediately. I agreed, and before leaving for the theater I wrote my notice, intending to turn it in that night. Running late, I rushed for the subway and would have done better walking. The train got stuck in its tunnel, and I arrived at the theater panting, late by half an hour.

Hal Prince and his co-producer, the late Bobby Griffith, were pacing the sidewalk at the stage-door entrance, wringing their hands.

"Where have you *been?*" they asked.

"Gee, I'm awfully sorry. The subway got

stuck, but I'll hurry. Anyway I don't go on till the middle of the first act."

"That's what *you* think! HANEY BROKE HER ANKLE THIS AFTERNOON AND YOU'RE ON RIGHT NOW!"

I was carrying my notice in my hand. I stuffed in back into my purse. The world spun around four times — once for each time I had watched Carol do the part. A horrible thought jumped into my mind and kept running: *I know I'll drop the derby in "Steam Heat," I know I'll drop the derby in "Steam Heat."*

"Steam Heat" opened the second act and it was the show stopper — a song-and-dance number for a trio of two men and a girl. The routine called for a derby to be tumbled, thrown, spun, and juggled throughout the number.

They hustled me to Carol's dressing room. I asked someone to call Steve. I shook so hard that someone else had to put the makeup on my face. (I was sure to drop the derby.) A wardrobe woman zipped up my first-act costume and it fitted. Relief. Then came the shoes. *Disaster*. Her size four wasn't even big enough for my big toe. I rushed to the basement where I always dressed and found a pair of my own black tennis shoes. They didn't go with the costume, but if the audience was looking at my feet I was in big trouble anyway.

Above me I heard the audience stamping, impatient because the curtain hadn't gone up.

John Raitt, the leading man, was learning the words to my songs in case I forgot them, and Eddie Foy, Jr., one of the co-leads, was so nervous that he was throwing up in his dressing room.

I raced up and waited in the wings as the stage manager walked out before the curtain and gestured for attention.

"Ladies and gentlemen," he said. "The management regrets to announce that Miss Carol Haney will not be performing tonight. Her role will be performed by a young lady named Shirley MacLaine. We hope you will enjoy the show."

His last words were drowned out as the audience set up a terrific boo. Many people rose and made straight for the box office to get their money back. *Chaos.* Hal Hastings, the conductor, stared up from the pit, a shaken man. He had no idea what key I sang in, or even if I sang at all, but resolutely he raised his baton. The musicians strightened in their chairs, and on cue they struck up the overture to try to drown out the hubbub that was still coming from the audience.

In the middle of the overture, Steve rushed in, and for a moment he just stood there, looking like a zombie.

He reached for my hand. "This should teach you patience," he said. "And remember — most people don't get this break in a whole lifetime, so, for everybody who waits, make the most of it."

Then, muttering the actors' good luck, *"Merde,"* he pat-patted me on the fanny and went out to join the audience. His napkin from dinner was trailing from the pocket of his jacket.

The overture ended. I had to go to the

bathroom so badly I was afraid to walk.

The curtain went up.

Taking a deep breath, I made it safely to center stage. From the corner of my eye I could see the cast lined up in the wings, watching. A hush came over the audience. They seemed to understand how I felt. The most important people in show business were out there. They had come to see Carol Haney, but I was onstage instead. I took another breath and spoke the first line. My high, raucous voice blasted in the ears. The line was supposed to get a laugh. It didn't. Just as I began the second speech, they laughed at the first one. I hadn't waited long enough, hadn't given them time. Just because I was ready didn't mean they were. I slowed the tempo of my delivery and soon we were on the same beat. I felt them relax, *en masse*, and I did too. There is nothing worse than an audience that's afraid for a performer. Suddenly the flow of communication that I had longed for all my life was there. It wasn't the applause and laughter that fulfilled me; it was the magnetism, the current, moving from one human being to the others and back again, like a giant pendulum. I was in time with the audience, no longer at odds with it.

John Raitt sang "Hernando's Hideway" for me, and I remember how strange Carol's song sounded in someone else's voice. For weeks I had been hearing the lines and songs in her voice, and now it took a combined effort to accomplish what she had done alone.

Then came the opening of the second act and "Steam Heat." Carol's black tuxedo fitted me

535

and even the derby, custom-made for her head, was fine.

The muted trumpet sounded in the orchestra pit as the curtain opened on the number that had already become a classic in musical comedy. The three of us held our opening positions until the applause of recognition had died down. I held my breath, feeling the weight and texture of the derby on my head, wanting to practice juggle the opening trick one more time.

In unison we danced our way to the footlights, threw our derbies into the air, and caught them simultaneously. The audience clapped again. Maybe I would get through it after all. The trumpet led the orchestra to a crescendo in a swinging wail and the theater seemed to rock. Each trick went perfectly. Then the music stopped: time for the *pièce de résistance*. We would execute it in silence.

Our backs were to the audience. In unison, we rolled the derbies from our heads, spilled them down our arms, flipped them high into the air and caught them at the last moment before the audience could figure out how it was done. Then it happened. I dropped my derby. There was a gasp from the audience. The derby crashed to the stage and rolled to the edge of the orchestra pit, where it mercifully decided not to fall in. Because my back was to the audience and because I just didn't realize that I wasn't in the chorus any more, I didn't think about controlling my reaction.

"Shit!" I muttered to myself, thinking that only the other two dancers could hear it.

The first three rows gasped again, and the word spread through the theater. Well . . . I thought. I come all this way, wait all this time, and now . . . what a way to end!

I rushed to the footlights, picked up the derby, put it on, shrugged a sort of apology to the audience, and finished the number. I remember little else. I can't remember whether or not they clapped after the routine, and I barely remember the rest of the second act.

The curtain rang down on the show and then up again for the curtain calls.

The audience stood. They cheered — and threw kisses. I felt as though a giant caress had enveloped me. The cast backed off, formed a semicircle around me, and applauded.

I stood there alone, wearing the black-and-white convict-striped pajama jacket that matched Eddie Foy's convict pants. I reached out, beckoning the cast to close in around me and share the applause, but they only backed off more and left me in the center to bask. I was overwhelmed with loneliness. When you've trained as a ballet dancer you are trained to be part of a team. You devote your talent to being a link that makes up the chain. You don't think in terms of being different or special. The desire lurks underneath, but you continually suppress it. And so with the night I went on in *Pajama Game* everything changed. I was out in front of the chain and I felt lonely, and yet at the same time I felt so much that I belonged. The curtain rang up and down to prolonged applause. I knew I could step out of the line and be myself any time

I wanted to now, I belonged to myself and from then on I would have to devote all of me to developing that self the best way I knew how. No more blacked-out front teeth and Servel ice makers. Everything had changed. A higher level of hard work, toil, and struggle was necessary now. Talent was nothing but sweat.

I returned to my dressing room to collapse. Steve was waiting. "We have a lot of work to do," he said. "Your drunk scene in the second act was phony, so the first thing is to take you out and get you drunk. Then you'll know what it's all about." Smiling, he wiped the perspiration from my face. "By the way — you were great."

"Was I really?"

"To them, yes. But you still have a long way to go."

"Thanks," I muttered, resenting him for not letting me rest on my laurels.

"By the way, that 'shit' shit was very quaint. I guess you can take the girl out of the chorus, but you can't take the chorus out of the girl. I've talked to Hal Prince. Haney will be out for three weeks. Now let's go get drunk."

The second night I was on for Carol I met another man who helped change the course of my life. Although I didn't know it then, eventually I would have to fight him in court as well as in arenas that had nothing to do with the judiciary. The words he spoke were the words every young American female supposedly longs to hear.

"Miss MacLaine," he said, "my name is Hal Wallis, and I'm prepared to offer you a movie contract. In Hollywood."

He had come backstage after the show and was waiting for me when I emerged from the dressing room.

Hal Wallis . . . .

What I saw was a well-dressed man of clearly more than average prosperity, slightly hunched, with cagy, calculating eyes, and a face like a suntanned pear. I knew the name; I knew he was a big producer. But I couldn't bring myself to swoon.

"Aren't you the one who makes all those movies with Dean Martin and Jerry Lewis?" I asked.

"Yes. I discovered them, too."

"Too?"

"Yes. I just discovered you. I was in the audience tonight."

"You mean you want me to be one of those girls who run up and down the stairs in a yellow sunsuit?"

"Does some other color sunsuit — ah — suit you better?"

It was only a first taste of what was to come.

At Wallis's suggestion, Steve and I met him later. I was wearing my blue jeans, which matched Steve's and we met him at the Oak Room of the Plaza Hotel to discuss his proposal.

The headwaiter, doubtless alerted for this or a similar breach, let us and our blue jeans in, and steered us toward a table in the corner, where Wallis, swallowing his concern for appearances and flashing a jaundiced grin, rose to greet us.

After drinks we had soup, salad, thick juicy steaks, baked potatoes and Cherries Jubilee. But

Wallis was content to nibble on Ry-Krisp, and as the conversation progressed, I understood why. He had a very special feeling for his forty-odd million. He couldn't bear to part with a dime of it.

What he was offering me was a seven-year contract with loan-out privileges — most of the privileges being his. After scooping up the last of the Cherries Jubilee, Steve and I decided it would be best to let the offer hang until we could find an agent to represent me. We also wanted to see if there would be other offers.

We thanked Wallis for the dinner and went up to the apartment to work on my drunk scene.

It doesn't take theatrical agents long to smell where the new flesh is. Waiting on my doorstep were men from three different agencies. If I'd tried to see the same men in their offices a week earlier, I'd never have gotten beyond the elevator. Watching Steve handle them, I wondered how I, or any young girl, could ever have coped with all this alone. I relied on him for everything.

While continuing to stave off Wallis, with Steve's help I concentrated on improving my performance in *The Pajama Game*. Every night after the show, Steve rehearsed me, bringing in some of his director friends for their advice and criticism. He also found me a reliable agent, one who was not part of an all-consuming corporation, and he saw to it that representatives of every major Hollywood studio came to watch my performance.

They came and they watched, and I wondered why they even bothered. When they talked to me, I found they were interested in only two things:

1. What were my measurements?
2. Would I pose for cheesecake?

Not one of them made me a concrete offer. That left only Wallis, the man with the nose of a bloodhound.

I asked Hal Prince for his advice. "Don't go to Hollywood now," he said. "You don't have enough experience. Stay on Broadway and do a few more shows first."

"In the *chorus?*"

"It doesn't matter. Go to Hollywood now and you'll never be heard from again."

My new agent worked out a deal slightly different from the contract Wallis had offered, one that would bind me only five years instead of seven.

I signed with Wallis.

Hal Prince lamented: *"You'll be sorry."*

Carol Haney returned to the show; I went back to the chorus and waited for Hal Wallis to call me to Hollywood.

Two months later Carol came down with a terrible case of laryngitis and was unable to speak. Once again I went on for her, and once again there was someone special in the audience — this time a representative of Alfred Hitchcock.

He came to my dressing room after the show. "Mr. Hitchcock is looking for a suitably fey creature to play the lead in his next picture, *The Trouble with Harry,*" he said. "I think you will do just fine."

"Me? But I already have a contract with Hal

Wallis," I wailed.

"Mr. Hitchcock knows that. He would like you to meet him in his suite at the St. Regis tomorrow. If he likes you, he can work something out with Wallis."

The next day at the appointed time I rang the bell of Hitchcock's suite. "Come in, my dear." The accent was unmistakable. He swung open the door. "Sit down — and tell me what motion pictures you have acted in."

Well, I thought, this will be over in a hurry. "None, sir I'm afraid."

Hitchcock looked at me and nodded. He began pacing. "Is there some television film I could see, then?"

"No, sir. I've never done a television show."

"Well — what Broadway plays have you had roles in?"

"None, sir. I'm a chorus girl."

He was still pacing. "You mean you've never acted in anything at all?"

"No, sir, I haven't — except as an understudy."

He came to an abrupt halt. Suddenly his leg shot up, his foot came down heavily on the seat of a chair, and his elbow came to rest on his knee, all in one lightning motion. "That makes you about the color of a shamrock, doesn't it?"

"Yes, sir, I suppose so." I stood up. "Should I go now?"

"Of course not. Sit down. All this simply means that I shall have fewer bad knots to untie. You're hired."

I fell back in my chair.

"I shall need you on location — in Vermont — in three days. Can you make it?"

I wanted to say, "Has a mule got an ass?" but I didn't know him well enough.

I left the St. Regis in a daze and floated back to the apartment, where Steve was waiting for me. I blurted out the news. Vermont — in three days! And I wouldn't have to run up and down the stairs in a yellow sunsuit after all.

Steve was happy. In addition to eveything else, we were going on location in the area where he had spent part of his boyhood.

But when we told Hal Prince and Bobby Griffith, they thought I was making a big mistake.

"But will you let me out of my chorus contract?" I asked.

"Why not?" was the answer. "You'll be back."

The next day, between the matinee and evening performances, Steve and I were married, surprising nobody.

After the ceremony I went back to the theater, made my farewell appearance in *The Pajama Game*, thanked Bobby and Hal for being so cooperative, told everyone goodbye — and went off to my wedding night, which was surely one of the craziest wedding nights in the annals of matrimony.

I once knew a couple who spent their wedding night stark naked playing parchesi. Ours wasn't quite that bad, but it was bad enough. And the reasons weren't even psychiatric. They were legal.

Before marriage, I was a minor under the laws of New York, and therefore my parents had signed my contracts with Wallis and with my agent. Now that I was married, even though I was still only twenty, legally I was no longer a minor, and I could, if I wished, declare both contracts invalid and renegotiate on my own.

At that time I had no desire to annul my contract with Wallis, but my agent — the one we had thought so reliable and independent — was another matter. Almost immediately he had sold a half interest in me to Famous Artists, a huge agency, and I felt I had a legitimate complaint against him.

Agents have a way of knowing when one of them has a falling-out with a "property." Once again I was fair prey, and the fact that I was making a picture for Hitchcock apparently gave me new luster.

I had sublet my apartment that morning; Steve had been living at the Lambs Club, where women were not allowed to cross the threshold. Since we didn't have enough money for anything better, we had taken a tiny room in the Piccadilly Hotel, just across the street from the theater.

After saying our farewells, we left the theater by the stage-door exit.

From then on, it was all Mack Sennett.

Blocking the way were six agents from Famous Artists. They were brandishing new contracts, flapping them in our faces, jockeying for position, jostling, stepping on each other's toes, screaming: "Re-sign! Re-sign! . . . Sign with us! . . . We'll make you a star . . . We'll put your name in lights . . . Get your new contract right here!"

We dodged back into the theater and slammed

the door in their faces. Racing around to the lobby entrance, we found another mob scene — a swarming pack, bright-eyed and drooling. When we appeared, one very small man tried to climb through the bars of the box-office window to get at us. Again we fled, running back to the night watchman and asking for help. Through a secret passageway so old it must have been used by Fanny Brice and Nicky Arnstein, we sneaked from the theater and made our way to the Piccadilly, thinking the worst was over.

When we stepped from the elevator and headed down the hall, we saw that the door to our room was wide open. Jammed into the room like stuffed olives in a slim bottle were more agents, oozing contracts, and jabbing at us with ballpoint pens.

The closet was empty. Our clothes were gone.

"For you I have reserved the honeymoon suite at the Sherry-Netherland Hotel — at the expense of Famous Artists Agency," said a swarthy man who happened to be president of Famous Artists. "And your clothes have been sent ahead to be pressed."

On the rickety coffee table was a huge bottle of champagne — a magnum — with iced caviar around it. A pudgy man with a crew cut gestured grandly toward the champagne. "With the compliments of the William Morris Agency," he said.

Perched precariously near the edge of our connubial bed was a three-foot-high wedding cake. On it was a note saying, "We'll be back later when the other bums have left!" It was signed MCA.

I burst out laughing.

Steve took over. "Now, gentlemen, what do you suggest we do? Obviously she can't sign with all of you."

The president of Famous Artists, who had moved us to the Sherry-Netherland, spoke up. "Shall we proceed to the honeymoon suite and talk this over in more pleasant surroundings?"

"Only if we can all come!" bellowed the others.

"A limousine is waiting, courtesy of William Morris," said the pudgy one. "Shall we go?"

Steve and I exchanged amused glances. "Shirley and I like to walk," he said. "We'll meet you there."

Their reaction was apoplectic. They thought we were trying to escape or that we were bent on a rendezvous with one of them at the expense of the others.

Eying us and each other suspiciously, they set to work. Like movers from a transfer-and-storage company, they gathered up the contents of the room and we all moved down to the sidewalk.

The strange caravan took off with Steve and me in the lead. Straggling behind us were agents and more agents, carrying champagne, caviar, and the huge wedding cake. The limousine and its mystified chauffeur cruised slowly along beside us.

On we went, eastward on Forty-fourth Street to Fifth Avenue, and then all the way up to Fifty-ninth to the Sherry-Netherland. The wedding cake was what did it; halfway there a passerby yelled, "Hey lady, which one is the husband?"

We trouped into the lobby of the Sherry-Netherland and were borne to the lush upper regions. The honeymoon suite was a fairy tale — peopled with more wicked agents. A royal buffet banquet was set out on a serving table twelve feet long covered with snowy damask and flanked by what looked like the Cold Stream Guards.

Our newly pressed clothes had been hung neatly in three closets in the bedroom, and a lady-in-waiting hovered nearby, should we decide to change.

The honeymoon bed was spread in crispy white Swiss lace, with bed lamps on either side that looked like fresh peach sundaes. The bathroom was all glass, with a sunken tub that looked like a swimming pool. The toilet rose like a white porcelain jewel from a sea of frothy pink carpet, and we could have held a polo match in the vast space between toilet and tub.

If a setting like this couldn't kill a marriage, nothing could.

"Hey Steve . . ." I called, listening to the echo of my own voice, "should we ask them if they want to stay and watch?"

There was no need to ask. The long night watch began.

Settling back in an easy chair, Steve opened a tower of champagne and invited everyone present to drink with him. The agents, impressed with this gesture of camaraderie, were quick to comply, as were the Gold Stream Guards. What they didn't know was that the more Steve drinks, the more he talks. In a drinking-talking marathon, he would win hands down.

The telephone rang incessantly — calls from the Hollywood offices of the various agencies to see what progress was being made. Steve intercepted each call and parried each question with a running commentary on the Brooklyn Dodgers and the prospects of abolishing nuclear testing.

The agents were perched on the window sill, the arms of chairs, the edge of the writing desk. Their eyes grew bleary and gradually Steve began to pick them off. Some time after midnight the Cold Stream Guards floated out on their hats.

I fell asleep on the sofa, and when I awoke at seven the next morning the agents were still there, passed out in all corners of the room. Steve was still talking.

Stealthily, we changed our clothes and packed. Before we left we jumped up and down on the luscious bed — just to be able to say we had used it. Then we went to the airport and headed for Vermont and the world of moviemaking. It seemed a long time since I had stood in the kitchen and smothered saltines with Tabasco sauce.

LOOKING FOR MEANING

HENRY DAVID THOREAU

from

WALDEN

Thoreau (1817–62) was an individualist and an eccentric, someone who thought for himself and acted on his beliefs and principles. In July 1845, he settled in a very small cabin on Walden Pond in Concord, Massachusetts, and lived there in solitude until September 1847, trying to throw off the burdens that he perceived dragged down the ordinary citizen — of earning a living but of having no time to live. Out of that experience he wrote the work that has become his most well-read piece, *Walden;* in the following excerpt, he talks of some of his observations on nature and solitude, and the nature of solitude.

This is a delicious evening, when the whole body is one sense, and imbibes delight through every pore. I go and come with a strange liberty in Nature, a part of herself. As I walk along the stony shore of the pond in my shirt sleeves, though it is cool as well as cloudy and windy, and I see nothing special to attract me, all the elements are unusually congenial to me. The bullfrogs trump to usher in the night, and the note of the whippoorwill is borne on the rippling wind from over the water. Sympathy with the fluttering alder and poplar leaves almost takes away my breath; yet, like the lake, my serenity is rippled but not ruffled. These small waves raised by the evening wind are as remote from storm as the smooth reflecting surface. Though it is now dark, the wind still blows and roars in the wood, the waves still dash, and some creatures lull the rest with their notes. The repose is never complete. The wildest animals do not repose, but seek their prey now; the fox, and skunk, and rabbit, now roam the fields and woods without fear. They are Nature's watchmen — links which connect the days of animated life.

When I return to my house I find that visitors have been there and left their cards, either a bunch of flowers, or a wreath of evergreen, or a name in pencil on a yellow walnut leaf or a chip. They who come rarely to the woods take some little piece of the forest into their hands to play with by the way, which they leave, either intentionally or accidentally. One has peeled a willow wand, woven it into a ring, and dropped it on my table. I could always tell if visitors had called in my absence, either by the bended twigs or grass, or the print of their shoes, and generally of what sex or age or quality they were by some slight trace left, as a flower dropped, or a bunch of grass plucked and thrown away, even as far off as the railroad, half a mile distant, or by the lingering odor of a cigar or pipe. Nay, I was frequently notified of the passage of a traveler along the highway sixty rods off by the scent of his pipe.

There is commonly sufficient space about us. Our horizon is never quite at our elbows. The thick wood is not just at our door, nor the pond, but somewhat is always clearing, familiar and worn by us, appropriated and fenced in some way, and reclaimed from Nature. For what reason have I this vast range and circuit, some square miles of unfrequented forest, for my privacy, abandoned to me by men? My nearest neighbor is a mile distant, and no house is visible from any place but the hilltops within half a mile of my own. I have my horizon bounded by woods all to myself; a distant view of the railroad where it touches the pond on the one hand, and of the fence which skirts the woodland road on the other. But for the most part it is as solitary where I live as on the prairies. It is as much Asia or Africa as New England. I have, as it were, my own sun and moon and stars, and a little world all to myself. At night there was never a traveler passed my house, or knocked at my door, more than if I were the first or last man; unless it were in the spring, when at long intervals some came from the village to fish for pouts — they plainly fished much more in the Walden Pond of their own natures, and baited their hooks with darkness — but they soon retreated, usually with light baskets, and left "the world to darkness and to me," and the black kernel of the night was never profaned by any human neighborhood. I believe that men are generally still a little afraid of the dark, though the witches are all hung, and Christianity and candles have been introduced.

Yet I experienced sometimes that the most sweet and tender, the most innocent and encouraging society may be found in any natural object, even for the poor misanthrope and most melancholy man. There can be no very black melancholy to him who lives in the midst of Nature and has his senses still. There was never yet such a storm but it was Aeolian music to a healthy and innocent ear. Nothing can rightly compel a simple and brave man to a vulgar sadness. While I enjoy the friendship of the seasons I trust that nothing can make life a burden to me. The gentle rain which waters my beans and keeps me in the house today is not drear and melancholy, but good for me too. Though it prevents my hoeing them, it is of far more worth than my hoeing. If it should continue so long as to cause the seeds to rot in the ground and destroy the potatoes in the lowlands, it would still be good for the grass on the uplands, and, being good for the grass, it would be good for me. Sometimes, when I compare myself with other men, it seems as if I were more favored by the gods than they, beyond any deserts that I am conscious of; as if I had a warrant and surety at their hands which my fellows have not, and were especially guided and guarded. I do not flatter myself, but if it be possible they flatter me. I have never felt lonesome, or in the least oppressed by a sense of solitude, but once, and that was a few weeks after I came to the woods, when, for an hour, I doubted if the near neighborhood of man was not essential to a serene and healthy life. To be alone was something unpleasant. But I was at the same time conscious of a slight insanity in my mood, and seemed to foresee my recovery. In the midst of a gentle rain while these thoughts prevailed, I was suddenly sensible of such sweet and beneficent society in Nature, in the very pattering of the drops, and in every sound and sight around my house, an infinite and unaccountable friendliness all at once like an atmosphere sustaining me, as made the fancied advantages of human neighborhood insignificant, and I have never thought of them since. Every little pine needle expanded and swelled with sympathy and befriended me. I was so distinctly made aware of the presence of something kindred to me, even in scenes which we are accustomed to call wild and dreary, and also that the nearest of blood to me and humanest was not a person nor a villager, that I thought no place could ever be strange to me again.

"Mourning untimely consumes the sad;
　Few are their days in the land of the
　　living,
　Beautiful daughter of Toscar."

Some of my pleasantest hours were during the long rainstorms in the spring or fall, which confined me to the house for the afternoon as well as the forenoon, soothed by their ceaseless roar and pelting; when an early twilight ushered in a long evening in which many thoughts had time to take root and unfold themselves. In those driving northeast rains which tried the village houses so, when the maids stood ready with mop and pail in front entries to keep the deluge out, I sat behind my door in my little house, which was all entry, and thoroughly enjoyed its protection. In one heavy thundershower the lightning struck a large pitch pine across the pond, making a very conspicuous and perfectly regular spiral groove from top to bottom, an inch or more deep, and four or five inches wide, as you would groove a walking-stick. I passed it again the other day, and was struck with awe on looking up and beholding that mark, now more distinct than ever, where a terrific bolt came down out of the harmless sky eight years ago. Men frequently say to me, "I should think you would feel lonesome down there, and want to be nearer to folks, rainy and snowy days and nights especially." I am tempted to reply to such, This whole earth which we inhabit is but a point in space. How far apart, think you, dwell the two most distant inhabitants of yonder star, the breadth of whose disk cannot be appreciated by our instruments? Why should I feel lonely? is not our planet in the Milky Way? This which you put seems to me not to be the most important question. What sort of space is that which separates a man from his fellows and makes him solitary? I have found that no exertion of the legs can bring two minds much nearer to one another. What do we want most to dwell near to? Not to many men surely, the depot, the post-office, the barroom, the meeting-house, the school-house, the grocery, Beacon Hill, or the Five Points, where men most congregate, but to the perennial source of our life, whence in all our experience we have found that to issue, as the willow stands near the water and sends out its roots in that direction. This will vary with different natures, but this is the place were a wise man will dig his cellar. . . . I one evening overtook one of my townsmen, who has accumulated what is called a "handsome property" — though I never got a *fair* view of it — on the Walden road, driving a pair of cattle to market, who inquired of me how I could bring my mind to give up so many of the comforts of life. I answered that I was very sure I liked it passably well; I was not joking. And so I went home to my bed, and left him to pick his way through the darkness and the mud to Brighton — or Brighttown — which place he would reach some time in the morning.

Any prospect of awakening or coming to life to a dead man makes indifferent all times and places. The place where that may occur is always the same, and indescribably pleasant to all our senses. For the most part we allow only outlying and transient circumstances to make our occasions. They are, in fact, the cause of our distraction. Nearest to all things is that power which fashions their being. *Next* to us the grandest laws are continually being executed. *Next* to us is not the workman whom we have hired, with whom we love so well to talk, but the workman whose work we are.

"How vast and profound is the influence of the subtile powers of Heaven and Earth!

"We seek to perceive them, and we do not see

them; we seek to hear them, and we do not hear them; identified with the substance of things, they cannot be separated from them.

"They cause that in all the universe men purify and sanctify their hearts, and clothe themselves in their holiday garments to offer sacrifices and oblations to their ancestors. It is an ocean of subtile intelligences. They are everywhere, above us, on our left, on our right; they environ us on all sides."

We are the subjects of an experiment which is not a little interesting to me. Can we not do without the society of our gossips a little while under these circumstances, have our own thoughts to cheer us? Confucius says truly, "Virtue does not remain as an abandoned orphan; it must of necessity have neighbors."

With thinking we may be beside ourselves in a same sense. By a conscious effort of the mind we can stand aloof from actions and their consequences; and all things, good and bad, go by us like a torrent. We are not wholly involved in Nature. I may be either the driftwood in the stream, or Indra in the sky looking down on it. I *may* be affected by a theatrical exhibition; on the other hand, I *may not* be affected by an actual event which appears to concern me much more. I only know myself as a human entity; the scene, so to speak, of thoughts and affections; and am sensible of a certain doubleness by which I can stand as remote from myself as from another. However intense my experience, I am conscious of the presence and criticism of a part of me, which, as it were, is not a part of me, but spectator, sharing no experience, but taking note of it; and that is no more I than it is you. When the play, it may be the tragedy, of life is over, the spectator goes his way. It was a kind of fiction, a work of the imagination only, so far as he was concerned. This doubleness may easily make us poor neighbors and friends sometimes.

I find it wholesome to be alone the greater part of the time. To be in company, even with the best, is soon wearisome and dissipating. I love to be alone. I never found the companion that was so companionable as solitude. We are for the most part more lonely when we go abroad among men than when we stay in our chambers. A man thinking or working is always alone, let him be where he will. Solitude is not measured by the miles of space that intervene between a man and his fellows. The really diligent student in one of the crowded hives of Cambridge College is as solitary as a dervish in the desert. The farmer can work alone in the field or the woods all day, hoeing or chopping, and not feel lonesome, because he is employed; but when he comes home at night he cannot sit down in a room alone, at the mercy of his thoughts, but must be where he can "see the folks," and recreate, and as he thinks remunerate, himself for his day's solitude; and hence he wonders how the student can sit alone in the house all night and most of the day without ennui and "the blues"; but he does not realize that the student, though in the house, is still at work in *his* field, and chopping in *his* woods, as the farmer in his, and in turn seeks the same recreation and society that the latter does, though it may be a more condensed form of it.

Society is commonly too cheap. We meet at very short intervals, not having had time to acquire any new value for each other. We meet at meals three times a day, and give each other a new taste of that old musty cheese that we are. We have had to agree on a certain set of rules, called etiquette and politeness, to make this frequent meeting tolerable and that we need not come to open war. We meet at the post-office, and at the sociable, and about the fireside every night; we live thick and are in each other's way, and stumble over one another, and I think that we thus lose some respect for one another. Certainly less frequency would suffice for all important and hearty communications. Consider the girls in a factory — never alone, hardly in their dreams. It would be better if there were but one inhabitant to a square mile, as where I live. The value of a man is not in his skin, that we should touch him.

I have heard of a man lost in the woods and dying of famine and exhaustion at the foot of a tree, whose loneliness was relieved by the grotesque visions with which, owing to bodily weakness, his diseased imagination surrounded him, and which he believed to be real. So also, owing to bodily and mental health and strength, we may be continually cheered by a like but more normal and natural society, and come to know that we are never alone.

I have a great deal of company in my house; especially in the morning, when nobody calls.

Let me suggest a few comparisons, that someone may convey an idea of my situation. I am no more lonely than the loon in the pond that laughs so loud, or than Walden Pond itself. What company has that lonely lake, I pray? And yet it has not the blue devils, but the blue angels in it, in the azure tint of its waters. The sun is alone, except in thick weather, when there sometimes appear to be two, but one is a mock sun. God is alone — but the devil, he is far from being alone; he sees a great deal of company; he is legion. I am no more lonely than a single mullein or dandelion in a pasture, or a bean leaf, or sorrel, or a horsefly, or a humblebee. I am no more lonely than the Mill Brook, or a weathercock, or the North Star, or the south wind, or an April shower, or a January thaw, or the first spider in a new house.

I have occasional visits in the long winter evenings, when the snow falls fast and the wind howls in the wood, from an old settler and original proprietor, who is reported to have dug Walden Pond, and stoned it, and fringed it with pine woods; who tells me stories of old time and of new eternity; and between us we manage to pass a cheerful evening with social mirth and pleasant views of things, even without apples or cider — a most wise and humorous friend, whom I love much, who keeps himself more secret than ever did Goffe or Whalley; and though he is thought to be dead, none can show where he is buried. An elderly dame, too, dwells in my neighborhood, invisible to most persons, in whose odorous herb garden I love to stroll sometimes, gathering simples and listening to her fables; for she has a genius of unequalled fertility, and her memory runs back farther than mythology, and she can tell me the original of every fable, and on what fact every one is founded, for the incidents occurred when she was young. A ruddy and lusty old dame, who delights in all weathers and seasons, and is likely to outlive all her children yet.

The indescribable innocence and beneficence of Nature — of sun and wind and rain, of summer and winter — such health, such cheer, they afford forever! and such sympathy have they ever with our race, that all Nature would be affected, and the sun's brightness fade, and the winds would sigh humanely, and the clouds rain tears, and the woods shed their leaves and put on mourning in midsummer, if any man should ever for a just cause grieve. Shall I not have intelligence with the earth? Am I not partly leaves and vegetable mould myself?

What is the pill which will keep us well, serene, contented? Not my or thy great-grand-father's, but our great-grandmother Nature's universal, vegetable, botanic medicines, by which she has kept herself young always, outlived so many old Parrs in her day, and fed her health with their decaying fatness. For my panacea, instead of one of those quack vials of a mixture dipped from Acheron and the Dead Sea, which come out of those long shallow black-schooner-looking wagons which we sometimes see made to carry bottles, let me have a draught of undiluted morning air. Morning air! If men will not drink of this at the fountainhead of the day, why, then, we must even bottle up some and sell it in the shops, for the benefit of those who have lost their subscription ticket to morning time in this world. But remember, it will not keep quite till noonday even in the coolest cellar, but drive out the stopples long ere that and follow westward the steps of Aurora. I am no worshiper of Hygeia, who was the daughter of that old herb-doctor Aesculapius, and who is represented on monuments holding a serpent in one hand, and in the other a cup out of which the serpent sometimes drinks; but rather of Hebe, cupbearer to Jupiter, who was the daughter of Juno and wild lettuce, and who had the power of restoring gods and men to the vigor of youth. She was probably the only thoroughly sound-conditioned, healthy, and robust young lady that ever walked the globe, and wherever she came it was spring.

MAY SARTON

from

JOURNAL OF A SOLITUDE

In these intimate journal entries, writer **May Sarton** draws us into her world like a close personal friend, sharing with us her keen delight in her surroundings and her love of her work as well as the inevitable disappointments and anger that beset most humans. In recent years, she has lived almost entirely alone and has studied the benefits and costs of living a life of intense solitude — broken only by short episodes of lecturing and visiting friends.

Born in 1912, May Sarton grew up in Cambridge, Masachusetts, where her father was a professor at Harvard. Originally interested in the theater, she later turned to teaching, writing, and lecturing, and has published prolifically — forty volumes of prose and poetry. She now lives in York, Maine, where she continues to keep a journal reflecting on the events, major and minor, that constitute her life.

———

Begin here. It is raining. I look out on the maple, where a few leaves have turned yellow, and listen to Punch, the parrot, talking to himself and to the rain ticking gently against the windows. I am here alone for the first time in weeks, to take up my "real" life again at last. That is what is strange — that friends, even passionate love, are not my real life unless there is time alone in which to explore and to discover what is happening or has happened. Without the interruptions, nourishing and maddening, this life would become arid. Yet I taste it fully only when I am alone here and "the house and I resume old conversations."

On my desk, small pink roses. Strange how often the autumn roses look sad, fade quickly, frost-browned at the edges! But these are lovely, bright, singing pink. On the mantel, in the Japanese jar, two sprays of white lilies, recurved, maroon pollen on the stamens, and a branch of peony leaves turned a strange pinkish-brown. It is an elegant bouquet; *shibui*, the Japanese would call it. When I am alone the flowers are really seen; I can pay attention to them. They are felt as presences. Without them I would die. Why do I say that? Partly because they change before my eyes. They live and die in a few days; they keep me closely in touch with process, with growth, and also with dying. I am floated on their moments.

The ambience here is order and beauty. That

is what frightens me when I am first alone again. I feel inadequate. I have made an open place, a place for meditation. What if I cannot find myself inside it?

I think of these pages as a way of doing that. For a long time now, every meeting with another human being has been a collision. I feel too much, sense too much, am exhausted by the reverberations after even the simplest conversation. But the deep collision is and has been with my unregenerate, tormenting, and tormented self. I have written every poem, every novel, for the same purpose — to find out what I think, to know where I stand. I am unable to become what I see. I feel like an inadequate, a machine that breaks down at crucial moments, grinds to a dreadful halt, "won't go," or, even worse, explodes in some innocent person's face.

Plant Dreaming Deep has brought me many friends of the work (and also, harder to respond to, people who think they have found in me an intimate friend). But I have begun to realize that, without my own intention, that book gives a false view. The anguish of my life here — its rages — is hardly mentioned. Now I hope to break through into the rough rocky depths, to the matrix itself. There is violence there and anger never resolved. I live alone, perhaps for no good reason, for the reason that I am an impossible creature, set apart by a temperament I have never learned to use as it could be used, thrown off by a word, a glance, a rainy day, or one drink too many. My need to be alone is balanced against my fear of what will happen when suddenly I enter the huge empty silence if I cannot find support there. I go up to Heaven and down to Hell in an hour, and keep alive only by imposing upon myself inexorable routines. I write too many letters and too few poems. It may be outwardly silent here but in the back of my mind is a clamor of human voices, too many needs, hopes, fears. I hardly ever sit still without being haunted by the "undone" and the "unsent." I often feel exhausted, but it is not my work that tires (work is a rest); it is the effort of pushing away the lives and needs of others before I can come to the work with any freshness and zest.

September 17th

Cracking open the inner world again, writing even a couple of pages, threw me back into depression, not made easier by the weather, two gloomy days of darkness and rain. I was attacked by a storm of tears, those tears that appear to be related to frustration, to buried anger, and come upon me without warning. I woke yesterday so depressed that I did not get up till after eight.

I drove to Brattleboro to read poems at the new Unitarian church there in a state of dread and exhaustion. How to summon the vitality needed? I had made an arrangement of religious poems, going back to early books and forward into the new book not yet published. I suppose it went all right — at least it was not a disaster — but I felt (perhaps I am wrong) that the kind, intelligent people gathered in a big room looking out on pine trees did not really want to think about God, His absence (many of the poems speak of that) or His presence. Both are too frightening.

On the way back I stopped to see Perley Cole, my dear old friend, who is dying, separated from his wife, and has just been moved from a Dickensian nursing home into what seems like a far better one. He grows more transparent every day, a skeleton or nearly. Clasping his hand, I fear to break a bone. Yet the only real communication between us now (he is very deaf) is a handclasp. I want to lift him in my arms and hold him like a baby. He is dying a terribly lonely death. Each time I see him he says, "It is rough" or "I did not think it would end like this."

Everywhere I look about this place I see his handiwork: the three small trees by a granite boulder that he pruned and trimmed so they pivot the whole meadow; the new shady border he dug out for me one of the last days he worked here; the pruned-out stone wall between my field and the church. The second field where he cut brush twice a year and cleared out to the stone wall is growing back to wilderness now. What is done here has to be done over and over and needs the dogged strength of a man like Perley. I could have never managed it alone. We cherished this piece of land together, and fought together to bring it to some semblance of order and beauty.

I like to think that this last effort of Perley's had a certain ease about it, a game compared to the hard work of his farming years, and a game where his expert knowledge and skill could be well used. How he enjoyed teasing me about my ignorance!

While he scythed and trimmed, I struggled in somewhat the same way at my desk here, and we were each aware of the companionship. We each looked forward to noon, when I could stop for the day and he sat on a high stool in the kitchen, drank a glass or two of sherry with me, said, "Court's in session!" and then told me some tall tale he had been cogitating all morning.

It was a strange relationship, for he knew next to nothing about my life, really; yet below all the talk we recognized each other as the same kind. He enjoyed my anger as much as I enjoyed his. Perhaps that was part of it. Deep down there was understanding, not of the facts of our lives so much as of our essential natures. Even now in his hard, lonely end he has immense dignity. But I wish there were some way to make it easier. I leave him with bitter resentment against the circumstances of this death. "I know. But I do not approve. And I am not resigned."

In the mail a letter from a twelve-year-old child, enclosing poems, her mother having pushed her to ask my opinion. This child does really look at things, and I can write something helpful, I think. But it is troubling how many people expect applause, recognition, when they have not even begun to learn an art or a craft. Instant success is the order of the day; "I want it *now!*" I wonder whether this is not part of our corruption by machines. Machines do things very quickly and outside the natural rhythm of life, and we are indignant if a car doesn't start at the first try. So the few things that we still do, such as cooking (though there are TV dinners!), knitting, gardening, anything at all that cannot be hurried, have a very particular value.

September 18th

The value of solitude — one of its values — is, of course, that there is nothing to *cushion* against attacks from within, just as there is nothing to help balance at times of particular stress or depression. A few moments of desultory conversation with dear Arnold Miner, when he comes to take the trash, may calm an inner storm. But the storm, painful as it is, might have had some truth in it. So sometimes one has simply to endure a period of depression for what it may hold of illumination if one can live through it, attentive to what it exposes or demands.

The reasons for depression are not so interesting as the way one handles it, simply to stay alive. This morning I woke at four and lay awake for an hour or so in a bad state. It is raining again. I got up finally and went about the daily chores, waiting for the sense of doom to lift — and what did it was watering the house plants. Suddenly joy came back because I was fulfilling a simple need, a living one. Dusting never has this effect (and that may be why I am such a poor housekeeper!), but feeding the cats when they are hungry, giving Punch clean water, makes me suddenly feel calm and happy.

Whatever peace I know rests in the natural world, in feeling myself a part of it, even in a small way. Maybe the gaiety of the Warner family, their wisdom, comes from this, that they work close to nature all the time. As simple as that? But it is not simple. Their life requires patient understanding, imagination, the power to endure constant adversity — the weather, for example! To go with, not against the elements, an inexhaustible vitality summoned back each day to do the same tasks, to feed the animals, clean out barns and pens, keep that complex world alive.

September 19th

The sun is out. It rose through the mist, making the raindrops sparkle on the lawn. Now there is blue sky, warm air, and I have just created a wonder — two large autumn crocuses plus a small spray of pink single chrysanthemums and a piece of that silvery leaf (artemisia? arethusa?) whose name I forget in the Venetian glass in the cosy room. May they be benign presences toward this new day!

Neurotic depression is so boring because it is repetitive, literally a wheel that turns and turns. Yesterday I broke off from the wheel when I read a letter from Sister Mary David. She is now manager of a co-op in the small town in South Carolina where she has chosen to work. Always her letters bring me the shock of what is really going on and the recognition of what one single person can do. "So," says Sister Mary David, "I am of course mostly involved in the co-op work, but I do find more and more of the desperate families which are so numerous in this state — people who are frustrated, lonely, sick, helpless.

571

One day I took an old man shopping. He was completely out of food and by some error his check had been stopped for three months. He bought what he needed and the bill came to $10.06. I emptied my wallet and what was in it came to *exactly* $10.06! So I suspect that the good Lord is at my elbow all the time. So many inexplainable things occur. Another day an elderly lady waited for me in the rain outside a second-hand furniture store to ask me to talk to a twelve-year-old boy who had tried to commit suicide. His father and stepmother had put him out — no clothes, no place to go. Well, he is better now. I bought him clothes and a folding bed which his old 'gran'ma' agreed to let him set up in her shack. I keep in touch, bought him a lunch box yesterday. They just seem to cross my path, dozens of them, and some disappear after the crisis."

I felt lifted up on the joy of sending a check and knowing that money would be changed at once into help. We are all fed up, God knows, with institutional charity, with three requests from the same organization in a week and often one to which a check had been mailed two weeks earlier. We are all, receivers and givers alike, computerized. It feels arid compared to the direct human way shown by Sister Mary David; she was not sent down by her order, but found her own way there on a summer project and then decided that she must stay, and somehow got permission to do so. This must be the tradition of the Sisters of Mercy.

The most hopeful sign, the only one, in these

hard times is how much individual initiative manages to make its way up through the asphalt, so many tough shoots of human imagination. And I think at once of Dr. Gatch who started in Beaufort, South Carolina to heal sick blacks on his own. Whatever his tragic end, he did force the situation down there — near starvation — on the attention of Congress and the people of the United States. We have to believe that each person *counts*, counts as a creative force that can move mountains. The great thing Gene McCarthy did, of course, was to prove this on the political scene. While we worked for him we believed that politics might give way to the human voice. It is tragic that the human flaws can then wreck everything — McCarthy's vanity, Gatch's relying on drugs to keep going. We can do anything, or almost, but how balanced, magnanimous, and modest one has to be to do anything! And also how patient. It is as true in the arts as anywhere else.

So . . . to work. It is not a *non sequitur*. I shall never be one of those directly active (except as a teacher, occasionally), but now and then I am made aware that my work, odd though it seems, does help people. But it is only in these last years at Nelson that I have know that for sure.

September 21st

Yesterday, Sunday, was Perley Cole's birthday. I went to see him in the afternoon and took him some pajamas. This time we were able to have a little talk. He is suffering from the change to a

573

new place, although to an outsider this seems such an improvement on the horrible old one, that dirty old farmhouse sinking into the ground, and the atmosphere of lies there and of neglect, a place where more than one child has simply abandoned a senile parent, buried him alive. But Perley had put out roots there, had to, to keep his sense of himself. And now those roots have been torn away. How long can it last? His hands are transparent, and only his eyes, their piercing look that says so much more than he can utter, remain Perley Cole.

Yesterday before I left on the sad expedition I had looked out and seen two elderly people standing at the edge of the lawn, then walking down the hill a way and coming back, obviously in the hope I would come out. So I did. Apparently they have come more than once, lovers of *Plant Dreaming Deep* and of the poems. They turned out to be Charlotte and Albert Oppler, German refugees from Hitler, who landed here and later were sent to Japan under Mac-Arthur, Albert as a legal expert who helped draw up the new Japanese constitution. Of course, they know Elizabeth Vining, whose autobiography I am reviewing for the *Times* these days. But why did I tell them, nearly in tears, of my depression? It is quite absurd to tell total strangers such things. I suppose I was taken by surprise like an animal in a lair. I had been writing all morning, was open from the inside out, unprepared for kindness and understanding such as they showed. Here the inner person is the outer person. It is what I want, but that does not make me any less absurd.

Found this in an old journal of mine — Humphry Trevelyan on Goethe: "It seems that two qualities are necessary if a great artist is to remain creative to the end of a long life; he must on the one hand retain an abnormally keen awareness of life, he must never grow complacent, never be content with life, must always demand the impossible and when he cannot have it, must despair. The burden of the mystery must be with him day and night. He must be shaken by the naked truths that will not be comforted. This divine discontent, this disequilibrium, this state of inner tension is the source of artistic energy. Many lesser poets have it only in their youth; some even of the greatest lose it in middle life. Wordsworth lost the courage to despair and with it his poetic power. But more often the dynamic tensions are so powerful that they destroy the man before he reaches maturity."

Must art come from tension? A few months ago I was dreaming of a happy work, a whole book of poems stemming from fruitful love. Now here I am back on the rack. But perhaps this is a sign of health, not sickness. Who knows?

Perley Cole died last night. I saw him at three thirty, only half conscious, so I did not try to rouse him, just stood by the bed for a few moments. At six the matron at the nursing home telephoned to say he was failing, and when I called back an hour later told me he had gone to the hospital in Keene in an ambulance. (Why didn't they let him die there in the nursing home?) Mary, his youngest daughter, miles away in Charlestown, told me he died in the ambulance. There will be no service, a cremation, the body shipped *alone* to Cambridge for that, and the ashes will be strewn in the Hillsboro cemetery. He had been separated from his wife for years because of her long illness. It is the loneliest dying and the loneliest death I ever heard of. How many times he has said to me in these last months, "I never thought it would end like this."

How is one to accept such a death? What have we come to when people are shoveled away, as if that whole life of hard work, dignity, self-respect, could be discarded at the end like an old beer can?

He taught me a great deal. His slow steady way of working taught me patience — "Easy does it." His infinite care about small tasks, the way he knelt to clip around the trees after cutting the grass, the way he worked, not for me but to hold up his own standards of a good job — and he must have known very well that half the time I could not really appreciate what that "good job" had involved. I loved him, loved that streak of wildness in him that might make him lay down his tools and walk off, at war with some demon. He lived in a state of intense personal drama, and that, perhaps, is what lifted him out of the ordinary. Deep down we recognized each other long ago as of the same breed, passionate, ornery, and proud. I say it at the end of my poem about him, *A Recognition*.* Let me remember that now, the man as he was:

A Private Mythology

576

Now Perley says, "God damn it!" — and
    much worse.
Hearing him, I get back some reverence.
Could you, they ask, call such a man your
    friend?
Yes (damn it!), and yes world without end!
Brancusi's game and his make the same
    sense,
And not unlike a prayer is Perley's curse.

So let the rest go, and heel down, my boy,
And praise the artist till Hell freezes over,
For he is rare, he with his scythe (no toy),
He with his perils, with his skill and joy,
Who comes to prune, to make clear, to
    uncover,
The old man, full of wisdom, in his prime.
There in the field, watching him as he
    passes,
I recognize that violent, gentle blood,
Impatient patience. I would if I could,
Call him my kin, there scything down the
    grasses,
Call him my good luck in a dirty time.

"That's the way it is," he used to say.

September 25th

Yesterday picked mushrooms on the front lawn,
and a cup of raspberries for Mildred. The leaves
are falling fast, but so far the colors are gentle,
not the blaze of October yet. And we are having
tropical air, humid, depleting.

The sun is out. I woke to lovely mists, dew on spider webs everywhere, although the asters look beaten down after the rain and the cosmos pretty well battered. But these days one begins to look up at the flowering of color in the leaves, so it is easier to bear that the garden flowers are going one by one.

Mildred is here cleaning. I think of all the years since she first began to come here and how her presence, so quiet, humorous, and distinguished, has blessed all that is here. The solitude is animated but not broken. I sit at my desk and work better because I know her sensitive hands are busy dusting and making order again. And when we sit down at ten for coffee and a talk, it is never small talk. Today she told me that she had seen a perfect round cobweb in the branches of the chokecherry outside her back window, sparkling with the dew on it. She and I have lived through a lot of joy and grief together and now they are "woven fine" through all that we exchange.

I am an ornery character, often hard to get along with. The things I cannot stand, that make me flare up like a cat making a fat tail, are pretentiousness, smugness, the coarse grain that often shows itself in a turn of phrase. I hate vulgarity, coarseness of soul. I hate small talk with a passionate hatred. Why? I suppose because any meeting with another human being is collision for me now. It is always expensive, and I will *not* waste my time. It is never a waste of time to be outdoors, and never a waste of time to lie down and rest even for a couple of hours. It is then that images float up and then that I plan my work. But it is a waste of time to see people who have only a social surface to show. I will make every effort to find out the real person, but if I can't, then I am upset and cross. Time wasted is poison.

That is why Nelson has been good for me, for my neighbors here are never pretentious, rarely smug, and their coarseness, where it exists, is rough and healthy. I could not be bored by the Warners, by Mildred, by Arnold Miner, just as the truly cultivated and sophisticated person (as rare as hens' teeth around here) never bores — I bask in Helen Milbank's rare visits. Best of all are the true intimates such as Anne Woodson, K. Martin, or Eleanor Blair, the old true friends with whom the conversation becomes a bouquet of shared joys and a shared vision of life. Eleanor has just been here for the weekend. We had a marvelous picnic, high up over the Connecticut valley in a field. We spread our blanket in the shade at the edge of woods, and spent a heavenly hour, absorbing the hazy gentle hills, the open space, the presence of the river with its nineteenth-century atmosphere. The whole scene might have been an engraving, because, I suppose, the river is not navigable, so even the bank has hardly changed in a hundred years. Near at hand we listened to many small chirring sounds of autumn insects, and on the way back Eleanor pointed out to me an amazing bright green, longwinged insect like a grasshopper. Further along she picked two branches of barberry rich in the red fruit, now lovely in the Japanese jar on the mantel here.

Nevertheless, getting ready for a guest and cooking meals seemed an almost insuperable effort because I am so depressed. Depression eats away psychic energy in a dreadful way. But of course it did me good to make the effort. I stuffed an eggplant with ham and mushrooms, a dish new to Eleanor and very good; it looks so grand too, the wrinkled purple eggplant standing up in a bowl surrounded by sweet potatoes.

All this pleasure was marred at the end by my fatigue and exasperation at a small remark about flowers in a vase being faded, blowing off in a classic example of my irrational angers. I must have screamed terribly loudly as I have lost my voice today! The punishment fits the crime perfectly. I feel crippled, unable to speak, having uttered horrible things. These angers are crippling, like a fit when they happen, and then, when they are over, haunting me with remorse. Those who know me well and love me have come to accept them as part of me; yet I know they are unacceptable. I must try to solve them, to learn how to head them off, as an epileptic learns to head off an attack with medicine. I sometimes feel it is a Laocoön struggle between anger and my life itself, as if anger were a witch who has had me in her power since infancy, and either I conquer her or she conquers me once and for all through the suicidal depression that follows on such an exhibition of unregenerate behavior.

Sometimes I think the fits of rage are like a huge creative urge gone into reverse, something dammed up that spills over, not an accumulated frustration that must find a way out and blows off at some tiny irrelevant thing. I have had these fits since I was an infant; the story goes back to Womdelgem when I was two years old. On a rainy winter day I was taken out in my white fur coat and became fascinated by a bowl of goldfish in a shop window. I wanted it passionately and when I was told "No," I flung myself, white coat and all, into a mud puddle. The tantrums worried my parents and on medical advice they tried putting me, fully clothed, into a tepid bath when it happened again. Next time I screamed in my rage, "Put me in the bath! Put me in the bath!" This suggests that at that age I was aware even while in the tantrum that somehow it had to be controlled, that I needed help, as we say these days.

But there is a difference between wanting something and not being given it and the episode the other day. That exploded from what I felt (irrationally) to be criticism of an unjust kind. Tension had built up simply by my trying to cope with the mundane side of having a guest. I had tried hard to make it in every way a good time for Eleanor, old and dear friend. And I felt in a quite idiotic way attacked. Of course, I also take pride in the flower arrangements and cannot bear having faded flowers around. But the reaction was wildly out of proportion, and that was what made it frightening. At such times I really feel as if my head were going to burst and there is no doubt that the tantrum itself is a release. But it is paid for very heavily in guilt and shame.

"Anger is a short madness," says Horace.

I have sometimes wondered also whether in people like me who come to the boil fast (*soupe au lait*, the French call this trait, like a milk soup that boils over) the tantrum is not a built-in safety valve against madness or illness. My mother buried her anger against my father and I saw the effects in her of this restraint — migraine headaches and tachycardia, to name only two. The nervous system is very mysterious. For the very thing that made her an angry person also gave her amazing strength with which to meet every kind of ordeal. The anger was buried fire; the flame sustained my father and me through the hard years when we were refugees from Belgium and slowly finding our place in American life.

The fierce tension in me, when it is properly channeled, creates the good tension for work. But when it becomes unbalanced I am destructive. How to isolate that good tension is my problem these days. Or, put in another way, how to turn the heat down fast enough so the soup won't boil over!

E. B. WHITE

from

ONE MAN'S MEAT

E. B. White (1899–1985) was one of the writers responsible for the stylish writing of the *New Yorker* magazine. His collected essays and letters have recently appeared in several volumes where one can enjoy his skillful style and his gentle bantering view of the world. His children's books, particularly *Charlotte's Web* and *Stuart Little*, are favorites with children and their parents.

In this piece, called "Once More to the Lake," he captures the many emotions of returning to a favorite childhood haunt with his own son. This essay appears with great frequency in anthologies, and the elegance of the writing is self-evident.

———

One summer, along about 1904, my father rented a camp on a lake in Maine and took us all there for the month of August. We all got ringworm from some kittens and had to rub Pond's Extract on our arms and legs night and morning, and my father rolled over in a canoe with all his clothes on; but outside of that the vacation was a success and from then on none of us ever thought there was any place in the world like that lake in Maine. We returned summer after summer — always on August 1st for one month. I have since become a salt-water man, but sometimes in summer there are days when the restlessness of the tides and the fearful cold of the sea water and the incessant wind which blows across the afternoon and into the evening make me wish for the placidity of a lake in the woods. A few weeks ago this feeling got so strong I bought myself a couple of bass hooks and a spinner and returned to the lake where we used to go, for a week's fishing and to revisit old haunts.

I took along my son, who had never had any fresh water up his nose and who had seen lily pads only from train windows. On the journey over to the lake I began to wonder what it would be like. I wondered how time would have marred this unique, this holy spot — the coves and streams, the hills that the sun set behind, the camps and the paths behind the camps. I was sure the tarred road would have found it out and I wondered in what other ways it would be desolated. It is strange how much you can remember about places like that once you allow your mind to return into the grooves which lead back. You remember one thing, and that suddenly reminds you of another thing. I guess I remembered clearest of all the early mornings, when the lake was cool and motionless, remembered how the bedroom smelled of the lumber it was made of and of the wet woods whose scent entered through the screen. The partitions in the camp were thin and did not extend clear to the top of the rooms, and as I was always the first up I would dress softly so as not to wake the others, and sneak out into the sweet outdoors and start out in the canoe, keeping close along the shore in the long shadows of the pines. I remembered being very careful never to rub my paddle against the gunwale for fear of disturbing the stillness of the cathedral.

The lake had never been what you would call a wild lake. There were cottages sprinkled around the shores, and it was in farming country although the shores of the lake were quite heavily wooded. Some of the cottages were owned by nearby farmers, and you would live at the shore and eat your meals at the farmhouse. That's what our family did. But although it wasn't wild, it was a fairly large and undisturbed lake and there were places in it which, to a child at least, seemed infinitely remote and primeval.

I was right about the tar: it led to within half a mile of the shore. But when I got back there, with my boy, and we settled into a camp near a farmhouse and into the kind of summertime I had known, I could tell that it was going to be pretty much the same as it had been before — I knew it, lying in bed the first morning, smelling the bedroom, and hearing the boy sneak quietly out and go off along the shore in a boat. I began to sustain the illusion that he was I, and therefore by simple transposition, that I was my father. This sensation persisted, kept cropping up all the time we were there. It was not an entirely new feeling, but in this setting it grew much stronger. I seemed to be living a dual existence. I would be in the middle of some simple act, I would be picking up a bait box or laying down a table fork, or I would be saying something, and suddenly it would be not I but my father who was saying the words or making the gesture. It gave me a creepy sensation.

We went fishing the first morning. I felt the same damp moss covering the worms in the bait can, and saw the dragonfly alight on the tip of my rod as it hovered a few inches from the surface of the water. It was the arrival of this fly that convinced me beyond any doubt that everything was as it always had been, that the years were a mirage and there had been no years. The small waves were the same, chucking the rowboat under the chin as we fished at anchor, and the boat was the same boat, the same color green and the ribs broken in the same places, and under the floor-boards the same fresh-water leavings and debris — the dead helgramite, the wisps of moss, the rusty discarded fishhook, the dried blood from yesterday's catch. We stared silently at the tips of our rods, at the dragonflies that came and went. I lowered the tip of mine into the water, tentatively, pensively dislodging the fly which darted two feet away, poised, darted two feet back, and came to a rest again a little farther up the rod. There had been no years between the ducking of this dragonfly and the other one — the one that was part of memory. I looked at the boy, who was silently watching his fly, and it was my hands that held his rod, my eyes watching. I felt dizzy and didn't know which rod I was at the end of.

We caught two bass, hauling them in briskly as though they were mackerel, pulling them over the side of the boat in a businesslike manner without any landing net, and stunning them with a blow on the back of the head. When we got back for a swim before lunch, the lake was exactly where we had left it, the same number of inches from the dock, and there was only the merest suggestion of a breeze. This seemed an utterly enchanted sea, this lake you could leave to its own devices for a few hours and come back to, and find that it had not stirred, this constant and trustworthy body of water. In the shallows, the dark, watersoaked sticks and twigs, smooth and old, were undulating in clusters on the bottom against the clean ribbed sand, and the track of the mussel was plain. A school of minnows swam by, each minnow with its small individual shadow, doubling the attendance, so clear and sharp in the sunlight. Some of the other campers were in swimming, along the shore, one of them with a cake of soap, and the water felt thin and clear and unsubstantial. Over the years there had been this person with the cake of soap, this cultist, and here he was. There had been no years.

Up to the farmhouse to dinner through the teeming, dusty field, the road under our sneakers was only a two-track road. The middle track was missing, the one with the marks of the hooves and the splotches of dried, flaky manure. There had always been three tracks to choose from in choosing which track to walk in; now the choice was narrowed down to two. For a moment I missed terribly the middle alternative. But the way led past the tennis court, and something about the way it lay there in the sun reassured me; the tape had loosened along the backline, the alleys were green with plantains and other weeds, and the net (installed in June and removed in September) sagged in the dry noon, and the whole place steamed with midday heat and hunger and emptiness. There was a choice of pie for dessert, and one was blueberry and one was apple, and the waitresses were the same country girls, there having been no passage of time, only the illusion of it as in a dropped curtain — the waitresses were still fifteen; their hair had been washed, that was the only difference — they had been to the movies and seen the pretty girls with the clean hair.

Summertime, oh summertime, pattern of life indelible, the fade-proof lake, the woods unshatterable, the pasture with the sweetfern and the juniper forever and ever, summer without end; this was the background, and the life along the shore was the design, the cottages with their innocent and tranquil design, their tiny docks with the flagpole and the American flag floating against the white clouds in the blue sky, the little paths over the roots of the trees leading from camp to camp and the paths leading back to the outhouses and the can of lime for sprinkling, and at the souvenir counters at the store the miniature birchbark canoes and the post cards that showed things looking a little better than they looked.

This was the American family at play, escaping the city heat, wondering whether the newcomers in the camp at the head of the cove were "common" or "nice," wondering whether it was true that the people who drove up for Sunday dinner at the farmhouse were turned away because there wasn't enough chicken.

It seemed to me, as I kept remembering all this, that those times and those summers had been infinitely precious and worth saving. There had been jollity and peace and goodness. The arriving (at the beginning of August) had been so big a business in itself, at the railway station the farm wagon drawn up, the first smell of the pine-laden air, the first glimpse of the smiling farmer, and the great importance of the trunks and your father's enormous authority in such matters, and the feel of the wagon under you for the long ten-mile haul, and at the top of the last long hill catching the first view of the lake after eleven months of not seeing this cherished body of water. The shouts and cries of the other campers when they saw you, and the trunks to be unpacked, to give up their rich burden. (Arriving was less exciting nowadays, when you sneaked up in your car and parked it under a tree near the camp and took out the bags and in five minutes it was all over, no fuss, no loud wonderful fuss about trunks.)

Peace and goodness and jollity. The only thing that was wrong now, really, was the sound of the place, an unfamiliar nervous sound of the outboard motors. This was the note that jarred, the one thing that would sometimes break the

589

illusion and set the years moving. In those other summertimes all motors were inboard; and when they were at a little distance, the noise they made was a sedative, an ingredient of summer sleep. They were one-cylinder and two-cylinder engines, and some were make-and-break and some were jump-spark, but they all made a sleepy sound across the lake. The one-lungers throbbed and fluttered, and the twin-cylinder ones purred and purred, and that was a quiet sound too. But now the campers all had outboards. In the daytime, in the hot mornings, these motors made a petulant, irritable sound; at night, in the still evening when the afterglow lit the water, they whined about one's ears like mosquitoes. My boy loved our rented outboard, and his great desire was to achieve singlehanded mastery over it, and authority, and he soon learned the trick of choking it a little (but not too much), and the adjustment of the needle valve. Watching him I would remember the things you could do with the old one-cylinder engine with the heavy flywheel, how you could have it eating out of your hand if you got really close to it spiritually. Motor boats in those days didn't have clutches, and you would make a landing by shutting off the motor at the proper time and coasting in with a dead rudder. But there was a way of reversing them, if you learned the trick, by cutting the switch and putting it on again exactly on the final dying revolution of the flywheel, so that it would kick back against compression and begin reversing. Approaching a dock in a strong following breeze, it was difficult to slow up sufficiently by the ordinary coasting method, and if a boy felt he had complete mastery over his motor, he was tempted to keep it running beyond its time and then reverse it a few feet from the dock. It took a cool nerve, because if you threw the switch a twentieth of a second too soon you would catch the flywheel when it still had speed enough to go up past center, and the boat would leap ahead, charging bull-fashion at the dock.

We had a good week at the camp. The bass were biting well and the sun shone endlessly, day after day. We would be tired at night and lie down in the accumulated heat of the little bedrooms after the long hot day and the breeze would stir almost imperceptibly outside and the smell of the swamp drift in through the rusty screens. Sleep would come easily and in the morning the red squirrel would be on the roof, tapping out his gay routine. I kept remembering everything, lying in bed in the mornings — the small steamboat that had a long rounded stern like the lip of a Ubangi, and how quietly she ran on the moonlight sails, when the older boys played their mandolins and the girls sang and we ate doughnuts dipped in sugar, and how sweet the music was on the water in the shining night, and what it had felt like to think about girls then. After breakfast we would go up to the store and the things were in the same place — the minnows in a bottle, the plugs and spinners disarranged and pawed over by the youngsters from the boys' camp, the fig newtons and the Beeman's gum. Outside, the road was tarred and cars stood in front of the store. Inside, all was just as it had always been, except there was more Coca-Cola and not so much Moxie and root beer and birch beer and sarsaparilla. We would walk out with a bottle of pop apiece and sometimes the pop would backfire up our noses and hurt. We explored the streams, quietly, where the turtles slid off the sunny logs and dug their way into the soft bottom; and we lay on the town wharf and fed worms to the tame bass. Everywhere we went I had trouble making out which was I, the one walking at my side, the one walking in my pants.

One afternoon while we were there at that lake a thunderstorm came up. It was like the revival of an old melodrama that I had seen long ago with childish awe. The second-act climax of the drama of the electrical disturbance over a lake in America had not changed in any important respect. This was the big scene, still the big scene. The whole thing was so familiar, the first feeling of oppression and heat and a general air around camp of not wanting to go very far away. In midafternoon (it was all the same) a curious darkening of the sky, and a lull in everything that had made life tick; and then the way the boats suddenly swung the other way at their moorings with the coming of a breeze out of the new quarter, and the premonitory rumble. Then the kettle drum, then the snare, then the bass drum and cymbals, then crackling light against the dark, and the gods grinning and licking their chops in the hills. Afterward the calm, the rain steadily rustling in the calm lake, the return of light and hope and spirits, and the campers running out in joy and relief to go swimming in the rain, their bright cries perpetuating the deathless joke about how they were getting simply drenched, and the children screaming with delight at the new sensation of bathing in the rain, and the joke about getting drenched linking the generations in a strong indestructible chain. And the comedian who waded in carrying an umbrella.

When the others went swimming my son said he was going in too. He pulled his dripping trunks from the line where they had hung all through the shower, and wrung them out. Languidly, and with no thought of going in, I watched him, his hard little body, skinny and bare, saw him wince slightly as he pulled up around his vitals the small, soggy, icy garment. As he buckled the swollen belt suddenly my groin felt the chill of death.

JOHN CIARDI

"WHAT IS HAPPINESS?"

Born in Boston, Massachusetts, **John Ciardi** (1916–86) published many volumes of poetry and childrens book's, and served as the poetry editor of the *Saturday Review*. In this inquiry, he argues that the essence of happiness derives from the *pursuit* itself — from the effort we put into our lives. "The mortal flaw with the advertised version of happiness," he says, "is . . . that it purports to be effortless."

The right to pursue happiness is issued to Americans with their birth certificates, but no one seems quite sure which way it ran. It may be we are issued a hunting license but offered no game. Jonathan Swift seemed to think so when he attacked the idea of happiness as the "the possession of being well-deceived," the felicity of being "a fool among knaves." For Swift saw society as Vanity Fair, the land of false goals.

It is, of course, un-American to think in terms of fools and knaves. We do, however, seem to

594

be dedicated to the idea of buying our way to happiness. We shall all have made it to Heaven when we possess enough.

And at the same time the forces of American commercialism are hugely dedicated to making us deliberately unhappy. Advertising is one of our major industries, and advertising exists not to satisfy desires but to create them — and to create them faster than any man's budget can satisfy them. For that matter, our whole economy is based on a dedicated insatiability. We are taught that to possess is to be happy, and then we are made to want. We are even told it is our duty to want. It was only a few years ago, to cite a single example, that car dealers across the country were flying banners that read "You Auto Buy Now." They were calling upon Americans, as an act approaching patriotism, to buy at once, with money they did not have, automobiles they did not really need, and which they would be required to grow tired of by the time the next year's models were released.

Or look at any of the women's magazines. There, as Bernard DeVoto once pointed out, advertising begins as poetry in the front pages and ends as pharmacopoeia and therapy in the back pages. The poetry of the front matter is the dream of perfect beauty. This is the baby skin that must be hers. These, the flawless teeth. This, the perfumed breath she must exhale. This, the sixteen-year-old figure she must display at forty, at fifty, at sixty, and forever.

Once past the vaguely uplifting fiction and feature articles, the reader finds the other face of the dream in the back matter. This is the harness into which Mother must strap herself in order to display that perfect figure. These, the chin straps she must sleep in. This is the salve that restores all, this is her laxative, these are the tablets that melt away fat, these are the hormones of perpetual youth, these are the stockings that hide varicose veins.

Obviously no half-sane person can be completely persuaded either by such poetry or by such pharmacopoeia and orthopedics. Yet someone is obviously trying to buy the dream as offered and spending billions every year in the attempt. Clearly the happiness-market is not running out of customers, but what is it trying to buy?

The idea "happiness," to be sure, will not sit still for easy definition: the best one can do is to try to set some extremes to the idea and then work in toward the middle. To think of happiness as acquisitive and competitive will do to set the materialistic extreme. To think of it as the idea one senses in, say, a holy man of India will do to set the spiritual extreme. That holy man's idea of happiness is in needing nothing from outside himself. In wanting nothing, he lacks nothing. He sits immobile, rapt in contemplation, free even of his own body. Or nearly free of it. If devout admirers bring him food he eats it; if not, he starves indifferently. Why be concerned? What is physical is an illusion to him. Contemplation is his joy and he achieves it through a fantastically demanding discipline, the accomplishment of which is itself a joy within him.

Is he a happy man? Perhaps his happiness is only another sort of illusion. But who can take it from him? And who will dare say it is more illusory than happiness on the installment plan?

But, perhaps because I am Western, I doubt such catatonic happiness, as I doubt the dreams of the happiness-market. What is certain is that his way of happiness would be torture to almost any Western man. Yet these extremes will still serve to frame the area within which all of us must find some sort of balance. Thoreau — a creature of both Eastern and Western thought — had his own firm sense of the balance. His aim was to save on the low levels in order to spend on the high.

Possession for its own sake or in competition with the rest of the neighborhood would have been Thoreau's idea of the low levels. The active discipline of heightening one's perception of what is enduring in nature would have been his idea of the high. What he saved from the low was time and effort he could spend on the high. Thoreau certainly disapproved of starvation, but he would put into feeding himself only as much effort as would keep him functioning for more important efforts.

Effort is the gist of it. There is no happiness except as we take on life-engaging difficulties. Short of the impossible, as Yeats put it, the satisfactions we get from a lifetime depend on how high we choose our difficulties. Robert Frost was thinking in something like the same terms when he spoke of "The pleasure of taking pains." The mortal flaw in the advertised version of happiness is in the fact that it purports to be effortless.

We demand difficulty even in our games. We demand it because without difficulty there can be no game. A game is a way of making something hard for the fun of it. The rules of the game are an arbitrary imposition of difficulty. When the spoilsport ruins the fun, he always does so by refusing to play by the rules. It is easier to win at chess if you are free, at your pleasure, to change the wholly arbitrary rules, but the fun is in winning within the rules. No difficulty, no fun.

The buyers and sellers at the happiness-market seem too often to have lost their sense of the pleasure of difficulty. Heaven knows what they are playing, but it seems a dull game. And the Indian holy man seems dull to us, I suppose, because he seems to be refusing to play anything at all. The Western weakness may be in the illusion that happiness can be bought. Perhaps the Eastern weakness is in the idea that there is such a thing as perfect (and therefore static) happiness.

Happiness is never more than partial. There are no pure states of mankind. Whatever else happiness may be, it is neither in having nor in being, but in becoming. What the Founding Fathers declared for us as an inherent right, we should do well to remember, was not happiness but the *pursuit* of happiness. What they might have underlined, could they have foreseen the happiness-market, is the cardinal fact that happiness is in the pursuit itself, in the meaningful pursuit of what is life-engaging and life-revealing, which is to say, in the idea of *becoming*. A nation is not measured by what it possesses or wants to possess, but by what it wants to become.

By all means let the happiness-market sell us minor satisfactions and even minor follies so long as we keep them in scale and buy them out of spiritual change. I am no customer for either puritanism or asceticism. But drop any real spiritual capital at those bazaars, and what you come home to will be your own poorhouse.

GOLDA MEIR

from

MY LIFE

Golda Meir (1898–1978) was born in Kiev in the Ukraine and emigrated to the United States at age eight. In 1921 she resettled in Palestine and in 1969 was elected prime minister of Israel; she remained in office until 1974.

In this brief passage, she tells of returning to her old school in Milwaukee and of giving some sound advice to the schoolchildren there.

I started school in a huge, fortresslike building on Fourth Street near Milwaukee's famous Schlitz beer factory, and I loved it. I can't remember how long it took me to learn English (at home, of course, we spoke Yiddish, and luckily, so did almost everyone else on Walnut Street), but I have no recollection of the language ever being a real problem for me, so I must have picked it up quickly. I made friends quickly, too. Two of those early first- or second-grade friends remained friends all my life, and both live in Israel now. One was Regina Hamburger (today Medzini), who lived on our street and who was to leave America when I did; the other was Sarah Feder, who became one of the leaders of Labor Zionism in the United States. Anyhow, coming late to class almost everyday was awful, and I used to cry all the way to school. Once a policeman even came to the shop to explain to my mother about truancy. She listened attentively but barely understood anything he said, so I went on being late for school and sometimes never got there at all — an ever greater disgrace. My mother — not that she had much alternative — didn't seem to be moved by my bitter resentment of the shop. "We have to live, don't we?" she claimed, and if my father and Sheyna — each for his and her own reasons — would not help, that didn't mean I was absolved of the task. "So it will take you a little longer to become a *rebbetzin* [a bluestocking]," she added. I never became a bluestocking, of course, but I learned a lot at that school.

More than fifty years later — when I was seventy-one and a prime minister — I went back to that school for a few hours. It had not changed very much in all those years except that the vast majority of its pupils were now black, not Jewish, as in 1906. They welcomed me as though I were a queen. Standing in rows on the creaky old stage I remembered so well, freshly scrubbed and neat as pins, they serenaded me with Yiddish and Hebrew songs and raised their voices to peal out the Israeli anthem "Hatikvah" which made my eyes fill with tears. Each one of the classrooms had been beautifully decorated with posters about

Israel and signs reading SHALOM (one of the children thought it was my family name), and when I entered the school, two little girls wearing headbands with Stars of David on them solemnly presented me with an enormous white rose made of tissue paper and pipe cleaners, which I wore all day and carefully carried back to Israel with me.

Another of the gifts I got that day in 1971 from the Fourth Street School was a record of my grades for one of the years I had spent there: 95 in reading, 90 in spelling, 95 in arithmetic, 85 in music and a mysterious 90 in something called manual arts, which I cannot remember at all. But when the children asked me to talk to them for a few minutes, it was not about book learning that I chose to speak. I had learned a lot more than fractions or how to spell at Fourth Street, and I decided to tell those eager, attentive children — born, as I myself had been, into a minority and living, as I myself had lived, without much extravagance (to put it mildly) — what the gist of that learning had been. "It isn't really important to decide when you are very young just exactly what you want to become when you grow up," I told them. "It is much more important to decide on the way you want to live. If you are going to be honest with yourself and honest with your friends, if you are going to get involved with causes which are good for others, not only for yourselves, then it seems to me that that is sufficient, and maybe what you will be is only a matter of chance." I had a feeling that they understood me.

VIKTOR FRANKL

from

MAN'S SEARCH FOR MEANING

Viktor Frankl's personal experiences in a Nazi concentration camp formed the basis of his later work as a psychiatrist and a professor of psychiatry in Vienna. In this excerpt, he describes the power of the remembered image of the people he loved — particularly his wife — to sustain him in his most agonizing moments. He sensed that "love is the ultimate and the highest goal to which man can aspire." Born in 1905, Dr. Frankl is the founder of logotherapy, a form of therapy that attributes an individual's neurotic suffering to a failure to find some larger meaning for his or her life.

———

In spite of all the enforced physical and mental primitiveness of the life in a concentration camp, it as possible for spiritual life to deepen. Sensitive people who were used to a rich intellectual life may have suffered much pain (they were often of a delicate constitution), but the damage to their inner selves was less. They were able to retreat from their terrible surroundings to a life of inner riches and spiritual freedom. Only in this way can one explain the apparent paradox that some prisoners of a less hardy make-up often seemed to survive camp life better than did those of a robust nature. In order to make myself clear, I am forced to fall back on personal experience. Let me tell what happened on those early mornings when we had to march to our work site.

There were shouted commands: "Detachment, forward march! Left-2-3-4! Left-2-3-4! Left-2-3-4! Left-2-3-4! First man about, left and left and left and left! Caps off!" These words sound in my ears even now. At the order "Caps off!" we passed the gate of the camp, and searchlights were trained upon us. Whoever did not march smartly got a kick. And worse off was the man who, because of the cold, had pulled his cap back over his ears before permission was given.

We stumbled on in the darkness, over big stones and through large puddles, along the one road leading from the camp. The accompanying guards kept shouting at us and driving us with the butts of their rifles. Anyone with very sore feet supported himself on his neighbor's arm. Hardly a word was spoken; the icy wind did not encourage talk. Hiding his mouth behind his upturned collar, the man marching next to me whispered suddenly: "If our wives could see us now! I do hope they are better off in their camps and don't know what is happening to us."

That brought thoughts of my own wife to mind. And as we stumbled on for miles, slipping on icy spots, supporting each other time and again, dragging one another up and onward, nothing was said, but we both knew: each of us was thinking of his wife. Occasionally I looked at the sky, where the stars were fading and the pink light of the morning was beginning to spread behind a dark bank of clouds. But my mind clung to my wife's image, imagining it with an uncanny acuteness. I heard her answering me, saw her smile, her frank and encouraging look. Real or not, her look was then more luminous than the sun which was beginning to rise.

A thought transfixed me: for the first time in my life I saw the truth as it is set into song by so many poets, proclaimed as the final wisdom by so many thinkers. The truth — that love is the ultimate and the highest goal to which man can aspire. Then I grasped the meaning of the greatest secret that human poetry and human thought and belief have to impart: *The salvation of man is through love and in love.* I understood how a man who has nothing left in this world still may know bliss, be it only for a brief moment, in the contemplation of his beloved. In a position of utter desolation, when man cannot express himself in positive action, when his only achievement may consist in enduring his sufferings in the right way — an honorable way — in such a position man can, through loving contemplation of the image he carries of his beloved, achieve fulfillment. For the first time in my life I was able to understand the meaning of the words, "The angels are lost in perpetual contemplation of an infinite glory."

In front of me a man stumbled and those following him fell on top of him. The guard rushed over and used his whip on them all. Thus my thoughts were interrupted for a few minutes. But soon my soul found its way back from the prisoner's existence to another world, and I resumed talk with my loved one: I asked her questions, and she answered; she questioned me in return, and I answered.

"Stop!" We had arrived at our work site. Everybody rushed into the dark hut in the hope of getting a fairly decent tool. Each prisoner got a spade or a pickax.

"Can't you hurry up, you pigs?" Soon we had resumed the previous day's positions in the ditch. The frozen ground cracked under the point of the pickaxes, and sparks flew. The men were silent, their brains numb.

My mind still clung to the image of my wife. A thought crossed my mind: I didn't even know if she were still alive. I knew only one thing — which I have learned well by now: Love goes very far beyond the physical person of the beloved. It finds its deepest meaning in his spiritual being, his inner self. Whether or not he is actually present, whether or not he is still alive at all, ceases somehow to be of importance.

I did not know whether my wife was alive, and I had no means of finding out (during all my prison life there was no outgoing or incoming mail); but at that moment it ceased to matter. There was no need for me to know; nothing could touch the strength of my love, my thoughts, and the image of my beloved. Had I known then that my wife was dead, I think that I would still have given myself, undisturbed by that knowledge, to the contemplation of her image, and that my mental conversation with her would have been just as vivid and just as satisfying. "Set me like a seal upon thy heart, love is as strong as death."

This intensification of inner life helped the prisoner find a refuge from the emptiness, desolation and spiritual poverty of his existence, by letting him escape into the past. When given free rein, his imagination played with past events, often not important ones, but minor happenings and trifling things. His nostalgic memory glorified them and they assumed a strange character. Their world and their existence seemed very distant and the spirit reached out for them longingly: In my mind I took bus rides, unlocked the front door of my apartment, answered my telephone, switched on the electric lights. Our thoughts often centered on such details, and these memories could move one to tears.

As the inner life of the prisoner tended to become more intense, he also experienced the beauty of art and nature as never before. Under their influence he sometimes even forgot his own frightful circumstances. If someone had seen our faces on the journey from Auschwitz to a Bavarian camp as we beheld the mountains of Salzburg with their summits glowing in the sunset, through the little barred windows of the prison carriage, he would never have believed that those were the faces of men who had given up all hope of life and liberty. Despite that factor — or maybe because of it — we were carried away by nature's beauty, which we had missed for so long.

In camp, too, a man might draw the attention of a comrade working next to him to a nice view of the setting sun shining through the tall trees of the Bavarian woods (as in the famous water color by Dürer), the same woods in which we had built an enormous, hidden munitions plant. One evening, when we were already resting on the floor of our hut, dead tired, soup bowls in hand, a fellow prisoner rushed in and asked us to run out to the assembly grounds and see the wonderful sunset. Standing outside we saw sinister clouds glowing in the west and the whole sky alive with clouds of ever-changing shapes and colors, from steel blue to blood red. The desolate gray mud huts provided a sharp contrast, while the puddles on the muddy ground reflected the glowing sky. Then, after minutes of moving silence, one prisoner said to another, "How beautiful the world *could* be!"

Another time we were at work in a trench. The dawn was gray around us; gray was the sky above; gray the snow in the pale light of dawn; gray the rags in which my fellow prisoners were clad, and gray their faces. I was again conversing silently with my wife, or perhaps I was struggling to find the *reason* for my sufferings, my slow dying. In a last violent protest against the hopelessness of imminent death, I sensed my spirit piercing through the enveloping gloom. I felt it transcend that hopeless, meaningless world, and from somewhere I heard a victorious "Yes" in answer to my question of the existence of an ultimate purpose. At that moment a light was lit in a distant farmhouse, which stood on the horizon as if painted there, in the midst of the miserable gray of a dawning morning in Bavaria. *"Et lux in tenebris lucet"* — and the light shineth in the darkness. For hours I stood hacking at the icy ground. The guard passed by, insulting me, and once again I communed with my beloved. More and more I felt that she was present, that she was with me; I had the feeling that I was able to touch her, able to stretch out my hand and grasp hers. The feeling was very strong: she was *there*. Then, at that very moment, a bird flew down silently and perched just in front of me, on the heap of soil which I had dug up from the ditch, and looked steadily at me.

A LATER PERSPECTIVE

JOHN D. MONTGOMERY

from

AFTERMATH

John D. Montgomery, professor of public administration at the Kennedy School of Government,
Harvard University, writes about an event that
took place forty years earlier. Montgomery
describes his well-remembered visit to what had
been the city of Hiroshima and recalls how even
the location of the streets had been thoroughly
obliterated by the first atomic bomb ever
dropped — just six months earlier.

The purpose of his visit was to help the
Japanese with plans for rebuilding the city — a
task that was of little interest to the U.S. military
government then running Japan. Since the war
had ended so recently and feelings were still so
bitterly charged, he was able to provide the local
officials with moral rather than any financial or
material support. Despite the indifference of his
superiors to the task, Montgomery describes his
own personal efforts to encourage the Japanese
with their plans to reconstruct their city around
a central peace park; at that first meeting he
suggested that they incorporate, in the museum
at ground zero, an institute devoted to research

613

on international peace.

After the experiences of a lifetime, Montgomery reassesses the decision to drop the bomb, made originally to limit the loss of American lives and to speed the end of the war — and analyzes the aftermath of that decision.

The Aftermath of War

Hiroshima provided my first experience of the aftermath of a great decision. Although I had not participated in the decision to use the bomb or in its implementation, I had fully appreciated its cargo of bitter hope. Like most other soldiers, I was awed by its initial success, but when I went there as a military government officer I was appalled at the indifference and neglect that followed. . . .

Planning a New Hiroshima

My first rather uncomplicated visit to the ruins of Hiroshima was in the early spring of 1946, six months after the most devasting bomb in history had destroyed it. My isolated efforts to help the city rise from its ashes began with a visit to the City Hall to meet with planners and other municipal officials. My credentials were meagre enough: I was the lowest-ranking officer in the military government of that region. No one of higher status, however, had the slightest interest in the aftermath of the bombing of Hiroshima.

And I did have some knowledge of the arts of city planning and a concern for the future prospects of the first horrid symbol of the nuclear age.

I came into the city from my military government office in Kure, less than an hour's drive away, where an American team was providing liaison services between the MacArthur headquarters in Tokyo and local offices of the Japanese government, and also with the British Commonwealth Occupation forces in southern Honshu. Hiroshima's acting mayor and the City Reconstruction Planning Commission had asked for an advisor. I was not only the youngest officer in the military government team but also its most recent (indeed, only) graduate in municipal administration and city planning. Violating a military principle of long standing, I had volunteered for the assignment.

In those days, officers — even second lieutenants — were allowed to drive their own Jeeps out of the small motor pool that served our company (twelve officers and sixty enlisted men), and though I did not know my way around Hiroshima yet, I could at least find the city and I commanded enough spoken Japanese to ask directions when I got there. For the meeting, of course, I would need an interpreter if any serious discussions got under way, as I intended even at that first meeting they should.

City Hall was easy to find — what was left of it. It was still standing in proud defiance against the atomic blast that had removed most of the surrounding buildings, and until I approached the front steps it looked official and serviceable. A reception committee showed me up those stone steps (on which stray rubble still crunched underfoot), through the central hall (where no plaster survived, and no desks of people could be seen), up a flight of divided stairs (illuminated by daylight streaming through where windows and a roof had been), to a large council chamber (where I sighted the only furniture in the whole building — long tables arranged in what the Army likes to call a hollow square).

More impressive than this sign of bureaucratic opulence was the company of formally dressed, somber-faced Japanese officials, probably 40 or so in number, who rose as I entered and offered a somewhat unnerving round of applause as I approached the designated seat at the head of the table. Nearly all of the Japanese I was to meet in my official capacity there were 20 or more years my senior and much more experienced in the arts of war and peace than I. Their cultivated politeness neutralized any psychological advantage I might have enjoyed had I been tempted to trade on my status as a representative of the conquering forces. In any case I was not so tempted; we shared an interest in reconstructing, as well as resources would permit, the most dramatically destroyed city in history.

The Scope of Destruction

Of course I knew something even then about the extent and nature of Hiroshima's devastation, but only as a sightseer. War's destruction is always awe-inspiring, but this was different. Here the ruins were even more distressing than those of the bombed-out strip that ran 50 kilometers or so from Tokyo to Yokohama or those in other cities which had been even more completely destroyed. No one who had lived in such places could remain unimpressed by the amount of damage a modern army can inflict without an invasion or an artillery barrage; no one who had served in the infantry could bring himself to resent that dreadful efficiency. The Air Corps, then part of the Army, had done its work well in Hiroshima. What it had destroyed, troops would not be called upon to take by house-to-house fighting if that planned American invasion had been necessary. Hiroshima had demonstrated, indeed, something that the sustained strategic bombing effort could not. The ultimate goal of inducing surrender without invasion was better served by a single dramatic stroke than by a hundred fire bombings of the Tokyo-Yokohama type. For the horrors and the ruins left by those saturation bombings were terrifying enough, but they were incremental; after months of apparently random targeting, the population had almost become immune to terror.

Whether we liked it or not, those of us who lived near Hiroshima became experts in massive bombing effects. Before Hiroshima I had spent a month or so in Kofu, near Mount Fuji, a city resembling Hiroshima in that it, too, had been destroyed by a single raid. The accounts of citizens fleeing to the river in panic sounded very much like events that occurred a few months later in Hiroshima. But several of Kofu's fireproof buildings had survived, and when our military government company arrived to set up a regional headquarters there, we could live in a grand mansion, assigning three or four officers to a room, and enjoy the luxury of situating our offices in another still usable building at the edge of the old business section, to which we could commute on foot. What was different about Hiroshima was the uniformity of the destruction, which leveled houses and office buildings in the central area so completely that it was no longer possible to tell where the streets had been, and which left only random parts of walls and built-in safes standing, surrounded by pocket-sized chunks of plaster, glass, stone, and brick. It was the thoroughness of the destruction, the aftermath of a single moment (8:15 A.M. on Monday, August 6, 1945) that inspired awe even in those like me, who considered themselves seasoned observers of destroyed cities.

Unlike most Japanese cities, Hiroshima had been built to withstand an earthquake, and its concrete buildings were designed to accommodate a safety load nearly double that considered standard in the United States. It had been expecting an air raid, too; of all Japan's major cities, few others besides Kyoto had been spared, and the inhabitants knew their time was coming and were preparing for it. Hiroshima was an important military command and communications center; it would have served as imperial head-quarters if Tokyo had fallen. The army had planned a defense-in-depth on the ground. It had built up stockpiles of lewisite and hydrogen cyanide gas to cover any retreat that became necessary. Hiroshima was doomed, whatever happened. All these facts were well known to the residents, who by August 1945 had spent many sleepless nights because of repeated air-raid warnings and had lost accumulated daylight hours as well waiting in assigned shelters for the all clear. By then 100,000 persons had been evacuated from the city, bringing the resident population down to 250,000.

The suddenness of the attack by a single, peaceful-looking plane contributed to the way the public responded to the destruction of their city. There had been many air-raid warnings before in Hiroshima but no actual air raids. Since only one enemy aircraft was detected on the fatal morning (the companion planes that rode shotgun on this raid were watching off-shore), the authorities felt secure in sounding the routine all-clear signal, upon which the few people who had obediently retreated to their civil defense shelters now emerged into the sunlight, while the majority of the citizens — who were just getting up — continued with their rituals of awakening. Boredom with the war and the numerous false alarms that had been sounded in Hiroshima might have contributed to the surprise; its citizens had suffered none of the sustained misery and pain that had dominated the consciousness of the people of Tokyo and other air-raid targets. After the bomb had fallen, panic and uncertainty distinguished Hiroshima's response from the dull disciplined behavior that characterized the aftermath of "normal" air raids in other cities. The survivors fled unbelievingly to parks and rivers, which were not very safe but offered some refuge from the fire storm of the city and undoubtedly saved some lives. There was, in fact, no other place to go, and even there no one was available to render help. It was several hours before military teams came through the area promising relief to the dazed survivors, which in the end never came. Yet there were individual heroes even in those hours, as the less severely wounded tried to save their families and friends or to help strangers. In a horrible way it may have been Hiroshima's finest hour up to that time, but it did not last long: In only a few days looters and petty chiselers reached the scene, and it was several weeks before there were signs of a return to law and order.

Gradually, however, the life of the city resumed, muted and subdued. When I visited it a few months later a quiet calm prevailed. Old residents were still sifting through the rubble of their homes, salvaging the few unbroken pieces of pottery and the small personal possessions that remained. The most vivid sound I recall was the trickle of water: Everywhere it was spouting or dripping from broken pipes and faucets. The fallen power lines, which no longer carried electricity, were still exposed. Essential services were operating, however, as they had been only a few weeks after the bombing. There were even a limited number of telephones and one or two public conveyances for those with cash or, preferably, barter goods.

I wondered whether better civil defense would have reduced the suffering, but in the end I concluded that no precautions Hiroshima could have taken in August 1945 would have reduced the death toll very much. Even if the air raid warning had continued, any lives that the shelters might have protected against the bomb blast would have been lost in the next few hours of the fire storm, against which even the most secure structure would have offered little protection. Nor could the existing fire-fighting teams have done much with their scant 16 pieces of standard equipment if there had been a sustained alert. The Japanese government was unable to mount a rescue mission to the city for 30 hours. A naval hospital ship was promised but it never arrived; the city's hospitals were mostly in ruins, and those that could still function were invaded by hordes of injured and frightened people, the vast majority of whom they could not help at all. There was Hiroshima's army base hospital, but a special form of triage had to be practiced even there: First priority was given to the mildly wounded, so that the limited staff could help the largest number in the shortest time. And very soon, military rule took over there, too; after five days all civilians were evacuated because new military casualties were arriving. Still no one knew what had happened. For a full week, the population had no idea of the nature of the catastrophe they had experienced. The term "atom bomb" was first used only two days before the Emperor's voice announced the shocking surrender.

The Beginnings of Rehabilitation

Six months later, when I entered City Hall to work with the city planners, the shock was well behind them. And before them were maps, lists, and estimates, a readiness to plan, and a hope that help was coming. After I seated myself at the assigned place at the head of the table, Acting (and former) Mayor Hichiro Kihara, who had been recalled from retirement to serve again, rose, introduced me, and spoke of the history and destiny of Hiroshima:

> This city was a military one, developing as a military depot when the Sino-Japanese War broke off about 50 years ago. . . . But by the disastrous atomic bomb raid, the military city of Hiroshima was completely wiped off the face of the earth and became a city of debris in a moment. This bomb-raid, however, caused the eradication of evil militarism from the heart of the whole nation, and brought the war to an end. When we think about this, instead of sorrow over the past, this attack has become the voice of peace, and our city is given the opportunity of being reborn as a peaceful symbol. . . .

At that time, I had no idea of the extent of rehabilitation that the citizens had already started. The City Hall, ruined beyond repair, was the first building I had entered. Few others in that part of the city had even the hint of a roof. Four

622

and a half square miles — the commercial center of the city where three-quarters of the population lived — were almost completely destroyed. Of the thousands of buildings in the heart of the city, only 50 were still standing and only 5 of them could be repaired. Nearly all of the bridges were down. Many of the roads were passable only by vehicles with four-wheel drive. Railway cars and trolleys had been tossed off their tracks. Only the industrialized zones located on the outskirts of the city, built up after 1931, had survived. There Nippon Steel, Hiroshima Ship Building, a rifle manufacturer, and an auto plant, which together had produced half of Hiroshima's output, were untouched; and about 75 percent of the small industries in the same area could resume operations within a month.

By the time of my arrival, rehabilitation efforts had not brought much improvement to the central city. There was, of course, no evidence of the immediate or subsequent human suffering, since relief activities there had begun on August 22, when the army started distributing clothing. In another week, electric power was restored to some of the hospitals, and even mail deliveries started. Residents who had fled to the countryside had been permitted to return in the first week of September, and sightseers began arriving soon thereafter. Fortunately in those early days there had been no epidemic — perhaps because of the fire, though no one knows for sure, for swarms of flies had appeared August 25, apparently harmless but then so numerous that people swallowed them and walked on them. By

November 1st the population had risen to 137,000, only a few of whom, however, were living in the central section.

In November the trolleys began running again, tracks being easier to clear than streets. The trolleys were an important symbol of urban life when I arrived, even though their schedule was infrequent. There was yet "no place to go" and little occasion for commuting; people did have to go to the central city for the few purchases then possible, since it was there that the black market was beginning to flourish. Most of the goods that were available were not rationed, but merely scarce. One doctor told me that the only source of glass to replace the broken windows of his hospital had been the black market — so called, perhaps, more because profit-making still seemed inappropriate in the wake of such devastation than because it was illegal. Demobilized soldiers, returning from duty overseas, were beginning to enter Hiroshima, and a few of them managed to obtain potentially valuable property which they claimed the former owners had "abandoned" downtown.

On my drive to City Hall, I had seen only a few signs of revival, shacks, and improvised shops a mile or so from "ground zero." I had not stopped to talk with any of the population, and did not know whether or not they shared Mayor Kihara's vision of a reborn Hiroshima.

Allied Indifference

I had no statement of allied plans to present to my Japanese colleagues (as I was soon to consider

624

them). No instructions had come with my designation as allied counselor to the city. So far as the army of occupation was concerned, the Japanese were a defeated enemy who had started the war and waged it savagely on the islands in the Pacific and in the Kamikaze-infested airspace off the main island of Honshu. Non-fraternization rules had been announced for the troops, though of course military government teams like mine had all kinds of business to transact with the Japanese.

My other duties in the military government included encouraging the formation of democratic trade unions and arranging the supply of 15,000 Japanese laborers a day to support the British Commonwealth Occupation Forces, along with visits to industrial plants that had been manufacturing poison gas and other munitions and were now seeking licenses to make pesticides, rayon, and salt (from seawater). For me, Hiroshima was a sideline.

Hiroshima's reconstruction was, in fact, an afterthought to the allied government as well. I had no reason to think military General MacArthur's headquarters would provide any funds or material help to the city fathers and mothers of Hiroshima. (They didn't.) I could offer no help except moral and, perhaps, technical. And even for those purposes I was on my own.

Having so little knowledge of the immediate past or the insistent present of Hiroshima, and no guidance at all on its long-term future, I could do little at that first meeting but encourage the Japanese to plan for the reconstruction that I thought was sure to come. I could recall to them, by way of encouragement, the hiatus that had followed the original planning of Washington, D.C., which had lain neglected for over a decade when suddenly the War of 1812 brought enough devastation to the capital to permit a completely new city to emerge. I could recall, too, the close alliance that had grown up in the years following that war between the United States and its British enemy. I urged the Planning Commission to make its plans as specific as it could, so that the improvised reconstruction that was beginning to serve the needs of the returning population would not preclude the building of a great new city on the ashes of the old.

I learned later that the Commission had already had several meetings and reached one or two decisions of symbolic but permanent importance. The planners wanted to use the delta land where the seven rivers flowed out to the sea as the basis for a great park system. They hoped to take advantage of the fire lanes that had been cleared before the bombing and to add some land from the devastated areas of the city, to build several boulevards a hundred meters wide through the commercial center, and to extend the green belt zone as far inland as they could.

During our first meeting we discussed the possiblity of preserving an area in the center of the city as a peace park, leaving standing the ghostly ruins of the Industrial Arts Museum (which was near ground zero), and building near it a new working museum to house the exhibits of the hideous fantasies created by the atomic flash — the shadows etched on stones, diffused glass, metal and ceramic fragments, and photographs or samples of the crazily twisted poles, godowns, trolleys, and other artifacts of the flash and the fire storm. I suggested as well that the new museum be part of an active institute of international peace, dedicated to research on the avoidance of war and to activism on behalf of strategies for resolving international disputes before they reached the conflict stage.

My vision of Hiroshima was, in fact, an entirely personal perspective. I was a staff officer to nobody at that moment. Hiroshima officials had invited me to come in the hope of enlisting sympathy, which in the end they did through the good offices of the press, not those of the Supreme Commander of Allied Powers or his Tokyo headquarters. The only other concrete suggestion I made came later, after I had toured the city with the chief engineer. As we discussed rezoning and land use, I thought it might be possible to amalgamate land parcels by swapping titles among different owners so as to give planners maximum flexibility in designing the city's physical layout. Since there was no longer a distinguishable commercial center or any other reserved areas, such as military camps, I thought that land previously in private hands could now be pooled and redistributed, retaining some portion of each parcel for public use while permitting the owners to rebuild following the natural contours of the seven rivers on which the city lay. Such a zoning scheme was actually applied later, covering 1,093 hectares and producing major improvements in the city's amenities and appearances.

Financial Constraint

The financial resources available at the time were limited. The Committee on Ways and Means, organized in May 1946, was — as the mayor put it — "buried in anxiety." It was formally appointed by the major, who named the chief of the financial bureau of the city, eight political leaders, a few professors, and a half-dozen businessmen to represent the interests of the New Hiroshima. Its resources for a "five-year plan" amounted to ¥780 million, of which ¥660 million would come from the city itself. It was all to be Japanese money, but whatever was to be added to the city's own resources would have to come from the prefecture. The central government was preparing to help any city that claimed war damage, but it was making no special allowances for Hiroshima, and the amounts involved would be small. The hope that the allies would contribute to the reconstruction — probably the primary reason for my being there — was never realized.

Not only could I offer no encouragement in that hope, but I was pretty sure no one else was interested in Hiroshima's problems. I knew enough about what was happening in Tokyo to realize that the allies would see no advantage in Hiroshima's reconstruction as a memorial city. I went to Tokyo to ask, but I could not summon up a convincing argument for an American contribution to Hiroshima's rebuilding. Foreign aid had not yet been invented; no one thought of Japan as a potential friendly power; reverse reparations to the attackers of Pearl Harbor were unthinkable. Moreover, like most members of the occupation forces in those early months, I believed the decision to drop the bomb inevitable. This belief was reinforced by my own knowledge and observations of the Japanese homeland defenses that U.S. troops would have faced in an invasion.

The Decision to Use the Bomb

By coincidence, the troop carrier that had brought our military government team to Tokyo Harbor left California on what we learned was to have been D-Day for the Allied invasion. During the first days of the occupation we all felt we owed our acquiescent reception in Japan to the *Enola Gay* and the atomic cargo it delivered to Hiroshima. In subsequent years, there would be teatime and cocktail party discussions about alternatives to the Hiroshima drop, such as a demonstration of the atomic bomb on an uninhabited island near Honshu by way of a final warning to the Japanese — rehearsals of arguments that had already appeared at Alamogordo and in Washington, only to be suppressed by authorities in the Manhattan Project, the War Department, and the White House. And despite the afterthoughts of a guilt-laden generation, the feasibility of this alternative still seems dubious to me. The bomb was, after all, still experimental:

what if it had failed to go off? The scientists themselves were far from certain that it would work, or how powerful it would be if it did. No one who had been in the army more than a few months expected any military technology to perform perfectly, especially a complex one. What if it had worked in a demonstration but the Japanese observers were to decide that a bomb delivered by one plane was no worse than many bombs delivered from an apparently inexhaustible air arsenal? We were aware that only two or three atomic bombs were then in existence. (More were promised, but the technology was still changing and nothing was certain.) None of us considered a demonstration in force technically possible. And where could such a demonstration take place without danger to human life, yet be within reach of the top Japanese leaders or any other credible observer? How could the two sides assure each other's safety during the approach or the demonstration itself? What intermediary could bring together negotiators representing two mortal enemies and arrange conditions for bargaining? And, for that matter, who would the negotiators be, especially for Japan: the stubborn military leaders? the inaccessible emperor? the discredited politicians? Even if they were persuaded, who would dare to assume that Japanese people would accept surrender without some almost miraculous event visible to all, after they had suffered so much already? Even now the revisionists' thoughts about an alternative to bombing Hiroshima seem to me more like visions.

One curious discovery my own military government team had made as it moved from place to place in Japan was that the population had accepted defeat in direct proportion to the damage they had themselves experienced. The greatest resentment we encountered was in cities like Matsue that were unscathed by the war. We had little reason to believe that the gradual attrition of Japanese strength would bring the people to the point of surrender.

Almost to a man, the American GIs and their officers in the occupation thought the atomic bomb, once invented, inevitably would be used. Nor can I believe that even now, in our present state of grace, many Americans would be willing to accept the casualties an invasion of mainland Japan would bring in order to avoid being on the side that first used the bomb. Such is the logic of war.

An Extension of the Philosophy of Guilt

What seems more unequivocally reprehensible in the American position is that the cruel logic to use the bomb also defined the official attitude toward reconstruction. No one doubted that "the Japanese" had brought the war on themselves; even the Roosevelt-haters in our ranks would have disbelieved the later theory that his ambition to become a war president produced an American diplomacy designed to bring on Pearl Harbor. Some of my fellow officers were then begrudging even the U.S. contributions to the rehabilitation of Britain or France; I never heard anyone suggest that we had an obligation to help our enemies

631

rebuild. By then I had developed an admiration for the Japanese people and culture, but even I did not doubt that the destruction of their empire was "their" own doing.

In those days military government doctrine prescribed that humanitarian assistance should be offered to civilians of both sides in the aftermath of war, if possible, but the field manuals were concerned with preserving law and order for the safety of the occupying troops. It was a revolution in the doctrine of military government when General MacArthur proposed to introduce institutional changes that would convert a militaristic society into a peaceful one, but rebuilding destroyed cities was not on his mind at all. I was not surprised at finding no concern in his headquarters over Hiroshima's future, though I pleaded my case as eloquently as I could, laying stress on the symbolic importance of the gesture and the possible significance of an institute for international peace located at Hiroshima. In my opinion, the one inhumane cruelty the U.S. occupation displayed was its profound neglect of Hiroshima's immediate needs.

Rebirth of the City

Hiroshima today is a beautiful, modern city with three times its pre-war population. It has splendid commercial buildings, high-tech industries, parks and green belts, new schools, an old university about to be relocated 30 miles to the East, and fairly orderly traffic jams during rush hours. One of the few visible reminders of the past is the trolley cars, still running quietly and efficiently on the old tracks through a city that remembers how well they served the public when nothing else moved. Since few Japanese cities still have streetcars, Hiroshima has shrewdly bought up the leftovers from elsewhere, including one car from Dortmund that makes its rounds still displaying its German advertising posters. The hundred-meter roads, along with the peace park, are almost the only other visible records of our 1946 plans. My suggestions for creating a research institute on peace in conjunction with the university and for consolidating private lands before rezoning the central city were forgotten by the city officials I spoke with in 1984. There is still talk about peace research but as yet no evidence of a serious effort to carry it out, although there are tourists and museums and peace marches in honor of the Hiroshima symbol.

In short, private initiative, with or without zoning, had built a city better than most of its size in Japan or elsewhere. As planned — indeed, inevitably — Hiroshima is an international symbol. It entertains 11,000 tourists a year, including some 500 VIPs who have to be personally received by the mayor. Its older citizens regularly travel abroad to remind the world of the horrors of nuclear war, often at their own expense.

The route to the present was not the result of carefully laid plans. For the city could not begin its unique reconstruction as a city of parks and boulevards until its financial resources became adequate, and that occurred almost by accident. In 1949 Mayor Hamai was able to prevail upon a sympathetic military government officer, my old friend Justin Williams, in General Mac-Arthur's headquarters, to help. He had no way of helping me in 1946, but American politics had ripened over the two years after I had abandoned my military government career. He could now insist that the Japanese central government pass the Peace City Law. This belated law, enacted only after American intervention, turned military properties in the heart of Hiroshima over to the city for development purposes. That fortuitous event could never have occurred within the Japanese political system itself, which was prepared to show no favoritism to Hiroshima or Nagasaki, and it would not have been possible at all if Mayor Hamai had waited until after the Korean War had begun, when General Mac-Arthur's headquarters had lost whatever enthusiasm it ever possessed for the symbolism of peace. That act, perhaps the only atonement the American army (at no cost to itself) made for the atomic bombing, freed Hiroshima from the constraints binding other municipal governments. In the process of releasing these unique resources, the law lifted Hiroshima above the deadening system of standardized city governments that had so long discouraged local innovations in Japan. And it gave Hiroshima's leaders enough of a boost to encourage the new investments on which the new city began to thrive.

Before the war Hiroshima had not distinguished itself in culture, political leadership, or the other arts of peace. One elderly citizen told me in 1984 that only 5 of the 19 pre-war mayors had been able to complete their terms of office, the others having been forced out by various political pressures and aborted get-rich-quick schemes. No important national political leaders had come from Hiroshima, either, nor were there any unusual community enterprises to its credit. Kihara was probably right in dismissing pre-war Hiroshima as a military city. The social effects of the bombing — the destruction of family and neighborhood life — provided the early post-war rallying point for the loyalties of an apathetic population, and it inspired the early mayors and councillors to assert new political aspirations for the community.

Reconstruction did not begin as a spiritual renaissance in Hiroshima; political reality merged heroism with venality. A few soldiers who entered the city early in the period of chaos gained control of disputed land; some farmed it cooperatively for a time and some became and remained rich. Many of the small land owners who lost their property in the bombing were impoverished further when the city took over centrally located lands for public purposes, offering token compensation. The merchants of those early days when I was sitting with the Planning Commission opposed the Peace Memorial Park and the 100-meter boulevards as pointless and extravagant.

During the next decades, however, all of them began to share a civic pride that Hiroshima had not enjoyed before. Among those active in commerce and public life in the 1980's I encountered exuberant optimism. The city today looks more impressive than others of its size in Japan, though its actual growth rate since World War II was below the average of other cities of its class. A huge but attractive public housing development for low-income groups has risen in the center of the city (not on the outskirts, as is usually the case) on lands once assigned to military uses. In 1984 there were new aspirations everywhere: a new campus for the university, a new cultural center, and a more positive commitment to study the structural and political dimensions of peace.

The Lesson of Hiroshima

Hiroshima is a microcosm of Japan's success story as a nation. It is rooted in a great historical setback, the aftermath of which was the release of energies that had been diverted by militarism. Militarism was lifted from the soul of Japan by history's most terrible bombings and the experience of unequivocal defeat. The reconstruction of Hiroshima called for the same cultural attributes of disciplined hard work, shared decision making, and political economy that have been responsible for the nation's remarkable productive achievements in the third quarter of the twentieth century. For Hiroshima, rebuilding the civic center was financed by a policy of demilitarization made possible by the unplanned interventions of a few American military government officers. The nation reconstructed itself in the model of peaceful industrialization without much encouragement and guidance from General MacArthur's headquarters. Today I drive a Japanese car whose design, workmanship, and price of nine years ago (it has lasted well) far excel those of its contemporary American competitors.

Could the Americans have done better in Japan? Not by rejecting the use of the bomb and thus prolonging the war, I say, but by taking more care of its immediate aftermath. There was, for example, no need to suppress information about radiation sickness. (The work of the Atomic Bomb Casualty Commission specialists was classified when I was in Hiroshima.) Nor was there any need to ignore the efforts of the civilians in the bombed-out cities to rebuild or any advantage in leaving to the reluctant American military command the tasks of institutional reconstruction in the wake of dictatorship. All of these post-war dimensions were fully knowable, and indeed were recognized at intermediate levels of the planning bureaucracies whose voices could not reach the decision makers in Washington and Tokyo.

In some ways Japan has learned more than America from World War II. Its once self-perpetuating militarist leaders succeeded only in bringing about the nation's destruction, after which — with a little help from their former enemies — the creativity and initiative of the population was asserted. Thus far the Japanese people have rejected American pressures to take even a modest step toward remilitarization. The roles of the pre-war period are almost reversed: The Japanese have retained a balance veering as far away from militant nationalism as the United

States has tilted toward it in recent years.

The lesson of Hiroshima has been different for the Japanese and the Americans. The Japanese reject an army larger than a self-defense force, while the United States urges rearmament. Japan has become an international economic force, but America still uses it military power to deter any major threat to its primacy or political preferences. The irony of Hiroshima is that Japan learned — and therefore gained — more from it than did the Americans.

MARY HEATON VORSE

from

THE AUTOBIOGRAPHY OF AN ELDERLY WOMAN

This selection describes the ironic role reversal that takes place when the elderly are taken care of by their children — or so it would seem from reading this account. But things are not always what they seem. Upon further investigation, it turned out that this so-called autobiography of an elderly woman was actually written by a young woman who modeled her writing on her mother's thoughts and life.

Mary Heaton Vorse initially published this book as an anonymous autobiography in 1911 at age thirty-five, and she succeeded in capturing the authentic tone of an elderly lady peeved at the restrictions imposed by her well-meaning family. In her own memoirs, published in 1935, Vorse wrote: "I knew exactly how my mother felt about age — or rather about growing old, for she never was old except in years and retained her gusto for life until shortly before her death."

Other writers have played with the autobiographical form, including Gertrude Stein in her *Autobiography of Alice B. Toklas.*

As I look back over my life, it divides itself into four parts. First come all the years before I married, and as I look back on my childhood and my short girlhood, it seems to me as though I were remembering the life of some other woman, for during these many years I know that I have changed several times from one person to another, and the world about me has had time to change also. All that early part swims in a fog, with here and there events popping out of the mist, more distinct than those a week past, — often meaningless and trivial events these; I cannot tell by what caprice memory has elected to keep them so clear. Lately I find myself returning to certain opinions and prejudices of my girlhood, that I had long forgotten. Time, after all, has not obliterated them, nor have I walked away from them. It is rather as though I had gone in a circle, and as I come to the completion of it I find my old thoughts and opinions, changed and grown older, waiting for me.

With my marriage begins the part of my life that seems real to me, — it is as if I had dreamed all that went before. I loved the time when my children were little, and I have often wished that I could put them and myself back in the nursery again. I pity the women whose children come too late for them all to be in some sense children together. But however young a mother is, there is a great gap between her and her babies. My little children were of a different generation from me. And for all our striving to understand, they were babies and my husband and I "grown people," though as I look back we seem mere boy and girl.

We worried over our babies, — there were four of them, all in the nursery at the same time, — we sat up nights gravely discussing their "tendencies," and their education — only to find that the very tendencies over which we worried most they outgrew, and that when the time for education began in earnest, all the conditions had changed and new methods had been evolved.

It will always be this way, — mothers and fathers will always sit up late nights, as we did, discussing the "futures" of their little two-year-old sons.

We tried so hard to do right; we thought back through the years and said: —

"I felt this and this when I was little. I thought this way and this — such and such things frightened me. My father seemed unjust when he punished me for this offense; my mother made such and such mistakes. I will not make these mistakes with my children."

And so, thinking to avoid all the mistakes of our own parents, we made, all unknowing, fresh mistakes of our own.

When I was little, for instance, I was very much afraid of the dark; so much so that the fears of my childhood haunted my whole life, — an unlighted staircase has terrors for me even to this day. And I made up my mind that no child of mine should suffer from fear of darkness as I did. So my first child had a light in his room.

He was always naughty about going to bed, and he grew to be a big boy before I found out that this was because the gray twilight of the room was horrible to him, and that he was very much afraid of the uncertain shapes of the furniture he saw in the dim light of the lamp, though not at all afraid of the dark. It is with such well-intentioned blunders that one brings up one's children.

Grandmothers know that this is so, and for that reason all the various "systems" seem like foolish words to them. They have learned that there will be mistakes made where there are parents and children, — yes, and that there will be cruelties and injustices, and that the only way to deal with very little children is to love them very much and let them feel this love.

The time my children took in growing up seems to me phenomenally short; one day they were babies and the next they were young people to be reckoned with, having wills and personalities of their own. Other mothers tell me that their children grew up as quickly, but this I have hard work to believe.

When my oldest son was nearly a man and the others crowding on his heels, my dear husband died, and my son grew up overnight, and in the next few years — years that were very full ones, for all their sadness — my other children stole a march on me and grew up too; almost, I might say, behind my back. While I was taking on myself the new responsibilities of my so altered life, and while the world seemed yet very empty of companionship, I found that my children were becoming my comrades, and so I entered on the third quarter of my life.

My boys and girls all at once belonged to my generation; we had common interests, common tastes and amusements — for all practical purposes we were the same age. It was at this time that the warning voice sounded in my ear, but I seemed to myself almost as young as my children, so no wonder I didn't recognize it as the voice of age calling to me. It is a very pleasant time when one is still on the great stage of life, playing one's small part shoulder to shoulder with one's children; shoulder to shoulder, too, with people a score of years one's senior. This is the golden moment when time holds its breath for a while and one imagines that, however old one may get, one will forever stay in spirit at the same smiling "middle way." Age, considered at that time, seems rather the result of some accident or some weakness of will than the result of living a great number of years in the world. So for many years my children and I did our work side by side, I helping and advising them, they aiding and advising me in the common partnership of our lives.

The fourth part of my life, my present life about which I am going to write, began when again I became of a different generation from my children — with the difference that they now are the strong, I the weak; that they treasure me and care for me, worry over me and weep over me, — a spry old lady, and, I am afraid, sometimes a defiant old lady, impatient of the rules which they lay down for me, as once they were of the rules that I made for them.

How did this come about? When did it happen?

There was a time when I was more of a comrade than a mother to my daughters; when I was the adviser of my sons. Now I am not. I do not know when the change came, nor do they, if indeed they realize it at all. There was a time when I was of their generation, now I am not. I cannot put my finger on the time when old age finally claimed me. But there came a moment when my boys were more thoughtful of me, when they didn't come to me any more with their perplexities, not because I had what is called "failed," but because they felt that the time had come when I ought to be "spared" every possible worry. So there is a conspiracy of silence against me in my household. "We mustn't worry mother," is the watchword of my dear children, and the result of their great care is that I am on the outside of their lives.

Shadows come and go among them; they talk about them; I feel the chill of their trouble, but I'm never told what it's about. Before me they keep cheerful; when I come, the shadow passes from their faces and they talk with me about all the things that they think will interest me. I move in a little artificial, smiling world away from all the big interests of life. If one of them is sick away from home, I am not told until it is all over; if there is any crisis among them, they do all they can to keep me from hearing of it. But in the end I always do know, for no one can live in the shadow of any anxiety and not be aware of it.

So the great silence enfolds me more and more. I live more alone and solitary among those I love, groping in the silence, watching the faces of my children to find what is passing in their lives. I often think how sweet it would have been if my husband had lived, and we could have grown old together, understanding and giving companionship to each other.

I can remember the very day when I *realized* that age had claimed me at last. There is a great difference between being a thing and realizing it. A woman may say a hundred times that she is ugly; she may be ugly; but unless she realizes that she is ugly, it will make very little difference. It is the consciousness of our defects which undoes us, — and so with age.

This great readjustment began with the most trivial of events. I happened to see a little dust on the table and around on the bric-a-brac — it seems to me that dusting is a lost art — and I was just wiping it off. I was enjoying myself, for I belong to a generation which was taught to work with its hands and to delight in doing its work nicely, when I heard Margaret's step on the stairs; she is my youngest daughter, home on a visit. My first impulse was to sit down and pretend to be reading, but I resolved to brazen it out, — after all, there is no reason why I shouldn't dust my own bric-a-brac in my own home if I choose.

She came into the parlor.

"*What* are you doing, darling?" she said.

"I am dusting the vases on the mantel," I answered, and I tried to keep any note of guilt from my voice.

"Why couldn't you have called Annie?" she asked me, with tender reproach.

"I like to stir around myself sometimes," I said, and for the life of me I couldn't help being a little defiant.

"Well, then, why couldn't you let me do it? You might have called me," she went on in the same tone.

"I told you I like to do it."

"It isn't good for you to stand on your feet so much. Give me that duster, mother. You'll tire yourself all out."

"I get tired *sitting*," I broke out.

"I always have said that you ought to take more exercise in the open air." By this time she had taken away my duster. "Why don't you go out and take a little walk? Come — I'll go with you."

Presently she had finished dusting, but I saw ever so many little places that I should have to wipe up later on, furtively. I should have enjoyed finishing that dusting myself.

"I'll run up and get your things," said Margaret.

Now, I cannot abide having any one trifle with my bureau drawers, and it isn't because I'm old enough to have middle-aged sons and daughters, either. Ever since I can remember, I have put my things away myself. I keep my bonnets in the little drawers and my gloves and veils — my everyday ones, that is — beside them; and I know that I shall never be able to find anything again once Margaret has been among them.

Besides that, I do not like going to walk. Walking aimlessly for exercise has always seemed most futile to me; a feeble stroll that has no objective point, not even the post office, annoys me more than any other way of spending my time. I have never walked except when I had something to walk for, and I don't intend to begin at my time of life.

"I don't think I'll go to walk, dear. I'm going out this afternoon — "

Now, though I said this indifferently enough, in a tone which didn't invite discussion, yet I braced myself inwardly; I knew what was coming.

"Oh, mother darling," my daughter cried. "You're not going to that lecture, with your cold, in that drafty hall! And you always catch more cold in a crowd! You won't go, will you?"

"Well, well — " I temporized.

"You won't go — promise."

Then the door-bell rang, and I made my escape to my own room and locked my door after me. I knew well enough what would happen, — how Margaret would tell the others at dinner that I was going out, and how they would protest. And I made up my mind, as I often have before, that since I am old enough to know what is best for me, I would go to that lecture, let them talk as they might; so I got ready for the battle, resolving for the hundredth time that I would not be run by my children.

As I sat in my room plotting — yes, plotting — how I should outwit my daughter, it came over me what a funny thing it was that I should be contriving to get my own way, for all the

647

world like a naughty, elderly child, while my daughter was worrying about my headstrong ways as if she were my mother instead of my being hers.

How increasingly often I hear as the years go on, not only from my own children, but from other people whose mothers are already old: "Mother will not take care of herself!" And then follow fearsome stories of mother's latest escapade, — just as one tells how naughty Johnnie is getting and how Susie kicks her bedclothes off, — stories of how mother made a raid on the attic and cleaned it almost single-handed when all the family were away; stories of clandestine descents into the perilous depths of the cellar; hair-raising tales of how mother was found on a stepladder hanging a window curtain; how mother insisted on putting down the preserves and pickles, — rows and rows and rows of shining glasses of them, — herself, and how tired she was afterwards, as if putting down the preserves tired only women who were past middle age. And a certain indignation rose within me as I remembered that I can visit my own attic and my own cellar only by stealth or with a devoted and tyrannical child of mine standing over me to see that I don't "overdo." For the motto of all devoted sons and daughters is: "Nag mother to death, if necessary, but don't let her overdo."

Well, what if I should overdo? Before one is old, one is allowed to shorten one's life unchecked; one may have orgies of work undisturbed. And I, for one, would far rather shorten my life by overdoing than have it lengthened out by a series of mournful, inactive years. Again I said I would not be run by my children. And as I got to this point in my meditation I heard my son Dudley coming up the stairs. I knew he would come to see me, so I unlocked my door.

I had said that I would not be run by my children. Now see to what depths constant nagging reduces a naturally straightforward woman. I know that Dudley watches me very closely, and I often wish he would sometimes ignore my moods as I do his; but this time I was ready for him, pulling a long face when he came in.

He said at once — I knew he would: —

"You look blue, old girl."

"I never," I burst out, "can do the least thing without you children interfering. I can't read *all* the time, you know; but whenever I propose to do anything, I meet with such opposition that for the sake of peace I give up at once."

I spoke more warmly than I felt as far as this particular instance was concerned for I was fighting for a principle.

"Who's been bothering you?" Dudley demanded.

"It isn't 'bothered' I've been," I remonstrated. "It's that you children are needlessly anxious about me. It's far better for me to go out now and then than to sit in the house from morning till night. And what's more," I added determinedly, "I am going to the lecture this afternoon no matter what Margaret or any one else says!"

Dudley laughed.

"There, there," he said, patting my hand.

"You *shall* go, no one is going to oppose you. You'll go if I have to take you there in a carriage myself."

So I knew I had won the day, for in our family Dudley is the important member. But I made up my mind, just the same, that I would go on my own two feet to that lecture, for there was no need at all of a carriage. And I did go, alone and walking, though I slipped out of the front door so quietly that it was hardly dignified, — "sneaked," was what Margaret called it.

As Dudley went down the hall, I thought how a similar warfare is being carried on all over this country to-day, wherever there are elderly mothers and middle-aged sons and daughters, — the children trying to dominate their parents with the end in view of making them take abnormal care of their health, and the older people fighting ever more feebly and petulantly for their lost independence. Not only struggling to have their own way, not only chafing at the leading-strings in which their watchful, devoted children would keep them, but fighting, too, for the little glimmer of youth that is yet left them.

For all this care by one's children means but one thing, and that is — age. While you slept, old age came upon you. You count the number of your years by the way your daughter watches your steps, and you see your infirmities in your son's anxious eyes; and the reason of all this struggle — why our own attics and cellars are forbidden ground to us; why our daughters take our dusters from us and tenderly nag us — is that they are valiantly, if tactlessly, striving to delay by their care the hour which they know must come, while we try to ignore its approach.

We like to kill the days, which sometimes crawl past us so slowly, with an illusion of activity, and we do not like to be reminded day by day, hour by hour, that we are old, that there is no work we need do, no "ought" calling us any more; that our work in the world is being done by other people and our long vacation has already begun.

As I sat alone that evening and soberly went over the events of the day, I clearly realized the meaning of Margaret's taking away my duster. I realized that there was no work in the world that I ought to do but take care of myself. I realized that I was old, and from that day, though I often forget it, the world has looked a little different to me; my point of view has, in some subtle way, shifted. It was on that day that I sat down to think how it was that I had come to be old and what the invisible milestones were that I had passed along the way.

The first time age touched me it was with so light a finger that I did not recognize the touch; I didn't know what had happened. Indeed, the touch of age at first irritated me; then I laughed at it, and finally I became a little bewildered, realizing confusedly that a new element had come into my life to stay. But I did not know that it was the shadow of age which was upon me, that it was always there, invisible, quiet, persistent, and, patient as death, waiting to claim me.

This first touch of age comes when our children begin to dictate to us.

The other day I saw the youth of a woman begin to wither under my very eyes. She didn't know what was happening, but I knew what shadow was over her. To me she seems young, for I have seen her grow up, and though she has big daughters, I never thought of her as approaching middle age until the last time she and the girls came to see me.

Edith is a big, handsome, buoyant woman, but there was a subdued air about her for which I couldn't account until her eldest daughter said sweetly, but with decision: —

"Mother isn't looking well; she ought to have some sea air."

And Edith replied with the note of helpless irritation that I have come to know so well: —

"I have told the children so often that I dislike leaving my comfortable home in the summer."

Then I knew why Edith seemed changed: her children had begun to run her.

So the finger of age touches all of us in much the same fashion. The warning may not always come through some dear child, though with mothers it is oftenest in that way; but the voice of the valiant new generation speaks in one way or another to every man and woman, and from the moment you have heard that voice you have set your face old-agewards, though twenty years or more may pass before you are really old. The strong new generation, eager and clamorous, is at your heels ready to take your place, anxious to perform your tasks. Already your children are altering the world that you know; already they are meditating the changes that they will make when the reins of power fall into their hands; and one day you will wake up in a new world, an unhomelike place to which you must adjust yourself as a baby must adjust himself to his surroundings, but with the difference that every day the baby makes progress, whereas every day you will find the new conditions harder to understand, — as I have, and as your mother has.

After my husband's death I was very anxious to have my own mother make her home with me, and at the time I couldn't understand why she wouldn't. Now I know. She lived instead in a little house in the town where she had spent her life, and for all companionship she had a "girl" nearly as old as herself. We used to worry about her a great deal, about her loneliness, her lack of care of herself, — all the things that my children worry about now; but she met all our pleading to live with us with the baffling smile, and the "Well, well, we'll see," that she had used with us when we were little children.

One time I accompanied her home after a visit she had made us, in spite of her protests that it was ridiculous for me to do so. It had stormed and the roads were bad, and I was afraid to let her travel alone. She strode ahead of me, straight as a pine tree, up the brick path which led to her house, and opened the front door. The gesture of welcome she gave her lonely little home, and the long breath she drew, as of relief, I didn't then understand, though I always remembered them. I understand now. She had come back to herself, to her own life, to her memories. Here she could think her own thoughts and lead her life as she wished. She could even sit in a draft without an affectionately officious child following her up with a shawl, and her little home, lonely as it was, was less lonely than the strange world we lived in. I have often taken the duster from my mother's hands as Margaret did from mine the other morning. And I suppose the same little drama will be enacted in every family until the end of time by mothers and daughters.

BERTRAND RUSSELL

REFLECTIONS ON MY EIGHTIETH BIRTHDAY

At the ripe age of eighty, **Bertrand Russell** (1872–1970) added the following few pages as a moving postscript to his autobiography.

Russell spent an active and productive life as a mathematician and philosopher (best known for his work *Principia Mathematica* written with Alfred North Whitehead), as a pacifist after World War I, and later as a supporter of nuclear disarmament.

Russell here sums up his thinking on the condition of the human race: "I am convinced that intelligence, patience, and eloquence can, sooner or later, lead the human race out of its self-imposed tortures, provided it does not exterminate itself meanwhile."

The serious part of my life ever since boyhood has been devoted to two different objects, which for a long time remained separate and have only in recent years united into a single whole. I wanted, on the one hand, to find out whether anything could be known; and, on the other hand, to do whatever might be possible toward creating a happier world. Up to the age of thirty-eight I gave most of my energies to the first of these tasks. I was troubled by scepticism and unwillingly forced to the conclusion that most of what passes for knowledge is open to reasonable doubt. I wanted certainty in the kind of way in which people want religious faith. I thought that certainty is more likely to be found in mathematics than elsewhere. But I discovered that many mathematical demonstrations, which my teachers expected me to accept, were full of fallacies, and that, if certainty were indeed discoverable in mathematics, it would be in a new kind of mathematics, with more solid foundations than those that had hitherto been thought secure. But as the work proceeded, I was continually reminded of the fable about the elephant and the tortoise. Having constructed an elephant upon which the mathematical world could rest, I found the elephant tottering, and proceeded to construct a tortoise to keep the elephant from falling. But the tortoise was no more secure than the elephant, and after some twenty years of very arduous toil, I came to the conclusion that there was nothing more that *I* could do in the way of making mathematical knowledge indubitable. Then came the First World War, and my thoughts became concentrated on human misery and folly. Neither misery nor folly seems to me any part of the inevitable lot of man. And I am convinced that intelligence, patience, and eloquence can, sooner or later, lead the human race out of its self-imposed tortures provided it does not exterminate itself meanwhile.

On the basis of this belief, I have had always a certain degree of optimism, although, as I have grown older, the optimism has grown more sober and the happy issue more distant. But I remain completely incapable of agreeing with those who accept fatalistically the view that man is born to trouble. The causes of unhappiness in the past and in the present are not difficult to ascertain. There have been poverty, pestilence, and famine, which were due to man's inadequate mastery of nature. There have been wars, oppressions, and tortures which have been due to men's hostility to their fellow-men. And there have been morbid miseries fostered by gloomy creeds, which have led men into profound inner discords that made all outward prosperity of no avail. All these are unnecessary. In the regard to all of them, means are known by which they can be overcome. In the modern world, if communities are unhappy it is often because they have ignorances, habits, beliefs, and passions, which are dearer to them than happiness or even life. I find many men in our dangerous age who seem to be in love with misery and death, and who grow angry when hopes are suggested to them. They think hope is irrational and that, in sitting down to lazy despair, they are merely facing facts. I cannot agree with these men. To preserve hope in our world makes calls upon our intelligence and our energy. In those who despair it is frequently the energy that is lacking.

The last half of my life has been lived in one of those painful epochs of human history during which the world is getting worse, and past victories which had seemed to be definitive have turned out to be only temporary. When I was young, Victorian optimism was taken for granted. It was thought that freedom and prosperity would spread gradually throughout the world by an orderly process, and it was hoped that cruelty, tyranny, and injustice would continually diminish. Hardly anyone was haunted by the fear of great wars. Hardly anyone thought of the nineteenth century as a brief interlude between past and future barbarism. For those who grew up in that atmosphere, adjustment to the world of the present has been difficult. It has been difficult not only emotionally but intellectually. Ideas that had been thought adequate have proved inadequate. In some directions valuable freedoms have proved very hard to preserve. In other directions, specially as regards relations between nations, freedoms formerly valued have proved potent sources of disaster. New thoughts, new hopes, new freedoms, and new restrictions upon freedom are needed if the world is to emerge from its present perilous state.

I cannot pretend that what I have done in regard to social and political problems has had any great importance. It is comparatively easy to have an immense effect by means of a dogmatic and precise gospel, such as that of Communism. But for my part I cannot believe that what mankind needs is anything either precise or dogmatic. Nor can I believe with any wholeheartedness in any partial doctrine which deals only with some part or aspect of human life. There are those who hold that everything depends upon institutions, and that good institutions will inevitably bring the millennium. And, on the other hand, there are those who believe that what is needed is a change of heart, and that, in comparison, institutions are of little account. I cannot accept either view. Institutions mould character, and character transforms institutions. Reforms in both must march hand in hand. And if individuals are to retain that measure of initiative and flexibility which they ought to have, they must not be all forced into one rigid mould; or to change the metaphor, all drilled into one army. Diversity is essential in spite of the fact that it precludes universal acceptance of a single gospel. But to preach such a doctrine is difficult, especially in arduous times. And perhaps it cannot be effective until some bitter lessons have been learned by tragic experience.

My work is near its end, and the time has come when I can survey it as a whole. How far have I succeeded, and how far have I failed? From an early age I thought of myself as dedicated to great and arduous tasks. Nearly three-quarters of a century ago, walking alone in the Tiergarten through melting snow under the coldly glittering March sun, I determined to write two series of books: one abstract, growing gradually more concrete; the other concrete, growing gradually more abstract. They were to be crowned by a synthesis, combining pure theory with a practical social philosophy. Except for the final synthesis, which still eludes me, I have written these books. They have been acclaimed and praised, and the thoughts of many men and women have been affected by them. To this extent I have succeeded.

But as against this must be set two kinds of failure, one outward, one inward.

To begin with the outward failure: the Tiergarten has become a desert; the Brandenburger Tor, through which I entered it on that March morning, has become the boundary of two hostile empires, glaring at each other across a barrier, and grimly preparing the ruin of mankind. Communists, Fascists, and Nazis have successfully challenged all that I thought good, and in defeating them much of what their opponents have sought to preserve is being lost. Freedom has come to be thought weakness, and tolerance has been compelled to wear the garb of treachery. Old ideals are judged irrelevant, and no doctrine free from harshness commands respect.

The inner failure, though of little moment to the world, has made my mental life a perpetual battle. I set out with a more or less religious belief in a Platonic eternal world, in which mathematics shone with a beauty like that of the last Cantos of the *Paradiso*. I came to the conclusion that the eternal world is trivial, and that mathematics is only the art of saying the same thing in different words. I set out with a belief that love, free and courageous, could conquer the world without fighting. I came to support a bitter and terrible war. In these respects there was failure.

But beneath all this load of failure I am still conscious of something that I feel to be victory. I may have conceived theoretical truth wrongly, but I was not wrong in thinking that there is such a thing, and that it deserves our allegiance. I may have thought the road to a world of free and happy human beings shorter than it is proving to be, but I was not wrong in thinking that such a world is possible, and that it is worth while to live with a view to bringing it nearer. I have lived in the pursuit of a vision, both personal and social. Personal: to care for what is noble, for what is beautiful, for what is gentle; to allow moments of insight to give wisdom at more mundane times. Social: to see in imagination the society that is to be created, where individuals grow freely, and where hate and greed and envy die because there is nothing to nourish them. These things I believe, and the world, for all its horrors, has left me unshaken.

ACKNOWLEDGMENTS

Clover Adams from *The Letters of Mrs. Henry Adams: 1865–1883*, edited by Ward Thoron. © renewed 1964 by Mrs. Louise Thoron. By permission of Little, Brown Company.

Henry Adams from *The Autobiography of Henry Adams*. Courtesy of the Massachusetts Historical Society.

Russell Baker from *Growing Up*. Copyright © 1982 by Russell Baker. Reprinted by permission of Congdon & Weed, Inc.

Clyde Beatty. Excerpt from *Facing the Big Cats* by Clyde Beatty. Copyright © 1964, 1965 by Clyde Beatty and Edward Anthony. Reprinted by permission of Doubleday and Company, Inc.

Candice Bergen from *Knock Wood*. Copyright © 1984 by Candice Bergen. Reprinted by permission of Linden Press, a division of Simon & Schuster, Inc.

Agatha Christie from *An Autobiography*. Reprinted by permission of Dodd, Mead & Company, Inc., from *An Autobiography* by Agatha Christie. Copyright © 1977 by Agatha Christie Limited.

John Ciardi, "What is Happiness?" Copyright © 1964 *Saturday Review* magazine. Reprinted by permission.

Richard P. Feynman from *Surely You're Joking, Mr. Feynman!* by Richard P. Feynman, with the permission of W.W. Norton & Company, Inc. Copyright © 1985 by Richard P. Feynman and Ralph Leighton.

Anne Frank. Excerpts from *Anne Frank: The Diary of a Young Girl*. Copyright 1952 by Otto H. Frank. Reprinted by permission of Doubleday & Company Inc. Canada: Reprinted by permission of Vallentine Mitchell & Co. Ltd.

Viktor Frankl from *Man's Search for Meaning*. Copyright © 1959. Revised Edition copyright © 1962 by Viktor Frankl. Reprinted by permission of Beacon Press.

Patricia Hampl from *A Romantic Education*. Copyright © 1981 by Patricia Hampl from *A Romantic Education*, published by Houghton Mifflin Co., Boston.

Lillian Hellman from *An Unfinished Woman: A Memoir* by Lillian Hellman. Copyright © 1969 by Lillian Hellman.

Index

A note on the text
Large print edition designed by
Kristina Hals.
Composed in 16 pt Plantin
on a Mergenthaler Linotron 202
by Modern Graphics, Inc.